Christopher Nolan

ALSO BY DARREN MOONEY

*Opening* The X-Files: *A Critical History of the Original Series* (McFarland, 2017)

# Christopher Nolan
*A Critical Study of the Films*

Darren Mooney

McFarland & Company, Inc., Publishers
*Jefferson, North Carolina*

LIBRARY OF CONGRESS CATALOGUING-IN-PUBLICATION DATA

Names: Mooney, Darren, 1987– author.
Title: Christopher Nolan : a critical study of the films / Darren Mooney.
Description: Jefferson, North Carolina : McFarland & Company, Inc., 2018 |
Includes bibliographical references and index.
Identifiers: LCCN 2018041214 | ISBN 9781476674803 (softcover : acid free paper) ∞
Subjects: LCSH: Nolan, Christopher, 1970– —Criticism and interpretation.
Classification: LCC PN1998.3.N65 M66 2018 | DDC 791.4302/33092—dc23
LC record available at https://lccn.loc.gov/2018041214

BRITISH LIBRARY CATALOGUING DATA ARE AVAILABLE

ISBN (print) 978-1-4766-7480-3
ISBN (ebook) 978-1-4766-3461-6

© 2018 Darren Mooney. All rights reserved

*No part of this book may be reproduced or transmitted in any form
or by any means, electronic or mechanical, including photocopying
or recording, or by any information storage and retrieval system,
without permission in writing from the publisher.*

Front cover: A scene from the 2017 film *Dunkirk* (Warner Bros./Photofest)

Printed in the United States of America

*McFarland & Company, Inc., Publishers
Box 611, Jefferson, North Carolina 28640
www.mcfarlandpub.com*

# Table of Contents

Preface 1

1 • *Following* 3
2 • *Memento* 13
3 • *Insomnia* 27
4 • *Batman Begins* 36
5 • *The Prestige* 51
6 • *The Dark Knight* 67
7 • *Inception* 85
8 • *The Dark Knight Rises* 99
9 • *Interstellar* 117
10 • *Dunkirk* 131

Appendix: Interview with Jeremy Theobald 147
Chapter Notes 155
Bibliography 209
Index 211

# Preface

Christopher Nolan is undoubtedly one of the most influential and successful directors working in contemporary Hollywood. To date, his films have grossed over $2 billion at the United States box office and over $4.5 billion internationally. His work has prompted in-depth discussion and analysis from both film critics and academics.

This book aims to provide an exploration of the director's first ten films, from *Following* through to *Dunkirk*. There is a heavy emphasis on the popular discourse around these films, the culture upon which they comment and also the culture which they have shaped. The goal is to explore Nolan's methodology as a storyteller, both in how he constructs those stories and in how those stories seem to speak to the cultural moment.

Particular attention is paid to the bridging of subjectivity and objectivity in Nolan's work; the translation of stories that are deeply personal to the director into films with an incredibly wide appeal.

This examination of Nolan's filmography aims to provide a context for his work, both in terms of his craft and technique and also how those films resonate in the cultural context of the early twenty-first century. It does so through a variety of means: quotations from interviews with Nolan and his collaborators, engagement with the critical discourse around his work, and also broader cultural commentary on the political and social realities of the wider world.

# 1

## *Following*

To quote the cliché, form tends to follow function.
In the films of Christopher Nolan, function tends to follow form.
Nolan's films often seem reverse-engineered. In terms of basic storytelling, he tends to create from the outside in. Repeatedly in his filmmaking, he seems to settle upon a particular style or technique that he wishes to use and then designs the film around it. Certain elements of his work are dictated by forces external to the films themselves, and the process of cinematic creation becomes an act of back-filling.

This is perhaps most obvious in *Batman Begins*, where a large chunk of the narrative is built around Bruce Wayne's decision to dress up as a giant bat to fight crime. *Batman Begins* essentially reverse-engineers its own core intellectual property, interrogating the core premise of an internationally recognizable brand.[1]

This logic also applies to many of Nolan's other films. A lot of his interest in *Inception* came from designing a movie where the exposition would not exist in service of the plot, but where the plot might serve as an engine for exposition.[2] Part of the creative process for *Interstellar* was in asking Hans Zimmer to come up with a piece of music inspired by an abstract and emotional short story, which then fed back into an epic science fiction movie.[3]

This is particularly true of Nolan's feature-length debut *Following*. Its content was designed very much from the outside inwards. Its narrative, its tone, its themes, the cinematic technique—these aspects were all secondary to the production realities that Nolan knew that he would face in bringing the film to life. *Following* was cannily designed with those constraints built into it, potential limitations woven into its architecture.

Like many cinematic debuts, *Following* is ruthlessly utilitarian, a feature-length work that is largely defined by the boundaries imposed on its production by issues like budget and resources. However, what is most striking about this aspect of it is how perfectly it reflects Nolan's filmmaking aesthetic. He adopted this approach throughout his life, from his earliest forays into filmmaking through to his status as a brand-name director.

Christopher Nolan was born in London on July 30, 1970. His father was a British advertising executive who worked as a creative director. His mother was an American flight attendant who would later work as an English teacher. The family split their time between London and Chicago, with their children traveling back and forth across the Atlantic.

Nolan fell in love with cinema at a very early age. "I went to the movies a lot as a kid," he recalls of his childhood. "That first *Star Wars*, that George Lucas directed, came out in 1977 when I was seven years old. It made a huge impression on me, in terms of the scope of it and the idea that you could create an entirely different experience for the audience, literally any world, more than one world, a whole different galaxy."[4]

*Star Wars* would be a formative influence on young Nolan, even beyond the direct connection that might be drawn to the blockbuster aesthetic of his films after *Batman Begins* or even the obvious stylistic debt owed in his own gigantic family-saga-as-space-opera epic *Interstellar*. In many ways, *Star Wars* inspired Nolan to become a storyteller.

Returning to London, Nolan regaled school friends with his account of *Star Wars*, which had yet to be released in the United Kingdom.[5] This was a formative experience as a storyteller. He later likened his interest in narrative and storytelling to the art of organic conversation, suggesting that his interest in non-linear narratives reflects the way in which people verbally share stories.[6]

*Star Wars* influenced more than just Nolan's storytelling. It inspired the child to take up the art of filmmaking. At age seven or eight, Nolan titled his cinematic homages *Space Wars*,[7] cast his younger brother Jonathan as an extra[8] and filmed using sets constructed from clay, flour, egg boxes and toilet rolls.[9] An uncle who worked at NASA helpfully provided footage from the Apollo missions, which Nolan spliced into his films.[10]

According to Jonathan, the Nolan family still has copies of these early home movies stored on their hard drives,[11] and Nolan remains a *Star Wars* fan. In the lead-up to the 2015 release of J.J. Abrams' belated sequel *Star Wars: Episode VII—The Force Awakens*, Nolan joked about what it must have felt like to work under the pressure of the expectations of "forty-somethings like me who live and die with each new bit of information about *Star Wars*."[12] Nolan tangentially contributed to *The Force Awakens*, mailing an IMAX lens to Abrams.[13]

*Star Wars* might have been a key and formative experience for the young Nolan, but it was not the only film to heavily influence the would-be filmmaker. His first memory of seeing a film in the cinema was the re-release of *Snow White and the Seven Dwarfs*, and he remembered being so terrified of the Witch that he would hide behind the cinema seats.[14] He also recalls a re-release of *2001: A Space Odyssey* making a powerful impression on him a year after *Star Wars*.[15]

The film *2001: A Space Odyssey* may have had a significant influence on how Nolan approached filmmaking, with the director stressing that the film's infamously ambiguous narrative was largely irrelevant to a young child just taking the experience in. Nolan reflects, "I don't remember being remotely concerned about what it meant or whether it was elusive or confusing."[16]

Nolan decided very early in his life that he wanted to construct films. "You know how you're supposed to have a character arc in a screenplay?" asks Jonathan Nolan. "My brother would not make a good character. There's a straight vector line, straight out of the womb: Filmmaker. Didn't waver, didn't wrestle with any of the doubts that plague the rest of us."[17]

Nolan's family encouraged him. Nolan has said that his parents were both creative; "I think they were thrilled that I was interested in doing something creative and they lent me their camera—which, you know, I wound up breaking. I strapped it to the bottom of a car and bottomed out, smashing it, which my dad wasn't very happy about."[18]

Nolan's interest in becoming a filmmaker informed a lot of his subsequent life choices. At University College London, he studied English Literature. "I didn't really have anything else to do," Nolan recalled. "My dad was very encouraging, but pointed out that you might want to get a degree in something unrelated to what you want to do because it gives a different take on things."[19]

This was in some ways a pragmatic and utilitarian decision. Nolan's primary influences tend to be rooted in cinema rather than literature.[20] He was in part interested in studying the mechanics of storytelling as a mechanism to enable his filmmaking.[21] As a young filmmaker, he would either have to write his own material to direct, or find a writing partner to write specifically for him.

Nolan's literary interests reflected what would become his own narrative style. He cites Graham Stiles' *Waterland* as a major influence on his own storytelling, particularly in its subjective and non-linear style that served to render the reader an active participant in the narrative. Nolan remarks of the book, "It's structured with a set of parallel timelines and effortlessly tells a story using history—a contemporary story and various timelines that were close together in time (recent past and less recent past), and it actually crosscuts these timelines with such ease that, by the end, he's literally sort of leaving sentences unfinished and you're filling in the gaps."[22] Nolan's other literary fascinations extended to pulp and genre fiction: Raymond Chandler, James Ellroy, Jim Thompson.[23]

Nolan consciously decided not to study film at third level. He preferred that his experience and understanding of film remain subjective and personal, rather than rendering it academic or objective.[24] Nolan has argued that his emphasis on hands-on experience with filmmaking rather than a third-level education provided him with "a very organic approach to understanding all the different bits of the craft."[25] The only film class that Nolan ever attended was given by Philip Horne as part of his English Literature course.[26]

Nolan reportedly chose University College London in large part due to the facilities afforded to its student filmmakers.[27] "It was a very fun environment because they had 16mm equipment," Nolan recalls. "I wasn't doing courses or anything—it was totally a student-run thing that we were able to do, and I think that was kind of the fun of it. There was no discipline whatsoever. It was literally just access to equipment and other like-minded people, you know?"[28] Nolan very quickly became president of the film society and began using its resources to further his filmmaking.[29]

While in college, Nolan began producing short films. Finished in 1989, *Tarantella* was a surrealist short produced with his childhood friend Roko Belic.[30] It was televised on *Image Union* on the public broadcasting station in Chicago, an impressive accomplishment for a college student who had yet to turn 20.

Nolan became more active and more prolific in the mid–nineties. In 1995, his short film *Larceny* was shot using University College London equipment, and it played at the 1996 Cambridge Film Festival. Although not made available to the public, it is considered one of the finest short films that University College London ever produced.[31]

*Larceny* also marked the first collaboration between Nolan and his college friend Jeremy Theobald.[32] Theobald would play the lead roles in Nolan's next two projects.[33] In 1997, Nolan would cast Theobald as the lead character in his three-minute short film *Doodlebug*.

*Doodlebug* is much more surreal than the bulk of Nolan's feature-length output.[34] In it, a man hunts a miniaturized version of himself through a dingy apartment, crushing the smaller version of himself just in time to be crushed in turn by a larger version of himself. *Doodlebug* is the earliest of Nolan's work that is still widely available to curious cinephiles, inevitably making the rounds on various film sites every time a major Nolan project is released in cinemas.[35]

Although very different in terms of storytelling than many of Nolan's later works, *Doodlebug* does share some of the same fascinations. The recursive structure of the story, with a man crushing himself before being crushed by himself, recalls Nolan's fascination with nested narratives; this recurs throughout his work.[36] Perhaps fittingly, given its status as the most personal of Nolan's films, *Interstellar* has the strongest connection to *Doodlebug*, both films hinging on the image of rooms within rooms piled on top of one another recursively.[37]

Nolan acknowledges his interest in these recursive structures. "I'm very inspired by the prints of M.C. Escher and the interesting connection-point or blurring of boundaries between art and science, and art and mathematics," Nolan concedes. "Also, the writing of Jorge Borges, the great Argentinian writer, wrote all kinds of incredible short stories that dealt with paradox. But I feel like films are uniquely suited towards addressing paradox, recursiveness, and worlds-within-worlds."[38]

After these three shorts, Nolan embarked upon a more ambitious creative effort. *Following* was the director's second attempt to make a full-length film; the first was never completed due to technical limitations.[39] In many ways, Nolan reverse-engineered *Following* from the technical limitations imposed upon it.

Many of the creative decisions on *Following* were a result of outside concerns. "If we shoot black and white, so we can get a bit of an expressionist style, cheaply and quickly," he explains. "If we do it predominantly handheld camera, so we're not trying to ape larger moviemaking techniques with the dolly and so forth, things that require a large amount of money."[40] These formal decisions then informed the core of the movie; the decision to shoot in black-and-white with a handheld camera was reflected in the choice of story being told, a subjective neo-noir about shifting loyalties and identities.

*Following* developed as an extrapolation from *Larceny*. Nolan recalls, "We made an eight-minute film about a burglary, shot in B&W on 16mm costing us £200. When I wrote *Following*, one of the things going on in my head was, 'We can make an eight-minute movie for £200 so that means we can make an 80-minute movie for £2000.' As it turns out that was pretty much what we did."[41]

While working on *Following*, Nolan had a full-time job making corporate videos.[42] This job taught him a lot of the efficiency that he would bring to bear on *Following*, in particular a mindfulness about getting coverage on a tight schedule.[43] Working on a budget of $6000,[44] Nolan and his crew shot the film on weekends over the course of a year; the entire production team and their equipment would cram into the back of a taxi to get from one location to another.[45] Nolan used his parents' house as a primary shooting location.[46]

Nolan developed a lot of his directorial hallmarks while working on *Following*, techniques and philosophies that he carried over to bigger budget filmmaking. A lot of this was simple efficiency and pragmatism. On an average film, roughly 15 minutes of film are shot for every one minute seen on-screen; Nolan produced one minute of usable footage for every two and a half minutes shot.[47] Nolan earned a reputation as a director who could come in under-time and under-budget on blockbusters.[48]

Nolan would have his actors extensively rehearse their scenes, so that he could capture everything that he needed in only one or two takes. "I thought we could [go] to a location that we had for an hour, jump in, do a scene we'd done 100 times before and film it, and give them one or two takes—most of the film is first takes, some are second."[49] While Nolan occasionally had difficulty recording sounds, he would have the actors record "dry takes" of audio only to loop over the footage, a technique that he later employed when working with the loud IMAX cameras on *The Dark Knight*.[50]

*Following* features many of Nolan's stylistic quirks and preferences, but a lot of them derived from production limitations. In terms of Nolan's signature narrative tropes, *Following*'s non-linear structure was driven by the realities of its production. "The non-linear chronology helped us keep continuity in an organic way," he explains.[51] Similarly, he retained his preference for the use of a single camera even when working on films with budgets large enough to support multiple cameras. Beyond that, Nolan's editorial fondness for crosscutting and inserts originated with the practical no-frills filmmaking of *Following*, where he discovered that crosscutting and inserts could help to conceal gaps in coverage.[52]

In some ways, the narrative of *Following* is largely a result of a variety of outside factors, from Nolan's clear desire to make a feature-length film to the understandings of the technical limitations of a film produced in the only manner available to him. It might be clichéd to suggest that artists put part of themselves in their work, but that cliché has some currency; whether apocryphal or not, there is some truth in the observation frequently attributed to Oscar Wilde that "in every first novel the hero is the author as Christ or Faust."[53]

As with a lot of Nolan's films, *Following* plays as meditation on the act of creation.[54] Its two central characters are presented as voyeurs, observers of human nature. This has obvious parallels with the act of moviemaking, an inherently voyeuristic process that invites the audience to take an extended look into the lives of these central characters.[55] Nolan reinforces this connection between the act of moviemaking and the act of voyeurism.

Due to technical constraints, the bulk of *Following* was shot with a hand-held camera; this gives the film an intimate quality.[56] Similarly, the use of real-life locations rather than sets forced Nolan to place the camera in a physical space. This positioning suggests that audience members are navigating these surroundings rather than existing objectively "outside" of them.

Even beyond budgetary and technical constraints, Nolan uses subjective shots repeatedly over the course of the film, most notably in the early stalking sequences. The audience is invited to feel the same vicarious thrill as the protagonist as he follows his subjects through crowded spaces. Through the framing device of an interrogation between a police officer and the protagonist, the audience is keenly aware that they are seeing the events of the film through the eyes of the protagonist.[57]

This use of voyeurism and subjectivity lends itself to the trappings of *film noir*. Nolan has acknowledged that at least part of his interest in the genre is that it allows young writers and directors to step outside some of the more self-indulgent clichés of amateur film. "For a young filmmaker it's a great genre. It draws on your real-life neuroses, your real-life paranoia, your real-life fears," he says. "I think particularly it's a good genre when you're younger—unless you want to make films about college grads looking for a job, or trying to get into the film business. Which I don't particularly."[58]

Writers tend to enjoy writing about writers,[59] just like Hollywood tends to enjoy making movies about Hollywood.[60] For Nolan, the trappings of *film noir* provided a mechanism with which he could sidestep that potential hurdle. Even with that caveat in mind, *Following* still suggests a correlation between the act of voyeurism and the art of creation, with the protagonist revealed as a failed writer.[61] More than that, the protagonist is a very particular sort of writer. To maintain control of his obsession, he has to impose order upon it. "I had to start making up rules to … just try and keep it under control," the character says. As many (including Nolan) have noted, he is a writer who tends to structure his stories around rules that are very clearly articulated to the audience.[62]

*Following*'s narrative fascination with subjective viewpoints is reflected in how Nolan approaches the mechanics of filmmaking. Nolan's tendency to wear a video monitor around his neck has become a mimetic mutation,[63] a special subset of the Internet's wry fascination with his sartorial style[64] and shorthand for his own brand of directorial eccentricity.[65] However, it serves a very clear purpose in terms of how Nolan approaches filmmaking.

Nolan is a subjective director, one who literally puts himself in the position of the camera when trying to capture a shot. The shot exists in his head, and the goal is to translate that to film. "That's always felt the right way to approach storytelling to me," he explains, "to know the shot that's going to be on-screen at any moment, and taking the camera and putting it on the shot."[66] From Nolan's perspective, he is always the primary audience for his own storytelling.[67] This subjectivity bleeds over into *Following*.

*Following* is obsessed with the act of looking and observing. Both of its central characters are essentially voyeurs. The protagonist stalks people through the streets, but comes into contact with a like-minded individual who pushes that idea even further. Cobb is a burglar, a man who breaks into people's homes and rifles through their belongings in order to get a snapshot of their lives. Cobb intrudes into family homes and couples' apartments, getting a read on who these people are on a fundamental level.

This act of peering is mirrored in Nolan's directorial style. The opening sequence of *Following* features a character putting on surgical gloves before exploring the spoils of a particular raid. The camera captures this inquiry through a set of inserts, focusing on the items in loving detail. These inserts would become a hallmark of Nolan's directorial style, an effective means of visual exposition frequently cut into monologues and conversations to effectively communicate information to the audience. However, in *Following*, this directorial tic becomes an obsession of itself.[68]

*Following* owes a conscious debt to Alfred Hitchcock, Nolan establishing a strong connection to the Master of Suspense with his feature-length debut.[69] Nolan has often expressed a kinship with Hitchcock and a respect for his cinematic techniques.[70] In particular, Nolan appreciates Hitchcock's mastery of plot and his ability to convey information in a clear and effective manner.[71]

It has become something of a cliché to compare these two directors.[72] The similarities are quite striking. Both Nolan and Hitchcock are directors who straddle the Atlantic, caught between the United Kingdom and the United States. Both Nolan and Hitchcock bring an incredible level of technical craft to work often considered "genre" entertainment, and have perhaps been overlooked and dismissed by institutions like the Academy because of that.

*Following* feels very much structured in the style of Hitchcock. Lucy Russell as is credited only as "The Blonde." The black-and-white cinematography, coupled with the 1.37:1 aspect ratio, evokes the texture of Hitchcock's films, particular in the sequences of the Blonde lounging around her apartment and scheming with Cobb.

Cobb acts like a consciously Hitchcockian antagonist. He is dapper and playful, his assumed intimacy with the protagonist evoking the perversion that underscores *Rope*. The movie's central plot hinges upon Cobb physically transforming the protagonist into a facsimile of himself through buying expensive clothes and restyling his hair, recalling the basic premise of *Vertigo*.

However, the most obvious point of comparison between Nolan and Hitchcock is their shared interest in subjective voyeuristic cinema—in placing the camera in such a position as to suggest that the audience is inhabiting the world of the film.[73] Hitchcock would invite the audience to peer, and even leer, into his films[74]; *Rear Window* was a point-of-view tale in which the voyeur was cast as the protagonist,[75] *Rope* was structured to resemble an extended unbroken take that creates the impression of a gaze held for 80 minutes,[76] while *Psycho* provided a more concrete connection between the voyeur and the audience.[77] Nolan tends to treat the camera in the same way, as a subjective audience for what is happening in a scene, right down to his methodology of mapping out a shot in his head and through his eye before trying to capture it on film.

As much as *Following* invites these comparisons between Nolan and Hitchcock, it also underscores key distinctions between them. Hitchcock's films tend to sublimate violence and sexuality in a provocative manner.[78] This is perhaps most obvious in Hitchcock's recurring fascination with asphyxiation.[79] It has been argued that many of Hitchcock's most famous films are "erotic thrillers."[80]

*Following* is perhaps Nolan's most sexually explicit work.[81] During the burglaries, Cobb expresses a curiosity in the sexual lives of the occupants, even catching one member of a couple engaged in an affair while framing the other for infidelity. While looting the Blonde's apartment, Cobb sniffs her underwear; both burglars help themselves to some of her undergarments. Later, the protagonist engages in a sexual affair with the Blonde, only for the film to reveal she is already sleeping with Cobb. *Following* makes a point to link sex and violence through comparing and contrasting how the Blonde and Cobb interact with the protagonist.

"Did you have to beat him?" the Blonde challenges Cobb. Cobb responds, "Did you have to sleep with him?" The Blonde seeks to coerce and control the protagonist through sex, while Cobb lashes out at him through violence. Together, the two characters serve to intertwine the twin Hitchcockian obsessions with sex and violence. "Did you enjoy it?" Cobb asks the Blonde. The Blonde replies, "Did you enjoy beating him up?"

However, even *Following* betrays Nolan's discomfort dealing with matters like sex and sexuality. The opening voiceover exposition stresses that the protagonist's obsession is not a sexual dysfunction of itself. "So you followed women?" the police officer asks.

The protagonist clarifies, "No, I didn't follow women. It wasn't a sex thing. I followed anybody." During one conversation, the Blonde refers to "the kind of kinky, voyeuristic shit men get into." The protagonist awkwardly shrugs it off. "I'm sorry. I'm not into any of that." It seems like *Following*'s protagonist only finds himself out of his depth when he allows sex to intrude into his voyeuristic pastime.

Despite this clear discomfort with sex and sexuality, *Following* is still the most candidly sexual of Nolan's films. Outside of the awkward and stilted sexuality of *Following*, Nolan's filmography is remarkably asexual.[82] His protagonists tend to be chaste and devoted, with female characters existing as romantic ideals rather than as objects of sexual desire.[83] In *Memento*, the protagonist is primarily motivated by the romantic memory of his dead wife.[84] In *Batman Begins* and *The Dark Knight*, Rachel Dawes exists as a romantic alternative to Bruce Wayne's life as Batman.[85] Even when the male protagonists find some measure of familial fulfillment at the end of *The Prestige*, *Inception* and *Interstellar*, their family relationships tend to be defined in wholesome and asexual terms: fathers returning home to their sons and (primarily) daughters.[86]

Any comparison between Nolan and Hitchcock must acknowledge that Nolan is more interested in Hitchcock's techniques than in his recurring themes. Nolan is a director who is a lot less comfortable incorporating sexuality into his work, and that is quite evident in the way that *Following* attempts to balance its obligations as a Hitchcock pastiche with Nolan's relative lack of interest in human sexuality.

The narrative of *Following* was inspired by a real-life event. Nolan returned home one day to discover that his flat had been burglarized. This prompted an existential realization in the young director. "I realized that the door was just plywood, and that was never keeping anybody out," he said. "What was keeping people out was the social protocols that we have that allow us to live together."[87] *Following* is very invested in this idea of transgression and the breakdown of social order, something that rather overtly prefigures his later work on *The Dark Knight*, *The Dark Knight Rises* and *Dunkirk*.

The character of Cobb haunts Nolan's later narratives. Most obviously, Cobb shares his name with the protagonist in *Inception*; both characters are master thieves and it could be argued that they share a gift for mental manipulation. But Cobb also shares a certain sensibility with the Joker from *The Dark Knight*, in that he represents a corrupting and corrosive figure who attacks social norms.[88]

*Following* is a movie very keenly invested in the idea of disruption and transgression. Cobb positions himself as a disruptive force, randomly entering people's lives and sowing the seeds of chaos; he scatters keepsakes, hides belongings, stages infidelity. The film goes so far as to suggest that the protagonist is ultimately doomed in the moment that Cobb convinces him to break his most important rule.[89] Had the protagonist remained within the structures and boundaries that he set for himself, by confining his stalking to public areas rather than intruding directly into the lives of others, he would have been safe.[90]

*Following* sets up a recurring dynamic in Nolan's filmography, the idea of a transgression that serves to reinforce social norms. Cobb argues that his intrusions and disruptions only reinforce the existing structures and bonds. "That's what it's all about: interrupting someone's life, making them see all the things they took for granted," Cobb advises his new friend. "You take it away and show them what they had." This in many ways outlines the narrative and emotional logic of Nolan's scripts, the idea that disruptions to the lives of various characters are useful in that they serve to strengthen and reinforce existing structures.[91]

*Following* serves as an interesting template for the rest of Nolan's extended filmography. It demonstrates a lot about how Nolan approaches both the craft of storytelling and the technique of filmmaking. This is perhaps most obvious in how Nolan chooses to structure the film. His films are frequently structured in a non-linear manner, often with a nested or recursive structure. This has become something of a calling card for the director, shorthand in critical discourse around his work.[92] One of the more frequent criticisms of his output is that he allows this non-linear style to overwhelm his work and to crowd out his storytelling.[93]

*Following* features a lot of narrative tics that recur throughout Nolan's filmography. The storytelling is non-linear, with scenes transitioning between three separate timelines: the first encounter between Cobb and the protagonist; the protagonist after he suits up and seduces the Blonde; the protagonist after parting ways with Cobb. Scenes transition from one time period to the next, with little rhyme or reason. According to Nolan, "I decided to structure my story in such a way as to emphasize the audience's incomplete understanding of each new scene as it is first presented."[94]

There are obvious parallels with his other work. *Memento*, *Batman Begins* and *The Prestige* all feature storylines that crosscut their narratives across time and space, juxtaposing the characters' forward movement through time with events that occurred in the past. *Dunkirk* crosscuts through three time periods that all synchronize in one harrowing climax.

In *Following*, this crosscutting becomes a potent metaphor for trauma.[95] *Following* contends that violence and its consequences are never as clearly delineated as cause and effect, instead suggesting that they overlap and intrude upon one another. Repeatedly over the course of the film, the audience is forced to confront the consequences of a violent action before witnessing the violence itself.[96] In this way, the use of the non-linear narrative might be seen as an extension of Nolan's recurring fascination with social disruption and disorder as expressed through characters like Cobb in *Following* and the Joker in *The Dark Knight*. This fear of disorder and breakdown is so profound that it affects the very structure of the story.

At the same time, *Following* lacks the finesse that Nolan would bring to his later work. Even compared to the careful structuring and reveals of *Memento*, there is a clumsiness to the film's non-linear storytelling. Most notably, the varying narrative threads never quite come together in harmony and synthesis at the climax, as Nolan's story threads do in *Memento*, *Inception* and *Dunkirk*. Instead, *Following*'s crosscutting climax takes place within the framing device rather than between the three competing narratives, with the police interrogation of the protagonist juxtaposed with Cobb's murder of the Blonde almost as an afterthought.

These two structural elements—the multiple narrative threads and the crosscutting climax—would become a hallmark of Nolan's work. However, he had not yet figured out how to integrate them into one another. The film does not build its multiple narrative threads into a crosscutting climax; it instead resolves them before transitioning into the big reveal. There is an inelegance to that creative decision, one that undercuts a lot of the potential pay-off and creates the impression of a film that stops and then starts so that it might stop once again. There is an experimental quality to *Following*, a sense that Nolan is playing with storytelling tools that he will use to greater effect in his later work.

The director's first feature-length film, *Following* is clumsy and awkward in the way that many feature-length debuts tend to be. A lot of the film is very clearly reverse-engineered from Nolan's technical interests and the production limitations, the narrative serving primarily as an explanation or justification for the restrictions imposed on the creative team. However, it shares a lot of DNA with the features yet to come.

# 2

## *Memento*

Appropriately enough, the origins of *Memento* are hazy, even to those directly involved in its creation.

Nolan's then-girlfriend (and later wife) Emma Thomas had moved to Los Angeles to take a job with the production company Working Title.[1] Meanwhile, Nolan had been struggling to raise money or to generate interest within the British film industry, finding the environment to be "clubby."[2] He decided to travel to the U.S. to be with Thomas, and hoping to be able to take *Following* on the American festival circuit.[3]

Nolan stopped in Chicago to pick up his brother Jonathan, and the pair embarked upon a cross-country road trip.[4] They made small-talk for part of the journey before they ran out of things to talk about, "as brothers do."[5] To fill the silence, Jonathan shared an idea for a short story upon which he had been working.[6] Jonathan hoped to adapt the premise as a short story, while Christopher thought it might make for an interesting movie.[7] The two developed the concept in parallel, with Jonathan's short story published in *Esquire* around the same time that Christopher's movie went into limited release.[8]

This is certainly a compelling origin story for a cult movie. However, there is a slight wrinkle in the tale. According to Christopher, this conversation took place on the first day of the journey, no further than Wisconsin. According to Jonathan, it took place on the second day of the journey, past Minnesota.[9] Memory plays tricks.

Jonathan Nolan was one of his brother's earliest collaborators. "Some of my earliest memories are of Chris making stop-motion space films in our garage," Jonathan recalls. "I would help out to the degree a two-year-old was capable of helping out."[10] Jonathan remained a creative collaborator as Nolan become more professional. He worked as a grip on both *Doodlebug* and *Following*. Beyond contributing the story for *Memento*, Jonathan also worked with his brother as a writer on *The Prestige*, *The Dark Knight*, *The Dark Knight Rises* and *Interstellar*.[11]

Six years younger than Christopher, Jonathan became more Americanized than his sibling. While Christopher studied in London, Jonathan attended Georgetown University.[12] While there, Jonathan attended a psychology lecture on memory loss.[13] Jonathan seems to have been paying particular attention; *Memento* has been described as "an honorable exception" to the clichés of cinematic amnesia which "accurately describes the problems faced by someone with severe anterograde amnesia."[14]

Jonathan dropped out of college for a semester and traveled the world.[15] As he did, the ideas that would become *Memento* percolated and turned in his head. He and Christopher have a strong creative bond, frequently bouncing ideas off one another. "My brother and I have this kind of symbiotic relationship," says Jonathan. "When you're a writer, you're always looking to see if [your scripts] pass the jealousy test. Like, 'Damn, I wish I was doing that project.'"[16]

Jonathan and Christopher Nolan share a lot of similar interests and fascinations. According to Jonathan, "Collaborating with my brother is such a fun thing to do because, in many ways, we have similar minds, having grown up with the same references. I'm the younger brother, so I grew up watching all the hand-me-down VHS cassette tapes of all the films that he loved."[17] It makes sense that they would have a similar frame of reference. Jonathan explains, "You just get down to work and we have that shorthand, having grown up watching the same movies and reading the same books."[18]

Given their shorthand and their recurring collaborations, it can be difficult to divorce the creative visions of Christopher and Jonathan Nolan. It seems fair to suggest that their outlooks and perspectives might overlap significantly. At the same time, it is possible to see certain thematic strands develop in their work apart from one another, to suggest which interests are most strongly shared and which can be more forcefully attributed to one brother or the other.

For example, both Jonathan and Christopher have a recurring interest in non-linear storytelling structures. In particular, narratives that start in different places at different times and then collide at the climax. Christopher used this approach in *Dunkirk*, where three different storylines converge at the end. Similarly, the climax of Jonathan's work on the first season of *Westworld* hinges on the revelation that the story has been unfolding across three different time periods.[19] Apparently this is an interest shared by the two siblings.

Similarly, both Jonathan and Christopher are fascinated with the idea of "rules" and "structures" that ground a narrative. Christopher's films can occasionally be described as puzzle boxes, games that establish rules and then ask the audience to play along.[20] In Christopher's world, characters frequently set rules for themselves, many of which they skirt and break.[21] More than that, Christopher's films frequently articulate a set of rules to the audience that informs the action as it unfolds across the rest of the film.[22]

Even in Jonathan's work on television, this internal logic applies. The first season of *Westworld* portrays the eponymous theme park as a complex system laid out as a mystery to be unraveled by both the audience and the characters.[23] Ford maps out a path to self-awareness through a metaphorical "Maze." The Man in Black treats this artificial environment as a game to be defeated.[24] Treating the theme park as a bleak Hobbesian metaphor for the capitalist system itself, the Man in Black states, "This world is just like the one outside. A game. One to be fought. Taken. Won."[25]

As such, this fascination with rules and systems is shared by both Nolan brothers. Describing his condition over the phone in *Memento*, Leonard insists, "You really do need a system, if you're going to make it work." To both Christopher and Jonathan, narratives frequently seem to follow this logic, existing as carefully regimented and structured systems in which the controlled release of information is governed by rules that are often literalized by exposition from the characters.

In contrast, there are certain recurring ideas that appear to appeal more strongly to one sibling than the other. Identity might be one such example. Identity overlaps with Christopher's fascination with subjectivity in narrative. Indeed, a logical extension of telling a story from a certain point of view is to question that perspective. Identity comes up as a theme in a few of Christopher's early films that do not credit Jonathan as a creative collaborator: *Doodlebug* and *Batman Begins*.

Christopher's interest in identity is perhaps strongest in the films on which he collaborated with his brother: Leonard's existential crisis in *Memento*, the life shared between Fallon and Borden in *The Prestige*, the Joker's multiple-choice history in *The Dark Knight*, Bane's anonymity in *The Dark Knight Rises*. More than that, Jonathan carries over that fascination with identity into his own projects, with a potent political subtext.

Anonymity and identity were recurring fascinations in *Person of Interest*, a television show co-created by Jonathan. It's about a CIA agent turned vagrant who teams with a reclusive billionaire to battle the surveillance state.[26] Christopher has acknowledged the similarities between the artificial intelligence at the center of *Person of Interest* and a similar surveillance device at the climax of *The Dark Knight*. That device was added to early drafts of the *Dark Knight* script by Jonathan.[27]

Similarly, Jonathan's work on *Westworld* is similarly tied up in themes of identity and politics that reflect his work on *Memento* and *The Dark Knight Rises*. *Westworld* characters are rarely who they claim to be, with several revealed to be robots with implanted memories designed to create a sense of continuity and narrative much like Leonard cultivates his own story to account for his lack of memory. One of the Internet's favorite pastimes while watching the first season of *Westworld* was to guess which cast member was secretly a robot.[28]

Like *Person of Interest* before it, *Westworld* was overtly political in a way that evoked Jonathan's collaborations with Christopher. However, while *Person of Interest* inherited the paranoia about the surveillance state from *The Dark Knight*, *Westworld* was more interested in the possibility of revolution suggested by *The Dark Knight Rises*. Both *Westworld* and *The Dark Knight Rises* are predicated upon the assumption that a marginalized class will inevitably rise up against their oppressors.[29]

It seems fair to suggest that Christopher's most overtly politically charged work came in collaboration with Jonathan. Nevertheless, the two writers inform and play off one another. *Memento* is a particularly interesting example because Christopher's film was developed in parallel with Jonathan's short story, both drawing from the same core idea. It is interesting to compare and contrast the two finished versions of this particular story, the film *Memento* and the short story "Memento Mori."

There are any number of superficial changes, such as the difference in name afforded to the lead character. In *Memento*, Guy Pearce plays a man named Leonard. "Memento Mori" is narrated by a character named Earl. There are other differences made to the story necessitated by the shift in medium. "Memento Mori," a short story, can play more clearly with subjective and objective narratives than a feature film.[30] More to the point, *Memento* is driven by something resembling a linear plot, and so needs a more dynamic (rather than reflective) protagonist.[31]

The most profound and telling difference between "Memento Mori" and *Memento* is the manner in which the film adaptation embraces subjective ambiguity while the short story consciously avoids it. In "Memento Mori," it is very strongly suggested that the protagonist has brought his wife's killer to justice and that the tragedy lies in the fact that he will never remember this.[32] In contrast, *Memento* suggests that the protagonist has constructed an elaborate and unsolvable puzzle for himself so that he will never have to face that sense of futility and listlessness. This emphasis on subjectivity and ambiguity, on the idea that Leonard's personal narrative will not bend to the outside world, is very much in keeping with Christopher's storytelling sensibilities.[33]

Christopher worked on the script for *Memento* while *Following* was in postproduction.[34] But he adopted a different approach to the scripting of his second feature-length film. "With *Following* I determined the structure that I wanted to use, then I wrote the script chronologically and reordered the scenes according to the structure I wanted," he recalls. "One of the reasons I wrote *Memento* differently was that I had to do a tremendous amount of rewriting in order to get the flow that I wanted within its fragmented structure."[35] He consciously wrote the script in the same way that audiences would watch the movie, underscoring the subjective manner in which he approaches his storytelling. There is no linear version of *Memento* that has been chopped up to produce the released feature film; that non-linear quality is woven into the film's fabric.

Nolan had a finished script ready by the time he took *Following* on the festival circuit. This gave him an advantage over other young independent filmmakers vying for attention. Christopher: "The timing was great because very often, if you can get a little bit of attention, a little bit of success on the festival circuit, people say, 'Well, what would you want to do next?' And the tricky thing is, if you don't have a specific thing, you can't capitalize on that moment. I already had the script done so it was like, 'Well, this is what I'm going to do.'"[36] In fact, Nolan was so well-organized that he had actually finished shooting *Memento* by the time that he was giving interviews for the small-scale cinematic release of *Following*.[37]

Nolan optioned his *Memento* script to Newmarket Films at the San Francisco International Film Festival in 1998.[38] Nolan directed the film from his own screenplay, filming in California over 25½ days.[39] It was an interesting transition for a director who had filmed his first feature-length film with friends on weekends over the course of a year. According to Nolan,

> People will often ask me about taking on *Batman* or whatever, but the truth is that the biggest leap I ever made in my career was from *Following* to *Memento*. It was from working with friends, spending my own money, and then risking our time and effort, to spending millions of dollars of somebody else's money and having a proper crew there with trucks and trailers and all sorts of things going on.[40]

It was a process of transition from the amateur production of *Following* to the professional filmmaking of *Memento*. In some ways, it was more difficult to make *Memento* on a much larger budget than it had been to film *Following* on a part-time basis. Nolan says,

> This was a union film and out here I realized that to make a film for a million dollars is very difficult, because you're in this in-between world where you can kind of afford certain things but you can't quite afford to pay people properly and you don't have any money to do anything. After *Following*, I thought I could make a film for $500k then I started looking at what I could do, and it wasn't enough![41]

More than that, working on a professional film meant delegating a lot of the work that Nolan had previous done himself. He needed to bring on board a cinematographer; Nolan's eye was no longer the only one guiding the camera. "For me, that was a source of a great deal of concern, because all of my filmmaking to that point had been me with the camera, directing through the lens."[42]

Wally Pfister began his career as a news cameraman, covering politics on Capitol Hill.[43] (He was recruited by Robert Altman to play a news cameraman in *Tanner '88*; Pfister also shot the b-roll.[44]) Pfister was working as director of photography on the small film *Rustin*, shooting in Alabama, when he read the *Memento* script. He was immediately taken with the Nolans' backwards narrative, and convinced his agent to arrange an interview with the young director. Although Pfister maintains that the interview did not go particularly well, he got a call back for the job. "Apparently, his first four choices weren't available," Pfister jokes.[45]

It is hard to overstate the importance of a cinematographer to the look and feel of a film, and there have been countless great (and underrated) director-cinematographer combinations.[46] A lot of the look of the French New Wave can be traced to the work of cinematographer Raoul Coutard, who worked with Jean-Luc Godard, François Truffaut and Jacques Demy. Coutard's handheld camerawork and emphasis on natural lighting helped define the texture of the movement.[47] The tone that defined many of Ingmar Bergman's later films was set in collaboration with cinematographer Sven Nykvist.[48] Many Powell-Pressburger classics owe a lot to cinematographer Jack Cardiff.[49]

Nolan and Pfister became one the defining director-cinematographer combinations of the twenty-first century.[50] The two men understood one another, and worked from a similar foundation. Nolan's experience in low-budget filmmaking and Pfister's background as a news cameraman gave them both an appreciation of the physical and the natural. In particular, they shared an affinity for natural lighting. According to Pfister,

> I think that there's a simplicity that you can go back to after you learn a lot about lighting and after you learn the complicated lighting setups, and sort of relearn how to shoot and embrace natural light photography. It was always something that Chris Nolan and I had in common. We both love naturalistic look and feel, and the speed associated with it.[51]

This emphasis on natural lighting was something that Nolan carried over from *Following*, like his affection for insert shots as a cost-effective way of establishing the world within which his characters operate. "It's something I talked to Wally a lot about on *Memento*," Nolan reveals. "And *Memento*—for narrative reasons—is full of inserts. But also, when you're up against it in terms of trying to give a style to a film, it's a lovely way to be able to give the audience some feeling of texture in the world that's harder to get in the wider shots, when you don't have time and money and a lot of production value."[52]

In particular, the inserts in *Memento* tend to serve as character exposition. It is possible to tell a lot about Leonard by the close-ups on the dog-eared case file. A quick shot of a dirty plate establishes a sense of dilapidation within Natalie's home. They serve the same purpose as Cobb's narration about such items in *Following*, these objects suggesting a life for these characters outside the boundaries of the frame. These inserts are quick and economical, but also very effective at getting a point across in a way that isn't simple plot-driven exposition. In the filmography of Christopher Nolan, these insert shots often suggest a totemic quality to the objects with which these characters interact.[53] It frequently seems these objects serve as concrete markers of the world in which they live, invested with an emotional weight otherwise left largely unspoken.[54]

They also provide a grounding for a script that is very subjective in its storytelling.

Leonard tells Natalie about the importance of these small certainties in providing some frame of reference for his condition: "There are things you know for sure. I know what that's gonna sound like when I knock on it." He knocks on a table. "I know what that's gonna feel like when I pick it up." He picks up a plate. The inserts do something similar for the audience.

*Memento* also inherits the non-linear structure of *Following*. Nolan designed the bulk of *Memento* to unfold backwards in order to "deny the audience the same information that was denied the protagonist."[55] Because the audience does not know the context heading *into* any given segment of the film, *Memento* places the audience within Leonard's subjective perspective.

Subjectivity was very important to Nolan when it came to structuring *Memento*, and he repeatedly placed the camera so as to put the audience in Leonard's position. Nolan: "What we tried to do with *Memento* was simply block the film from the character's point of view as much as possible. He walks into a room and you're looking over his shoulder, exploring the room as he does."[56] The structure of the film is designed to replicate Leonard's condition.

In some ways, *Memento*'s structure is designed as a purer distillation of the approach that Nolan took to *Following*. Inspired by his work on *Larceny* and *Doodlebug*, Nolan had approached the production of *Following* as a series of short films stitched together. "What we did with *Following* was, we made a short film every weekend," he recalls.[57] However, *Following* still had a clear overarching plot, and its transition between time periods could often seem arbitrary.

In contrast, *Memento* is actually structured so that it can play like a series of short films stitched together. Because of the narrative's unique structure, Nolan needs to ensure that every segment of the film has enough going on to hold the audience's attention, even with the pattern of the overall arc withheld. That means that each five-minute block of the film needs to offer some self-contained nugget of storytelling. Sometimes that nugget can arbitrary, like a really clever hook that sustains the audience until the next jump back. Sometimes that nugget is character-driven, like the short scenes between Leonard and the prostitute. Most of these sequences are structured to contain something resembling a bite-sized arc that *also* enriches the larger picture.

*Memento* inherits the theme of trauma from *Following*, albeit handled in a much more direct manner. Once again, trauma is presented as something that disturbs an individual's sense of continuity.[58] Leonard's life has clearly been thrown into disarray, right down to his efforts to disassociate from his own trauma by projecting the tragic death of his wife onto the story of Sammy Jankis. Recalling the bruises on Bruce Wayne's body early in *The Dark Knight*, Leonard's tattoos become markers of his trauma and reminders of the loss that he has suffered.[59] William G. Little argues that, through these tattoos, Leonard "is replaying the original trauma on the field of his body."[60]

Nolan repeatedly reinforces this idea of replaying trauma through the use of mirroring and repetition. Framing and inserts provide a strong juxtaposition between certain objects and events, suggesting that trauma plays out in vicious and repeating cycles that can be difficult to break.[61] There is a sense that the characters are trapped within repeating narratives and events, with little capacity to break free of them.

As with *Following*, *Memento*'s non-linear narrative flow serves to literalize the experience of trauma, but in a more overt manner. Due to the narrative flow of *Memento*, the audience is frequently confronted by the *aftermath* of violence before witnessing the violence itself.[62] Bruises and scars are provided without context, effect divorced from cause in a way that evokes the discontinuity of trauma.

*Memento* also streamlines the non-linear flow that Nolan employed in *Following*, alternating between two major threads instead of three. The primary thread flows backwards from Leonard's murder of Teddy, in color. The secondary thread progresses linearly in black-and-white, with Leonard providing exposition about his condition and imparting other plot-centric information. Whereas *Following* bungled its crosscutting climax by resolving its three threads *before* heading into the big reveal, *Memento* cleverly dovetails its two threads, allowing the climax of the story to serve as a pivot point between the two arcs.[63]

*Memento* is largely inseparable from its primary narrative device, the plot woven tightly into its stylistic sensibilities. Nolan concedes that its basic plot is straightforward, with the movie only complicated by its structure:

> The whole dynamic of the script is aimed at taking a really very simple story and putting the audience through the perceptual distortion that Leonard suffers, thereby making this simple story seem incredibly complex and challenging, the way it would be for someone with this condition. Which isn't to say that there aren't all kinds of complexities at the end of the story, but the basic plotting is actually very simple.[64]

During pre-production, it was suggested that the story could be restructured to play out in a more linear manner. "People were asking me to do that, and I always refused," Nolan recalls.[65] When the distributor insisted on editing a linear version of the story for the DVD, Nolan reveals, "I told them they could release it, but only with the repetitions because they are all different in slightly different ways. I also insisted that it was a hidden feature so it seemed less of a legitimate way to watch the film."[66]

Nolan was inspired to tell the story in this way by classic cinema. He contends that *Citizen Kane* was a narratively ambitious piece of work, but that cinematic storytelling grew increasingly conservative in the decades that followed. Nolan could point to one clear culprit. "I think what happened is TV," he explains. "TV is the most intensely linear format, and it's become the primary ancillary market for motion pictures. So you've got to create something where someone can start watching ten minutes late, and still absorb the whole thing over an hour on TV."[67] Nolan describes this as "the pizza delivery scenario," elaborating, "If a pizza arrives while you're watching TV, you have to answer the door, deal with the man and then be able to get straight back into the story, having missed three or four minutes."[68]

*Memento* makes a point to incorporate this criticism into the affliction affecting the movie's protagonist. Projecting himself onto Sammy Jankis, Leonard seethes with contempt as he describes the amnesiac as "this guy who couldn't follow the plot of *Green Acres*." *Memento* repurposes Nolan's observations about linear television plotting as a pinpointed insult within the narrative itself.

*Memento*'s ambitious structure is another example of how Nolan's storytelling logic allows function to follow form. Much like the narrative of *Following* was reverse-engineered from the production constraints of making a no-budget film in his spare time, *Memento* is designed as a cinematic experience that is not friendly to television broadcast. This would become a recurring fascination for Nolan, a desire to design films that took full advantage of the format.

In some respects, *Memento* arrived at the right cultural moment. Its unique structure is designed to reward re-watching. The movie does not hinge on a twist or anything that invalidates the rest of the movie to that point. Instead, the reveals within *Memento* are structured as to retroactively provide context for what came before. Quentin Tarantino contends,

> Part of the appeal of *Memento* is he's challenging you in a game to poke holes in the mystery, and the scenario, and the storytelling. As opposed to something like *The Sixth Sense* or *Fight Club* where you watch it, and then you want to see it a second time to poke holes in it. He's actually challenging you to do that. If you find a hole in it, that's almost as much fun as not finding a hole.[69]

Nolan had great difficulty securing a distributor for the film. Many studios showed an interest in the project, but expressed skepticism about whether the film could find an audience.[70] With the support of Steven Soderbergh, Nolan convinced Newmarket to distribute it themselves. *Memento* went into limited release in March 2001 and went wide two months later. The studio got a $25 million return on their $9 million investment.[71]

The DVD was released in September 2001. Three months later, DVD sales topped VHS sales for the first time.[72] The arrival of DVD represented a significant change in home media. DVDs offered a higher resolution than VHS, and one that did not deteriorate with each use.[73] They also offered more control over navigation and configuration.[74] Beyond this, they provided special features that allowed them to be packaged as complete multimedia experiences.[75] *Memento* capitalized on this interest in DVD as a new technology. The special edition gave viewers a series of questions to answer.[76] It also provided them with an alternate cut of the film.[77]

*Memento* arrived at a point where the Internet was going mainstream. In August 2000, 51 percent of American households were online, up from 42 percent in December 1998.[78] The Internet had become a hub for people to share interests and media with one another. Napster, launched in May 1999, allowed Internet users to share music files across vast geographical distances.[79] The first wave of film fan sites were going up, creating forums for fans to share gossip and to discuss movies. *Ain't It Cool News* was launched by Harry Knowles in 1996, *Film Threat* went exclusively online in 1997, and *Cinematic Happenings Under Development* was founded by Nick Nunziata in 1999.

There was a massive online community ready to process and dissect cinema. It was such a potent emerging cultural force that movies were beginning to acknowledge it. Kevin Smith released *Jay and Silent Bob Strike Back* in August 2001, only a few months after *Memento*. In that film, the character of Holden takes a direct shot at this obsessive side of online committing: "The Internet is a communication tool used the world over where people can come together to bitch about movies and share pornography with one another."[80]

Nolan's films attracted a devoted online following of fans willing to discuss and dissect his work.[81] This relationship began with *Memento*, which generated considerable online chatter and hype.[82] The plot's somewhat complicated nature proved perfectly suited to this changing form of film discourse.[83]

*Memento* arrived at a point in time when there was an audience for adventurous non-linear storytelling, and when a format and a forum were emerging that allowed that audiences to properly dissect and analyze the film, something that would not have been practical for a mass audience before that point. This became a cornerstone of Nolan's filmography, a following eager to pick apart and analyze the work that he was producing.[84] In many ways, Nolan was the right director with the right storytelling sensibility at the right time. Nolan's directorial arc seems to define twenty-first century filmmaking.

At the same time, *Memento* is a movie that is anchored in the late 1990s. It was shot between September 7 and October 8, 1999,[85] and did not premiere until the Venice Film Festival in October 2000.[86] Even allowing for its theatrical run the following year, the film exists within the cultural context of the nineties. There is a credible argument to be made that the nineties as a cultural moment spanned from the fall of the Berlin Wall to the destruction of the World Trade Center.[87]

Like a lot of Nolan's other films, *Memento* is fundamentally engaged with the art of narrative. In *Following*, the protagonist makes up stories about people that he follows. In the *Dark Knight* trilogy, Bruce Wayne transforms himself from man into myth. In *The Prestige*, Fallon and Borden live their lives as lies in order to preserve one impossible magic trick. In *Inception*, corporate spies hijack dreams with powerful stories. In *Interstellar*, parents become little more than ghosts to their children. In *Dunkirk*, a story of defeat is repurposed as a patriotic triumph.

However, *Memento* is particularly engaged with the idea of narrative as conspiracy theory. Leonard fashions an epic narrative around the death of his wife, positioning himself as a lone crusader hoping to avenge her death. He concocts an elaborate mythology about her murder scrounged together from incomplete information and vague clues that provide him with a sense of purpose and direction. There are drug dealers and warnings, torn pages and redacted information.

Conspiracy theories had always been a part of American popular discourse.[88] They became increasingly common after the assassination of John F. Kennedy.[89] During the seventies, events like Watergate shook public confidence and inspired all kinds of fringe speculation.[90] Of particular interest was the 18-minute gap in Nixon's tapes, a lacuna that drove all manner of feverish conjecture.[91]

Conspiracy theories entered the mainstream during the nineties. A number of factors made it possible for these fringe beliefs to enter public discourse. Writers (for example, Oliver Stone and Chris Carter) engaged with the notion of conspiracy in popular and successful media like *JFK*, *The X-Files* and *Nixon*, blurring the line between history and speculation while making it acceptable to openly discuss these ideas.[92] Similarly, the development of the Internet made it easier for people to discover conspiracy theories and to share them with like-minded individuals.[93]

The political climate of the nineties also contributed to the mainstreaming of conspiracy culture. The Clintons were subject to allegations of murderous cover-ups, shared and spread through right-wing media.[94] For their part, the Clintons publicly speculated about the sinister manipulations of a "vast right-wing conspiracy."[95] These conspiracy theories fueled media that could no longer be dismissed as fringe.[96]

At the same time, postmodernism was creeping into popular discourse.[97] Free of the rigid ideological dichotomy of the Cold War, there was room to debate and discuss notions of cultural identity and shared history.[98] History itself was treated as something subjective, long-accepted beliefs challenged and debated.[99]

More than that, it was easy to see the appeal of conspiracy theories, particularly in the nineties. After the end of the Cold War, America was largely unchallenged as a geopolitical power. Charles Krauthammer described this strange interlude as "the unipolar moment,"[100] while Francis Fukuyama more ambitiously insisted that it was "the end of history."[101] Whatever it was, it represented a moment at which the United States had no clear external enemy.

At the same time, complex social and political forces were at work. Globalization was radically changing the communities, reconfiguring economies and shifting demographics.[102] A culture war was raging to define American identity into the twenty-first century.[103] Even though crime was down in the nineties,[104] there was a moral panic about waves of violence on American streets.[105] Despite reassurances that the American GDP rose significantly during the decade, many Americans did not feel the benefits.[106]

Conspiracy theories are narratives that make sense of a seemingly arbitrary and chaotic world. They offer reassurance and reinforcement that *somebody* is in control. Even if that *somebody* is an evil conspirator, it is somehow more assuring than accepting that the universe is random and that individuals are subject to forces beyond any mortal or moral reckoning.[107]

This is the key to any conspiracy theory, from the assassination of JFK to the belief in a secretive "deep state." It serves to make sense of what would otherwise be a frighteningly random series of events. "They can't accept that someone as inconsequential as Oswald could have killed someone as consequential as Kennedy," author Robert Dallek says of Kennedy conspiracy theorists. "To believe that only Oswald killed Kennedy—that there wasn't some larger plot—shows people how random the world is, how uncertain. And I think it pains them; they don't want to accept that fact."[108]

The mythology that Leonard cultivates for himself in *Memento* plays into this idea. In his final (or first) conversation with Teddy, Leonard discovers that he has been creating gaps in his own narrative in order to prolong his search for meaning. "You don't want the truth," Teddy argues. "You make up your own truth, like your police file. It was complete when I gave it to you. Who took out the 12 pages?" When Leonard refuses to make the leap, Teddy presses the point: "It was you." Leonard is offended. "Why would I do that?" Leonard explains, "To create a puzzle you could never solve."

Leonard is stuck in a world without any meaning to him. He has no real identity. The climax reveals that Leonard has been walking around in a dead man's clothes and driving a dead man's car. "You don't know who you are," Teddy taunts in the movie's opening scene. He repeats the accusation later in the film. Leonard responds, "I'm Leonard Shelby. I'm from San Francisco." Teddy: "No, that's who you were."

Without a memory or an identity, Leonard has no frame of reference for his experiences and no direction for his life. He is trapped in weird postmodern limbo, without a past and without a future. In many ways, this encapsulates a lot of the anxieties of living in America during the nineties. Leonard cannot imagine a world without an enemy against which he might define himself, so he cultivates a conspiracy and a mythology to imbue his life with a grander sense of purpose.

The cruelest irony of *Memento* is the implication that Leonard's condition is not obscuring anything particularly important. In the climactic scene, Teddy explains what happened to Leonard's wife. They killed the attacker a long time ago, but there was no meaning to the act. "Does it matter who?" Teddy asks, and the film suggests that he has a point. "No reason, Lenny, no conspiracy, just bad fucking luck. Couple of junkies too strung-out to realize your wife didn't live alone." There was no grand meaning to this, no massive sinister force at work. Instead, Leonard and his wife were victims of pure chance in a chaotic world.

More than that, the climax reveals that Leonard's wife survived the assault. Instead, she suffered the same fate that Leonard has projected onto the wife of Sammy Jankis.[109] Leonard killed his wife by over-administering her insulin. Leonard is effectively hunting himself, an irony that the film underscores repeatedly by dressing him in the clothes and giving him the car of the last "Johnny G" and by having Teddy instruct him, "Maybe it's time you started investigating yourself." Leonard takes great pride in his ability to detect truth in other people. As an insurance investigator, that was his job. "I had to see through people's bullshit. It was useful experience, because now it's my life." The irony is that Leonard lacks the capacity or the willpower to turn that perception back on himself.

This is a reflexive twist on the conventions of *film noir*, with Leonard's investigation ultimately illuminating his own psyche.[110] It represents Nolan's devotion to subjective storytelling. Everything in *Memento* ultimately reflects back to Leonard himself. Experiences and events are defined primarily as they relate to Leonard. Even his desire to avenge the death of his beloved wife serves as an attempt to exorcise his own guilt and avoid a sense of powerlessness. Leonard's love for his wife is something that gives him pleasure, but has little objective value beyond that. "Tell me about her again," Natalie urges Leonard. "Why?" he asks. Natalie responds, "Because you like to remember her."[111] Leonard insists that his attempt to avenge her death has objective value, even if he can't remember it. "My wife deserves vengeance, and it doesn't make any difference whether I know about it," he tells Natalie. However, the climax suggests that Leonard's experience of that retribution is the *only* thing that matters, because he needs to keep reliving that cycle of violence to give his life meaning.

*Memento* repeatedly suggests that Leonard's condition simply allows him to rationalize what people do every day. As Leonard points out, human memory is fallible and prone to distortion to support a subjective viewpoint. "Memory can change the shape of a room; it can change the color of a car," Leonard assures Teddy. "And memories can be distorted. They're just an interpretation, they're not a record, and they're irrelevant if you have the facts." Leonard is correct to point out that subjectivity and fallibility of memory render eyewitness testimony suspect in criminal cases.[112] In fact, the very act of remembering an event involves rewriting the memory of that event, often with the emphasis shifted.[113] Memory is a jumble, a mess of subjective experiences subsequently filtered through subjective remembrances. The human brain is not a hard disk drive, and memory is not film.

*Memento* suggests that Leonard's condition has just literalized a very familiar process, creating a more efficient and systemic process whereby Leonard can engage in the day-to-day process of self-delusion. "So you lie to yourself to be happy," observes Teddy. "There's nothing wrong with that. We all do it. Who cares if there's a few little details you'd rather not remember?" Leonard just has a more literal excuse for this self-deceit than most people.[114]

Leonard is very much an archetypal Nolan protagonist, in that he has set up a system of rules and structures to dictate his day-to-day existence. The world is a complicated place, and Leonard imposes a system upon it so that it might make sense. "Sammy Jankis wrote himself endless notes," Leonard explains. "But he'd get mixed up. I've got a more graceful solution to the memory problem. I'm disciplined and organized. I use habit and routine to make my life possible." Like other major Nolan characters, Leonard uses his system to build a framework to navigate a chaotic and random existence.

*Memento* acknowledges that Leonard's system works relatively well. He is functional in a way that Sammy Jankis was not, able to navigate the mundane world. However, like so many Nolan characters, Leonard transgresses and faces repercussions for that. He breaks the rules of his own system. Like the protagonist in *Following* and Cobb in *Inception*, Leonard's disintegration begins the moment that he ignores the rules that he had carefully put in place. He decides to edit information and to manipulate data in a way that undermines and corrupts his system. This leads to a breakdown in moral order, and to Leonard's descent.

*Memento* embraces the subjectivity of its narrative in a way that reflects many late nineties movies. Without any memory or cohesive identity, Leonard repeatedly questions whether the world outside of himself actually exists.[115] This represents a more fundamental existential crisis than most Nolan protagonists, with the possible exception of *Inception*'s Cobb. Nolan began working on *Inception* around the time that *Memento* was released, so it makes sense that it would share some thematic concerns.[116]

Pop culture in the late nineties was particularly concerned with notions of the subjective experience of an objective reality. *Memento* even shares two major actors with perhaps the most iconic of these movies, *The Matrix*.[117] However, at the turn of the millennium, television and film repeatedly suggested that reality itself was an elaborate illusion: *Dark City, The Truman Show, The Thirteenth Floor, Harsh Realm, V.R. 5, eXistenz, Pleasantville*. All of these stories were built around the idea that there was a gulf between what the characters experience as reality and the objective nature of reality itself.

It has been suggested that this anxiety about the nature of reality ties back to cultural and technological concerns at the end of the twentieth century. Randy Laist, Associate Professor of English at Goodwin College, speculates that this existential crisis was prompted by both "the end of the Cold War" and the "the proliferation of new reality-bending technologies."[118] This makes a certain amount of sense, given the broader uncertainty created by the end of the Cold War and the massive social and technological advances such as the Internet and the computer-generated imagery in nineties blockbusters like *Independence Day* and *Jurassic Park*.[119]

Even if the world outside of Leonard can be confirmed to exist, the character's condition means that he has no appreciation of time as a concept. Time is the key to continuity and progress. Motion and change are only possible through time. Leonard is denied any possibility of growth. "How can I heal?" he wonders at one point. "How am I supposed to heal if I can't feel time?"

In some ways, Leonard is expressing an anxiety about existing at "the end of history." If there is no more history, then there is no more time. If there is no more time, there is no more progress. To many observers, the nineties appeared like a time period trapped in amber with little material social progress to accompany the vast technological advances. The nineties seemed like they could exist in perpetuity. Jean Baudrillard said that for "these generations which no longer expect anything from some future 'coming,'" it was entirely possible that "the year 2000 will not perhaps take place."[120] To some cultural observers, it feels like the nineties never actually came to an end, whether in terms of art[121] or fashion.[122]

Leonard is in many ways an embodiment of the cultural anxieties at the transition to the new millennium. Leonard exists without any sense of time or without any sense of history. He is a man who can no longer be certain of the history that he took for granted, but who also lacks a clearly defined direction in which he might go. As a result, Leonard is listless. Without any memory, Leonard becomes a man without an identity.

*Memento* feels like a snapshot of its cultural moment, one taken by Leonard with his Polaroid camera that slowly materializes on the print. It is too much to say that *Memento* is defined by the nineties, that its themes are unique within Nolan's body of work. However, the emphasis on those themes is filtered through the cultural anxieties of the decade around it. The rest of Nolan's films were released after 9/11, and so would exist within that particular cultural context. This is particularly true of his *Dark Knight* trilogy and *Inception*, but it informs all of his later films to a greater or lesser degree.

*Memento* was a striking piece of work when it was released. It generated considerable debate and speculation, with many audience members trying to figure it out and disentangle it. "I've seen it five times, and I've seen it differently each time," observed actor Carrie-Anne Moss.[123] Jonathan Nolan argued that the slight wrinkles in the movie's reverse timeline structure added to the complexity of the narrative. "If it was a straight-backwards film, you could just take that two-dimensional timeline and flip it over, but you can't do that with this film. Later on down the line, you realize that this film doesn't run back; it's a Möbius strip."[124]

Given the movie's structure and ambiguity, along with the narrative emphasis on rules and logic, it is understandable that many viewers approached it as a puzzle to be solved.[125] After its Venice premiere, the cast and crew sat down to enjoy dinner together. Jonathan recalls, "Someone realized after a few drinks that everyone there—the stars, the producers, my brother, myself—everyone had a different interpretation of what that film meant."[126]

While touring with the film, Christopher frequently fielded questions as audiences looked to him to explain the ending to them. At one early screening, he took the question at face value and decided to answer it. "Somebody had asked about my interpretation of the ending and I said, 'Well, it's all up to the audience but this is what it means to me,' and I gave them in great detail what exactly the ambiguities of the film meant to me," he recalls. That answer was never recorded.[127]

Jonathan admits to being somewhat frustrated by the fact that Christopher answered the question in the first place:

> I clocked him right afterwards and said, "You're a fucking bonehead." He has this one interpretation of the way the film goes, but by doing that he's misinterpreted the whole film. We all had a nice long argument about it. There is no objective truth. It would totally betray the concept of the film.[128]

"It's the last time I ever opened my mouth," Christopher says.[129]

More to the point, Christopher rejects the idea that his film endings are puzzle boxes that can be solved to provide a singular objective truth. Nolan prefers that his films are just experienced subjectively by the audience rather than picked apart or deconstructed.

"What I've found is, people who let my films wash over them—who don't treat it like a crossword puzzle, or like there is a test afterwards—they get the most out of the film."[130]

In some ways, this reflects a recurring theme of Nolan's work itself. His films are full of characters who attempt to make sense of a chaotic world by imposing structures upon them. However, these structures cannot account for human emotion or human need, and so the characters inevitably fracture or distort those systems in a way that results in horrific consequences. In the world of Christopher Nolan, with the notable exception of *Interstellar*, the universe is chaotic and arbitrary in a way that cannot be controlled or regulated or rationalized.

It makes sense that Nolan's films would adhere to a similar logic. Nolan is a writer and director who pays "meticulous attention" to the plotting of his films.[131] With that in mind, it is revealing that the director would make a point to leave gaps and lacunas in his otherwise carefully calibrated narratives.[132] Like Leonard, Nolan is constructing a puzzle that cannot be solved, that does not have a clear objective answer. However, *un*like Leonard, Nolan understands that this is the point of the exercise. The real world is full of empty space and hanging questions, people eagerly filling those gaps with conspiracy theories and speculation.

*Memento*'s ending is intended to leave questions for the audience to answer on their own. That audience includes the two brothers who first conceived of the story somewhere on a road trip between Chicago and Los Angeles, even if neither is entire sure where.

Jonathan adds, "Chris and I still disagree about the end of *Memento*, by the way, so I feel like that's as it should be."[133]

# 3

## *Insomnia*

*Insomnia* is unique in the Nolan canon.

Ironically, given its position directly following *Memento*, it has been described as "the Christopher Nolan movie that nobody seems to remember."[1] The word "forgotten" is apparently mandated in any retrospective discussion of *Insomnia*.[2] It's strange that a movie starring Al Pacino and Robin Williams could be forgotten.

There are multiple reasons why *Insomnia* is overlooked in the larger context of Nolan's filmography. Most obviously, it is the only Nolan film on which he did not receive a screenplay credit, although he was involved in the creative process and revised several drafts with Hillary Seitz.[3] Given Nolan's own collection of tropes and storytelling techniques, his modest involvement in *Insomnia*'s creative process would always set it apart.

Similarly, *Insomnia* falls in an awkward place in the Nolan canon. It followed *Memento*, which was a film that had a *huge* cultural impact.[4] It led into *Batman Begins*, which would spawn a sequel that became one of the defining films of the twenty-first century.[5] A well-made psychological thriller remake could get lost in the shuffle.

At the same time, *Insomnia* feels like a crucial step in the evolution of Christopher Nolan. It provides a sharp contrast to the rest of his filmography, while also serving as an important transition from the indie movie aesthetic of *Following* and *Memento* towards the more polished studio filmmaking of *Batman Begins* and *The Prestige*.

*Insomnia* might be easy to overlook, but it is also vitally important.

*Insomnia* is notable among Nolan's other films because it is explicitly a remake of another director's film: It shares a premise and title with Erik Skjoldbjærg's 1997 Norwegian film.[6] Nolan had seen and appreciated that film, and had expressed an interest in remaking it even before he began working on *Memento*.[7] Nolan had no luck convincing studios to invest in a untested young director, so he decided to work on *Memento* instead. Nevertheless, he remained interested in the possibility of an adaptation. "I kept my eye on the project when I found out that Warner had the remake rights," he explains.[8] Warner Brothers assigned Hillary Seitz to work on the screenplay.

When Nolan finished working on his memory-loss thriller, he turned his attention to the possibility of the remake. "When I finally finished *Memento*, I came back to Warner Brothers and showed them the film and was able to get on to the *Insomnia* project as the director. I then collaborated with Hillary Seitz on several drafts."[9]

Nolan was repeating a pattern that had served him well in the transition between *Following* and *Memento*, lining a potential new project in order to capitalize on the pre-release hype around his most recent work. There was never a lull in his early career, never a moment of indecision or hesitation, even as he was struggling to get *Memento* distributed.

> I was able to keep trying to push my career forward, as well, while the film sort of sat there in limbo. And so I was already signed up with Warners to do *Insomnia* by the time *Memento* kind of had its moment and that was great. I've had a lot of fortunate things happen to me, but that was one of the most fortunate because I wasn't put in the position of everybody saying, "Oh, you've done this very different, extreme thing. What are you going to do next? How do you top that?" I wasn't in that position at all because I was already making another film that was a relatively straightforward studio thriller, which I loved doing and poured myself into, and it was a great experience.[10]

*Insomnia* is not a Christopher Nolan film in the way that *Following* and *Memento* might be described that way. Nolan certainly had less creative impact on *Insomnia* than he did on *Batman Begins* and *The Prestige*. At the same time, there are certain elements of the film that stand out as Nolan's work, certain aspects of how the story is told that reflect his sensibilities as a filmmaker. Some of these are undoubtedly pre-existing elements that drew him to the project in the first place, and some of these elements were developed and expanded by Nolan through the writing process.

Most obviously, *Insomnia* is a modern *film noir* in the same way that *Memento* is. Both films subvert the expectations of the genre by constructing these seedy narratives against brightly lit backdrops; *Memento* is set in sun-drenched California, while *Insomnia* unfolds against an Alaskan wilderness where the sun never sets.[11] As with many modern (and color) *noir* films, these bright surroundings provide an effective contrast to the underbelly being explored.[12]

Although they unfold in very different parts of America, both *Memento* and *Insomnia* are ineffably tied to the American landscape and surroundings. "For me, there needs to be a strong relationship between the landscape of the film and the characters, and for the last two films that has been uniquely American," Nolan said when asked about the films.[13] They are the most archetypal of American narratives: They are fundamentally frontier stories, albeit ones that contrast sand and snow.[14]

In cinema, geography is often psychology.[15] Landscapes often exist as physical representations of the emotional and mental states of the people who inhabit them. In *Memento*, Leonard seems to be living on the very fringe of society, among the forgotten and the downtrodden.[16] In *Insomnia*, Dormer navigates a landscape that reflects his own psychological unease, the fog during the botched stakeout reflecting his own moral confusion.

In some ways, the archetypal Nolan protagonist is an extension of the hero of frontier myth. In Nolan's films, the characters frequently attempt to impose order on a chaotic world. Although buried a little deeper in the script, this is every bit as true of Dormer as it is of Leonard. "The situation isn't yours to control, Will," Finch tells Dormer over the phone. Nevertheless, it is clear that Dormer believes he can control the situation even as it spirals beyond his grasp.

This desire to build structures to contain and control the world reflects the core of the frontier mythology. The history of the American frontier is populated with tales of rugged European settlers who sought to tame a vast wilderness by imposing their notions of "civilization" upon it.[17] In the words of Frederick Turner, the western frontier offered settlers "a new field of opportunity, a gate of escape from the bondage of the past."[18]

This is what characters like Leonard and Dormer want; Leonard wants a landscape where he can constantly reinvent himself and relive his heroic revenge narrative over and over, while Dormer flees to Alaska to escape from the eyes of Internal Affairs. There is some irony that Leonard and Dormer both find themselves in westerly states where the continent gives way to the unyielding Pacific. Both Leonard and Dormer have literally run out of west.[19] Appropriately enough, neither manages to find what they were looking for.

Although the emphasis of Nolan's filmmaking would shift slightly after *Memento* and *Insomnia*, the frontier would simmer across his work. In *Inception*, the dream world is treated as a new frontier to be explored by pioneers and exploited by corporate interests,[20] feeling very much like an internalized psychological reflection of anxieties about cyberspace as a new frontier during the eighties and nineties.[21] The frontier imagery and symbolism is more overt in *Interstellar*, with the movie's branding and advertising consciously evoking Kennedy-era enthusiasm for the "new frontier."[22]

Nolan has a deep and abiding affection for American culture, perhaps owing to his childhood split between London and Chicago or his early encounters with *Star Wars*. Many of Nolan's films build upon iconic American imagery. With his *Dark Knight* trilogy, Nolan was embracing one of the most recognizable characters in American popular culture.[23] In *Interstellar*, he took the audience from stereotypical images of the American heartland into deep space.[24] Unlike movies like *Sunshine* and *The Europa Report*, *Interstellar* was explicitly about American space exploration.[25]

Nolan did not make a movie that felt exclusively and completely British until *Dunkirk*, which makes a certain amount of sense given the deeply personal nature of *Interstellar*.[26] This may also have been a pragmatic decision. After finishing *Following*, Nolan moved to the United States to be with Emma Thomas. However, his move was in part motivated by the fact that he could never generate support or interest from British production companies for the films that he wanted to make.

"To be honest, it's a very clubby kind of place," Nolan said of the British film industry. "In Hollywood there's a great openness, almost a voracious appetite for new people. In England there's a great suspicion of the new. In cultural terms, that can be a good thing, but when you're trying to break into the film industry, it's definitely a bad thing. I never had any luck with interesting people in small projects when I was doing *Following*. Never had any support whatsoever from the British film industry."[27] It is interesting to wonder how Nolan's career might have been different had he been able to finance projects in Britain.

*Insomnia* is an interesting and important film in his filmography because it established a strong relationship between the director and Warner Brothers. Warners would handle distribution on *Insomnia* and the seven films that followed.[28] Given that those eight collaborations returned $4.7 billion box office-wise, it makes sense that Warners would be happy with this longstanding creative partnership.

Among the major studios, Warner Brothers has a reputation for being "unusually director-friendly" in their cultivation of talent.[29] Even their blockbuster slate of superhero movies has been marketed by studio insiders as being "filmmaker-driven" rather than directed by heavy-handed studio interference.[30] There is some indication that this policy was in part inspired by the success of their relationship with Nolan[31] and there were suggestions that incoming president Toby Emmerich was trying to get away from that auteur-driven model when he took over in June 2017.[32] Nevertheless, Warner Brothers had cultivated longstanding and mutually beneficial relationships with directors Clint Eastwood and Stanley Kubrick dating back decades.[33]

Nolan credits a lot of his constructive interactions with the studio to advice given by Steven Soderbergh, who has also developed a lot of his films with Warner Brothers:

> I think I went into [*Insomnia*] taking a lot of advice from Steven Soderbergh, one of the executive producers. He told me the best way to deal with lots of producers was to be communicative and not to be defensive or fight all the time. We're brought up being told how bad the studio will behave and that expectation can actually create those problems. So it was a valuable lesson to be able to talk to the studio and gain people's trust and then you can work more easily.[34]

Warner Brothers has historically trusted Nolan to develop his own ideas on his own terms, with a minimum of interference. In recent years, this faith was based on past performance, but the studio also placed a great of faith in Nolan when entrusting him with the remake of *Insomnia* and the rebooted *Batman Begins*.[35] It is very difficult to imagine another filmmaker cultivating a relationship strong enough to convince the studio to invest in creative visions like *Inception*, *Interstellar* and *Dunkirk*, allotting huge sums of money to films unrelated to established intellectual properties or franchises.[36]

As part of his process, Nolan agrees on his approach with the studio, setting clear boundaries and understandings before he begins working on a movie. "I felt very supported in everything we tried to do with the film," he says of his experience working with Warners on *Insomnia*. "Importantly, they never tried to make the film something that it wasn't and we agreed early on to what film we were making."[37]

Nolan also retains control of his projects by working efficiently and effectively. As a director, he tends to come in under-time and under-budget. He famously *returned* some of the budget on the massive productions *The Dark Knight, Inception, The Dark Knight Rises* and *Interstellar*. "What he realized very early on was that the moment you give the studios an excuse to come in, you've lost it," Emma Thomas explains. "The moment you go over budget, you've lost the creative control than an obsessive director like Chris needs. He's always been extremely strategic about it."[38]

Nolan's control over his projects extends to second unit footage, which is often outsourced to other parties because the director is busy overseeing the rest of production. "Chris does his own second unit and that makes it a lot easier for all of us," says editor Lee Smith, who worked on all of Nolan's films from *Batman Begins* onwards. "I'd hate to say this for second unit directors but in an ideal world I would have the main unit shoot the second unit. Sometimes it's not practical and if you don't have the speed of operation of someone like Chris who also has a profound sense of the schedule, then that would be a disaster unto itself."[39]

This sense of control was obvious even working on *Insomnia*. Veteran actor Al Pacino was impressed that Nolan did not need to bring him back for any reshoots after primary production wrapped.[40] "It all comes down to editing," Nolan says of his avoidance of the dreaded reshoot, "just craft, just hammering it with my editor every day, trying radical cuts, pulling things out, abandoning bits of exposition, saying, 'Okay, does the audience really need to understand this? What if they don't?'"[41]

However, there is considerable skill in ensuring that the director and editor have everything that they might need going into the post-production phase.[42] In particular, Lee Smith notes that Nolan is "very knowledgeable about coverage," in providing the editor with all material that they might possibly use to stitch together a scene.[43]

This is particularly impressive given that Nolan tends not to storyboard his scripts. He does not work from shot lists. According to Nolan, this affords him a greater freedom when working with actors:

> I think that it's very important to be open to changing the way you shoot the scene depending on what the actors want to do in moving around the scene. The physicality of the scene is very important to the actor. I like to try and give them room to maneuver so that in our rehearsals we can find the best way to play a scene and the best way to photograph it.[44]

A lot of this is also down to the fact that Nolan tends to construct the film inside his own head and then attempt to capture it on film. Nolan's filmmaking is so subjective that it seems to spill right from his mind's eye onto the screen. As Lee Smith says of Nolan's creative process, "Chris has made the movie [in his head] and then makes the movie in the camera."[45] Reportedly, Warner Brothers president Alan Horn was surprised to note how calm Nolan was amid the helicopters and hundreds of extras working on *Batman Begins*, noticing the that the director sat there with "no notes. It was all in his head."[46]

This explains why Nolan's direction is so perfectly tailored for his own movies. But it does create a problem when Nolan is working on a story that did not originate inside his own head. *Insomnia* was already filtered through two other creative minds before Nolan inherited it: original writer-director Erik Skjoldbjærg and screenwriter Hillary Seitz. As a result, it provides an interesting control case for Nolan as a director, in that it allows the audience to separate Nolan-as-pure-creative-force from Nolan-as-director.

To be clear, Nolan did work on the *Insomnia* script. There are certainly elements that play into his recurring interests and fascinations. In particular, Nolan engaged with the idea of *Insomnia* as a film wherein Dormer and Finch wrestled with one another for control of the narrative. Nolan says,

> What you wind up with is a story that starts to write itself, the characters inside it start to write it. I enjoyed that idea a lot and encouraged the screenwriter, Hillary Seitz, to push it in that direction so that Robin's character wasn't just a writer so that he could know about crime and be clever in that respect, it was also this notion that the characters would write the film themselves halfway through.[47]

In a significant departure from the plot of the original film, the investigator and the killer spend an extended portion of *Insomnia* trying to entrap one another within narratives. In the original, Detective Jonas Engström comes up with the idea of framing the deceased's boyfriend for the murder using the murder weapon. In the remake, Detective Will Dormer attempts to plant evidence to point the police to the real murderer Walter Finch, while Finch tries to lead the police away from him and towards the boyfriend. This idea of characters thrown into conflict by competing narratives recurs in Nolan's work, whether in Borden and Angier's competing "Transported Man" in *The Prestige* or in Batman and the Joker's competing views of human nature in *The Dark Knight*.

The characters in the remake of *Insomnia* are quite clearly Nolan characters. "I did do a last draft myself just for small issues relating to Pacino's character, because he wanted to see what I wanted to do on paper but I never strayed very far from what I thought were the important things Hillary had put in," Nolan says of his contributions to the script.[48] Engström in the original film is a much more contemptible figure than Dormer in the remake; Engström shoots a dog in order to retrieve a bullet to get himself off the hook for his partner's shooting,[49] sexually assaults a teenage girl[50] and attempts to force himself on the hotel receptionist.[51] Dormer is a much more conventional Nolan protagonist in that he has trapped himself within a lie and is forced to watch as that lie collides with reality.

Much like Leonard in *Memento*, Dormer has transgressed in attempting to manipulate and falsify a narrative. Dormer's decision to plant evidence on the guilty party is the original sin in *Insomnia*. The image of blood soaking through fabric plays through the opening credits, positioned in such a way that the audience might believe that they are witnessing the murder of Kay Connell. Then it is revealed that the audience is watching Dormer plant evidence at the house of a child-killer who would otherwise escape justice. As with Leonard, Dormer seems to have trapped himself within a self-perpetuating cycle of moral decay, with one lie leading to another and another.[52]

More than that, *Insomnia* adheres to Nolan's interest in subjective perspective. "*Insomnia* is a terrific companion piece to *Memento*, because they're both very subjective films that take you inside the central character's experience," says producer Steven Soderbergh.[53] This is most apparent both in the fact that the opening credits are crosscut with Dormer's (rather than Finch's) indiscretion and in the way that Finch haunts the narrative as a voice on the phone or a shape in the distance for an extended period before actually appearing.[54]

Early in *Insomnia*, Dormer accidentally shoots his partner during a botched stakeout. Because his partner was about to testify to Internal Affairs and perhaps implicate him, Dormer covers up the murder. While Dormer is clearly guilt-ridden, the film repeatedly suggests that Dormer might have *wanted* to murder his partner. However, the script also emphasizes that Dormer *does not know himself* whether he did it intentionally. "Did you think about it before that moment?" Finch asks. "What would it be like if he wasn't there any more? Doesn't mean you did it on purpose." The film never answers the question clearly one way or another, instead leaving it open for the audience in the same way that Finch leaves it open to Dormer.

There is also a very clear sense that Nolan remains at a distance from the narrative that drives *Insomnia*. "If someone else has written the script, then you can retain your objectivity a lot longer," he says.[55] More to the point, it is very clear that *Insomnia* is not a story that has been particularly constructed to play to Nolan's directorial sensibilities. It has not been reverse-engineered in such a way as to perfectly marry it to his style. It did not begin as a movie within Nolan's own head before being transferred to film; there were more intermediate stages than usual.

This was quite apparent in the edit. While Nolan makes a point to arrive in editing with all of the material that he could possibly need, he very rarely has a surplus. Nolan's scripts tend to be constructed with enough efficiency that there are very few deleted scenes. "Pretty much with all my films, there are very few deleted scenes, which always disappoints the DVD crowd," he says.[56] Nolan's efficiency means that there is typically very little waste generated between his construction of the narrative and his completion of the film.

*Insomnia* is the exception to that rule, perhaps reflecting the fact that it did not begin as his own narrative. "When we went to the edit suite, we were able to have a longer version of the film, we were able to pull out certain scenes, we could track things and play around," he says.[57] He admits that the movie is not as lean and tidy as he would like: "There are various mistakes in the film, but all of them are as a result of editing."[58]

This is quite apparent, watching the movie: It often seems like there are elements that do not add up. For example, when Dormer visits Finch's apartment at around the midpoint, the audience sees Dormer disturb a piece of cardboard that had been placed in the door and clumsily misplace it. This seems like a set-up for a reveal where Finch will see the relocated piece of cardboard and realize that somebody has been in his apartment. However, Dormer catches sight of Finch outside of the apartment, chases him, and then heads back to the apartment where the two men have another phone conversation.

The piece of cardboard in the door serves to illustrate small details relating to the two characters. It tells the audience that Finch is careful and that Dormer is careless. However, it also feels somewhat extraneous given the attention paid to it. It feels surplus to requirement. There are several elements in *Insomnia* that have that sense of superfluity, lacking the clockwork precision that is present in films like *Memento* and *Batman Begins*.

*Insomnia* remains an interesting case study because it is the Nolan film where his directorial style can be most cleanly divorced from his writing and his story construction. *Insomnia* is the least distinctly "Nolan" film in his body of work, but it is still shot and edited in a distinctly "Nolan" way, which allows for a cleaner dissection of how Nolan's directorial eye works separate from his own storytelling.

Most obviously, *Insomnia* applies a lot of Nolan's favored directorial techniques in service of a story where they are never integral nor innovative. In the Norwegian film, Skjoldbjærg tends to capture a sense of weariness and dislocation through holding long shots to disorient the audience.[59] The camera follows Engström down corridors and pans as he moves around rooms. Repeatedly, the long takes are used to convey the distortion of time, with transitions happening *within* the take itself; characters arrive in shots where they shouldn't be, based on the audience's awareness of the space.

In contrast, Nolan's remake eschews this technique in favor of his own stylistic sensibilities. There are lots of quick cuts and edits employed.[60] While Skjoldbjærg tries to overload the senses with long takes, Nolan attempts to overwhelm the audience with quick flashes. It is a very different approach to the same idea.

To be fair, Nolan's style somewhat suits the material. His love of quick cuts and inserts is perfectly suited to a psychological thriller, using these mechanisms to impart useful information to the audience rapidly and effectively. Like Leonard in *Memento*, Dormer makes a point to ground himself in the sort of small material details that are conveyed through these inserts. "It's all about small stuff," Dormer tells Burr. "You know, small lies, small mistakes. People give themselves away same in misdemeanors as in murder cases. It's just human nature." Later, Dormer urges Burr, "The second you're about to dismiss something, think about it. Look at it again." The inserts allow the audience to get that second look, to interpret that information.

At the same time, there is nothing particularly innovative about this approach. Nolan's use of edits and inserts to convey information was just a more confident and stylized cinematic variant of the technique employed by contemporary procedural television series like *CSI*.[61] Indeed, Nolan's techniques are quite blunt and literal-minded in *Insomnia*. As Dormer studies the body of Kay Connell, his exposition is translated into quick inserts depicting the acts of clipping described.[62] This literalism is also applied to Dormer's more subjective experiences. "You seeing anything yet?" Finch asks about his sleep deprivation. "Those little flashes of light?" The film dutifully cuts to "little flashes of light" so that the audience can confirm that Dormer is in fact seeing them.[63]

In *Insomnia*, Nolan's techniques never quite gel in the way that they do on projects that he designed from the ground up. This is perhaps most obvious in conversational scenes, where Nolan tends to cut across his actors to get reaction shots. Many of the conversational scenes in *Insomnia* were stitched together from relatively few takes, but the film seems unable or unwilling to hold its gaze for an extended period of time.[64] This approach works very well in films where Nolan has tighter control over the release of information, such as *The Prestige* and *Inception*, where the cuts within a conversation reveal more information than simple character responses. In *Insomnia*, it just seems restless.

Similarly, the climax of *Insomnia* uses Nolan's techniques in a story that has not been designed to accommodate them. Nolan attempts to crosscut the final confrontation between Dormer and Finch, as he did with the climaxes of *Following* and *Memento*. The problem is that *Insomnia* doesn't really have any other plot threads running at the same time. As a result, the climactic confrontation between cop and killer is intercut with repeated shots of Burr restrained and tied up that add little to the narrative except to maintain the tempo of the edit.[65]

This is a perfectly reasonable approach to the material. At his weakest, Nolan is a director with a gift for conveying information to the audience and with a strong sense of rhythm in the edit. Nolan's rapid-fire and disorienting use of cuts to convey Dormer's exhaustion is just as valid as Skjoldbjærg's use of long takes, even if it's less artful. Nolan's use of inserts is a tried and true way of conveying information to the audience about the case at the center of the story. *Insomnia* is not a bad film by any means. It is a well-constructed psychological thriller.[66]

At the same time, *Insomnia* demonstrates how closely Nolan's directorial style is anchored to broader storytelling concerns. Nolan's techniques are effective and efficient when applied to a standard genre piece, but Nolan's true strength as a storyteller comes from an ability to reverse-engineer his stories in such a way as to capitalize (and even enhance) his technical craft. *Insomnia* serves as a clear contrast to films that are more quintessentially "Nolan."

Still, the impact of *Insomnia* on Nolan's filmography should not be overlooked. *Insomnia* was massively important in the director's development. Nolan acknowledges that the movie's importance is often lost in discussions of his career:

> When people look at what I did with the Batman franchise, for example, they say, "Well, the guy did this little indie film and then went and did that." And it's like, no, I did a medium-sized studio film, where I certainly felt a lot of pressure, unquestionably, but I did not feel the pressure that you feel when you take on a beloved character in a huge franchise, you know? So I had agreeable timing and

I was able to build my relationship with the studio through that film and learn how to deal with the pressures of big-budget Hollywood filmmaking.[67]

The skills that Nolan learned working on *Insomnia* are not to be underestimated. In the wake of his success, several major studios have made a point to recruit smaller indie directors to work on big-budget projects.[68] The goal seems to be to emulate Nolan's transition from the independent cinema credibility of *Memento* to the broad commercial success of his *Dark Knight* trilogy.

There have been cases where this approach has paid dividends, both critically and commercially.[69] There have also been cases where studios have butted heads with directors who are not necessarily prepared for the demands of producing a blockbuster-scale project. Some of these creative disagreements have been spectacular in scale,[70] while others have been handled with more discretion and grace.[71] A few of these indie directors have even left projects before the shoot commenced[72] or outright declined the opportunity to work with major studios for fear of the creative compromises involved.[73]

With all of that in mind, the importance of a film like *Insomnia* becomes clear. *Insomnia* was a mid-budget film with relatively low stakes that allowed Nolan to establish a relationship with Warner Brothers, to demonstrate what he was capable of doing with studio resources and to understand what the studio would want in return. From Warners' perspective, it demonstrated that he could be trusted to work with a budget and with a cast, and turn in good work under professional conditions. *Batman Begins* would not have been possible without *Insomnia*.

A lot of the cinematic techniques that Nolan employed on *Batman Begins* were honed on *Insomnia*. There is a very conscious similarity in the look and feel of the film. The atmospheric establishing shots of the icy Alaskan wilderness during the opening credits are echoed in similar shots early of the Icelandic landscape in *Batman Begins*. The cold blue-and-white color scheme from *Insomnia* would shade Gotham in *The Dark Knight* and *The Dark Knight Rises*.[74]

*Insomnia* also afforded Nolan his first opportunity to really work with action sequences on a budget. The quick-cut wrestling match between Dormer and Finch is shot in the same style as many of the hand-to-hand combat sequences in the *Dark Knight* trilogy, a collection of quick cuts to capture the disorientation of combat. Even the shots of Dormer chasing Finch into the tunnels beneath the shack in *Insomnia* recall the visual language of all the sequences in the *Dark Knight* trilogy where characters jump into tunnels, especially Gordon's foray into the sewers in *The Dark Knight Rises*.

*Insomnia* may be Nolan's least distinctive film, but it is still an informative glimpse at his evolution as a filmmaker. It is a solidly constructed psychological thriller that not only demonstrated Nolan's ability work within the studio system, but which also serves to illuminate by contrast how much of Nolan's directorial style is tied to the stories that he crafts.

# 4

## *Batman Begins*

Following *Insomnia*, Christopher Nolan decided that his next film would be about an eccentric billionaire and American cultural icon.

Nolan's previously three films had all bled into one another, with Nolan optioning *Memento* while working the festival circuit with *Following* and landing the role of director on *Insomnia* while trying to secure distribution for *Memento*. After *Insomnia*, Nolan had a bit more time and space to develop his ideas and to focus on what he wanted to do.[1]

In that time, Nolan began working on a script about the life of business magnate Howard Hughes. Reportedly, the script was to focus on the later and stranger years of its subject's life.[2] This seemed a strange choice for a director primarily working in *film noir*, to construct a biopic around one of the most influential Americans of the twentieth century. "Not a biopic is what I keep saying," he jokes.[3] He was adamant that the project would still be a Christopher Nolan film. "It will have strong connections with the films I've already made," he promised.[4] Acknowledging that earlier attempts to adapt the life of Howard Hughes for the screen had failed to materialize, Nolan asserted in interviews, "I don't know why it has a reputation as being cursed, and I don't intend to find out."[5]

Jim Carrey was very quickly attached to the film, which put Nolan in the novel position of writing a script with a leading actor already invested in the process. "It is different sitting down to write, and sitting down to write [while] already knowing who is going to play the part," he said during the press cycle for *Insomnia*. "We have met several times to discuss the specifics of the direction we were going in and Jim has some fantastic ideas which are close to my ideas. We are having quite a bit of fun."[6]

Nolan quickly fell victim to the "curse" which he had jokingly dismissed. Reports began to surface that director Michael Mann was working on a similar project with actor Leonardo DiCaprio.[7] That project eventually developed into *The Aviator*, with Martin Scorsese stepping in to direct after Mann departed to work on *Collateral*.[8]

Hollywood has a long history of "dueling movies" dealing with similar material released in close proximity[9] (Nolan came out on the favorable side of such comparison when *The Prestige* went head to head with *The Illusionist*). The development of *The Aviator* undercut Nolan's Howard Hughes project. Recalls Nolan, "I was definitely like, 'Fuck!' I think it's the best script I've ever written, and I had a really wonderful experience writing it. Yeah, it was a frustrating experience that the other movie got going."[10] So Nolan moved on to other projects. His Howard Hughes script would haunt a lot of his later work.[11]

The *Batman* cinematic franchise had been lying dormant since the release of *Batman & Robin* in June 1997, and deservedly so.

The second film in the series directed by Joel Schumacher, *Batman & Robin* had landed with a resounding critical thud. The movie earned 11 nominations for "Golden Raspberry" Awards, a celebration of the worst that Hollywood has to offer.[12] Beyond the critical humiliation, the film underperformed at the box office. It dropped 63 percent in its second weekend, signifying a rejection by mass audiences.[13] It was the lowest-grossing film in the *Batman* series.[14]

This torpedoed any hope for a potential sequel directed by Schumacher, who had reportedly been eyeing a darker tone for *Batman: Triumphant*.[15] Interestingly, Schumacher had hoped to cast Nicolas Cage as the Scarecrow,[16] the villain who would ultimately appear in all three films in the *Dark Knight* trilogy.[17] The *Batman* franchise faded into the background.

Things changed at the turn of the new millennium. In July 2000, 20th Century–Fox released *X-Men*. It was directed by Bryan Singer, best known for his work on low-key indie films (*The Usual Suspects*, *Apt Pupil*). The film was a grounded adaptation of the eponymous team of mutants, proving that superheroes could transition faithfully to film, quite apart from the looser adaptations of the nineties.[18] In May 2002, Sony Pictures released *Spider-Man*. Again the director was a somewhat unconventional choice. Sam Raimi was best known for his weird indie horror film *The Evil Dead*.[19] The following April, 20th Century–Fox released *X-Men II*.

Taken together, these films created a "superhero boom" in Hollywood.[20] The superhero genre has been likened to the western as one of *the* dominant forms of crowd-pleasing blockbusters during the twenty-first century. (Some observers predict that the genre will undergo a similar implosion due to oversaturation.[21]) Somewhat ironically, westerns have undergone their own miniature revival in the new millennium, albeit in a slightly warped and skewed form.[22]

There are any number of reasons why the superhero became so popular in the early years of the twenty-first century. Most superficially, computer animation finally reached a point where it was able to convincingly depict the weird imagery and the scale of action that unfolded on comic book pages.[23] Practically, the consolidation of media ownership meant that major studios could effectively purchase comic book publishers to act as in-house loss-leading research and development labs for intellectual property.[24] Existentially, the superhero archetype is particularly suited to the anxieties of the War on Terror.[25]

In times of global political uncertainty, there is something reassuring about the character of the superhero. These figures embody the ideal of a powerful individual who can protect the world from the chaotic forces of evil.[26] The superhero is inevitably a defender of the *status quo*, which makes them particularly comforting at times of instability and ambiguity.[27] The superhero offers reassurance.

The superhero has inevitably been affected by the War on Terror. The way in which pop culture approaches the figure of the lone vigilante has changed a great deal.[28] This is particularly apparent in *Batman Begins*, where Batman's war on crime is contextualized in terms of the War on Terror. Wayne Enterprises is revealed to be a military contractor, and Bruce Wayne forges his identity using prototypes designed for military use.[29] Nolan's *Dark Knight* trilogy became the first superhero movies to actively engage with this subtext, to process through what it meant to be a superhero film in a post–9/11 world.

As the superhero genre became increasingly popular, Warner Brothers looked to revive their core superhero franchises. The studio ran through a number of proposals for *Batman*, looking at ways to modernize the character and make him acceptable to contemporary audiences. In 2000, Boaz Yakin was a candidate to direct an adaptation of the animated series *Batman Beyond*.[30] Fresh off the success of *Requiem for a Dream*, Darren Aronofsky pitched a rather surreal (and radical) adaptation of Frank Miller and David Mazzucchelli comic *Year One*.[31] Fourteen years before the film eventually materialized, director Wolfgang Petersen was considered for *Batman vs. Superman*.[32] These are just a few of the more high-profile failed adaptations.

Nolan did not actively seek out the job, but heard about it through his agent. He recalls, "My agent, Dan Aloni, called and said, 'It seems unlikely you'd be interested in this, but Warners is sort of casting around for what they would do with Batman.' It had reached the end of its last sort of life, if you like."[33] Nolan was interested.

As with *Insomnia*, Nolan worked very hard to communicate his intentions for the film ahead of time. He met with Paul Levitz, the head of DC Comics, to ensure that his interpretation of the character would not cause any friction to those more familiar and more invested in the character and his continuity.[34]

Nolan's plans for his *Batman* project were rooted in a desire to direct a classic old-fashioned blockbuster in the style of movies that he had enjoyed as a child. He affectionately recalled the impact that those movies had on him. "Going to see them with my parents would give me the feeling of the potential for geography, for landscape, for scale and escapism," he says. It was important that his big-budget *Batman* film capture that sensibility. "I really wanted to give it that scope which was so important to me in the blockbusters I watched when I was very young."[35]

As with most of Nolan's films, he was designing a movie that would appeal to him as a viewer. In particular, he was appealing to his own inner child. "Tonally, I always knew in making a *Batman* film that I wanted it to appeal to a wide range of ages," he said when asked if he ever would have pushed for a higher age rating. "I certainly didn't want to exclude the sort of 10- to 12-year-olds, because as a kid I would have loved to see a movie like this."[36] As a result, a lot of *Batman Begins* was reverse-engineered from that starting point. Nolan pushed hard for a bombastic spectacular third act, even though it was hard to reconcile that with the more intimate opening act. "It was the thorniest issue we grappled with," recalls co-writer David S. Goyer, "not making it seem like they were two separate movies."[37]

Nolan's chief cinematic influence in constructing *Batman Begins* was Richard Donner's classic *Superman* (1978). "It made a huge impression on me," Nolan admits. "I can remember the trailers for it...."[38] In terms of direct influence on the construction of *Batman Begins*, Nolan cites the all-star supporting cast of *Superman* as an inspiration in building a similarly impressive ensemble for the Caped Crusader. "We dared to ask some of the finest actors to take on these roles and I was able to put together really a dream cast," he says, leading to a situation where most of the movie's exposition is delivered by Morgan Freeman.[39]

*Batman Begins* was not the only superhero production at Warner Brothers to be influenced by *Superman* around this time. After completing work on *X-Men II*, Bryan Singer moved to Warner Brothers to reboot the long-dormant *Superman* franchise. In doing so, the director hoped to reconnect the franchise with its roots. *Superman Returns* would emerge as a nostalgia-driven superhero epic, one that borrowed production design, plot points and even footage of Marlon Brando from *Superman* and *Superman II*.[40]

Developed in parallel with *Batman Begins*, *Superman Returns* provides an interesting counterpoint in approach. *Superman Returns* aims to glorify the past and to trap it in amber. The belated follow-up fetishizes the early Superman films to an obsessive degree, often feeling like a big-budget fan production.[41] In contrast, *Batman Begins* makes a clear break with what came before in order to build its central character from the ground up.

Audiences would largely reject *Superman Returns*. Although its budget had been inflated by costs from previous failed attempts to revive the franchise, *Superman Returns* struggled to break even at the box office.[42] In contrast, given Nolan's careful management of his budget and meticulous attention to detail, *Batman Begins* turned a very tidy profit for the studio.[43] In many ways, this triumph of the bold innovation of *Batman Begins* over the empty nostalgia of *Superman Returns* shaped the direction of superhero cinema for the next decade.[44]

To be fair, a lot of Nolan's freedom came from the fact that *Batman & Robin* had turned the earlier *Batman* franchise into a punchline. Even Nolan would make jokes at its expense, promising interviewers that "there are *no* nipples on Batman's suit!"[45] However, there was also an understanding that Nolan wanted to create a *Batman* film that would stand apart from the earlier films by Joel Schumacher and Tim Burton, without pandering to nostalgia or trying to compete on their terms.

Recruiting composers Hans Zimmer and James Newton Howard, Nolan helped to craft a unique soundscape for the film. "I thought of approaching it strictly from 'This is a Chris Nolan movie' and completely forgetting that there were any other Batman movies before," Zimmer explains of his creative process. "You know what I mean? It's boring. You don't want to go and do what anybody else has done before."[46] Zimmer carried that attitude over to his later collaborations with Zack Snyder on rebooted interpretations of Batman and Superman, making a conscious effort to create new musical themes for these characters to differentiate them from early interpretations.[47] This approach contrasted with Danny Elfman's more nostalgic approach to *Justice League*, when he would incorporate John Williams' theme from *Superman* and his own theme from *Batman* into the film.[48]

Nolan decided early in the process that his *Batman* film would not attempt to compete with the stylized aesthetic of Tim Burton's *Batman*.[49] His decision to imbue *Batman Begins* with a more grounded aesthetic was very much in response to the look and feel of the earlier film. "I desired a world that wasn't stylized and overly fanciful because I didn't want to compete with Anton Furst's wonderful work in the 1989 *Batman*," Nolan says.[50]

"Realism" has become critical shorthand for the *Dark Knight* trilogy, with most discussions of the films fixating upon the grounded nature of this adaptation of the character.[51] However, that is a gross oversimplification of Nolan's approach to the character. There are elements of *Batman Begins* that are quite consciously stylized rather than explicitly realistic. Batman's cape seems to alternate in length between atmospheric establishing shots and more dynamic action scenes. The Narrows resemble a grim and overcrowded future dystopia, the movie's most overt homage to *Blade Runner*.[52] More to the point, *Batman Begins* is a movie in which organized crime in a major American city is upended by a man in a scarecrow mask and cult of ancient ninja assassins.[53]

It is perhaps more accurate to describe Nolan's approach as "verisimilitude," the same approach employed by Richard Donner.[54] It is not that the films themselves are particularly realistic, it is that they impose their more outlandish and cartoonish elements upon a world that is recognizable to the audience. This was exactly how Nolan pitched the movie during its development. "The world of Batman is that of grounded reality," he explained. "Ours will be a recognizable, contemporary reality against which an extraordinary heroic figure arises."[55] In retrospect, Nolan clarifies, "We wanted to have an ordinary world so that the figure of Batman would stand out and be extraordinary."[56]

Nolan's reputation for "realism" is arguably grounded more in his technique than in his output. Nolan's films are not especially grounded and realistic. It could reasonably be argued that *The Prestige*, *Inception* and *Interstellar* are all science fiction epics, predicated on advanced technology beyond anything currently feasible. Similarly, Nolan's *Dark Knight* trilogy places a heavy emphasis on the science fiction elements of the character's "wonderful toys."[57] The subject matter of Nolan's films is not realistic in the slightest.

However, Nolan's technique is grounded in practical and in-shot effects. *Batman Begins* was shot on sets constructed for the film rather than location[58] and did feature digital enhancement to the establishing shots of Chicago to add elements like the elevated train and the Narrows.[59] However, it is quite telling that *The Dark Knight* and *The Dark Knight Rises* both forgo these filmmaking compromises and use real locations as much as practical.[60]

Nolan prefers to capture as much of an effect in-shot as possible, with a minimum amount of post-production computer-generated enhancement. "I insisted on doing things for real rather than employing visual effects, so there was a tremendous amount of stunt work and so forth," recalls Nolan of his approach to spectacle on *Batman Begins*. "And I insisted on doing everything main unit, not using any second unit action crews. We wanted the whole film to have a consistency that applied to the action set pieces as well as to the character scenes."[61]

Nolan made a point to shoot some footage of real bats for the sequences involving the creatures, despite the complications that this created. "Bats are a complete nightmare," he observes. "They're extraordinarily difficult to train, and they can only do basic tricks. We had to [digitally] multiply them into thousands and thousands of bats, but I was determined to get some hero bats on screen, so the visual effects crew could see the reality we were holding them to."[62]

This is one of the more interesting paradoxes of Nolan's filmmaking. Nolan embraces the idea of the subjective and the spectacular, anchoring movies in the perspectives of unreliable narrators and building plots around technologies and concepts that are impossible by any modern reckoning. However, for all that Nolan's stories dabble in the fantastical, his filmmaking technique is grounded in more objective elements.

As a director, Nolan works hard to convince the audience to invest in the physicality and reality of the world in which his outlandish stories unfold. In his earlier films, his use of inserts focusing on objects and details serve to provide the audience with a texture of the world that assures them of its corporeality. In his later films, his emphasis on practical special effects and use of physical space serves the same purpose on a much larger scale. The texture of Nolan's films might be "realistic," but the substance of them is not. This is one of his defining attributes as a filmmaker.

Nolan's *Dark Knight* trilogy represents a fusion of the director's British and American sensibilities. *Memento* and *Insomnia* were fundamentally American films, tales of men lost on the frontier. In contrast, *Batman Begins* offers something of a blend between the United Kingdom and the United States. This is arguably related to the character of Bruce Wayne. Batman is a character perhaps more rooted in European traditions than the twentieth-century American mythology of Superman.[63] Bill Finger named Bruce Wayne in part for the Scottish patriot Robert Bruce.[64] It should be noted that many of the more influential and iconic *Batman* writers have been of British extraction.[65] Nolan cast Welsh actor Christian Bale as Bruce Wayne. (Bale made a point to do a lot of the publicity in an American accent.[66])

*Batman Begins* took Nolan back to working in Britain for the first time since *Following*. A lot of downtown Gotham was built on sets in hangars near Bedford, just outside of London.[67] "Stately Wayne Manor" was represented by Mentmore Towers in Buckinghamshire.[68] There was something slightly surreal in the fact that Nolan had struggled to find support in the British film industry, then returned home at the helm of a studio blockbuster. He admits, "I don't dispute that it's ironic that it was Warner Brothers that brought me back to film in England."[69]

However, *Batman Begins* was a homecoming in another sort of way. Gotham City has conventionally been associated with New York.[70] Indeed, the standard logic at DC comics is that both Metropolis and Gotham represent different notions of New York City in the popular imagination.[71] However, while planning *Batman Begins*, Nolan saw something different in that fictional city. "When Nathan Crowley, my production designer, first set up here in my garage, putting together composites of what Gotham might be, we started imagining a city with all these layers, with bridges and subterranean streets and tall skyscrapers. And at a certain point I said to him, 'I know where this is. This is Chicago.'"[72] Nolan would use Chicago much more thoroughly in *The Dark Knight*.

Like *The Prestige*, *Batman Begins* serves as a synthesis of the director's British and American sensibilities, something that played out across a lot of his later work.[73] His films often seem to straddle the Atlantic, and that is particularly true of *Batman Begins* and *The Prestige*.

Nolan approached *Batman Begins* with a fondness for the character, and with a casual familiarity with the character's world. "As a little boy, I was a huge *Batman* fan from the Adam West TV show," Nolan recalls. "Growing up in later years, I got into the comics and graphics novels, but I wouldn't describe myself as a particularly knowledgeable, avid fan—certainly not compared to the people I've met and collaborated with on this project. However, I've always loved the character and his story, and I'm a big fan of *Batman: The Long Halloween*."[74] Nolan and Goyer provided an introduction to the prestige collected edition of *The Long Halloween*, acknowledging it as an influence on their approach to the character and his world.[75] Although Nolan did not have a particularly in-depth appreciation of the character's history and continuity, Warner Brothers enlisted David S. Goyer to work on the script and to provide necessary attention to continuity.[76]

Although the production design of *Batman Begins* changed a lot of elements established in the source material, Nolan argued that this was simply a process of adaptation from one medium to another:

> *Batman Begins* isn't intended to be a radical approach; it's more about trying to create certain things on film that worked well in the comics and graphic novels. If you look at the way comics used to be printed, there was a certain ambiguity as to whether Batman's suit was blue or black; it depended on the four-color printing. Dick Grayson's hair appears blue at certain points in the comics, but you have to interpret it as black. That suggests a certain shading in Batman's costume.[77]

The core of Nolan's *Batman Begins* pitch was to tell a story that had never been depicted in live action. He recalls that he sold Warner Brothers on this idea: "Nobody's ever made this origin story in this way and treated it as a piece of action filmmaking, a sort of contemporary action blockbuster."[78] Nolan had a point. Previous live action adaptations had largely glossed over Bruce Wayne's transformation into Batman.[79] The Adam West *Batman* television show had dispensed with the murder of the Waynes.[80] Tim Burton's *Batman* seemed to unfold early in the character's career, but introduced him fully formed, attacking criminals on Gotham roofs.[81]

It is strange to think that it took Warner Brothers so long to produce a *Batman* origin film. Origin stories are arguably the superhero stories best suited to cinematic adaptation. Comic book heroes tend to exist within a relatively static *status quo*, because the assumption is that readers need to be able to join the comic at any point in its run.[82] A quote accredited to Stan Lee suggests that comics were intended to offer readers "the illusion of change" without altering the central character's world in any significant way.[83] However, cinematic narratives tend to hinge on ideas of growth and change for central characters. Even when characters have not changed, such as Leonard in *Memento*, the audience's understanding of them has fundamentally altered.

This is why origin stories are so appealing for cinematic adaptations of superheroes. By definition, origin stories are adventures where the central characters are allowed to grow and change over the course of the story. Peter Parker is noticeably different before the spider bite as compared to when he becomes Spider-Man, Clark Kent is very different as a child than he is when he chooses to become Superman. The superhero origin story conforms to the familiar three-act structure.[84] One of the bigger issues with superhero sequels is attempting to tell a story with growth and change *within* the familiar *status quo* established at the end of the first film.[85]

Still, the lack of a pre-existing cinematic origin for the central character meant that *Batman Begins* was exploring new ground with Batman in cinema, even though it was drawing upon more than 60 years of comic book storytelling. Any number of classic comics were an influence on the story that Nolan chose to tell. Denny O'Neal and Dick Giordano's *The Man Who Falls* bleeds through in the film in several ways.[86] The nonlinear structure of the story, the imagery of Bruce traveling the world and growing a beard to learn how to be Batman, even the recurring references to falling as a learning experience all hark back to *The Man Who Falls*.[87]

Frank Miller and David Mazzucchelli's *Year One* was also a massive influence on the story.[88] However, *Batman Begins* is more inspired by *Year One* than slavishly devoted to it.[89] To Goyer, *Year One* was more effective for what it suggested, rather than what it depicted. Goyer singles out "the moment in *Year One* when Bruce Wayne is returning to Gotham after a multi-year absence. I was captivated by that. I wanted to explore what had happened in those intervening years."[90]

The storytelling in *Batman Begins* is very much pure Christopher Nolan. He was heavily involved in early drafts of the screenplay with Goyer, but he took complete control of the narrative when Goyer had to leave to work on his own directorial debut, *Blade: Trinity*. "I ended up doing a draft and a half of the script," Goyer recalls. "After that, I said they have to do their own revisions."[91] Goyer was also quite removed from the production, particularly during its time in England.[92]

*Batman Begins* is fundamentally a Nolan movie in how it approaches the eponymous character. Nolan's approach to storytelling is frequently to invent the story from the outside in, in some ways literalizing the non-linear structure of *Memento*. The director had decided that his cinematic debut *Following* would be a psychological thriller based primarily on the fact that he would be shooting on black and white with a handheld camera. *Batman Begins* does something similar with the central character. By necessity, it was always going to be a *Batman* film, but Nolan's approach to the character was to fundamental reverse-engineer that core concept.

This is most obvious in Bruce Wayne's superhero identity. The internal logic of superhero secret identities is fairly straightforward and intuitive, with Batman acknowledging as much in an early conversation between Bruce Wayne and Carmine Falcone, wherein Falcone threatens Bruce's friends and family with harm. Alfred happily summarizes why superheroes need an alter ego: "I assume that—as you take on the underworld—this symbol is a persona to protect those you care about from reprisals?" Alfred inquires, articulating Bruce Wayne's decision to create a specific persona to fight crime.

However, the very concept of *Batman* requires a more profound justification. Even Bruce's faithful manservant finds his patience for this enterprise tested by that decision. "Why bats, Master Wayne?" inquires Alfred Pennyworth. Bruce does not respond by pointing to the title of the film or the iconic intellectual property upon which it has been built. Instead, *Batman Begins* dedicates an extensive amount of its running time to explaining why Bruce Wayne chose to disguise himself as a flying rodent rather than *literally anything else*.

This is something that the comics had dealt with only fleetingly. The character's co-creator, Bob Kane, was inspired by a variety of visual influences in creating "The Bat-Man," but never quite explained the character's thematic connections to bats beyond the aesthetic appeal of the design.[93] Bill Finger radically reworked and redesigned the character before he went to print, but never really explained the bat motif.[94] The character's origin story suggested that Bruce had been inspired to dress like a bat when the creature flew in through the open window in Wayne Manor.[95] Later interpretations of the same scene imbue it with a mythic quality.[96] Still, there is something vaguely unsatisfying in the idea that Bruce Wayne's choice of costumed identity hinges on the coincidence of the right animal being in the right place at the right time.[97]

However, *Batman Begins* takes that idea and reverse-engineers it even further. Nolan's film roots this idea in childhood trauma, in an encounter that young Bruce had with bats nesting on the grounds of his family manor a short while before the murder of his parents, reinforcing an unconscious association with the death of Thomas and Martha Wayne by having the family attend a performance of *Mefistofele* at Gotham Opera House before their murder. During that performance, Bruce is terrified by acrobats performing as gigantic bats. Bruce panics and asks his parents to leave the opera house. Thomas opts to leave via the back door, which leads the family into the alleyway where they are murdered.

*Batman Begins* moves with laser-point precision towards explaining and articulating the psychology of Bruce Wayne. The film explains why he could be so driven. He was already traumatized from an experience with bats shortly before the death of his parents, and was responsible for them leaving the opera before it finished in response to his fear of the performers dressed like bats, which led to the attempted mugging and to their deaths. Bruce's anger towards criminals is reinforced by the response of the adults around him in the aftermath of the murders. "We got him," Commissioner Loeb assures Bruce that night in the police station, suggesting that bringing Joe Chill to justice imposes order on the situation. Later, when Bruce admits his sense of guilt to Alfred, the butler attempts to reassure him by placing the blame squarely on Joe Chill. "It was nothing that you did. It was him, and him alone." When Ra's Al Ghul asks whether Bruce still feels responsible for the deaths of his parents, Bruce makes it clear that he has sublimated his guilt into anger. "My anger outweighs my guilt."

Everything in the movie is constructed efficiently to point towards this characterization, even the music. "Batman's parents die at the beginning of the movie," Hans Zimmer explains. "I did this crazy thing with this choirboy whereby he's singing a fairly pretty tune and then he gets stuck, it's like froze, arrested development. Just little things like that, just little psychological ideas in there."[98] Bruce's single-minded determination to overcome his own fear is rooted in the last words spoken by his father, suggesting that he never quite moved past that moment.[99]

All of this serves to contextualize Bruce Wayne as a Nolan protagonist. Like Leonard in *Memento*, Bruce has buried his own sense of guilt and shame over the death of his loved ones. Leonard and Bruce instead choose to cultivate a personal mythology to avoid confronting their own sense of responsibility. They are somewhat kindred spirits.[100] Of course, Leonard's situation is bleaker than that of Bruce. In some ways, Leonard serves as a cautionary tale for Bruce, a freakish reflection of what might have been.[101]

Central to Nolan's conception of Bruce is that the character must work according to his own internal logic. Nolan refuses to use any shorthand to justify aspects of the character, taking pains to explain almost every aspect of his persona. In some ways, *Batman Begins* serves as a feature-length "Frequently Asked Questions" section on the character of Batman. Why does Batman have a cape? *Because he realizes that he will be escaping off a lot of rooftops.* Why does Batman have scallops on his gloves? *They were very useful at stopping him falling off the edge of a giant mountain while training, and are also useful for snapping swords into pieces.*

Central to Nolan's thesis on *Batman Begins* was the idea that everything in the movie had to make sense on its own terms. For the movie to hold together, Bruce's decisions had to come from somewhere recognizable rather than existing in comic book shorthand. Nolan contends:

If Bruce knew of Superman or even of comic books, then that's a completely different decision that he's making when he puts on a costume in an attempt to become a symbol. It's a paradox and a conundrum, but what we did is go back to the very original concept and idea of the character. In his first appearances, he invents himself as a totally original creation.[102]

Nolan approached his *Batman* films as self-contained cinematic works. He was never signed up to more than one *Batman* film at a time, allowing him the freedom to treat each individual series entry as its own story.[103] He has stated that the seeming cliffhanger ending to *Batman Begins* was not intended to set up the Joker's appearance in *The Dark Knight*, but instead to signify that Batman's origin story was complete.[104] This phase of the journey was over.[105]

Even the decision to have the Wayne family murdered at the opera rather than after a screening of *Zorro* (as in comic book continuity) was intended to keep the film self-contained.[106] "We wanted nothing that would undermine the idea that Bruce came up with this crazy plan of putting on a mask all by himself," Nolan insists. "That allowed us to treat it on our own terms. So we replaced the *Zorro* idea with the bats to cement that idea of fear and symbolism associated with bats."[107]

*Batman Begins* makes a conscious effort to invest in Bruce Wayne as a fully formed character. The earlier live-action *Batman* films suffered from criticisms that Bruce Wayne was never as interesting or compelling as the colorful foes that he faced.[108] While this is something of a generalization that glosses over Michael Keaton's restrained performance and Tim Burton's presentation of Bruce as a socially awkward individual, that argument has *some* legitimacy. *Batman Begins* placed Bruce front and center, to the point of concealing its primary villain until the third act.[109]

"If we're successful, the thing that will be talked about a lot and on what we worked on the hardest is that the audience will really care about Bruce Wayne and not just Batman," David S. Goyer contended. "It doesn't matter how much you spend on special effects—if it feels hollow, no one gives a damn."[110] For Christian Bale, the idea of a *Batman* movie focusing on the psychology of Bruce Wayne was a large part of the appeal of working on *Batman Begins*. "We've established that Batman is just as interesting, and in my mind more interesting character than the majority of the villains."[111]

Part of this interesting psychological approach is the decision to consciously delineate between Bruce and Batman. Part of the reason that Hans Zimmer convinced Nolan to allow him to collaborate with James Newton Howard was to embody the "split personality" of the film, the gap between Bruce and Batman.[112] *Batman Begins* arguably places Batman secondary to Bruce. Although there is plenty of action and adventure in the opening act, the full Batman costume does not appear until over an hour into the film.[113]

This emphasis on Bruce explains the choice of antagonists. Both the Scarecrow and Ra's Al Ghul exist within *Batman Begins* not because they are popular or iconic in their own right, but because they fit within the larger arc that Nolan has mapped out for his central characters.[114] The Scarecrow reflects Bruce's desire to weaponize his own fear as a tool that can be employed against his enemies.[115] And Ra's Al Ghul exists as a cautionary tale for Bruce, a warning about what might happen if the character takes his obsessions too far and if he allows his anger to fester into nihilism.[116]

Ra's Al Ghul is arguably the most conventional supervillain in the *Dark Knight* trilogy, the character who seems most in keeping with the expectations of the comic book movie genre. Most superficially, he is appreciably older than the protagonist and played a formative role in his origin.[117] More fundamentally, the character ties back into the genre's fascination with overtly fascistic antagonists, something that applies both to the source material[118] and to the cinematic adaptations.[119]

Ra's is a moral absolutist who has led a secret ninja cult "for centuries," using the League of Shadows as "a check against human corruption."[120] However, Ra's also uses language that evokes fascism, talking a lot about "will" and "action."[121] This is perhaps most obvious in the training sequences. "Your parents' death was not your fault," Ra's assures Bruce. "It was your father's. Anger does not change the fact that your father failed to act." When Bruce insists that Thomas lacked the necessary training, Ra's responds, "The training is nothing! Will is everything! The will to act."

The decision to emphasize Ra's Al Ghul as a fascistic antagonist was a clever one. By establishing the extremism of Ra's Al Ghul's philosophy, *Batman Begins* can cannily sidestep any issues related to the more overtly fascistic elements of the Batman mythos. After all, Bruce Wayne is another character who acts outside of democratic structures to impose his will on society.[122] By positioning him in opposition to Ra's Al Ghul's attempted mass murder, *Batman Begins* can postpone explorations of the character's own more uncomfortable political subtexts to *The Dark Knight* and *The Dark Knight Rises*.[123]

There are other aspects of the character that mark Ra's Al Ghul as a more archetypal comic book movie villain than the characters in the subsequent films. As played by Liam Neeson, Ra's has much clearer and more conventional enunciation than the villains who followed, lacking the Joker's sing-song voice (*The Dark Knight*) and Bane's strange-accent-muffled-through-a-mask (*The Dark Knight Rises*).[124] More bluntly, in his expensive suits and without any facial scarring, Ra's Al Ghul lacks the sheer *weirdness* that defines the Joker and Bane.

In keeping with Nolan's desire to construct an archetypal blockbuster like the ones that he grew up with in the seventies and eighties, Bruce's journey is centered on his desire to find a replacement father figure.[125] Bruce spends most of the film trying to make peace with his father's legacy.[126] He completes his journey in *Batman Begins* when he casts off the shadow of Thomas Wayne, allowing Wayne Manor to collapse so that he might rebuild it on his own terms.[127]

The relationship between Bruce and Ra's Al Ghul is codified as a warped father-son dynamic. Bruce has lost his parents, with a particular emphasis on his father; he seems to find a surrogate father figure in Ra's Al Ghul. For his part, Ra's has been separated from his own family and sees Bruce as a potential surrogate son.[128] *Batman Begins* consciously mirrors the two. In keeping with the trilogy's emphasis on repeated dialogue, both Thomas Wayne and Ra's Al Ghul try to calm Bruce by assuring him, "Don't be afraid."

This is very much in keeping with the Joseph Campbell mythology that was infused through George Lucas' *Star Wars*.[129] Bruce's desire to fill a father-shaped absence in his life also evokes the broken families that recur within the films of Steven Spielberg.[130] There is also an argument to be made that cinema in the eighties—the movies Nolan grew up with—was populated by absent and failed fathers.[131] These flawed and dysfunctional father-son dynamics were most likely informed a variety of contemporaneous factors, from skyrocketing divorce rates to generation gaps over issues like Vietnam.[132]

Over the course of *Batman Begins*, Bruce learns to banish the specter of his biological father and eventually kills (through inaction) his surrogate father Ra's Al Ghul. There is a decidedly pop psychological undertone to *Batman Begins*, right down to the decision to cast psychiatrist Jonathan Crane as Batman's first costumed antagonist.[133] There is something Freudian in Bruce's journey over the course of *Batman Begins*, in his escape from the shadow of Thomas Wayne and in his participation in the murder of Ra's Al Ghul.[134]

There is an argument to be made that comic book movies are perfectly suited to these sorts of broad mythic themes. In fact, that was part of what drew Nolan towards working on a superhero movie in the first place. "Superheroes fill a gap in the pop culture psyche, similar to the role of Greek mythology," he observes. "I mean, Superman is essentially a god, but Batman is more like Hercules: he's a human being, very flawed, and bridges the divide."[135]

With all of this in mind, it makes sense that Nolan should adapt a somewhat stylized and exaggerated approach to this character and this world. As much as Nolan's direction anchors the film in a very physical and tangible world, *Batman Begins* has a very operatic quality in how it chooses to construct its story. In particular, Nolan embraces the tendency towards literalism that was evident in *Memento* and *Insomnia*.[136]

Nolan subscribes to the view that plot is best described as "the controlled release of information."[137] As such, it makes sense that one of Nolan's primary strengths is his ability to communicate information to the audience. He relays this information in any number of ways, from the dialogue through to the way in which he edits his films. He has an undeniable fascination with exposition, to the point that his earlier films can occasionally over-articulate themselves.[138] *Memento* turned this into something of a running joke, with Leonard frequently asking characters if he had explained his condition to them already.

*Batman Begins* really serves to emphasize Nolan's tendency toward what might be described as "thematic exposition." Characters in Nolan movies tend to explicitly articulate themes and ideas in abstract ways, with the narrative then serving to literalize those abstractions. This was very much a feature of Nolan's work on *Memento*[139] and even shone through a little bit in *Insomnia*.[140] However, *Batman Begins* doubles down on this approach to character and theme.

While training on the ice, Ra's Al Ghul drives Bruce into pure rage. Bruce manages to subdue Ra's. "You haven't beaten me," Ra's taunts, "you've sacrificed sure footing for a killing stroke." In that moment, Ra's is speaking literally; he cracks the ice beneath Bruce and sends him into the water. However, the movie makes it quite clear that he is also speaking in more abstract and metaphorical terms. Bruce's anger runs the risk of taking him to a very dark place, of sacrificing his "sure footing."[141]

In the world of *Batman Begins*, metaphors are often literalized. When Alfred talks about how Bruce's great grandfather was involved in the Underground Railroad, he is walking Bruce through a literal underground cavern.[142] Things reach critical mass when Ra's Al Ghul shows up at the climax, crashing Bruce's party and outlining his plan to destroy Gotham. "When a forest grows too wild, a purging fire is inevitable and natural," he tells Bruce of his plans to destroy Gotham, as his henchmen set *literal* fire to Wayne Manor. Later, he warns Bruce, "If someone stands in the way of true justice, you simply walk up behind them and stab them in the heart." At that same moment, one of his ninjas drops from the ceiling with a knife and tries to stab Bruce from behind.[143]

There are shades of self-awareness to all this. Ra's Al Ghul is particularly literal-minded. In the first act, Bruce destroys his mountain fortress and leaves Ra's in the custody of locals. In the third act, Ra's burns Wayne Manor to the ground. Ra's cannot resist the urge to acknowledge the dramatic irony. "Justice is balance. You burned my house and left me for dead. Consider us even." However, even allowing for Ra's heavy-handed literalism, he is still both impressed and taken aback when he confronts Batman at the climax. "You took my advice about theatricality a bit … literally." Ra's doesn't seem to be in any position to cast stones about being overly literal.

On a thematic level, *Batman Begins* is about Bruce learning to harness fear as a weapon in his war against crime. On a plotting level, the League of Shadows is plotting to do exactly the same thing with weaponized fear gas. Theme is literalized and overlaid with plot, abstract ideas rendered concrete through the film's storytelling mechanics. This very clever plotting mechanism works so well because it ensures that the plot is ultimately just the controlled release of information that feeds into the underlying thematic and character dynamics. It is a shrewd and elegant storytelling choice.

This sort of literal *and* metaphorical storytelling is perfectly suited to a comic book character like Batman, given that the genre is infused with a broad operatic quality.[144] It could reasonably be argued that one of Nolan's most lasting contributions to mainstream blockbuster cinema has been this emphasis on thematic exposition. In modern blockbusters, theme is not only articulated by plot and action, but it is also explicitly articulated by characters in such a way that is both metaphorical *and* literal.[145]

All of Nolan's films are concerned with narrative in one way or another. *Following* is about the cultivation and manipulation of narrative, whether through voyeuristic burglary or through Cobb's seduction of the protagonist. *Memento* is about the lies that the central character tells himself, and the idea of conspiracy theory as a personal narrative. The second act of *Insomnia* is about two oppositional figures trying to ensnare one another in their own separate stories. *Interstellar* focuses on how absent parents become stories told to their children. *Dunkirk* is about the imposition of a national myth on events larger than any one story.

But the five films following on from *Batman Begins* are more fundamentally and overtly about narrative than any other films within the larger Nolan canon. In *Batman Begins*, *The Prestige*, *The Dark Knight*, *Inception* and *The Dark Knight Rises*, Nolan engages more comprehensively and more thoroughly with the idea of narrative than at any other point in his filmography. He turns the idea over in his head, and on the screen, dissecting and analyzing it. And these five films all inform one another, allowing Nolan to take that central idea of narrative and play with it, to turn it inside out and to deconstruct it in specific relation to the other films in his filmography.

*Batman Begins* establishes that the character of Batman is fundamentally a story constructed by Bruce Wayne as a way to make sense of the world. Like Johnny G in *Memento*, Batman is not real or tangible in any sense until the protagonist literally constructs him.[146] However, while Johnny G is simply a revenge fantasy that serves Leonard's own sense of purpose and justice, *Batman Begins* understands that Batman's fantasy needs to be heroic in nature.[147] Reflecting its origins as a superhero story, and reflecting Nolan's desire to make a family-friendly blockbuster, the fantasy in *Batman Begins* is much more constructive than that in *Memento*.

The difference between Leonard and Bruce is reflected in the world around them. The world of *Batman Begins* is appreciably more humanistic and compassionate than that in *Memento*. Leonard is surrounded by people like Teddy and Natalie who seek to manipulate him for their own ends. Bruce is surrounded by people who genuinely want what is best for him and for Gotham.[148] Nolan's *Dark Knight* trilogy repeatedly stresses that Batman is not the sole creation of Bruce Wayne, but instead a process of mythic collaboration between Bruce and characters like Alfred, Fox and Gordon.[149] This is part of what makes the construction of the Batman myth so effective, that he is a process of creative collaboration between a variety of characters.[150]

If Leonard's obsession in *Memento* is an example of narrative as conspiracy theory, then Bruce's creation of Batman in *Batman Begins* is an example of narrative as mythology. Repeatedly in *Batman Begins*, characters talk about Bruce's idea as if it represents some sort of literal transcendence. "A vigilante is just a man lost in the scramble for his own gratification," Ra's Al Ghul suggests in his introductory sequence. "He can be destroyed or locked up. But if you make yourself more than just a man—if you devote yourself to an ideal and if they can't stop you—then you become something else entirely." Bruce takes the bait and asks the obvious follow-up question: "Which is?" Ra's responds, "Legend, Mr. Wayne."

This becomes a core mantra for Bruce. On his return to Gotham with Alfred, he explains, "As a man, I'm flesh and blood. I can be ignored, destroyed. But as a symbol ... as a symbol, l can be incorruptible. I can be everlasting." This sets up an interesting idea that plays out across *The Dark Knight* and *The Dark Knight Rises*, both of which explore the gap that exists between reality and mythology. Nolan's films repeatedly wonder whether there is value to be found in believing in something, even if that something is not true.[151] There is comfort and security to be found in fiction, and Bruce creates Batman as a work of fiction that is not only big enough to support him, but is also big enough to hold Gotham together in *The Dark Knight* and *The Dark Knight Rises*.

This embrace of Batman as modern mythology plays into a broader social context of treating comic books as something akin to a corporatized modern mythology.[152] This claim has been repeated so often that it is practically a cliché.[153] These figures loom large in the popular consciousness, and provide a broad metaphorical canvas against which they may meditate upon profound existential anxieties and uncertainties.[154] Superheroes are very archetypical and simplistic characters, but subject to the same cycle of reinvention and reconceptualization that defines so many mythologies.[155] *Batman Begins* literalizes that debate, by effectively having Bruce not only invent Batman, but inventing the very idea of superheroes.

*Batman Begins* has been somewhat overshadowed by its two sequels.[156] However, *Batman Begins* remains quietly influential. It arguably popularized the concept of "rebooting" comic book properties, particularly given its success relative to the more traditional and old-fashioned *Superman Returns*.[157] The term "reboot" was not in popular use in the industry while Nolan was developing *Batman Begins*, "I don't even know who was first banging around the term 'reboot' or whatever, but it was after *Batman Begins*, so we didn't have any kind of reference for that idea of kind of resetting a franchise."[158]

*Batman Begins* was frequently cited as an inspiration by directors hoping to take beloved franchises back to their roots, such as Matthew Vaughn on *X-Men: First Class*[159] and Alan Taylor on *Terminator: Genisys*.[160] It greatly informed the look and feel of the recent Marvel Netflix series, particularly *Daredevil* and *Iron Fist*.[161] This makes a certain amount of sense, given the shared influence of Frank Miller on both Batman and Daredevil.[162]

The lasting impact of *Batman Begins* would arguably be in the way that it set up the next stage of Nolan's career. The director was not under contract for a sequel, as he frequently reminded the press during the film's publicity cycle.[163] This afforded Nolan a great deal of freedom, both in how he approached the sequel and also in how he chose his future projects.

A blockbuster, *Batman Begins* was in many ways the story of how Christopher Nolan finally arrived.

# 5

## *The Prestige*

*The Prestige* is the most Nolanian of films.

The origins of the cinematic adaptation can be traced back to the earliest days of Nolan's career. Christopher Priest published *The Prestige* in 1995, to considerable acclaim. The book won the James Tait Black Memorial Prize for best fiction[1] and the World Fantasy Award for Best Novel.[2]

Producer Valerie Dean brought the novel to Nolan's attention while he was in the UK promoting *Memento*.[3] Intrigued by the novel, Nolan convinced Aaron Ryder of Newmarket Films to option the film rights.[4] The author was eager. "When I saw *Memento*, I realized that if Nolan were to adapt one of my own novels it would be a meeting of minds," Priest says.[5] The writer was optimistic about the possibility of the film making it into production. A lot of his novels get optioned, he says, "but they rarely go to the next crucial step. *The Prestige* was different, though. I had a hunch from the start that Nolan meant business."[6]

Nolan did not get started on the project right away. He turned his attention to *Insomnia*. Following the production of *Insomnia*, there was a brief gap in Nolan's schedule. Nolan's planned follow-up Howard Hughes project was stalling because of the threat posed by *The Aviator*. Nolan was attached to direct the as-yet-untitled *Batman* reboot, but there were signs that this project was stalling.[7]

Christopher asked his brother Jonathan to work with him on the *Prestige* script.[8] Priest was not actively involved in the adaptation process, stating, "I felt in safe hands. I backed off and let them get on with it. I've never regretted that."[9]

The Nolan brothers worked on the script on and off for about five years, between finishing up on *Insomnia* and getting ready to film it following *Batman Begins*.[10] This explains in part how Nolan was able to release *The Prestige* only 16 months after *Batman Begins*.[11] *The Prestige* benefited from Nolan's trademark organizational skills. It was filmed for just over one quarter of the budget of *Batman Begins*.[12] "It's definitely not a big effects movie. It's much smaller than *Batman*," says Nolan. "Compared to *Batman* it's tiny. I think it has a lot of exciting things in it, but it's much more contained."[13]

Nolan is correct. Despite its small scale, *The Prestige* is arguably the most thematically rich of Nolan's films. As with each of Nolan's previous films, it builds on what came before. It's a logical extension of the filmmaking on *Batman Begins*. This extends even to the cast and crew. The primary cast includes Christian Bale and Michael Caine.

Bale arrived in the film almost by accident. The actor says,

> I read *The Prestige* again after I finished *Batman*, but I wasn't sure if Chris just wanted to keep me as Bruce Wayne in his eyes and that was it, and he wouldn't want to work on anything else. So, I contacted him and raised that question. I really liked the character of Borden and just told him, "Hey look, this would be great. I could really do this very well." And he did believe me, so we got crackin'.[14]

*The Prestige* was the second of Nolan's collaborations with Michael Caine. Caine became one of Nolan's most steadfast collaborators, appearing in a variety of roles in each of the films following *Batman Begins*.[15] "He comes so prepared and he is just so good with such a minimal effort," Nolan says. "I cast him in every film just as an example to everyone else. He's just a lovely guy to be around. He jokes that he's my lucky charm. It was a very good strategy on his part."[16]

*The Prestige* employed a number of other regular Nolan collaborators. It was co-written by his brother Jonathan. It was edited by Lee Smith, who edited all of Nolan's films following *Batman Begins*. The production design was by Nathan Crowley, who served in that capacity on all of Nolan's post–*Batman Begins* productions with the exception of *Inception*.[17] The soundtrack was designed by David Julyan, who had gone to college with Nolan and had provided the soundtracks for *Following* and *Memento*.[18] The soundtrack was also produced by Hans Zimmer, who had worked with James Newton Howard on *Batman Begins* and would write music for the soundtrack to every Christopher Nolan film from *The Dark Knight* onwards.[19] Wally Pfister was cinematographer.

In his post–*Batman Begins* films, Nolan tends to work with the same people as much as possible. Occasionally, they will be unavailable due to other commitments and he will have to work with a replacement, but by and large the director has a team of frequent collaborators. This applies in front of the camera as well. Nolan has a troupe of actors with whom he clearly enjoys working.[20]

Talking about his creative collaborators, Nolan argued for the value of surrounding one's self with familiar faces and talents. "It makes it much easier and quicker to communicate with your team," Nolan says. "It also allows for a freer exchange of ideas with less defensiveness from myself, from my other collaborators. You're not fighting your corner so much; you're actually just trying to all contribute to the pool of ideas."[21]

This familiarity and this creative shorthand allowed Nolan to produce *The Prestige* in a timely and efficient manner. "We could really hit the ground running," Bale said of the movie's production. "Not only Chris, but obviously Wally Pfister—the d.p. Much of the crew, we'd all worked together before so there wasn't that kind of breaking-in period."[22] The result is a very polished movie that was meticulously constructed with ruthless efficiency on a tight schedule.

*The Prestige* represented something of an inversion of *Batman Begins* in terms of the relationship between America and Britain in Nolan's work. *Batman Begins* had used British locations and British sets to represent American locales like Gotham City and Wayne Manor. *The Prestige* uses American locations to substitute in for Britain; Los Angeles repeatedly stands in for turn-of-the-century London.[23] This included the theaters and stages, which were all real locations in and around L.A.[24] *The Prestige* provides another example of the blurred relationship between Britain and America in many of the films in the middle of Nolan's filmography.

As with a lot of Nolan's films, *The Prestige* feels like it has been constructed from the outside-in. It is perhaps Nolan's most structurally complex film, even when compared to the reverse narrative that drives *Memento* and the layered dreams in *Inception*. In many ways, *The Prestige* takes Nolan's familiar and favored narrative tropes and executes them in a very subtle and clever way.

This is most obvious in the framework of the film. Nolan tends to describe and explain his cinematic tricks before he employs them. As with *Memento*, the audience is invited to see the consequence before the action. This is obvious in the framing device, which opens with the death of Robert Angier and the conviction of Alfred Borden, before the audience has any real context for their relationship. However, this motif recurs throughout the film in several small ways. When Angier attends Borden's show, Nolan consciously avoids *showing* Borden performing "The Transported Man."[25] Instead, the camera focuses on Angier's and Cutler's reactions to the trick and the discussion of the mechanics of the illusion.[26] By the time the audience actually sees Borden perform the trick, it is deliberately anticlimactic.[27]

This is a microcosm of how Nolan approaches plotting on *The Prestige*. The movie has two central twists, in keeping with its fascination with duality. It very cleverly sets up and foreshadows these reveals in a way that feels organic and logical, despite the fact that these two twists are radically different in nature. The twist involving Borden is the more obvious of the two, because it conforms to genre expectations. *The Prestige* looks and feels like a period drama, and the reveal that Borden is actually a set of twins pretending to live a single life fits within those expectations. It is a grounded and practical reveal that makes sense within the context of a seemingly rational world.

*The Prestige* quite consciously mirrors Borden's devotion to his illusion in the character of Chung Ling Soo. Ching Ling Soo is named for a real-life stage magician. In the film, Chung Ling Soo spends his entire life performing as a cripple in order to preserve the mystery of his central illusion. In real life, Chung Ling Soo was the stage name of American performer William Ellsworth Robinson.[28] Robinson died when he was accidentally shot with a real bullet while attempting a bullet dodge.[29] Reportedly, Robinson's true identity was so well-concealed that audiences were surprised to hear him speak in unbroken English after he was shot.[30] But, to be fair, there is some suggestion that the contemporary press never particularly cared about his secret identity.[31]

*The Prestige* consciously seeds this twist through the narrative. Borden notes in the first two lines of his journal, "We were two young men at the start of a great career, two young men devoted to an illusion, two young men who never intended to hurt anyone." The way that the movie is set up, it initially appears like Borden *might* be referring to himself and Angier.[32] In hindsight, it is clear that Borden is talking about the two twins who inhabit that shared life. At several points in the journal, Borden uses the first-person plural ambiguously.[33]

More than that, the movie repeatedly hints at Borden's secret in early scenes. Borden deduces Chung Ling Soo's deception almost instantly, while Angier cannot fathom the possibility. In this case, Borden's subjective experience provides a key insight. Borden understands the sacrifice necessary to pull off one great trick, and so recognizes a similar deception in a fellow performer. Similarly, Sarah deduces early on that there are some days when her husband loves her and some days when doesn't. Elements like this very clearly set up the reveal of Borden's secret.[34]

*The Prestige* explicitly reveals how Borden does the trick almost as soon as Angier witnesses "The Transported Man." Before the audience sees the trick performed, before the audience even knows the substance of the trick itself, Cutler guesses the right answer. "How does he do it?" Angier demands. "He uses a double," Cutler responds. Angier dismisses the possibility out of hand, but it is subsequently revealed that Cutler is entirely correct. In fact, *The Prestige* never even bothers to advance a plausible alternative possibility, or to set up a viable red herring. However, because the film puts out the answer before raising the question, the twist is preserved without cheating the audience. It is a deft narrative accomplishment.

The twist involving Angier's trick—"The *Real* Transported Man"—is constructed in a similar manner. However, the narrative trickery involved is a lot cannier. Quite frankly, "The *Real* Transported Man" is a trick on the audience at home more than the characters in the film, because it hinges on a deception as to the true nature of *The Prestige*. The reveal behind the nature of "The *Real* Transported Man" makes no sense in the surroundings of a period drama, and so the audience never considers it as a real possibility. The period drama trappings of *The Prestige* become misdirection, designed to ensure that the audience is looking in the wrong direction as the film performs its narrative sleight of hand.

The production team working on *The Prestige* was careful to preserve the movie's central twist without directly lying to the audience, which is a very difficult line for production teams to walk in this era where the Internet forensically deconstructs a movie's pre-publicity hype cycle.[35] It is interesting to wonder whether the production team would have been able to preserve the twist if the film had not been based on a book[36] and if the film had been released after *The Dark Knight*.[37]

When it came to discussing *The Prestige*, the production team danced carefully around the issue of genre classification. "One of Chris' first notes to me on the film was that he didn't want a period score," says composer David Julyan. "The way the film is shot, it's a period setting but it's not a period film."[38] In interviews during production, Nolan avoided categorizing the film as a period drama. "I know you hear this from everybody, but it's genuinely hard to categorize, which is what I love about it," he told interviewers.[39] In the contemporary press, Christian Bale distinguished it from other period pieces.[40]

The big reveal about "The *Real* Transported Man" catches the audience off-guard because it exists outside the framework of the story. It is a trick pulled on the audience, in which Nolan effectively invites the audience to play the role of one of his protagonists. *The Prestige* looks and feels like a period drama, with its fantastic production design and impressive costuming, so the audience imposes the structures and framework of a period drama upon it. Much like Leonard structures his own life as a revenge narrative in *Memento*, and like Dormer and Finch try to trap one another in their narratives in *Insomnia*, the audience tries to fit *The Prestige* into a narrative framework based upon their experiences with films that look and feel like this film. However, as with Leonard at the end of *Memento*, the *Prestige* climax forces the audience to confront the fact that the reality presented to them does not conform to the structure that they have imposed upon it.

Robert Angier is directed to Nikola Tesla by Alfred Borden, who is trying to misdirect him. Borden's planted diary convinces Angier that Tesla developed the technology to enable Borden's illusion, so Angier reaches out to Tesla. Tesla designs a machine to Angier's specifications, with one horrific caveat. The device actually works. The device is no illusion. The device *actually* creates a copy of whatever is placed into it, one displaced in space. When Tesla puts Angier's hat through the machine, it creates dozens of copies. When Tesla puts a cat through the machine, it creates an identical twin. When Angier puts himself into the machine, he finds himself staring at a perfect copy of himself on the other side of the room. "The *Real* Transported Man" offers exactly what its title promises. The only illusion is the idea that it is an illusion.

"The *Real* Transported Man" is not a story element that belongs in a turn-of-the-century novel about class and obsession. It does not fit within the framework of a period drama. It is a story device right out of science fiction. Indeed, the core premise of the device that Tesla designs for Angier recalls one of the core existential dilemmas of the "transporter" in *Star Trek*.[41] In the world of *Star Trek*, the transporter allows the characters to "beam" from one location to another through a vaguely defined process of translocation where a body is broken down, transmitted as information and then reassembled at the destination.[42] The implications of this technology are obvious, with *Star Trek* infamously developing a "transporter malfunction" subgenre in which the device would split, combine or otherwise malform the characters.[43] However, there was an even more unsettling subtext to the device, the idea that the transporter effectively created a copy of every person who used it and destroyed the original, meaning that every *Star Trek* character is a copy of a copy of a copy.[44] As such, it seems like the twist involving Robert Angier belongs more to *Star Trek* than to the type of story that *The Prestige* initially appears to be.[45]

However strange a turn this might be, Nolan structures the set-up and reveal in the same way that he structures the reveal of the Borden brothers. Nolan puts all of the information that the audience needs up front, before they even know what they are seeing. The film's opening shot is the pile of duplicate hats from Tesla's experiment. Without any context in which to assess that image, the audience cannot deduce the twist at the end of the story.[46] However, this is far from the only such example of Nolan explaining the twist in very explicit terms.

During the court case, Cutler and the judge examine the device employed by Angier for "The *Real* Transported Man." In that short expositional scene, Cutler effectively lays down the rules of the trick: "This wasn't built by a magician. This was built by a wizard. A man who can actually do what magicians pretend to do." At this point, the audience has not yet met Nikola Tesla.[47] Similarly, the audience has not actually seen "The *Real* Transported Man" performed. Therefore, the explanation that the device actually works has no context. Nevertheless, Cutler gets even more explicit in his explanation of the device. "I'm sure beneath its bells and whistles, it's got a simple and disappointing trick," the judge says. Cutler responds, "The most disappointing of all, sir. It has no trick. It's real." This is not even a half-hour into the film, and Nolan has already spelled out the reveal.

*The Prestige* is a subtle demonstration of Nolan's non-linear storytelling.[48] It is structured in such a way that it offers up the answers to all of its mysteries before the audience even knows to ask the questions.[49] Nolan employs one of his tried and tested storytelling techniques in order to execute a cunning deception on the viewers. Several members of the production team likened the storytelling on *The Prestige* to a magic trick. Asked what made *The Prestige* stand out from other projects, Michael Caine said, "What is unique about it is you have no idea there is another magician called Christopher Nolan who is the writer-director, who is working behind you. The whole movie you're seeing is a two-hour trick, and I've never seen that done before."[50]

*The Prestige* even teases the audience by drawing attention to its misdirection. Cutler's opening monologue explicitly states as much, taunting the viewer. "Now you're looking for the secret, but you won't find it, because, of course, you're not really looking. You don't really want to know. You want to be fooled." The film is structured in such a way as to hoodwink the audience on initial viewing, employing the cinematic equivalent of sleight of hand in order to preserve its twists while also playing fair with the audience.[51]

There is a sequence later in the film where Tesla and Alley demonstrate how their machine works, with Angier's hat. The original hat remains in the machine, while a duplicate is created somewhere else on the Tesla estate. An objective and impartial audience member would realize that this effectively raises two questions about Angier's use of the machine: "What happens to the version of Angier in the machine?" and "What happens to the duplicate of Angier created by the machine?" A canny audience member would realize that the first question had been answered by the water tank in which Angier drowns. At the start of the film, and that the second question is setting up the reveal that Angier is still alive.

These tricks work because Nolan cannily prevents the audience from approaching *The Prestige* objectively, and instead invites them to think about it subjectively, in the context of what they expect from movies like this. The twist behind "The *Real* Transported Man" can hide in plain sight because the audience is never *really* looking for it, because it does not fit within their expectations of what makes sense in the context of a movie like this.

Nolan employs this approach even for smaller plot developments. The characters discuss the manner in which a bullet-catch might go wrong *twice* before the audience actually sees the bullet-catch go wrong.[52] Similarly, the possibility that Julia might not escape from the wrong knot is set up in an earlier argument between Cutler and Borden about the knot that he chose to tie and whether it was a "wet" knot. As with *Inception*, *The Prestige* is a great example of Nolan's capacity to convey information to an audience.

*The Prestige* embraces Nolan's love of subjective storytelling, of placing the audience within the perspective of Nolan's characters. What is particularly interesting about Nolan's use of non-linear storytelling in *The Prestige* is that he largely eschews visual storytelling cues to denote a shift in time or story. In *Following*, Nolan delineated between his three time frames by the physical appearance of his lead character and through the use of a black frame.[53] In *Memento*, the film shifts between color photography and black-and-white, providing a clear delineation between the scenes moving *forwards* in time and scenes moving *backwards* in time.[54] In the first act of *Batman Begins*, Bruce's colorful orange-tinted flashbacks are juxtaposed against the mostly gray-blue-and-white contemporary scenes with the League of Shadows.[55]

In contrast, *The Prestige* tends to avoid particularly obvious visual indicators to suggest a shift in time. The story does not clearly delineate between the particular sets of flashbacks. Instead, the script uses voiceover from Borden and Angier to suggest these transitions. As a result, the lines between various subjective accounts within *The Prestige* are consciously blurred.

A large portion of the film involves Alfred Borden reading the diary of Robert Angier. Within that narrative framework, Robert Angier is also reading a diary that he stole from Alfred Borden. There is a fascinating and compelling level of recursion there, with the audience receiving Borden's perspective filtered through Angier's perspective, back out to Borden again.[56] Nolan then cuts across various accounts of various events, from the perspective of various characters.[57] More than that, both layers of the subjective narrative are subsequently revealed to be false, constructed for the benefit of the audiences reading them; Borden's diary is a fake to lead Angier down dead-end paths, while Angier's diary is a taunt to the incarcerated Borden.

It has been noted that the structure of *The Prestige* consciously emulates the formula of the classic "discovered manuscript" genre, the narrative framework which formed the basis of Christopher Priest's novel.[58] Historically, the "discovered manuscript" serves to undermine ideas of historical credibility: unsettling readers by reminding them that humanity "can only (re)construct the past from the textual traces that have survived."[59] A large portion of *The Prestige* is devoted to trying to impose some objective order on the universe, to make sense of what happened; this is most apparent in the first act's framing device, the courtroom trial of Alfred Borden.[60]

However, cinematic adaptations of "discovered manuscript" stories do not have to preserve their structure and their style. After all, relatively few adaptations of *Dracula* and *Frankenstein* are particularly concerned with preserving the subjective framework of those stories. The decision to preserve the "discovered manuscript" framework in *The Prestige*, and to preference subjective storytelling over any objectivity, was a conscious decision on the part of Jonathan and Christopher Nolan.[61] In many ways, *The Prestige* builds upon the subjective framework established by *Memento*. In *Memento*, Leonard was simply lying to himself by translating subjective distortions into objective markers on notes, tattoos and photographs. In *The Prestige*, the characters are not only lying to themselves, but also lying to others.

Although *The Prestige* adheres to the textual format of traditional "discovered manuscript" stories, it should be noted that it emerged at around the time that contemporary cinema was embracing a modern variant of the format. "Found footage" horror films could be seen as a twenty-first century cinematic equivalent to the genre and format.[62] Although "found footage" films date back to Ruggero Deodato's *Cannibal Holocaust* at the very latest, the genre exploded in the twenty-first century.[63] Part of this was undoubtedly due to the success of the low-budget indie horror film *The Blair Witch Project* (1999), which became a multimedia phenomenon.[64] However, it has been argued that the found footage horror genre only *really* took off in the wake of 9/11.[65] There are any number of reasons why this might be. It is possible that found footage horror recaptures the aesthetic of the amateur footage of the attack and the aftermath, and so reflects a very modern sense of horror.[66] It might also be the case that the attacks on 9/11 represented a shattering of the concept of reality, which made these movies particularly appealing and unsettling in how they blur these same lines.[67]

In some ways, although *Memento* is anchored in the late nineties, it sets up Nolan as a director perfectly suited to the early twenty-first century. Nolan's protagonists are frequently individuals processing trauma and loss, and trying to make sense of the world through the lens of that loss. In *Memento*, Leonard has constructed a narrative to explain the death of his wife. In the *Dark Knight* trilogy, Bruce is haunted by the loss of his parents. In *The Prestige*, the characters are initially struggling to make sense of what happened on the night that Julia McCullough died.

For the first half of the film, Angier tries to comprehend and understand his wife's death. He holds his head under water so that he might experience what she experienced in her dying moments.[68] He holds Borden at gunpoint to get an answer, shooting his rival when none is forthcoming. The *Prestige* characters believe that Borden tied the wrong type of knot, but nobody *knows* for sure. Reading Borden's diary, Angier rages, "How can he not know? How can he not know? He must know what he did. He must."[69]

This desire to make sense of a chaotic world resonated in the wake of the 9/11 attacks. It is no exaggeration to state that the terrorist attacks changed the way that Americans saw the world.[70] There were undoubtedly a series of complicated (but understandable) social and politic influences that led directly to the 9/11 attacks, but to a lot of American observers (who had lived through a decade of peace and prosperity), the attacks seemed arbitrary and random.[71] A lot of Americans could not fathom why they had taken place, nor the motives behind them.[72] The attacks inflicted a trauma upon the American psyche.[73]

It makes sense that Nolan's tales of trauma and dislocation would resonate with post–9/11 America. Nolan's characters frequently try to narrativize their pain, to put that suffering in a broader context. This is a recurring theme in public discourse after 9/11: A lot of time and energy has been spent trying to make sense of the events through the prisms of conspiracy theories or wild speculation.[74] More than that, the twenty-first century has fragmented public discourse through advances in technology and self-selected data filtering.[75] Facts are no longer considered absolute within public discourse.[76] Reality appears frayed at the edges.[77]

Nolan's films present characters who are frequently trying to make sense of a chaotic world, to impose their own sense of order upon it. This recurring fascination with subjectivity plays out across *The Prestige*, where even the characters cannot make sense of their own actions. In Borden's diary, he ruminates upon the death of Julia McCullough. "I have fought with myself over that night," he states, "one half of me swearing blind that I tied a simple slipknot, the other half convinced that I tied the Langford double. I can never know for sure." Of course, in keeping with Nolan's fascination with literalizing his existential themes, *The Prestige* portrays this sense of internal division by having Borden *actually* be two people much like *Memento* literalizes the process of Leonard lying to himself by denying him the facility of memory.

*The Prestige* embraces subjectivity to the point that it is suggested that the characters themselves can never know their own secrets. Borden ruminates that each of the twins had "half of a full life," although that means neither had a life of their own. Angier is gripped with anxiety about his exploitation of Tesla's device and the existential questions that it poses. "It took courage to climb into that machine every night, not knowing if I'd be the man in the box or in the prestige." The film suggests that Angier is simultaneously both and neither.[78] Even then, the version of Angier in "the box" gets to answer the tough existential questions about what happened to Julia in her final moments, but the Angier in "the prestige" will never have the closure of knowing what his doppelganger experienced.

As with all of Christopher Nolan's films, *The Prestige* is engaged with the idea of narrative. *The Prestige* is arguably his most densely layered film. Its preoccupation with narrative spans multiple levels, in many ways building off the idea of narrative suggested by *Batman Begins* and setting up the idea of narrative that would be explored in *Inception*. If *Batman Begins* touches on the idea of narrative as mythology, then *The Prestige* engages with even more fundamental and existential questions. *The Prestige* is about one of the most fundamental narratives, one of the oldest structures created to impose order on a seeming random and arbitrary world. On one level, *The Prestige* is about religion.

*The Prestige* is a film built around dualities, invested in forces that exist in opposition to one another. The most obvious contrast is between dueling magicians Borden and Angier. However, the theme runs much deeper than that. The twins, who try to live one shared life as Alfred Borden, are often caught in a tug of war between their separate desires. Angier is caught between being "the prestige" and "the man in the box." Nikola Tesla and Thomas Edison caught up in their own rivalry in "the War of the Currents."[79] In discussing his art form, Cutler seems to suggest a division between "magician" and "showman." Appropriately enough, *The Prestige* itself would exist in opposition to *The Illusionist*, another magician-themed period piece released around the same time.[80]

At the core of *The Prestige* is an existential conflict between the materialism and spirituality. *The Prestige* consciously unfolds in a materialist world where value is measured in money and capital.[81] Various characters understand that their existence is dependent upon the ability to earn money off their creations. Early in the film, Cutler refuses to explain his tricks in front of an open courtroom. "The *Real* Transported Man is one of the most sought-after illusions in this business," Cutler insists. "I have the right to sell it on. If I reveal the method here, the trick is worthless."[82] Borden in particular exists in opposition to this materialist world, seeking to escape poverty through his innovations and improvisations.

The conflict between Angier and Borden is largely rooted in class. For Christian Bale, the film was an exploration of a very British sensibility. "You know your place," Bale states. "That's it. Do not try to get above your station at all. So, I'm sure, yeah, there is a certain amount of annoyance from Borden's part about Angier. He keeps that hidden, Angier, his actual resources and where he comes from."[83] It is revealing that the working-class Borden adopts the stage name "The Professor" once he becomes famous, as if trying to distance himself from his origins.

When Borden shows Sarah's nephew how to perform a simple sleight of hand, it comes with a grave warning. "Never show anyone," Borden explains. "They'll beg you and flatter you for the secret, but as soon as you give it up, you'll be nothing to them. You understand? Nothing." Borden understands that the trick has material value, even if he does not have innate value himself. So it makes simple economic sense for Borden to *become* the trick, in order that he might accrue economic value. He designs a trick that cannot be duplicated and mass-produced, so that its value cannot be divorced from his own. "A real magician tries to invent something new that other magicians will scratch their heads over," Cutler says. "Then you sell it to him for a small fortune." When Borden asserts that he has such a trick, Cutler replies, "Would you care to sell it to me?" Borden answers, "No. No one else can do my trick." Cutler states, "Any trick can be duplicated." Borden responds, "Wrong."

The bulk of *The Prestige* is given over to Angier trying to duplicate Borden's trick, trying mass-producing something that was originally unique and particular. In this way, *The Prestige* might be read as a broad critique of capitalist excess, of the horrors of unbridled materialism that seeks to replicate and control what is initially mysterious and ambiguous. *The Prestige* is a film that is consciously wary of such uncritical materialist thinking. At the same time, it understands the yearning of its characters to break beyond the confines of a cold and materialist world.

Reflecting on Chung Ling Soo's complete devotion to his art, Borden immediately understands what could drive a man to such sacrifice and commitment. Borden understands what it is to be poor and trapped, while Angier has no frame of reference. "It's the only way to escape," Borden notes. He taps on the hard concrete wall of the building beside him. "All this, you know?" Borden is obvious talking about the trick's capacity to elevate a person out of poverty, but he is also referring to something more fundamental. Borden is talking about magic's capacity to enable people to escape the trappings of the material world.

In his *General Theory of Magic* (1902), sociologist Marcel Mauss contextualizes magic in terms of both technology and religion.[84] *The Prestige* arguably does something very similar, juxtaposing the belief in something mystical against the cold hard rationality of science.[85] Repeatedly over the course of the film, characters find that scientific fact is rejected and dismissed by the public, because they don't *want* to believe it. Tesla watches his life's work destroyed in large part because people are not ready to confront the objective, scientifically verifiable reality of how the universe works. "The truly extraordinary is not permitted in science and industry," Tesla notes in his letter to Angier. "Perhaps you'll find more luck in your field, where people are happy to be mystified." The scenes of Edison's agents demolishing Tesla's laboratory recall sequences of angry mobs attacking mad scientists and freaks of science in classic horror films like *Frankenstein*.[86]

When Tesla builds a machine for Angier that can *literally and scientifically* accomplish what magicians create through illusion, the characters understand that it cannot be presented as it *really* is. Instead, it must be disguised. When Ackerman sees the trick performed, he is horrified. "You'll have to dress it up a little. Disguise it. Give them enough reason to doubt it." The implication is clear. The audience is not *ready* to confront the reality of how such things work. They prefer illusion and mysticism over cold rationality. As with the films in the *Dark Knight* trilogy, *The Prestige* is concerned with an overarching narrative that a society constructs in order to better function. In the *Dark Knight* trilogy, that fantasy is the myth of Batman. In *The Prestige*, that narrative is magic. However, it is also an overt metaphor for religion.

In the film's final moments, Angier explains the appeal of magic to Borden, as a rejection of the physical and materialist world. "The audience knows the truth," Angier says. "The world is simple. It's miserable, solid. Solid all the way through. But if you could fool them, even for a second, then you could make them wonder. And then you … then you got to see something very special." This is perhaps the most cynical argument in *The Prestige*, and in Nolan's filmography: that the audience *wants* to be fooled into believing that there is something more, because there *isn't*.[87]

This is a logical extrapolation of Nolan's core themes, albeit one that extends them to their logical conclusions. In *Memento* and *Batman Begins*, characters constructed narratives to make sense of their lives and the world around them. *The Prestige* extrapolates that outwards. The film plays sleight of hand with the audience, tricking them into imposing their own expectations about this sort of film onto the narrative. However, in the world of the film itself, Nolan builds off of Teddy's line to Leonard at the end of *Memento* and suggests that *everybody* builds these self-serving narratives around themselves and that society itself constructs such narratives.

This idea of a comforting lie plays out across *The Prestige*, most notably in the discussion around Julia's death. Early in the film, Cutler attempts to comfort Angier about the drowning of his wife. "I knew an old sailor once," Cutler recalls. "They told me he went overboard, tangled in the sails. They pulled him out, but it took him five minutes to cough. He said it was like going home." This is reassuring to Angier, a suggestion that Julia did not suffer as she died. However, it is also a lie. At the end of the film, confronting the horror of what Angier has done, Cutler decides to speak the truth. "I once told you about a sailor who described drowning to me," Cutler recalls. Angier responds, "Yes, he said it was like going home." Cutler bluntly corrects himself. "I was lying," Cutler reflects. "He said it was agony." This is the choice: the comforting lie or the horrific truth.

This reads very much as an exploration of the social role of religion.[88] Religion and superstition tend to provide a framework through which people can understand (and account for) a complicated and arbitrary world.[89] A particularly cynical view of religion might treat it as something that offers believers reassurance that the world makes sense, at least by some specific set of criteria.[90] Religion offers a narrative of the world for its adherents, one codified and structured through creation myths and commandments.[91]

To be clear, this is a very broad and generalized reading of religion. *The Prestige* positions religion in direct opposition to science, as one of the movie's central dichotomies. This ignores the fact that it is possible for a person to accept science *and* hold religious beliefs at the same time.[92] At the same time, *The Prestige* arrived in the midst of a broader culture war in which religion was frequently used as an objection against scientific principles like global warming and evolution.[93] Similarly, *The Prestige* was also released at a time when both the United Kingdom and the United States had elected leaders who believed themselves to be directed by divine purpose. President George W. Bush believed that God had chosen him to wage the War on Terror,[94] while Prime Minister Tony Blair used his religious belief to ground his understanding of the world.[95] As such, it seems like the film's decision to play up that contrast touches on that broader debate about religion and science as competing narratives of the world, and religion as the more comforting of those two narratives.[96]

Nolan has never talked about this interpretation of the film, but has acknowledged that part of what interested him about magic was the fact that the audience willfully does not *want* to know the secrets of the tricks:

> The real paradox, which is the paradox of magic, but this is to me what's interesting about the subject, is that much as the audience wants to know the secret, the secret ultimately will be disappointing. That's the nature of magic. And that's, to me, the key thing which I'm trying to do in the film.[97]

Films like *The Prestige* and *Inception* seem to suggest a rather cynical view of the world. Critic Keith Uhlich described the experience of watching *The Prestige* as witnessing

Nolan "pummeling the belief out of me. There is no trick. There is no God. There is no magic. Just an endless supply of self-same meat-bodies to be buried forever out of sight."[98] Nolan would appear to argue that there is only the rational and chaotic world, and the flawed systems which mankind imposes upon that world to make sense of it.

However, Nolan is not dismissive of those illusions; he is sympathetic to them. Angier creates a rational and scientific process that can successfully recreate Borden's illusion. Angier's rational and scientific recreation is presented as *truly* monstrous. "Take a minute to consider your achievement," Cutler sarcastically advises Angier, as the two of them stand surrounded by the drowned clones (and, possibly, the one original version) of the magician. Cutler's voice drips with contempt. Angier has found a way to recreate the illusion in a tangible and literal manner, and it is the stuff of nightmares. The illusion has value of itself, even though it is just an illusion. That is the paradox, and a recurring theme in Nolan's cinematic work.[99]

After all, the mostly commonly cited metaphor in *The Prestige* is Nolan's interrogation the idea of narrative as filmmaking. Nolan has confirmed this reading of the film:

> There's quite a strong relationship between what magicians do and what filmmakers do. The filmmaker is very similar to a magician in the way we release information, what we tell the audience and when and how we draw the audience in through certain points of view. We use our own techniques, blind alleys and red herrings, to fool the audience and, hopefully, to create a satisfying payoff. With *The Prestige*, there was an opportunity to really play with these concepts right before the audience's eyes.[100]

There is a sense that *The Prestige* allows Nolan to discuss his art form with the audience in a similar manner to the decision to edit his director's commentary on the DVD version of *Insomnia* so that the scenes play in the order in which they were shot. He saw that commentary as a potentially insightful tool for parties looking to understand the mechanics of how films are constructed. "We've given them a pretty unique insight into the filmmaking process that I don't think I've seen anywhere else."[101]

It could reasonably be argued that many of Nolan's films are *about* the process of filmmaking, whether overtly or in terms of Nolan's more subjective experience of the form.[102] However, *The Prestige* is especially candid about it. Says Nolan:

> For me, *The Prestige* is very much about filmmaking. It's very much about what I do. It is also intended to suggest to the audience some of those ideas about how the film itself is spooling its narrative out to the audience. You want people to be aware of the effect the film is having as it's unfolding before their eyes.[103]

The superficial parallels between the two processes are quite obvious. *The Prestige* imagines the central characters as performers. The twins play the roles of Borden and Fallon, swapping in and out while trying to preserve the illusion. Lord Caldlow disguises himself as Robert Angier and then rebrands himself as "The Great Danton." Both Borden and Angier blend narrative and spectacle in order to seduce and distract the audience.

The film's structure is even designed to mirror the framework of the magic trick. That was something of a breakthrough for Nolan when structuring the film, the decision "to structure the screenplay according to the same principles the magic trick is based on, the three-act structure of the trick: the pledge, the turn, the prestige."[104] In fact, the Nolan brothers make a point to change the descriptor "stage" in the novel to "act" in the screenplay to reinforce this parallel.[105]

However, *The Prestige* seems to be discussing some very particular aspects of filmmaking, particularly in contrast to Nolan's other film-related narratives like *Inception* and *Interstellar*. In some ways, *The Prestige* plays like a meditation upon filmmaking and spectacle, in particular the existential challenges that Nolan faced in transitioning to blockbuster filmmaking. *The Prestige* is positioned at the halfway point in Nolan's first ten films, and at a clear intersection between his origins as a low-budget filmmaker and his subsequent career as a blockbuster director.

*The Prestige* marks an end for a certain type of film produced by Nolan. *The Prestige* was his last film with a budget of under $100 million. It was also his last film to earn under $200 million at the worldwide box office. It was the last Nolan film distributed by Newmarket Films, the company that helped launch his career with *Memento*. It was also Nolan's last collaboration with his old friend David Julyan.

Working on *The Prestige*, Nolan took advantage of the freedom of this sort of filmmaking, which was radically different from the more controlled method that he had employed on *Batman Begins*. According to Christian Bale,

> Chris was a shape shifter in the way he went to very different styles of directing from *Batman* to this. He really wanted to be able to move very quickly, spin on a dime, and have us all ready to approach different scenes in different ways. "Maybe we are going to do this scene today, maybe we're going to do this one instead." Whereas with something like *Batman*, because it's such an enormous kind of setup, you really know that here is what we have to do. Any changes require an awful lot of time to switch around. So, it was nice to be working in a much more spontaneous manner.[106]

Free of the demands of excessively complicated stunt work and set pieces, Nolan could engage in a more relaxed cinematic style.

*The Prestige* often feels like Nolan is meditating upon the demands of big-budget and high-profile filmmaking, which makes sense in the context of questions and speculation about his potential involvement in the inevitable sequel to *Batman Begins*.[107] Nolan was not under contract for the film that would become *The Dark Knight* at the time that *Batman Begins* was released,[108] and was facing questions about what kind of filmmaker he wanted to be in the long term.[109]

Even the casting of *The Prestige* plays into this idea. The central roles of Borden and Angier are played by Christian Bale and Hugh Jackman, actors best known at the time for their lead role in popular superhero films.[110] The character of Tesla is played by rock star David Bowie, who Nolan cast due to his "iconic status."[111] Tesla's memorable and distinctive entrance walking through a field of lightning could be seen as a nod to the iconic lightning bolt across his face on the cover of *Aladdin Sane*.[112] Tesla's assistant Mr. Alley is played by Andy Serkis, who at that point was still best known for his motion-capture performances in the *Lord of the Rings* trilogy and *King Kong* (2005).[113]

*The Prestige* seems designed to straddle the gap articulated by Cutler in his discussion of Borden's technique, the space between the "magician" and "showman" or the engineer and the spectacle. Bale and Jackman might be best known for playing superheroes, but they are both cast as down-to-earth human beings. Bowie might be a rock god, but he is playing a misunderstood recluse. Andy Serkis revolutionized twenty-first century special effects, but his role is that of an ordinary human being. Asked if it was refreshing to star in a high-budget film where audiences could actually see his face, Serkis jokingly replied, "Yeah."[114]

*The Prestige* seems like a cautionary tale about the dangers of getting swept up in wondrous new technology. The film implies that Borden's "The Transported Man" is somewhat less monstrous than Angier's "The *Real* Transported Man," in that the film allows the surviving twin the opportunity to rebuild his life while Angier is completely lost to the horrific spectacle that he has created.[115] Cutler is perhaps the closest thing that *The Prestige* has to an objective center, and the movie's finale finds him aligning with the surviving Borden twin rather than whatever Angier has become.

In some ways, *The Prestige* could reflect Nolan's longstanding ambivalence towards technological innovation within the filmmaking industry. Nolan is a director who constructs subjective and ambiguous narratives, but likes to ground them in tangible trappings. He is wary of spectacle for the sake of spectacle. Nolan says,

> There are usually two different goals in a visual effects movie. One is to fool the audience into seeing something seamless, and that's how I try to use it. The other is to impress the audience with the amount of money spent on the spectacle of the visual effect, and that, I have no interest in.[116]

Borden's "The Transported Man" could be seen to embody the former style of special effects, with his understated delivery of a genuinely innovative trick in a very practical and organic manner. The characters take a moment to appreciate the texture and artistry of Borden's trick. Angier falls in love with its elegance and simplicity, calling it "the greatest magic trick I've ever seen." Angier, Cutler and Olivia fawn over the trick. Olivia even notes the *realism* involved. "It's the same man," she marvels. "He wears padded gloves to hide his damaged fingers, but, if you look closely, you can tell." However, despite its authenticity and craft, Borden's trick does not resonate with contemporary audiences. "Did they applaud when you saw it?" Olivia asks. Angier responds, "It was too good. It was too simple."

And so Angier reinvents the trick as "The *Real* Transported Man" in a manner that more consciously evokes the second type of computer-generated special effects. *The Prestige*'s introductory scene captures the awe-inspiring nature of Angier's illusion, with sparks and crackles of energy from a device that exists beyond the capacity of human imagination. It is disjointed and terrifying, grotesque and horrific. It is an illusion that threatens to break reality itself, reflecting the argument that the use of computer-generated imagery in film and television wanders into the uncanny valley.[117] Some more extreme philosophers would argue that advances in technology like computer-generated animation have contributed to a sense that reality is fractured and broken.[118] Either way, Angier's over-complicated and mechanized attempt to replicate a fairly simple and straightforward illusion is treated as an abomination.[119]

In keeping with the filmmaking metaphor at the center of the story, it could also be argued that *The Prestige* reflects Nolan's other anxieties about the direction of the medium. In particular, the film might be seen to reflect the discomfort with the shift towards digital photography in moviemaking.[120] Nolan is not a fan of the transition away from celluloid towards video, wryly remarking, "It's called filmmaking, after all."[121] He would become an outspoken proponent of physical film in his later career, particularly with the release of his subsequent films *Interstellar* and *Dunkirk* in prestigious formats like 70mm.[122] Nolan's attitude would arguably become clear with his next film, with his decision to produce portions of *The Dark Knight* on IMAX.[123]

Nolan has made a lot of arguments about the superiority of film over digital. However, it should be noted that he has never actually worked with digital.[124] His preference for celluloid comes from his experience having worked with it, his own subjective experiences on his short films and *Following*. It provided the director with some certainty in a rapidly changing world:

> I think that getting a strong technical grounding was very important for me, and learning how to photograph things on film, expose the film correctly, choose the film stocks, those kind of things, has served me extremely well as I've gone on to bigger and bigger films, and, frankly, had more and more a bewildering array of technical options. Things you can buy, and so forth. And massive pressure, frankly, from electronics companies and engineering firms and labs and however people are trying to push you. You're given endless misinformation. And, as a filmmaker, you literally watch that become currency.[125]

Nolan's preference for film over digital could be seen as an expression of the same core beliefs that inform his preference for practical effects. Although his films are obsessed with the subjective and the unreal, the director makes a point to ground them in something tangible and physical. Much like Leonard takes reassurance in the physicality of the world around him, Nolan seems to find comfort in the tangibility of film stock. He concedes this of both his use of film stock and his preference for practical effects: "I am a seriously strong believer in a tactile sense of things."[126]

In some ways, digital photography represents the antithesis of this approach. The technique came to prominence in the early years of the twenty-first century, when George Lucas decided to shoot *Star Wars: Episode II—Attack of the Clones* on digital rather than film.[127] Michael Mann became a champion for the form with *Collateral* and *Miami Vice*.[128] Robert Rodriguez demonstrated what was possible with the form with *Sin City*.[129] David Fincher came to embrace the opportunities and possibilities of this style of filmmaking.[130]

Notions of reality are among the biggest divides when it comes to debates between celluloid and digital. Digital filmmaking renders it a lot easier to manipulate the image, whether in terms of lighting or special effects. Post-production tends to be smoother on digital, where the image can be altered in profound ways depending on the director's preference.[131] Things that would never have been possible to create in the "real" world can be rendered efficiently through the distortion of the digital file.[132] It could also be argued that digital production pushes a film unconsciously into the realm of the uncanny in a way that is difficult to precisely measure. According to Heather Stewart, the British Film Institute's Creative Director, "People know. They feel it in their bodies, the excitement becomes more real."[133]

On a purely practical level, film is just more tangible than digital.[134] It is possible to physically hold a reel of film in hand, in a way that is impossible with a digital file stored on a hard disc.[135] Every film reel has actually existed in the world, and accrued some mark of that passage, sometimes denoted by imperfections that would not be present on a perfect copy of a perfect original. To proponents of celluloid over digital, these imperfections give celluloid texture, they make it feel substantial.[136] It is much more romantic and substantial than limitless copies of an original perfectly preserved digital file. It is more "real."

*The Prestige* seems to touch on this anxiety. Borden's version of "The Transported Man" is effectively an analog illusion. It is practical and grounded, rooted in the real world. Like those scratches and burns on old film footage, there is an authenticity to Borden's illusion. Olivia actively encourages Borden to proudly acknowledge his imperfections and to wear them for the audience watching in the auditorium. She suggests removing the padded glove that hides his missing fingers, those shot off by Angier during an earlier sequence.

"You hide this," Olivia observes. "I had to look very closely to spot it during "The Transported Man," but this makes you unique. It shows you aren't using a double. You mustn't hide it. You must display it proudly. I'm sure it takes great skill to perform illusions with one good hand." Borden concedes that it does. Olivia responds, "So let people know." In some ways, this is an argument for accepting the limitations of shooting on celluloid, accepting that those limitations provide an important grounding that adds legitimacy to the illusion being performed.[137]

In contrast, Angier's version of "The *Real* Transported Man" creates a perfect copy of the magician each and every night. There is no discernible difference between the "the prestige" and "the man in the box." There are no telling details, no obvious imperfections. It would be impossible to tell one from the other, to the point that even the coroner is fooled by the body drowned in the box. Angier is able to fashion a recreation of himself that is at once perfect *and* uncanny.[138] Angier's trick seems like an effective metaphor for the fears that certain celluloid-focused directors have about the shift in the industry towards digital photography.

Positioned at a turning point in Nolan's career, the halfway mark in his first ten films and the pivot point between Nolan's earlier small-scale productions and his subsequent blockbuster epics, *The Prestige* remains his most intricate and precise narrative. It is the most carefully calibrated and measured film in his filmography, the most densely layered of his work and perhaps the most rewarding to re-watch.

*The Prestige* remains perhaps Nolan's greatest trick.

# 6

## *The Dark Knight*

*The Dark Knight* is probably Nolan's biggest film, in terms of cultural impact.

It is not his longest film; that is *Interstellar*.[1] It is not his most expensive film; that is *The Dark Knight Rises*.[2] While *The Dark Knight* returned the highest box office grosses of any Nolan film in the U.S., *The Dark Knight Rises* returned a slightly higher worldwide total.[3]

However, *The Dark Knight* looms large over Nolan's filmography. Depending on how one measures such things, it *might* be Nolan's most critically acclaimed film.[4] It is *perhaps* his most popular.[5] It undoubtedly has the largest pop cultural footprint of any of Nolan's films, radically re-conceptualizing both summer blockbusters and superhero cinema.

It seems strange, then, that *The Dark Knight* was never particularly planned or orchestrated. The film builds off of *Batman Begins'* closing scene, which teased the arrival of the Joker in Gotham. However, Nolan had never intended for that closing scene to be an intentional sequel hook: "It wasn't really about setting up a sequel. I wanted [the audience] to leave the theater with their minds just spinning. Batman has arrived. That was always the snap of the ending. It wasn't really until months after the film came out that I said, 'Okay, now I want to know who the Joker is.'"[6] As Nolan reminded the press in the release cycle around *Batman Begins*, he was not under any contractual obligation to return for the sequel.[7]

According to *Batman Begins* co-writer David Goyer, "It wasn't really until maybe three months after *Batman Begins* came out that Chris sat down with me for lunch and said, 'Okay, let's talk about a sequel.'"[8] Nolan tended to play coy with the media in the immediate aftermath of the release of *Batman Begins*.[9] Warner Brothers confirmed the title of *The Dark Knight*, and the fact that Nolan was returning, a few months before the release of *The Prestige*.[10]

*The Dark Knight* was the first sequel in Nolan's filmography.[11] Unlike other directors working on franchise films, Nolan would not be rushed into production on a sequel or follow-up.[12] Instead, he arranged with Warner Brothers that he would be afforded the freedom and the opportunity to pursue projects that interested him outside of the larger franchise concerns.[13] He took the time to produce *The Prestige* between *Batman Begins* and *The Dark Knight*. Nolan says,

If you're really trying to grow and nurture a franchise, the thing that used to be understood, that I think now is a little harder to carve out with the studio because of the pressures they have, is you need time. And that doesn't mean necessarily even working full-time on it itself; it means time to throw some ideas together and then let them sit, go off and do something else, come back and see what still feels right and everything.[14]

What really drew Nolan was the character of the Joker. "I didn't have any intention of making a sequel to *Batman Begins* and I was quite surprised to find myself wanting to do it. I just got caught up in the process of imagining how you would see a character like the Joker through the prism of what we did in the first film."[15]

The character was ripe for reinvention. The Joker had been continually reimagined and conceptualized across his 68-year comic book history.[16] More than that, the success of *Batman Begins* had allowed Nolan to escape the shadow of Tim Burton and Joel Schumacher's earlier cinematic adaptations of Batman. The Joker could be considered fair game for adaptation, despite the fact that the character had been played by Jack Nicholson less than two decades earlier.

The public was hungry for a fresh take on the Clown Prince of Crime. Co-writer Jonathan Nolan recalls his experience of watching *Batman Begins* with an audience and the effect of that final reveal of the playing card. "Gordon flips over the Joker card at the end and the audience erupts like they're going to tear the place apart. I've never heard a noise like it."[17] The Internet was consumed with casting speculation, naming every actor from Paul Bettany[18] to Sean Penn.[19]

Nolan had first met with Heath Ledger as a candidate to play Bruce Wayne in *Batman Begins*: "He was quite gracious about it, but he said, 'I would never take a part in a superhero film.'"[20] Ledger was somewhat blunter: "I actually hate comic book movies, like fucking hate them, they just bore me shitless and they're just dumb."[21]

Nevertheless, Nolan pitched him on *Batman Begins* and Ledger expressed some interest in seeing how it would play out.[22] Indeed, it was *Batman Begins* that got Ledger interested in the possibility of playing the Joker in the sequel. "I thought what Chris Nolan did with [*Batman Begins*] was actually really good, really well directed, and Christian Bale was really great in it," the actor explained.[23] Ledger met with Nolan about the part. "I didn't know whether it was something he'd be interested in, but I sat and chatted with him in my office for a couple of hours," Nolan remembers of that fateful meeting. "We didn't have a script at that point, but—my brother was writing it at the time, and we knew kind of where that was going to go, and it was very much what Heath had in mind. And he just was determined to do it."[24]

Ledger and the Joker were baked into the concept of *The Dark Knight* from the outset, before Jonathan had even finished his first draft of the script.[25] It would be impossible to separate the two. Ledger's casting was initially deemed controversial by certain vocal online fans.[26] Ledger threw himself into the role, taking advantage of the time afforded by his early casting to really delve into the concept of the Joker. Ledger explained, "I sat around in a hotel room in London for about a month and I just locked myself away and formed a little diary and experimented with voices."[27] Ledger's diary included a list of concepts that the Joker would find funny like "land mines," "AIDS" and "brunch."[28] Ledger invested himself completely in the character.[29]

*The Dark Knight* represents a reinvention of the Joker as a character. It also goes back to the character's origins. In fact, the premise of the Joker taunting authorities by naming his victims and even the sequence in which the Joker removes his clown makeup to impersonate a police officer is taken directly from his first comic book appearances.[30] However, this was not a conscious decision on the part of Christopher and Jonathan Nolan. It happened almost by accident, as a result of the direction in which they always envisaged taking the character.[31]

This included going back to the character's original influences from silent expressionist cinema. The Joker had been created by Jerry Robinson, Bob Kane and Bill Finger as an adversary for the first issue of Batman's self-titled series in the spring of 1940.[32] He was such a compelling character that he appeared in two of the issue's four stories.[33] As with the character of Batman, the Joker was built inward from a compelling visual rather than outward from a core concept. The design of Conrad Veidt's character in Paul Leni's adaptation of Victor Hugo's *The Man Who Laughs* was a major influence on the design of the character.[34]

Once again, the Nolan brothers seemed to have landed on this subtle call-back to the character's origins by happenstance or parallel evolution rather than by design. Their version of the Joker was influenced by a *different* German expressionist director. Jonathan found writing for the Joker to be disarmingly easy. "Maybe I should see a shrink," Jonathan says. "Then I remember Chris making me watch Fritz Lang's take on *Dr. Mabuse* all those years ago. I fight the feeling that he's been planning this project since we were kids."[35] Christopher would later prescribe *Dr. Mabuse* as "essential research for anyone attempting to write a supervillain."[36] Ledger approached the character's physicality in the style of silent movie actors like Charlie Chaplin and Buster Keaton, which contributed to the character's uncanniness.[37]

The design of the Joker was very much grounded in the verisimilitude that defined *Batman Begins*.[38] The character's makeup design gave him a Glasgow smile, which prosthetics supervisor Conor O'Sullivan faithfully modeled on a delivery man who visited an estate near his workshop.[39] Costume designer Linda Hemming says of the character's sartorial style, "You've got to make it look like someone really dresses like this. It can't just be, 'Hello, I'm putting on my costume.' It's got to be wherever he lives and whatever he's been doing, he's been wearing that."[40] According to Nolan,

> What's strong about [the Joker] was this idea of anarchy, this commitment to chaos. He's not just a bank robber or an ordinary criminal who's out for any kind of material gain. I talked to Heath a lot about that even as we were finishing the script, and we both agreed that's the most threatening force, in a way, that society faces—that of pure anarchy by someone who really wants to do harm for its sake and for his own entertainment.[41]

This theory of the Joker explains why the character was so compelling to a director like Nolan. As a writer-director, Nolan is fixated upon notions of structures and control. His films argue for systems and frameworks that govern and constrain human behavior, punishing characters like Leonard in *Memento* and Dormer in *Insomnia* when they step outside those systems.

This is, to a certain extent, true of Nolan himself. Frequent collaborator Cillian Murphy has remarked how he is in awe of how "in control" Nolan is of his large-scale productions.[42] Nolan has cultivated a reputation as a director so efficient that his blockbusters come in ahead of time and under budget.[43] He tends to structure his films so carefully that he rarely generates any deleted scenes for the home media release.[44] Directors working on big-budget productions need to be able to maintain control, and Nolan is the epitome of that efficiency and effectiveness.[45]

Nolan has acknowledged that chaos is one of his core fears. Conceding that his characters tend to worry about their lives slipping out of their control, Nolan admits, "It's definitely something that I have a fear of—not being in control of your own life."[46] The Joker is very much a living embodiment of this fear, the personification of chaos. Jonathan saw the Joker as the representation of a particular mythological archetype, the trickster:

> I think the Joker particularly was a lesson for me because that character can connect to the peyote stories of Native American mythology, and Loki in Norse mythology, and there are so many examples of a Joker-like figure that you can endlessly reinvent that character.[47]

The Joker is a *particularly* terrifying force in the context of a Christopher Nolan narrative, where everything is structured and controlled. The Joker just tears through all of that. The film itself seems to bend and distort around the character as an avatar of chaos, as if the world is caught in his gravity.

Nolan is usually a very precise and very careful director, but he occasionally seems to cede control of the movie to his antagonist.[48] Nolan's directorial style noticeably loosens when the Joker is on screen, swirling wildly around the Joker when he invades the party at the Wayne Penthouse and slowly twisting around to face him head-on as he dangles from the half-constructed Prewitt Building.[49] Similarly, Nolan breaks the familiar and core "180°" rule" of filmmaking during the interrogation scene between Batman and the Joker, a scene in which the Joker taunts, "Tonight you're going to break your one rule."[50] Given the attention that Nolan typically pays to the technology that he is using, it is highly symbolic that the first shot of the Joker's face (as he peels off his mask at the end of the bank robbery) is slightly out of focus.[51]

The Joker's distortive effect on the film production itself carries over to the soundtrack. Hans Zimmer designed a soundscape for the character that sounds hostile and unsettling, in marked contrast to the more conventional cues associated with Ra's Al Ghul in *Batman Begins* and with Bane in *The Dark Knight Rises*. Says Zimmer,

> I had this idea that rather than what a note is in the context of the notes surrounding it, what could I do emotionally through a performance within one note? How much can I stretch the meaning of a single note and get it down to such minimalism. I failed slightly. I had to use two notes in the end.[52]

Part of what makes the Joker so unsettling is the effective and uncanny use of silence over several of his key scenes, particularly in places where the audience would expect swelling orchestral music. As sound designer and supervising sound editor Richard King noted, the big action set piece, built around the Joker's assassination attempt on the arrested Harvey Dent, is uncomfortably silent. "Chris decided to play the scene with sound effects and no music for the most part, which is rare for a scene like this," King recalls.[53]

The Joker is a very broadly drawn anarchist, a villain who wishes to destroy society itself. He makes for an interesting contrast from the fascists or nihilists who tend to populate these big-budget event pictures, in many ways typified by characters like Ra's Al Ghul and Bane. If pop culture tends to fixate upon cartoonishly exaggerated right-wing fascistic antagonists, then the Joker makes for a compelling take on a cartoonishly exaggerated left-wing anarchistic antagonist.[54]

The Joker is very clearly grounded in a set of twenty-first century fears. "It was about the threat of anarchy," Nolan says of his approach to the Clown Prince of Crime. "It was about anarchy being the most frightening thing there is. Chaos and anarchy in this day and age, and I think it is. It's certainly the thing I'm most afraid of."[55]

If movies like *Memento* and *The Prestige* demonstrated the storytelling sensibilities that established Nolan as an effective post–9/11 storyteller, then the *Dark Knight* trilogy fits within a particular subset of that. *Batman Begins*, *The Dark Knight* and *The Dark Knight Rises* are effectively pop cinema for the War on Terror, to the point that *The Dark Knight* has been described as "the first great post–Sept. 11 film."[56] Nolan's *Dark Knight* films provide a prism through which the early years of the twenty-first century might be explored in pulp fiction.[57]

To be fair, twenty-first century American film and television is largely defined by the events of 9/11 and the War on Terror.[58] The politics and imagery of the era is continually filtered back through these blockbuster properties, whether consciously or not.[59] There is a sense that American popular consciousness has been trying to make sense of this radical paradigm shift through the framework of blockbuster action and superhero stories.[60] Urban destruction in the film and television of the twenty-first century is inevitably influenced by those amateur recordings of 9/11.[61] Holes seem to constantly tear themselves open in the sky above major cities, particularly New York.[62] Planes and spaceships are constantly colliding and impacting with one another and with buildings.[63] What distinguishes the *Dark Knight* trilogy is the way in which it digs deeper than this imagery and iconography in an effort to parse something approaching meaning from these events.

In *The Dark Knight*, the Joker is explicitly branded as a terrorist.[64] More than that, his methodology is framed in terms of how Americans think of terrorism in the twenty-first century. The Joker talks to Gotham through ominous video statements, read by captives and featuring brutal executions. He uses improvised explosive devices activated by cellular telephones. He destroys buildings, leaving search and rescue to wander through the burned-out remains looking for signs of life.[65]

In practical terms, the Joker is able to disrupt a major metropolitan area with relatively few resources and a little innovation. "Look what I did to this city with a few drums of gas and a couple of bullets," the Joker says to Dent, recalling the damage and devastation that a handful of terrorists caused with utility knives and box cutters on 9/11.[66] The Joker's low-tech approach and resourcefulness taps into deep-seated fears about how easily modern terrorists can cause death and disruption in spite of security precautions and regulations, and about how arbitrary that violence can seem.[67] The Joker's fixation on disrupting established social structures rather than inflicting widespread casualties reflects the way in which modern terrorism has affected the American psyche.[68]

However, the Joker is an imperfect metaphor for the terrorism that defines the War on Terror, the militant actions of radical organizations like Al Qaeda and ISIS.[69] In some ways, this reflects a broader difficulty that modern blockbuster films have had in exploring the motivations of antagonists steeped in terrorist iconography.[70] American popular culture seems to struggle to understand the motivations for horrific terrorist attacks.[71] When that type of violence is portrayed on screen, blockbuster films tend to treat terrorism as an end of itself, rather than something that exists within a broader political context. The Joker is not a terrorist; he is the anthropomorphic embodiment of terrorism.[72]

This approach works in the context of *The Dark Knight*. It is not a film about terrorism; it is a film about the War on Terror. More precisely, it's a film about the western world's response to terrorism. Nolan was quite conscious that this would be an essential part of his approach to the *Batman* mythos when he signed on to *Batman Begins*. "Taking on an action film set in a great American city post–9/11, if we were going to be honest in our fears, then we would come up against the idea of terrorism," says Nolan.[73] This is particularly true when adapting a comic book character who originally justified his decision to dress like a giant creepy bat because criminals were "a superstitious and cowardly lot."[74]

Fear was a major theme of *Batman Begins*, a blockbuster built on the concept that Bruce Wayne dressed up as a giant bat as a way of conquering and projecting his own fear in order to honor his dying father's instruction, "Don't be afraid." The first film in the series featured a villain whose primary gimmick was weaponized fear gas, and a terrorist attack that was designed to create mass panic that would lead a major metropolis to "tear itself apart through fear." *Batman Begins* solidified its position as a War on Terror blockbuster by folding Wayne Enterprises into the military-industrial complex, with Bruce arming himself using abandoned military prototypes.[75]

But *The Dark Knight* is more engaged with the costs of the War on Terror. The Joker is immediately established as an adversary who operates beyond the established social framework. This is very much in keeping with the War on Terror, which presented global terrorism as an existential threat to the western civilization.[76] Confronted with the Joker's unyielding assault on Gotham City's institutions, the characters in the film wrestle with how best to stop this wave of terror. Bruce turns to Alfred, who tells him a story about his time serving as a mercenary in Burma. Alfred was hunting a bandit who was hiding in a vast forest and could not be found.[77] How did Alfred catch this bandit? "We burned the forest down."

Waging a war on organized crime in Gotham, and against the Joker in particular, Batman convinces his allies to cross lines. Gordon manages to plant "lightly irradiated bills" in mob banks, which is technology far beyond the realm of a major metropolitan police force and has obvious parallels with the militarization of local police departments during the War on Terror.[78] The characters frequently resort to torture for information; Batman breaks Sal Maroni's legs, Dent threatens to shoot Thomas Schiff, Batman beats the Joker in his prison cell. This reflects the normalization of torture in both American popular culture and American foreign policy during the War on Terror.[79] Both processes are interlinked, each feeding back into the other.[80]

When no information is forthcoming from these interrogations, Batman relies upon a device that allows him to use cellular telephone data from every person in Gotham City. This device was worrying when the movie was released, but considered speculative.[81] However, the device is even more unsettling given subsequent reveals about information gathering conducted by U.S. intelligence services on citizens through cellular devices and information technology.[82] The development of this technology by a private company also suggests the exploitation (revealed a decade later) of data on social networks by organizations that might have been working with foreign powers to influence domestic politics.[83]

This portrayal of extreme measures taken in pursuit of safety and security has been read as a defense of the conduct of the Bush administration during the War on Terror, an "ends justifies the means" approach to violations of civil rights and civil liberties.[84] This reading is somewhat justified by the cover-up at the end of the film, when Gordon and Batman agree to conceal the string of murders committed by Harvey Dent in order to preserve the public's faith in their civic institutions.

But this is an overly simplistic reading of the film and its politics.[85] Most obviously, *The Dark Knight* is a depiction of these methods and violations, rather than an endorsement.[86] On a purely metaphorical level, *The Dark Knight* suggests that Batman's response to the Joker only gives the villain what he wants. Batman's actions and behaviors have created a climate in which the Joker might thrive, much like these oppressive tactics in the War on Terror only fueled and begat more terrorism.[87] The U.S. foreign policy has become a recruiting tool for extremist organizations.[88]

This was a conscious theme when the Nolan brothers were developing *The Dark Knight*, building right off the closing scene between Gordon and Batman in *Batman Begins*. According to Nolan,

> Really, the key point is Gordon's little speech about escalation and the idea of [Batman's] radical response to crime then prompting [crime's] own radical nature. At the end of the first film where the Joker idea was presented, it's very clear that that was our idea of, "Yes, Batman succeeded, but at the same time he's definitely going to prompt a very extreme response." That's the jumping-off point for this film, the extreme response to Batman's war on crime.[89]

It may not be a perfect example of the escalation of the War on Terror, but it is effective. President Barack Obama would cite *The Dark Knight* as a perfect metaphor for how U.S. foreign policy had enabled the spread and increased the power of extremist ideologies by disrupting established systems. "There's a scene in the beginning in which the gang leaders of Gotham are meeting," Obama said, talking about how extremist groups like ISIS and ISIL had capitalized on the chaos created by military interventions in the region. "These are men who had the city divided up. They were thugs, but there was a kind of order. Everyone had his turf. And then the Joker comes in and lights the whole city on fire. ISIL is the Joker."[90] Within *The Dark Knight*, it is explicit that the Joker would never have been able to rise to prominence without Batman clearing the way.

In fact, *The Dark Knight* is quite clear that Batman and his allies are enabling and validating the Joker. Fire is a recurring thematic element in the *Dark* Knight trilogy, often associated with chaos consuming order.[91] Given the film's central antagonist, it is fitting that this fire imagery recurs most strongly throughout *The Dark Knight*. The movie's title card superimposes the iconic Batman logo over a gigantic explosion. Flames are tied most firmly to the Joker, a character with a confessed fondness for "dynamite, gunpowder and gasoline." Nolan's thematic literalism comes into play with a shot of the Joker standing in front of a mountain of money, saying, "It's about sending a message. Everything burns." Alfred even summarizes the Joker's motivations by saying, "Some men just want to watch the world burn."

With that in mind, Bruce's decision to "burn the forest down" is not defeating the Joker. Instead, Bruce is helping the Joker to complete his stated goals. It is perhaps telling that the Joker is the only *major* antagonist in the *Dark Knight* trilogy to survive his tussle with Batman, the Scarecrow notwithstanding. Batman cannot beat the Joker using these methods; he can only fight him to a draw. The Joker understands this, predicting, "I think you and I are destined to do this forever."[92]

Even in more specific ways, these violations of civil liberties are proven ineffective both within the context of *The Dark Knight* and also retroactively in *The Dark Knight Rises*. In the world of *The Dark Knight*, torture is useless. Batman breaks Maroni's legs, but does not get any information because Maroni does not have any to give. Dent threatens to execute Schiff, but Schiff is a low-level criminal without any useful intelligence. When Batman physically abuses the Joker in the interrogation room, the Joker simply laughs at his opponent's impotence. "You have nothing; nothing to threaten me with, nothing to do with all your strength."[93]

However, for all that the Joker claims to be an "agent of chaos," there remains an interesting paradox at the core of his character. On the surface, the Joker seems to embody the perfect antagonistic force within a Nolan film; the embodiment of sheer anarchy loosed upon a carefully structured narrative. However, there is also a suggestion that the Joker is ultimately a very twisted variant on the archetypal Nolan protagonist. Like Leonard in *Memento* and Dormer in *Insomnia* and Bruce in *Batman Begins*, the Joker is a character trying to impose his own narrative structure upon a world that does not conform to his belief systems.

"Do I really look like a guy with a plan?" the Joker asks Dent in the hospital. This is self-evidently untrue. The Joker has a variety of complicated and convoluted plans.[94] Indeed, the Joker is literally in the middle of one such complicated and convoluted plan while boasting to Dent that he has no plan. The Joker's hypocrisy marks him out as a villain in the world of the *Dark Knight* trilogy, a hypocrisy shared to a greater or lesser extent by Ra's Al Ghul and Bane.[95]

There is a scene in which the Joker's approach to planning reflects the way in which Nolan approaches storytelling, a tendency to reverse-engineer his plans backwards from the desired outcomes in order to disguise his intent. The Joker's threat to blow up a hospital unless somebody murders Coleman Reese is really a smokescreen in order to get him close to Harvey Dent. While the Joker clearly doesn't want Batman's identity exposed to the public, he also wants to get Dent out of hospital and this will give him that chance. Similarly, his attempt to murder Harvey Dent on his way to police custody is not part of his plan to kill Batman, but is instead reverse-engineered from his earlier plan to break Lau out of custody and return the mob's money; the Joker just needs to get arrested, and the attempt on Dent's life provides the perfect opportunity.[96]

The Joker claims to want to show Batman and Gotham "the truth" that "the only sensible way to live in this world is without rules." However, paradoxically, the Joker does this by imposing rules. No sooner has the Joker insisted that Batman needs to learn to live in this world without rules in order to save Harvey Dent or Rachel Dawes than he warns the Caped Crusader, "No, there's only minutes left, so you're gonna have to play my little game if you want to save one of them." When the Joker plays his game with the ferries at the climax, the character lays out a number of very precise and very exacting rules to cover the dynamics at play.[97]

With that in mind, *The Dark Knight* suggests that the Joker's primary motivation is not so much to create a world without rules, but instead to alter reality so that it conforms to the rules that he has set for himself. The Joker conspires to set Gotham City against itself, to watch the metropolis tear itself apart, in order to validate his own worldview.[98] The Joker bristles when people call him crazy, dropping his shtick to coldly insist that he is not.⁹⁹ Batman seems to grasp this at the climax of the film, as the Joker loses his patience with the ferries. "What were you trying to prove?" Batman demands. "That deep down, everyone's as ugly as you are? You're alone!" This is the moment when Batman subdues the Joker. The closest that the heroes come in *The Dark Knight* to defeating the Joker is in forcing him to acknowledge his own pettiness and hypocrisy.

*The Dark Knight* suggests that the Joker is fundamentally wrong about human nature, as demonstrated by the scene with the ferries. The Joker's worldview suggests that the civilians should murder the prisoners.¹⁰⁰ However, *The Dark Knight* suggests that people are, on a fundamental level, decent. In its own way, this is an extension of the core theme of *The Prestige*. The Joker might have a point about how the narrative of civilized society can allow people to dismiss horrific violence as long as it fits expectations, so long as that narrative has a clear and binding purpose. The world might be a cold and chaotic place, but the narratives that mankind constructs allow civilization to transcend that barbarism.

As such, despite his anarchistic leanings, the Joker is in some ironic way the *ultimate* Nolan protagonist. Unlike Leonard in *Memento*, the Joker is not just using his disjointed narrative to distort his own perspective and actions. Instead, he is trying to impose his own subjective worldview on society at large, trying to rewrite a larger social narrative, the narrative of civilized society. The Joker is not an inversion of characters like Leonard, Dormer and Bruce but an extrapolation. He just looks so alien and so antagonistic because *The Dark Knight* approaches him from a more objective and external perspective.

In some ways, the Joker suggests how a Nolan protagonist might look from the outside. Repeatedly over the course of *The Dark Knight*, characters refer to the Joker as a "freak." This recalls the way in which Natalie talked about Leonard in *Memento*. In the way that Leonard has his own skewed internal logic for his actions in *Memento*, the Joker's objectives initially seem ambiguous, but become clearer over the course of the film.

When working on *The Dark Knight*, it was important for Nolan that the audience never be allowed access to the Joker's subjective viewpoint. Nolan recalls, "Heath found all kinds of fantastic ways to humanize him in terms of simply being real and being a real person, but in narrative terms we didn't want to humanize him, we didn't want to show his origins, show what made him do the things he's doing because then he becomes less threatening."¹⁰¹ The Joker states a number of contradictory and mutually exclusive origin stories over the course of *The Dark Knight*, which further underscores how alien and unknowable the character is to the audience.¹⁰²

*The Dark Knight* underscores this sense of otherness by contrasting the structure of the film with the character of the Joker. *The Dark Knight* is notable as Nolan's first (and arguably *only*) linear film.¹⁰³ This is remarkable, given Nolan's long-standing reputation as a non-linear storyteller.¹⁰⁴ Nolan cheats somewhat by beginning the story *in media res* and having characters refer through exposition to actions that occurred in the space between *Batman Begins* and *The Dark Knight*, but the film never needs to pause for an extended flashback or to jump around in time.¹⁰⁵

There are points where *The Dark Knight* falters slightly under the strain of having to construct its narrative in a strictly linear fashion. This is most obvious when it comes to conveying important plot information to the audience, when it is clear that the audience needs to have particular information heading into a particular scene. For example, *The Dark Knight* has to interrupt the montage in which Bruce pulls fingerprints off a bullet shattered in a wall in order to include a short scene in which Coleman Reese tries to blackmail Lucius Fox. This scene is important in the context of the montage because Fox refers back to a piece of off-hand information from Reese in his very next scene with Bruce, so it was necessary from a continuity standpoint to place the thwarted-blackmail scene before that exchange between Bruce and Fox.[106] However, inserting a short and disconnected thwarted-blackmail scene into an otherwise self-contained montage throws off the rhythm of the sequence.[107]

In many ways, Nolan positions *The Dark Knight* as his most objective externalized narrative, which provides the anarchistic Joker with a structure against which he might rail and which also provides a sharp contrast to the Joker's more internal and subjective narrative of Gotham. The film seems to invert the traditional dynamic of Nolan's films. *Memento*, *Insomnia* and *Batman Begins* all align themselves with the subjective viewpoint of their central characters. *The Dark Knight* aligns itself in direct opposition to the Joker's perspective. This is a very clever and unsettling narrative trick.

The objective perspective of *The Dark Knight* is reinforced a number of different ways. Nolan develops Gotham into a fully fleshed-out world populated by a wide variety of characters. Repeatedly, he makes a point to emphasize that his characters are moving through a world populated with living people. *The Dark Knight* develops a clear infrastructure for Gotham City; there are a wide variety of characters from various walks of life. Populated with cops and robbers, politicians and reporters, Gotham feels like a tangible place. There is an emphasis on reaction shots, particularly during big action set pieces.[108] Even during small character moments, there is a recurring suggestion that characters other than the credited leads still have some agency within this fictional world.[109]

In much the same way that he did with *The Prestige*, Nolan plays with the idea of genre within *The Dark Knight*. On the surface, *The Dark Knight* looks and feels like a conventional crime film. Much more than *Batman Begins* could, *The Dark Knight* develops its police officers and its criminals in a way that conforms to expectations about the genre. Harvey Dent is a maverick prosecutor with Hollywood good looks and a mean right hook. Jim Gordon is an honest cop working in a corrupt town, surrounded by people he cannot trust. Sal Maroni is a criminal beginning to feel the squeeze of law enforcement around his neck. The world feels fleshed out.[110]

Nolan acknowledged *Heat* as a massive influence in terms how he approached the storytelling on *The Dark Knight*, another epic crime film unfolding against a stratified city backdrop. He said,

> In the case of *The Dark Knight*, we're attempting to tell a very large, city story or the story of a city. In the same way that, I don't know, Michael Mann's films, like *Heat* or something. That was sort of an inspiration. If you want to take on Gotham, you want to give Gotham a kind of weight and breadth and depth in there. So you wind up dealing with the political figures, the media figures. That's part of the whole fabric of how a city is bound together.[111]

Nolan is an avowed fan of *Heat*, even interviewing the cast and crew for a screening at the Academy.[112] The casting of William Fichtner in a small role as a criminal banker in the opening sequence of *The Dark Knight* is a nod to his similar role in *Heat*.[113]

Part of the thrill of *The Dark Knight* is watching the introduction of Batman and the Joker into this carefully ordered and constructed world. The film is built in such a way that is possible to imagine a blander and more conventional crime film in which

Gordon and Dent wage a slow, unproductive war on Maroni. It would feel like an inferior version of *Heat*, recalling that popular subgenre of cops-and-robbers social dramas including *American Gangster*, *Public Enemies* and *Den of Thieves*.[114] However, Batman and the Joker just tear through this established framework, the characters around them having no frame of reference for what is happening.[115]

Following *The Prestige*, each of Nolan's films plays with genre. They look like one thing, but are ultimately another thing entirely. *The Prestige* looked like a period drama, which made its science fiction twist all the more effective. *The Dark Knight* is a crime epic with Batman and the Joker thrown in on top. *Inception* was sold as a science fiction psychological thriller, but is really just a variety of action movies nested inside one another. *The Dark Knight Rises* had the marketing hype of a superhero movie, but became a social epic in the style of David Lean. *Interstellar* branded itself a science fiction movie transcending space and time, but was ultimately a more intimate story of a father who wanted to come home. *Dunkirk* is for all intents and purposes a survival horror dressed up with the trappings of a war epic.

Nolan's later films use this blending of genre as a way to catch audiences off-guard, understanding that the idea of genre imposes a storytelling framework that can then be subverted or undermined. The world of *The Dark Knight* is perhaps the most grounded world in any of Nolan's films; the narrative is linear, the genre is familiar, the surroundings appear realistic. This makes the juxtaposition of Batman and the Joker against this narrative starker than the contrast in *Batman Begins* and *The Dark Knight Rises*.

It has been argued that the superhero movie is the dominant genre of blockbuster in twenty-first century cinema.[116] Superhero movies are massively successful at the domestic and international box offices.[117] Major studios have produced slates with dozens of superhero movies projected years into the future.[118] Director Steven Spielberg has likened the genre to the western, which saturated American cinemas in the middle decades of the twentieth century. Spielberg speculates that the comic book movie bubble must eventually burst.[119]

Given the extent to which superhero movies power the modern box office, this is not an outcome that the major studios desire.[120] Part of the solution to this problem has been to blend the superhero movie with other genres in order to keep things fresh and interesting.[121] In particular, Marvel Studios devoted considerable energy in the second decade of the twenty-first century to hybridizing its superhero blockbusters to prevent fatigue from setting in.[122]

However, Nolan's work on the *Dark Knight* trilogy demonstrated the potential of blending genres long before other movie studios latched onto the idea. Marvel Studios were just launching their own brand with *Iron Man* and *The Incredible Hulk* when Nolan blended the superhero movie with the urban crime epic in *The Dark Knight*. Marvel Studios would only be releasing their first team-up in *The Avengers* when Nolan merged the superhero film with the revolutionary epic in *The Dark Knight Rises*. This is one of the more subtle and pervasive influences of *The Dark Knight* on blockbuster filmmaking.

In terms of positioning itself as an urban crime epic, *The Dark Knight* makes a much lesser effort to disguise Chicago than *Batman Begins* had done. *Batman Begins* had created Gotham on sound stages in London *and* on the streets of Chicago, while Nolan made a point to shoot as much of *The Dark Knight* as possible in Chicago. "The real world is built on a scale you could never reproduce in the studio," Nolan said of the decision.[123] Many of the city's landmarks are readily visible in Gotham, blurring the lines between the real city and fictional metropolis.[124] Cinematographer Wally Pfister made a conscious choice to move away from the more stylized orange lighting of *Batman Begins* towards a more natural lighting style on *The Dark Knight*.[125] Production designer Nathan Crowley said that the way that *The Dark Knight* approached the city's architecture spoke to the psychology of the characters in the story. "We were given access to these great modernist floors, and we felt that era of architecture was better suited for what we were trying to convey emotionally," he adds. "It's cold and it's vacant; there's no warmth to the environment."[126] The production team pushed this "coldness" even further in *The Dark Knight Rises*, setting the climax against the backdrop of winter in the city.

*The Dark Knight* also afforded Nolan the opportunity to work with IMAX technology. The director had a long-standing interest in the format, and had even arranged to film a few shots from *The Prestige* on IMAX cameras in order to get a sense of the feel and the texture of the technology.[127] In some ways, this fascination reflected Nolan's sensibilities as a filmmaker. Nolan likes to work with physical objects, and IMAX cameras and film are certainly tangible. "They're hand-built cameras, so each one has a bit of a personality," says Bob Hall, who long served as Pfister's first assistance cameraman.[128] The cameras were so bespoke and unique that there were less than 30 in the world when Nolan was filming *The Dark Knight*.[129] One of those cameras was destroyed during the car chase in the middle of the film.[130]

*The Dark Knight* included 28 minutes of IMAX footage.[131] However, this would just be a proof of concept for Nolan, who embraced the technology more thoroughly in his subsequent films. *The Dark Knight Rises* included 72 minutes of IMAX footage.[132] *Interstellar* featured over an hour of such footage.[133] *Dunkirk* included 79 minutes of footage shot by IMAX cameras.[134]

At a time when the film industry was looking to technology like 3D as the future of the medium, Nolan was very much invested in the traditional appeal of filming on IMAX. To him, the appeal of IMAX was that it represented an extrapolation of everything that he appreciated about film, at the highest quality. "I think IMAX is the best film format that was ever invented," Nolan states. "It's the gold standard and what any other technology has to match up to, but none have, in my opinion."[135] There were early reports that Warners originally wanted the sequel to *The Dark Knight* to be rendered in 3D.[136] However, Nolan made it clear very early in the process that he would not support such a decision.[137]

Part of Nolan's objection to 3D technology was philosophical: It removed the idea of an objective image being projected onto a screen. Nolan says,

> I find stereoscopic imaging too small-scale and intimate in its effect. Three-D is a misnomer. Films are 3D. The whole point of photography is that it's three-dimensional. The thing with stereoscopic imaging is it gives each audience member an individual perspective. It's well suited to video games and other immersive technologies, but if you're looking for an audience experience, stereoscopic is hard to embrace.[138]

This is another example of Nolan's fascination with objectively grounding depictions of subjective narratives, of anchoring subjective stories in objective filmmaking.

History vindicates Nolan on this point. 3-D enjoyed a minor resurgence around the time that he was releasing *The Dark Knight Rises*, in large part due to the success of James Cameron's *Avatar*.[139] But the technology could not maintain that momentum.[140] By the time that Nolan was generating press for the various 35mm, 70mm and IMAX prints of *Dunkirk*, 3D movies accounted for less than 20 percent of ticket sales.[141]

In contrast, *The Dark Knight* sparked a miniature revolution in IMAX filmmaking. It was the first narrative film to shoot sequences in IMAX.[142] However, a variety of other filmmakers followed suit, including Michael Bay, Brad Bird and J.J. Abrams.[143] It is perhaps telling that after George Lucas brought digital filmmaking mainstream with *Star Wars: Episode II—Attack of the Clones*, Abrams brought the franchise back to celluloid with *Star Wars: Episode VII—The Force Awakens*.[144] Nolan wasn't even the first director to film an entire movie in IMAX; that honor went to the Russo Brothers for *Avengers: Infinity War*.[145]

Nolan's use of IMAX cameras is an interesting development in his filmmaking, because filming on IMAX is fundamentally different from shooting on regular film stock. The form inevitably influences the function, with Nolan acknowledging that the technology

> makes you think differently about how you stage things, which is one of the things I enjoyed about our experience with it on *The Dark Knight*. There's more of a tableau element to composition; we let things come in and out of frame and move the camera a little more slowly. In some ways, it's more of an old-fashioned approach to finding the scale of the story.[146]

However, the unique of production of *The Dark Knight* means that Nolan was simultaneously framing his action sequences for both IMAX and for the more traditional 2.39:1 aspect ratio. *The Dark Knight* needed to be constructed in such a way that it was coherent for audience members who did not have access to an IMAX screen or did not have access to the film on Blu-ray.[147] As a result, Nolan's framing and composition tend to be loose so that a given shot could work if viewed in either aspect ratio.[148]

Nolan's precision when it comes to framing and composition has been subject to some debate, with critics contending that he does not always successfully communicate what he intends to within a given frame.[149] At least some of this confusion is down to the fact that many of the film's action scenes were shot in IMAX and subsequently cropped to more conventional aspect ratios.[150] The argument is that Nolan effectively papers over these gaps in visual storytelling through exposition and editing.[151]

These criticisms of Nolan's visual storytelling are not unfounded. In fact, he readily acknowledges this aspect of his filmmaking. He did not study film at college, but instead through practical experience. The director tends to use crosscutting and inserts to cover these gaps in his framing and composition. He says,

> In terms of protecting myself editorially, the thing that I developed on *Following* that I've carried on ever since that has most served me is cross cutting. So I'll always try to intercut scenes where possible. Because, if you know that you're cutting the scene with these two people here with the scene with the guy running down the street there, you know that if you've got a gap anywhere, if there was something that didn't work, if there's something that wasn't covered—you've got a very invisible was of getting around it. I enjoy the editing room, I wouldn't be doing it just for that reason. But I found it to be a great asset, as opposed to shooting very conventional coverage, where you know you have to cover everything exactly in a precise way.[152]

The vast majority of *The Dark Knight*'s action sequences are crosscut. The Joker is a very helpful co-conspirator in this regard, staging his plans so that they unfurl along multiple threads in multiple locations simultaneously. The bank robbery begins with the burglars entering from above and below, giving the sequence two strands to cut across. Later, his targeting of three individuals allows Nolan to build tension by cutting across three strands before the Clown Prince of Crime arrives at the party at Bruce Wayne's penthouse. Bruce's race to rescue Rachel is cut across the Joker's escape from captivity. The battle at the Prewitt Building unfolds on multiple levels, as Harvey Dent plots his revenge and the people on the ferries examine their options. *The Dark Knight* is Nolan's most linear film, but it is constantly crosscutting.

It's fair to suggest that Nolan's framing and composition lack the elegance and precision that many formalists demand.[153] However, narrative is more than just a collection of still images. It is about how those images fit together. One of Nolan's key strengths has always been communicating relatively complex information to the audience through a combination of editing and dialogue. It is an approach to storytelling and filmmaking that is perhaps less elegant than more conventional or traditional styles.[154]

In many ways, this is the biggest formal difference that exists between Nolan and other cinematic *auteurs* like Stanley Kubrick.[155] Kubrick came to filmmaking with a background as a photographer[156] and he tended to be very precise in his framing and composition.[157] Given his attention to detail and to framing, it is difficult to imagine Kubrick ever filming in an aspect ratio equivalent to IMAX and then allowing it to be released and distributed in the standard theatrical aspect ratio.[158]

It has been suggested that Nolan's action sequences are disjointed as a result of his use of crosscutting.[159] The filmmaker has been criticized for not adhering to continuity editing during his action scenes.[160] These are valid observations, even if they do not represent a holistic examination of Nolan's style. There is a valid criticism to be made of his approach to action sequences, where the director's rapid-fire quick-cutting technique denies the audience the particular pleasures expected of a more conventionally choreographed action sequence. Even in the director's action scenes, his primary objective is to convey information.[161]

"The action has to be exciting but we didn't want to make it any more complicated than it needed to be," says editor Lee Smith. "The action has to have cause and effect, to make the audience stay with us and not to wonder why something was happening." Smith screened these edited action scenes for friends and family, quizzing them on the content of the scene to ensure that all the information necessary to understand the sequence had been conveyed through the action and the edits.[162]

Nolan's ability to convey information visually is easily underrated, but *The Dark Knight* works in large part due to the director's attention to detail. Quick cuts provide a sense of the location of key players and their spatial relationship to one another, such as the split-second shot of the Joker scrambling for a gun during that attack on Bruce Wayne's penthouse that establishes where he is and what he is doing moments before he grabs Rachel as a hostage. Similarly, during the scenes in which the Joker goads Stephens into attacking him in the cell, the frame is constructed so as to include the broken glass that the Joker will fashion into a knife. In a larger sense, a model of the incomplete Prewitt Building is visible in all of the scenes set in Mayor Garcia's office, serving as set-up for its use later in the film. These little touches ensure a sense of clarity, even if they do not adhere to conventional continuity editing.

In some ways, this debate about the clarity and continuity of Nolan's action sequences demonstrates how *The Dark Knight* walks that fine line between order and chaos. One of the film's more interesting structural quirks is the fact that it seems to reach a climax and an ending during the Prewitt Building siege and then continues into what is effectively a secondary climax in which Batman and Gordon confront Harvey Dent in the remains of 250 52nd Street. The Joker has converted Dent into the villainous Two-Face, and Dent has taken it upon himself to avenge the death of Rachel Dawes.

This structural quirk was imitated with a surprising frequency after the success of *The Dark Knight*. It became a feature of contemporary blockbusters that included a large-scale heavily choreographed action climax, before settling into a quieter and more restrained final confrontation.[163] While *The Dark Knight*'s momentum carries it over the finish line, the resolution of the plot thread focusing on Dent still feels like something of an afterthought.

This is most likely down to David S. Goyer's original plan for *The Dark Knight*. After the release of *Batman Begins*, he outlined his vision for two more films to complete a trilogy. His second proposed film sounded very similar to *The Dark Knight*, right down to leaving the Joker alive at the end. However, Goyer proposed that Dent's transformation into Two-Face form the narrative backbone of the final film in the series. "In the third, the Joker would go on trial, scarring Dent in the process," he reveals.[164]

It seems clear why Nolan rejected this structure and instead made a point to follow Dent's story to its logical conclusion in *The Dark Knight* itself. "I don't think in terms of sequels," Nolan states. "I think in terms of making this film the best film it can be and the most complete film it can be."[165] Two-Face's inclusion in *The Dark Knight* was part of a conscious effort to avoid any dangling threads that would keep *The Dark Knight* from feeling like a satisfying movie experience on its own terms.

Released in July 2008, *The Dark Knight* was enthusiastically welcomed by critics and audiences alike. Roger Ebert wrote that Nolan had produced "a haunted film that leaps beyond its origins and becomes an engrossing tragedy."[166] A blockbuster behemoth, the film smashed records and took in $155 million in its first three days.[167] It was the fourth movie to break one billion dollars worldwide.[168] However, it is hard to quantify the sheer cultural excitement around and impact of *The Dark Knight* in terms as simple as box office returns. "Opening night, I watch 14 screens fill to capacity for a midnight showing at the Arclight in Hollywood," recalls Jonathan Nolan. "It seems like everyone is watching this movie, all at once—except for us. Warner can't find us tickets anywhere in Los Angeles county."[169]

It is no exaggeration to say that *The Dark Knight* changed the shape of Hollywood filmmaking and storytelling, even beyond the example already discussed. Blockbusters were quick to copy even the smallest innovations within *The Dark Knight*. Franchises like *Transformers* and *Thor* could not wait to cram words like "Dark" or "Knight" into the subtitles of their sequels.[170] *Star Trek Into Darkness*, *The Avengers*, *Thor: The Dark World* and *Skyfall* included second-act sequences in which the villains allow edthemselves to be trapped (usually in a brightly lit cage), only to get loose and cause more havoc.[171] The success arguably inspired a slate of self-serious reboots and reimaginings, including *Snow White and the Huntsman*, *The Amazing Spider-Man* and even *Man of Steel*.[172]

It goes without saying that many of these attempts at imitation were shallow and superficial, misunderstanding what had worked about *The Dark Knight*. The film's title was not the key to its success, nor was the complicated plotting. As much as it has become an accepted criticism to suggest that Nolan's films are dour or humorless,[173] the truth is that all of his *Dark Knight* films have a wry and arch sense of humor that stands in contrast to the more winking and ironic style of humor associated with contemporary blockbusters.[174]

*The Dark Knight* took on a much more important significance for a certain subset of its audience. "I have two teenage boys, and watching the reverence with which they saw it, again and again and again," says screenwriter David Koepp. "It really is like their generation's *Godfather*. It is absolutely a seminal film for teenage boys of that and this era."[175] *The Dark Knight* took on an almost mythic proportion for young male audiences, particularly those active online. On the Internet Movie Database, there was an organized effort by voters to manipulate the rankings and make *The Dark Knight* the top-rated movie of all time; this effort involved voting up *The Dark Knight* and voting down *The Godfather*.[176] The coordinated campaign was reportedly formulated on the film's official web boards.[177] This campaign was ultimately unsuccessful, eventually leading to a weird compromise where *The Shawshank Redemption* became the highest-ranked movie of all time on IMDb.[178]

Nevertheless, this spoke to the obsession that certain segments of the Internet felt towards *The Dark Knight*. This obsession heightened with the release of *The Dark Knight Rises* four years later. Critics who gave negative reviews reported receiving death threats from zealous fans.[179] The reviews aggregator Rotten Tomatoes suspended comments on reviews in an attempt to control these aggressive devotees.[180] Even though the immediate response to *The Dark Knight* did not reach that fevered pitch, the film still connected with a particularly aggressive strain of Internet fandom. To a certain extent, these fans have remained a part of the cultural background noise around Christopher Nolan since the release of *The Dark Knight*.[181]

In terms of *The Dark Knight*, this enthusiasm and this eagerness expressed itself through a campaign to secure Nolan and *The Dark Knight* major nominations at the Academy Awards the following year. Internet fans were obsessed with the notion that *The Dark Knight* was entitled to Best Picture and Best Director nominations.[182] Some establishment critics reacted with horror to the perceived absurdity of a comic book movie earning such major nominations.[183] Others believed that it was possible for *The Dark Knight* to secure the fifth place on either ballot, owing to a particularly weak year in terms of prestige cinema.[184]

This obsession within this Internet fan base perhaps speaks to the young male demographic that latched onto the film. In many ways, *The Dark Knight* seemed to legitimize comic book movies and broader genre fare, demonstrating that pulpy beloved characters could anchor serious films with important things to say.[185] A lot of that passion seemed to be tied up the notion of demonstrating to the world that comic books and superheroes were "not just for kids" and should be treated as "real art."[186]

Appropriately enough, this tension within Internet fandom reflected a similar anxiety in the comic book culture that had spawned the film. Nolan's *Dark Knight* trilogy had been inspired by late 1980s comic books like Frank Miller's *The Dark Knight Returns* and *Year One*.[187] Those books had in turn inspired a certain strain of comic book fandom to embrace and valorize them as proof of the genre's maturity and legitimacy.[188] Violence and brutality became shorthand for complexity in comic book publishing during the late eighties and into the nineties.[189] This in turn influenced the medium to become more violent and sexualized, failing to appreciate the difference between being "adult" and being "mature."[190] This was most likely tied up in the same anxieties that informed so much of this emotional investment in *The Dark Knight*, a desire for validation and affirmation about the worthiness and sophistication of a genre beloved by young men.[191]

These fans sorely misunderstood the inner workings of the Academy of Motion Picture Arts and Sciences. The precise membership of the organization's voting body is kept largely secret[192] but the institution's demographics skew noticeably older and more conservative, as reflected in their choice of nominees into the twenty-first century.[193] The awards body was highly unlikely to vote for a populist spectacle which featured on a man dressed as a bat engaged in existential struggle with a homicidal clown.[194] Following *Titanic*'s win of the Best Picture Oscar in 1998, the Academy had become increasingly fixated upon low-budget and independent films.[195]

*The Dark Knight* did not secure a Best Picture nomination, which became a source of Internet frustration and outrage.[196] Adding to that frustration was the fact that *The Reader* was nominated in its place, taking the fifth slot of the Best Picture and the Best Director nominees.[197] The story of a man who engages in a lifelong relationship (built upon a teenage fling) with an illiterate Nazi, *The Reader* had received lukewarm reviews and was generally perceived to be cynical Oscar bait.[198]

Heath Ledger did win for Best Supporting Actor, making Ledger only the second actor to posthumously receive an award.[199] *The Dark Knight* was the first comic book film to win a major prize at the Academy Awards.[200] However, there was some legitimate debate over whether Ledger would have received recognition for his work had he still been alive during the nomination cycle and had the Academy a later opportunity to award him for more conventional and prestigious fare.[201]

Nevertheless, the omission of *The Dark Knight* from the Best Picture and Best Director categories had a profound impact on the Academy Awards. Host Hugh Jackman dedicated an extended portion of his opening musical number to the snub, acknowledging the film's absence.[202] However, *The Dark Knight* would arguably make its biggest impact *after* the ceremony. In June 2009, the Academy announced plans to expand the Best Picture field from five to ten nominees.[203] The goal of expanding the field was to allow the Academy to recognize more populist movies in the hopes of driving up the show's declining ratings and cultural impact.[204] To certain industry insiders, this revision became known as "the *Dark Knight* rule," reflecting the shadow that the snub cast over the awards body.[205]

The impact of the rule in practical terms is subject to debate. The Academy revised it in subsequent years to allow for *up to* ten nominees rather than including a hard-and-fast rule of ten nominees.[206] There have been rumors that the Academy has considered returning to the familiar "five nominees" format.[207] More than that, the historically strong connection between the Best Picture category and the five-nominee Best Director field would lead many pundits to reflect that there were still only five "real" Best Picture nominees in any given race.[208] Nevertheless, it remains a significant overhaul to one of Hollywood's oldest and most venerated institutions.

The exclusion of *The Dark Knight* also played into attempts to broaden the membership of the Academy. In the years following the snub, the organization made a point to welcome younger and more diverse members in order to slowly shift the demographics away from an older and whiter membership that was seen as out of touch with contemporary culture.[209] It is open to debate whether a more diverse membership would have voted for *The Dark Knight* or would have been more likely to champion fringe and independent filmmakers over crowd-pleasing blockbusters.[210] At the same time, moves were made to remove voting rights from members who had not worked for an extended period of time, to ensure that those members casting a ballot were more likely to be in touch with the modern realities of film production.[211]

In the years following the *Dark Knight*-Oscar controversy, the Academy seemed to make some conciliatory gestures. Expanding the Best Picture field ensured that *Inception* secured a nomination, although Christopher Nolan was not included in the Best Director category.[212] However, the Academy would use that Best Picture nomination as an opportunity to invite several of Nolan's close collaborators into the organization later that year, including his producer and wife Emma Thomas.[213]

It is impossible to objectively measure cultural impact, but *The Dark Knight* was one of the defining films of the twenty-first century. It changed the language and structure of blockbuster storytelling, from the way that narratives were designed to the technology employed in telling them. Its impact can be measured through the fact that even the act of overlooking it led to real and tangible changes in an organization as conservative and traditional as the Academy.

*The Dark Knight* was not just a film, it was an event—an event orchestrated with the efficiency and effectiveness that define the rest of Nolan's output.

# 7

## *Inception*

After *The Dark Knight*, Christopher Nolan found himself in a strange position. He had nothing to do, no obvious next project on his plate. Each of his previous films had bled into one another, each assignment feeding directly into the next. His first six films had been released over roughly eight years between the small theatrical release of *The Following* to the epic blockbuster event that was *The Dark Knight*.

"While we were doing *The Prestige*, we knew we were going to do *The Dark Knight*," Nolan recalls. "While I was doing *Batman Begins*, I knew I was going to do *The Prestige*. That's basically five or six years that you're completely locked into a creative path." Regarding the gap after *The Dark Knight*, he says, "For the first time I was able to step back and go, okay, what do I want to do now? I'd always wanted to do *Inception*. I took six months to finish the script, and I found I could."[1]

Nolan had been nursing the idea that would become *Inception* for years. "I've been fascinated by dreams … since I was a kid, and I think the relationship between movies and dreams is something that's always interested me," Nolan says. "I liked the idea of trying to portray dreams on film." Nolan had been earnestly working on the script for about a decade before it was released.[2] In *Inception*'s opening scene, when Cobb says that ideas can be "the most persistent parasite," he may as well be talking about the film itself.

Nolan's original plan for the movie that would become *Inception* was to stage it as a horror story, submitting an 80-page treatment to Warner Brothers shortly after the release of *Insomnia*.[3] But it quickly became clear to the director that *Inception* would work better on a larger scale with a bigger budget aimed at a broader audience.

In that respect, *Inception* could never have been made at an earlier stage in the director's career, for several reasons. Even if the director had the ambition to attempt such an effort in those early days, he had not accrued the necessary skills. Nolan:

> It took a long time to write, and for me to learn how to make a film on the scale that I needed it to be. But it was born of a belief, when I sat at the Toronto Film Festival and watched *Memento* with an audience and heard them responding to it in a very mainstream way—a very clear-cut, communicative relationship between the audience and the story. I felt like you could do that on a big scale. You could do a big version of that and people would get it, would respond to it.[4]

It is perhaps revealing that the genesis of what would become *Inception* can be traced back to *Memento*, despite the nine years that separate the films. In some ways, *Inception* is the film that feels most akin to *Memento*, to capturing the perspective and the texture that defined Nolan's big break. It could reasonably be argued that *Inception* blends the non-linear psychological thriller aspects of *Memento* with the stylistic sensibilities of Nolan's later blockbusters *The Dark Knight* or *The Dark Knight Rises*.[5]

It took Nolan the better part of a decade working on a variety of films to figure out *how* to make *Inception*. However, it also took him years to develop the trust necessary to allow him to make *Inception*. There was a reason that he had the freedom to make *Inception* exactly when he did:

> With the success of *The Dark Knight*, we were in a position where the studio was prepared to put a lot of faith in us and trust in us to really do something special. Those opportunities are very rare for filmmakers, and I felt a responsibility to really try and do something memorable with it.[6]

It is hard to overstate just how much trust Warner Brothers invested in Nolan when they greenlit *Inception*. Cinema was undergoing a dramatic shift in the early years of the twenty-first century. Major releases were becoming a higher-stakes gamble for the major studios. The summer calendar was becoming increasingly crowded, with big movies competing with one another for space and publicity.[7] There were several conscious efforts to expand the summer movie season back into March to give these blockbusters room to breathe.[8] Studio spending on individual films was dramatically increasing.[9] With so much overcrowding in the peak months, opening weekends were becoming more important determinative factors in gauging the long-term profitability of these box office behemoths.[10]

These changes have had a number of consequences, shaping the output of major studios in the early years of the twenty-first century. This overcrowded blockbuster slate has led to the death of the respectable mid-budget movie, which has arguably migrated to prestige television along with writers, directors and actors.[11] At the same time, it has arguably overinflated budgets on franchise films forced to compete, leading to bizarre situations where sequels to cult hits like *Star Trek* or *Blade Runner* need to perform on the scale of a *Star Wars* film to turn a profit.[12]

As a result of these factors, studios become more conservative in their output. The key to summer blockbusters became franchise recognition, as building in an audience was an effective way to secure the massive financial investment necessary to produce a viable modern blockbuster.[13] Established intellectual property became currency, in the form of belated sequels and reboots and prequels.[14] Disney purchased Marvel Studios in August 2009 for $4 billion in order to secure a stable of intellectual property that would appeal to young boys.[15] They doubled down in October 2012, purchasing *Star Wars* from George Lucas for almost the same amount.[16] Due to the value associated with these franchise brands, it seems likely that these will fuel feature films for decades (if not generations) to come.[17]

There were still original films being produced, it just so happened that they were rarely among the big-budget summer releases that dominated pop cultural conversation.[18] Against this backdrop, it became increasingly difficult for studios to finance "event" movies built around original concepts and ideas.[19] The market seemed to be saturated with rehashes of familiar concepts and ideas.[20] Infamously, Sony launched three different versions of its *Spider-Man* franchise over the space of 15 years, leading to a situation where the previous iteration of the franchise was barely dead before the property was rebooted.[21] Warner Brothers waited just over a year after the release of *The Dark Knight Rises* to announce that Ben Affleck would play a *new* version of the Caped Crusader in *Batman vs. Superman*.[22]

With all of this in mind, it is surprising that Warner Brothers chose to invest $160 million in *Inception*—four times the budget of *The Prestige* and only $20 million less than *The Dark Knight*.[23] However, Warners had defined themselves as a director-friendly studio and cultivated a relationship with Nolan over his previous four films.[24] It has even been reported that the success of *The Dark Knight* encouraged Warners to invest $100 million in publicity and advertising for *Inception*.[25]

*Inception* is acutely aware of its own status as an original film in a landscape populated by sequels, reboots and remakes. It is positioned between the only two sequels that Nolan directed, *The Dark Knight* and *The Dark Knight Rises*. Repeatedly over the course of the film, the characters stress the need to dream new and original dreams, to create new ideas and to embrace new possibilities. While offering a tour of the dreamscape to Ariadne, Cobb warns her, "Never recreate places from your memory. Always imagine new places." Later, Ariadne discovers that Cobb has allowed himself to get lost inside dreams that he has created from his own memories. These memories trap Cobb and warp his sense of reality.

*Inception* seems wary of the wave of cultural nostalgia that surrounds it, suggesting that Cobb's subconscious is decorated with the ruins of a past of which he cannot let go. During the early years of the twenty-first century, pop culture came to be dominated by nostalgic tributes to a romanticized and fondly remembered past.[26] These films provided audiences with recycled and familiar imagery and ideas, offering comfort and security in an otherwise uncertain time.[27]

It has been argued that this wave of nostalgia has been getting faster all the time, perhaps enabled and fed by the short attention span and rapid consumption culture of the Internet.[28] This nostalgia seems to get closer and closer to the present all the time, inviting observers to speculate on what people might feel nostalgic about when they run out of past to romanticize.[29] In some ways, this nostalgia could feel uncanny, creating a sense of dissonance.[30] Over the years that followed, this nostalgia arguably seeped out of media and into other aspects of the popular consciousness, including politics.[31]

*Inception* repeatedly warns of the dangers of confusing dream with memory, and of embracing that warped memory over reality. "Building a dream from your memory is the easiest way to lose your grasp from what's real and what is a dream," Cobb says, and the film suggests that the character has learned this lesson first-hand. It stresses the importance of creating new dreams and constructing new worlds, rather than simply recreating old visions and inhabiting faded memories.

Nolan says that the studio understood this need to map out new conceptual ground with a big-budget summer blockbuster: "Maybe it's just particularly working with Warner Brothers, but in my experience with the studio system, they have always understood the need for freshness and not just something the audience has seen before."[32] Following *Inception*, Nolan was one of relatively few high-profile directors who could command a budget of over $100 million to develop an original intellectual property with minimal studio interference.

When *Inception* was released, one of the big criticisms was the fact that it wasn't *really* about dreams. Its depiction of its characters' dreamscapes was rigidly rational and meticulously structured, failing to accurately capture the surreal or intangible aspects of a dream state.[33] Nolan was criticized by certain reviewers for being "too literal, too logical, too rule-bound" in his depiction of the process of dreaming.[34] These are certainly fair observations of the world he created in *Inception*.

Nolan is a director too fixated on rules and structure to embrace the surrealism and absurdity of dreams. He would never produce anything like the Japanese animated film *Paprika*, which covered similar subject matter four years earlier.[35] Nolan was very conscious of the rules that he was imposing on the film, noting that they were the first thing that he concentrated on when writing the script.[36]

Rules are very important to Nolan's storytelling, in some ways reflecting the structures that his characters try to impose upon the world around them. Says Nolan,

> I spend a lot of time analyzing my response to other stories. It basically teaches you to look for a rule set. You can make up your own, but it has to be internally consistent. I've always had a lot of faith that if the rule set is clear, the audience will come along. *Inception* is the furthest I've pushed that relationship with the audience. We trusted that if we were diligent and consistent, the audience would trust it. You don't want to feel like a trick was played on you a little too obviously.[37]

However, it is very clear that *Inception* is not actually about dreams, it is about movies.[38] This is not a radical idea. Cinema has long been compared to and discussed in terms of dreams. During the early years of the twentieth century, for example, many critics employed the tools of psychoanalysis, including Freudian theory, to discuss cinema.[39] The construction of film narrative recalls the process of dreaming: the use of cuts to create narrative ellipses, the changing of character and location within an instant, the distortion of time, the acceptance of concepts and ideas that should be alien to a rational mind.[40]

This is not merely an abstract similarity. It has been argued that the ease with which audiences accept the irrational conventions of cinematic storytelling might be attributed to the human brain's experience with dreaming.[41] Scientific studies suggest that the process of watching a movie acts upon the same parts of the brain that are used while dreaming, suggesting a strong scientific basis for this comparison.[42]

Many directors liken their process of filmmaking to the act of dreaming. Ingmar Bergman has claimed that *all* of his films are dreams.[43] Akira Kurosawa fashioned his film *Dreams* from a set of dreams that had followed him since childhood.[44] Although director David Lynch insists that few of his ideas actually originate in dreams, the logic of his dreams informs those ideas.[45]

*Inception* even draws attention to the similarities, to the narrative conventions that the audience accepts readily in a cinematic framework. At one point, Cobb and Ariadne discuss the process of controlling dreams and visions. The scene comes immediately following their introduction, having moved the characters from inside a university to a street-side café. This is an accepted cinematic narrative convention, and the audience thinks nothing of the use a cut to make such a transition. However, Cobb quickly draws attention to the unreality of their situation.

"You never really remember the beginning of a dream, do you?" he challenges his companion. "You always wind up right in the middle of what's going on."[46] He presses the point: "So how did we end up here?" It is revealed that both Cobb and Ariadne are in a dream, demonstrating how the audience watching the film might confuse the logic of dreams with the logic of cinematic storytelling. Nolan is not trying to differentiate the normal process of filmmaking from the experience of dreaming, instead hoping to stress the similarities. As a result, it makes sense that the director would avoid the sort of consciously stylized or heightened approach employed by films like *Paprika* and *The Cell*.

However, Nolan is particularly interested in the idea of cinema as a shared dream. This is another example of the central tension in his work, between the subjective and objective. He repeatedly argues for the idea of an experience as objective, but of interpretation as subjective. To Nolan, film is objective but narrative is subjective. "I am fascinated by our subjective perception of reality, that we are all stuck in a very singular point of view, a singular perspective on what we all agree to be an objective reality," he observes. "Movies are one of the ways in which we try to see things from the same point of view."[47] This is part of the reason why he has historically declined to shoot or render in 3D, as it would serve to change the image for each individual viewer.[48]

Discussing the science fiction elements of *Inception*, Nolan wryly insists, "The only outlandish idea that the film presents, really, is the existence of a technology that allows you to enter and share the same dream as someone else."[49] He may as well be talking about the kind of technology employed in the projection booths of cinemas around the world, which allow audiences to share a singular perspective and vision on a regular basis.[50] Nolan acknowledges that he was particularly drawn to the idea of film as a collective experience and memory: "What I wanted was for the dream imagery to be resonant not just to me, but on some kind of shared level. And I think naturally, as a filmmaker, I just gravitate toward cinema as the collective memory we have of imagery and symbolism."[51]

In many ways, *Inception* can be seen as a metaphor for a group of people coming together to make a feature film. This is not a unique idea within Nolan's filmography, with *The Prestige* also exploring this thematic ground. However, *Inception* is more precise in its central metaphor. It is possible to map key characters to core roles in film production. Cobb is the director, trying to maintain control of the project[52]; Arthur is the producer, responsible for keeping the operation running; Ariadne is the production designer, working on sets and constructs[53]; Eames is the actor, capable of playing any role required[54]; Saito is the studio, bankrolling and micromanaging the project while demanding results; and Fischer is the audience. "In trying to write a team-based creative process, I wrote the one I know," says Nolan.[55]

It could reasonably be argued that Ariadne is as much the writer as the production designer. She is tasked with designing mazes, which obviously reflect physical sets and locations, and also reflect Nolan's approach to storytelling. "I always find myself gravitating to the analogy of a maze," Nolan says of his storytelling process. "Think of *film noir* and if you picture the story as a maze, you don't want to be hanging above the maze watching the characters make the wrong choices because it's frustrating. You actually want to be in the maze with them, making the turns at their side, that keeps it more exciting."[56] The plot of *Inception* literalizes that metaphor.[57]

Similarly, there is something very revealing in the internal logic of *Inception*. According to the movie's dream logic, the characters inside the dream world are the projections of the dreamer rather than of the designer; the characters inside Fischer's head might inhabit worlds designed by Ariadne and Cobb, but they are populated from his own subconscious. This reflects certain psychological theories about cinema, suggesting that audience members project themselves into the film.[58] Nolan has repeatedly said that this is very much the case with regard to his own work.[59]

A certain amount of the plot of *Inception* seems to have been reverse-engineered from the technical craft that Nolan employed in making the film. In particular, the dream worlds in *Inception* seem structured in such a way as to justify certain stylistic filmmaking decisions within the film's narrative framework. This is most apparent with the use of crosscutting, which has been a recurring fascination for Nolan as a director. *Inception* is structured in such a way that there is action unfolding across multiple "levels" of the story simultaneously, allowing Nolan to cut between those layers and to synchronize his action beats across various narrative threads. Nolan structures *Inception* so the story unfolds on five different planes, which has been suggested as the maximum amount of recursion that an audience can process.[60]

These different levels of the dream allow Nolan to distort and dilate time. This is important, because it also allows Nolan to justify the use of slow motion in certain sequences. He has been quite candid about his distrust of slow motion as an unmotivated stylistic quirk.[61] However, the entire plotting framework of *Inception* allows him the opportunity to use slow motion in a way that is explicitly justified by the rules of the story that he is telling.[62]

In fact, the bulk of *Inception* exists as a justification and vehicle for copious amounts of exposition. It is *constantly* explaining itself to its audience, providing new contextual information as it moves along.[63] "The only useful definition of narrative I've ever heard is 'the controlled release of information,'" says Nolan.[64] In those terms, *Inception* is undoubtedly his *most* narrative movie. It is perhaps revealing that *Inception* was followed by three films with much looser narrative frameworks, as *Inception* distills this idea of plot as controlled information to its purest form.

Much like the rules of the dreamscape within *Inception* exist to justify the use of filmmaking techniques like slow motion and crosscutting, *Inception*'s story was constructed in such a way as to justify Nolan's fascination with narrative-as-information. To that end, *Inception* was modeled upon a heist movie. Nolan says,

> One of the fascinating things about the heist movie, and one of the reasons I took this as the model, is that the type of exposition that in most films is problematic, boring, tricky, hard to get through—in a heist movie becomes the meat of it. It's part of the entertainment, simply because the process of a heist movie and that sort of procedure, the way they put things together, becomes the reason you're watching the story.[65]

To Nolan, the heist story within *Inception* is merely a mechanism for telling a story about the controlled release of information, which is effectively a narrative about Nolan's understanding of narrative.

While Nolan quickly grasped the mechanics of the story that he was telling, there were certain elements of *Inception* that did not come together as easily. He understood *Inception* on a logical level, but the film needed a stronger hook:

> I eventually realized that heist films are usually unemotional. They tend to be glamorous and deliberately superficial. I wanted to deal with the world of dreams, and I realized that I really had to offer the audience a more emotional narrative, something that represents the emotional world of somebody's

mind. So both the hero's story and the heist itself had to be based on emotional concepts. That took years to figure out.[66]

Interestingly, the story's emotional hook developed through Nolan's collaboration with his lead actor. Leonardo DiCaprio was the first member of the cast recruited, and Nolan reworked the screenplay in consultation with the performer. "I think I sort of grew into the project in a way," Nolan confesses, crediting DiCaprio as a major influence on the finished film:

> With his attention to the emotional life of the character and what that should mean to the audience, I think I finally found that emotional connection with the material that I depend on as a filmmaker, because what I've realized about myself over the years is, if I don't engage with something on that level, I'll never sustain my interest in it for the two years it takes to make it.[67]

DiCaprio most likely contributed to the success of the film in more than just storytelling terms. *Inception* arrived at a time when intellectual property was seen as the strongest box office draw in the business, with traditional movie stars very rarely attracting audiences outside of franchise films.[68] But DiCaprio was one of the few exceptions to the rule, a recognizable celebrity whose presence seemed to buoy the films in which he starred.[69] In some ways, he cultivated his own brand through shrewd collaborations with high-profile and prestigious directors like Martin Scorsese, Quentin Tarantino, Ridley Scott, Steven Spielberg, Clint Eastwood and Nolan.[70] Although it may be difficult to determine whether *Inception* helped boost DiCaprio's cinematic credibility or whether DiCaprio boosted *Inception*'s box office, the actor proved a good fit for the film.

If *Inception* is a movie about cinema, then this late emotional hook into the story is part of that discussion. The characters within *Inception* tend to talk about how films work, often in vaguely technical terms; they discuss the distortion of time and the suspension of disbelief necessary for storytelling. However, they also talk broadly about storytelling itself, and about the relationship that exists between the story being told and the audience that is responding to it. Much like *The Prestige* and the *Dark Knight* trilogy, *Inception* expresses a deep-seated ambivalence towards certain facets of storytelling and how they serve to distort reality.

Cobb is hired to plant an idea in the head of industrialist Robert Fischer. The idea is that Cobb will construct a narrative that will lead Fischer to make various life-changing decisions in service of Cobb's employer. Even on a conceptual level, this is very close to the profound (and sometimes random) influence that films can have on an individual.[71] For Nolan, this idea of a profoundly personal and emotional response to an idea became the crux of the story: "The idea that you would plot something that would have to grow in a particular way and you'd have to predict the chaotic way in which that thing might grow through somebody's mind—it seemed a much bigger payoff for the premise."[72]

In many ways, *Inception* serves as a meditation on the emotional mechanics of storytelling. Repeatedly over the course of the films, characters insist on dialing back information and exposition to its emotional core. After Cobb explains the plan to Eames, Eames offers his own take on the art of inception. "It's not just about depth," Eames insists. "You need the simplest version of the idea in order for it ... to grow naturally in your subject's mind." The word "simple" and its variations recur repeatedly in discussions about how best to get an idea lodged in an individual's subconscious.[73]

In some ways, this mirrors the idea that the many successful and enduring movies appeal on some very simple and archetypal level, resonating with ideas in a manner that is both straightforward and profound.[74] The idea is that films like *Star Wars* do not resonate on such a broad cultural level because of the specifics of their fictional universes, but because they speak to universal human experiences like the relationship between parents and children.[75] Many of the original generation of studio blockbusters were preoccupied with the dynamic between fathers and sons.[76] Nolan had been influenced by these blockbusters in constructing *Batman Begins*, as reflected in its own preoccupations with damaged father-son relationships.[77] It makes sense that he returned to that simple narrative when exploring the idea of moviemaking in *Inception*.

In some ways, *Inception* might be read as a self-aware narrative about a modern Nolanian protagonist and a classic Spielbergian protagonist who assist one another on their character arcs. Robert Fischer is very much an archetypal Spielberg protagonist.[78] A young man who has a strained relationship with an emotionally absent father, his life is defined by that dysfunctional relationship.[79] The actual process of "inception" within *Inception* begins with the death of Maurice Fischer, at which point Robert's father ceases to be emotionally absent and instead becomes *literally* absent.[80] Throughout *Inception*, Robert's journey is towards reconciliation with his absent father, a particularly Spielbergian journey.[81] Even outside of Fischer's character arc, there are aspects of *Inception* that recall the filmmaking of Steven Spielberg.[82]

Cobb represents something of an inversion of that archetype. He is an absent father trying desperately to reunite with his lost children. This is a recurring motif in Nolan films, first emerging in Alfred Borden's desire to reunite with his daughter in *The Prestige* and developing through Cobb's desire to return home in *Inception*. Even in the films less keenly focused on fathers, Nolan tends to build stories around father figures who clearly want to reconnect with their lost children.[83]

There is an interesting structural parallel between Cobb and Fischer. Cobb spends most of the movie trying to steer Fischer towards reconciliation with his emotionally distant father. At the same time, while embarking upon this journey, Cobb experiences his own character arc. All of this takes place while Cobb is on his own literal journey on a Boeing 747 between Sydney and Los Angeles. However, through his attempted inception of Fischer, Cobb is afforded some clarity on his own situation, forcing him to reconcile with his emotional issues as personified through the subconscious manifestation of his deceased wife.

*Inception* discusses the power of narrative to offer catharsis to audiences, as embodied by Fischer. Narratives provide a sense of meaning and framework, offering reason and logic that is often absent from real life. In the real world, events frequently happen beyond the control of an individual and without any clear or discernible purpose. Within a good story, everything has a purpose and a place, with every event controlled by an author outside the narrative. Nolan's films are typically about characters who try to impose their own personal narratives on a world that is more complicated and arbitrary than they are comfortable admitting. Perhaps this a universal experience of itself.[84]

In *Inception*, the characters argue that their attempt to break into Robert's mind will allow him some grand epiphany and insight into his relationship with Maurice. They decided to frame their corporate objective in simpler familial terms. On hearing of the strained relationship between Maurice and Robert, Eames wonders, "Do you play on that? Suggest breaking up his father's company as a 'screw you' to the old man?" Reacting like the director of a blockbuster, Cobb responds, "No. I think positive emotion triumphs negative emotion every time. We're all yearning for a reconciliation. A catharsis."

In many ways *Inception* is about providing that sense of reconciliation and catharsis. With Cobb's manipulation and guidance, Robert imagines his father supporting his decision to break up the company. Robert imagines that his father always loved him, and that any disappointment that the old man felt was rooted in Robert's refusal to travel his own path and to forge his own identity. Over the course of the story, Cobb undergoes his own emotional catharsis when he is forced to confront the part of his subconscious that manifests as his deceased ex-wife, Mal.[85]

This is one of the core appeals of narrative. The term "catharsis" as a dramatic device can be traced back to Aristotle's *Poetics*.[86] The concept remains an essential part of modern storytelling, especially in big-budget cinema.[87] This is what audiences expect from these stories, to the point that even adaptations of true stories may massage the details in order to offer audiences this sense of closure and satisfaction that is often elusive in real life.[88] As such, it makes sense for *Inception* to close with this sense of catharsis and release.

However, *Inception* is ambivalent about the catharsis offered by this sort of storytelling. The film makes a point of acknowledging that Robert's imagined reconciliation with his father is nothing but a heart-affirming fairy tale with no basis in reality. More than that, Cobb is blatantly manipulating Robert in ways that may actually harm him. "Shifting Fischer's antipathy from his father onto Browning should work," Cobb muses. Ariadne is shocked and appalled: "We're gonna destroy his one positive relationship?" she quite rightly asks.

More than that, Cobb is not hoping to reconcile Robert with his father out of some sense of altruism or charity. Cobb's motivation is not Fischer's well-being: He is doing this because Saito is paying him for his services, by allowing him to return home to the United States. Saito is doing this to destroy a corporate rival. In some ways, this moral ambiguity and complexity reflects the awkward relationship between individuals and corporately owned media. As much as the catharsis offered by big budget media might offer comfort and reassurance to audiences, it also represents a cynical economic process governed by capitalist concerns.

*Inception* is also ambivalent towards the emotional release experienced by Cobb when he vanquishes Mal and returns home to be with his children. In the closing shot, Cobb starts to spin his "totem" on the kitchen table, to determine whether he is truly in the real world or still dreaming. Then he decides to simply walk away before finding his answer. The camera holds on the spinning top, and then cuts away before offering a decisive answer. This closing scene sparked a wave of debate and discussion about whether Cobb was still trapped within his dream or whether the *entire* film had been a dream.[89]

In some ways, this insistence on treating *Inception* as a riddle to be solved rather than a movie to be watched reflected a lot of contemporary popular culture.[90] The television series *The X-Files* and *Lost*, along with the emergence of the Internet as a communications tool where film and television might be dissected in *incredible* detail, had contributed to an environment where everything was to be analyzed and debated.[91] Ambiguity was a source of heated discussion, with audiences expecting to determine objectively "correct" interpretations of the art presented to them. There was an increased emphasis on the idea of objectively verifiable interpretations of art, as opposed to subjective discussion of its meaning.[92]

In some ways, Nolan was perfectly suited to that cultural moment. His interest in blurring the line between subjective and objective, and his willingness to leave ambiguity lingering, encouraged this sort of speculation. His structuring of plot as the "controlled release of information" was perfectly suited to an age where even minor details were dissected at incredible length. The arrival of any Nolan film is inevitably met with speculation and theorizing as certain sections of the Internet compete to "solve" the puzzle in the most convincing manner.[93] The endings of Nolan's films frequently leave some ambiguity for the audience to discuss, a little space in which their subjective interpretation of the narrative might play out.

It is worth comparing Nolan's use of ambiguity and his engagement with Internet speculation culture to that of other writers and directors. Writer-director J.J. Abrams is avowedly fond of the "mystery box" as a storytelling tool, although he has acknowledged that he is indifferent as to what the box actually contains so long as it interests the audience.[94] In contrast, writer Steven Moffat has a tendency to set up teases and plot threads that lead to rampant fan speculation, only to brutally subvert that speculation when it comes to resolving the plot developments.[95] Nolan tends to be a lot more precise in his structuring of set-up and pay-off than either Abrams or Moffat, always aware of where his story is going and making a point never to undercut his own narrative set-ups. Instead, Nolan creates a layer of ambiguity distinct from plot, often rooted in character interpretation or inviting the audience to speculate on the meaning of such resolutions.

In keeping with that approach, Nolan has acknowledged that there is no clear-cut answer to that final shot of *Inception*, and that he will never explain to any interviewer whether Cobb was in the real world or the dream world.[96] This is because this intentional ambiguity, by its very nature, does not have a clear answer. The final shot is not designed to suggest that Cobb might be trapped in a dream world. Instead, it exists to suggest that Cobb *does not care* whether he is in the real world or the dream world.

Nolan has confirmed this reading of the closing scene. "The way the end of that film worked, Leonardo DiCaprio's character, Cobb—he was off with his kids, he was in his own subjective reality," offers Nolan. "He didn't really care any more, and that makes a statement: perhaps all levels of reality are valid."[97] Cobb has decided to accept the world placed in front of him, rather than to question or challenge it. Like Fischer, he has accepted his emotional catharsis at face value, and does not care that it may be based on a lie or that it may be untrue.

*Inception* seems rather ambivalent about the catharsis offered by cinema, inviting the audience to wonder whether the strong emotions that they feel in watching a story unfold are a genuine expression of some deep-set humanism or the cynical manipulations of the studio system.[98] This hints at a rather bleak worldview, but one that is very much in keeping with the thematic arc of this stretch of Nolan's filmography.

In *The Prestige*, much was made of the financial and economic forces that dictate and shape performance; that wonder was a commodity that could be traded upon by characters like Borden and Cutler as a means to escape poverty. More than that, *The Prestige* emphasized that narrative was essentially a lie designed to disguise the horrors of a harsh and cold world that was "miserable, solid all the way through." Even beyond that, *The Prestige* insisted that such narratives demanded the illusion of a happy ending, even if that ending was not true or earned. As Cutler explains, "Because making something disappear isn't enough; you have to bring it back."[99]

Similarly, the end of *The Dark Knight* suggests an ambivalent approach to the idea of political narratives: Harvey Dent is dead, killed following a murder spree and the attempted execution of James Gordon's family. But to boost Gotham's morale, Batman and Gordon conspire to cover up the crime and preserve Dent's reputation. *The Dark Knight* ends (and *The Dark Knight Rises* begins) with James Gordon eulogizing Dent, providing a falsified (but comforting and reassuring) narrative about Gotham's so-called "White Knight." Gordon even hints at his distortion of the historical record by acknowledging that the mythic Harvey Dent was "not the hero we deserved, but the hero we needed."

*The Dark Knight* pitches this fabrication and distortion of the historical record in service of a political narrative as something approaching catharsis for the community, much as the use of magic in *The Prestige* might be read as a meditation upon both cinema and religion. Bruce offers a similar argument to Borden, suggesting that sometimes a reassuring lie is more satisfying than cold reality. "Sometimes the truth isn't good enough, sometimes people deserve more," Bruce contends. "Sometimes people deserve to have their faith rewarded." However, these lies are at best ambiguous within the context of *The Dark Knight*, and are exposed as actively dangerous in *The Dark Knight Rises*. The lies at the end of *The Dark Knight* come back to haunt Gotham in *The Dark Knight Rises*, suggesting that these narratives of convenience come at a high price.

Nolan's later films continue to engage with the idea of narrative as a framework imposed upon reality.[100] However, that theme is never quite as strong as it is in the five films from *Batman Begins* to *The Dark Knight Rises*, wherein Nolan seems to grapple with the idea that all storytelling is effectively lying and the consequences that branch out from that.[101] In many ways, this reflects an extrapolation of the more personal narratives constructed by characters in films like *Following*, *Memento* and *Insomnia*, and applies those ideas to a broader social context. Films like *Batman Begins*, *The Prestige*, *The Dark Knight*, *Inception* and *The Dark Knight Rises* continue to explore the narratives that individuals build around themselves, but also explore the ways in which societies construct their own narratives and myths.

Nolan is not so cynical as to condemn the idea outright, understanding the appeal (and even the necessity) of these narratives for societies to function.[102] *Inception* is ambivalent about the catharsis that Cobb affords to Fischer and to the catharsis that Cobb achieves on his own terms. The film candidly acknowledges that Fischer's emotional closure is not grounded in anything that is objectively or verifiably real, and that it was a result of cynical and exploitative manipulation. However, the film also makes the case that Fischer's catharsis is no less real for that fact. Fischer has reached an understanding with his deceased father, and through that found a peace that would otherwise elude him.[103] Similarly, *Inception* allows the audience to make their own determination on whether it is a good or a bad thing that Cobb has ceased to worry about what is real when offered a chance to reunite with his children.

In some ways, this feels like an evolution in the broader thematic arc of Nolan's career. Nolan's early films *Following* and *Memento* suggested that their disjointed and confused non-linear narratives were anchored in ideas of loss and trauma, the structure of the films allowing audiences to empathize with the central characters' attempts to process that trauma. With that in mind, the exploration of catharsis and release in *The Prestige*, *The Dark Knight* and *Inception* might be read as the next step in that arc, an attempt to move past the trauma towards some sort of reconciliation. *The Prestige*, *The Dark Knight* and *Inception* are all fascinated by the mechanics of such reconciliation.

*Inception* is a movie that is more intrigued by emotion than engaged with it. It makes these observations about catharsis a safe distance from its emotional core, operating at a remove from the emotional release afforded by such narratives. With this in mind, and coupled with an impressive homage to an iconic visual from *2001: A Space Odyssey*, it is no surprise that *Inception* garnered a new wave of critical comparisons between Nolan and Stanley Kubrick.[104] However, this emotional distance within *Inception* allows Nolan the opportunity to explore not only blockbuster storytelling in general, but his own narrative sensibilities in particular. Indeed, *Inception* is preoccupied with a number of Nolan's recurring thematic and narrative preoccupations, serving as something of an exorcism within his own filmography.

Nolan's films tend to focus on driven and obsessive men; the protagonist in *Following*, Leonard in *Memento*, Dormer in *Insomnia*, Bruce Wayne in the *Dark Knight* trilogy, Borden and Angier in *The Prestige*, Cobb in *Inception*. In many cases, they are motivated by a deep loss. In the majority of cases, this loss is of a female character.[105] This is most obvious in explicit cases like Leonard's obsession with finding his wife's murderer in *Memento*, Angier's anger over the loss of his wife in *The Prestige* and the fact that Cobb is literally haunted by the death of his wife in *Inception*. However, it also plays out even in minor emotional beats; the suicide of Sarah Borden in *The Prestige*, the death of Rachel Dawes in *The Dark Knight*.[106]

To be fair to Nolan, this is not a problem unique to his films. An unreasonable proportion of films tend to focus on male heroes, and reduce their wives and families to motivational factors as narrative shorthand.[107] This is such a common narrative trope that it has entered critical discourse, with comic book writer Gail Simone coining the phrase "women in refrigerators" to refer to female characters who are killed off and humiliated in order to motivate a masculine hero.[108] The term has been accepted into broader popular culture, with the verb "fridged" or "fridging" used to denote a female character who has been treated in such a manner.[109] This is not to excuse Nolan's use of his female characters in this way, but instead to provide a sense of cultural context.

*Inception* confronts this issue head-on through the relationship that exists between Cobb and the part of his subconscious manifesting as his deceased wife Mal. As with Nolan's work in *Memento*, there is a sense of ambivalence about the relationship between the lonely, driven protagonist and his deceased wife, a lingering question about how much of the character's motivation can be traced back to the deceased wife and how much of it is simply a reflection of the protagonist's own obsessive tendencies.[110] In doing so, Nolan offers a slight twist on the classic "women in refrigerators" cliché by approaching the idea as an archetype to be deconstructed rather than as a plot device to be taken at face value.[111] Nolan's characters often seem motivated by an abstract idea of something that has been lost, rather than through a strong emotional attachment of itself, and his films suggest that these are not healthy behaviors.[112]

Whatever ambiguity exists in Nolan's early films, *Inception* tackles this narrative crutch head-on. Cobb's projection of Mal is in many ways Nolan's archetypal "lost love," a bitter and destructive source of obsession that leads to damaging patterns of behavior and fuels dangerous obsessions.[113] *Inception* repeatedly makes the case that Cobb's difficulty in reconciling himself to the loss of Mal puts himself (and everyone else) at risk; it happens during the opening sequence and again during the central plot. Cobb believes that he is holding onto the memory of his dead wife, keeping her locked away in his literal subconscious. However, the truth is that his memory of her has served to trap him. Cobb's projection of Mal haunts every moment, keeping the character on edge. This projection is part of the reason that Cobb cannot create any more, to the point that the people working with him cannot trust him.

*Inception* seems like a reflexive piece of self-criticism from Nolan, with the writer-director acknowledging his over-reliance on the character archetype so effectively represented by Cobb's projection of Mal. In terms of Nolan's filmography, *Inception* represents an attempt to exorcise those tendencies within his own writing, to confront this aspect of his storytelling directly and to vanquish it. Indeed, Nolan's approach to female characters changes dramatically in the movies that follow *Inception*.[114] There is a conscious sense of a storyteller assessing his own work and trying to do better.

It could be argued that the only truly heroic character in *Inception* is also its only female character, Ariadne.[115] The male characters are willfully blind to Cobb's deep-seated issues with Mal; they often enable and excuse Cobb's poor judgment and risky behavior. Arthur is aware of how unstable Cobb has become, to the point that he can warn Ariadne about it. But Arthur never takes any steps to confront Cobb about it. Similarly, Yusef is actively complicit in Cobb's instability, administering chemicals that allow Cobb to dream and converse with Mal. Yusef allows himself to be manipulated by Cobb, sending the team into a deep trance in return for Cobb's full share of the job's profits. *Inception* seems to suggest that men tend to cover for one another when it comes to matters of poor judgment and poor impulse control.[116]

Ariadne is the one character capable of confronting Cobb about the danger he poses to the team, explicitly calling out Arthur's failure to do so. She is largely responsible for the success of the mission. On top of designing the mazes that the characters must navigate, she insists on accompanying the team into Fischer's mind and then insists on accompanying Cobb on the culmination of his journey to recover Fischer and confront Mal. Ariadne becomes the film's moral compass and its most technically proficient character.[117] In many ways, the contrast between Mal and Ariadne would inform the way in which Nolan approached his female characters in *The Dark Knight Rises*.[118]

The character of Ariadne is not entirely unproblematic. The contrast between Ariadne and Mal evokes the classic Madonna-Whore dichotomy that informs so many female characters in popular culture.[119] Mal is sultry, seductive and evil; Ariadne is pure, inspiring and good.[120] Once again, Nolan complicates the criticism by making it clear that the version of Mal who appears in *Inception* is merely Cobb's projection of the woman. More than that, *Inception* makes a point to afford Ariadne her own agency in terms of the overall plot.[121]

*Inception* is a culmination of some of the recurring fascinations that played through the first six films in Nolan's filmography. It feels like a director working through both the conventions of blockbuster storytelling and his own narrative sensibilities, taking stock of how these stories work and picking them apart in order to understand the mechanics at play. *Inception* is arguably Nolan's tightest and coldest of films, the film that is constructed most mechanically and at the greatest emotional distance from its subjects. It is both a showcase for his sheer technical craft and a vehicle for introspective analysis of his storytelling.

Nolan's films following *Inception* are dramatically different from the films leading up to it, and many of those differences feel like a direct response to the elements identified in *Inception*. It occasionally feels like Nolan has taken apart his own storytelling in order to reconstruct it in the films that follow. The plotting of *The Dark Knight Rises* and *Interstellar* is noticeably looser than the plotting of *Inception*, their narratives moving in a more circuitous route towards their destinations, in contrast to the unrelenting forward momentum of *Inception*. Similarly, *The Dark Knight Rises* and *Interstellar* feature more complex and developed female characters than his earlier films. On a similar note, *The Dark Knight Rises* and *Interstellar* are less ambivalent about their narrative catharsis than *The Prestige*, *The Dark Knight* and *Inception*. *Inception* is the point of this pivot.

In some ways, *Inception* plays as both a dream and an awakening.

# 8

## *The Dark Knight Rises*

*The Dark Knight Rises* is arguably the only *true* sequel in Nolan's filmography.

There were rumors, based on the success of *Inception*, that Warner Brothers wanted to develop sequel films to the box office smash.[1] Nolan remained open to the possibility in press and interviews around the film.[2] However, none of those sequels ever entered development or progressed beyond a stage of idle speculation.[3]

*The Dark Knight* was clearly a sequel to *Batman Begins*. The film's themes and antagonist had been set up in its direct predecessor.[4] At the same time, *The Dark Knight* is relatively self-contained in terms of plot and character. The audience watching *The Dark Knight* might appreciate some key details and ironies having seen *Batman Begins*, but they will be able to follow the film without any prior knowledge.[5]

In contrast, *The Dark Knight Rises* is very explicitly a sequel to both *Batman Begins* and *The Dark Knight*. It is a film that would be very difficult to appreciate without an in-depth knowledge of the storytelling dynamics and character arcs from the previous films.[6] *The Dark Knight Rises* pays off certain ideas and plot beats from both *Batman Begins* and *The Dark Knight*, arguably constructed as a more satisfying end to those two films than as a cohesive piece of narrative in its own right.[7] In this regard, *The Dark Knight Rises* is unique in Nolan's filmography.

There is some suggestion that Nolan had planned on developing a sequel to *The Dark Knight* during its production. On the one hand, the writer and director had restructured David S. Goyer's original plan for the film in such a way that it did not demand a sequel, closing various narrative loose ends like Harvey Dent's transformation into Two-Face in order to create a more self-contained and cohesive narrative.[8] However, Heath Ledger's family has confirmed that the actor had intended to reprise the role.[9] This sentiment was shared by various members of the production team who had worked on *The Dark Knight* with Nolan and Ledger.[10]

It was very clear that the studio *wanted* a sequel to the Batman blockbuster. Goyer recalls a studio executive laying out plans during the opening weekend, stating, "It's gonna be the Riddler, and we want it to be Leonardo DiCaprio...."[11] A lot of the Internet users agreed with that anonymous executive, and pop culture discussion over the next couple of years was dominated by fantasy casting of the role of the Riddler in a potential sequel to *The Dark Knight*.[12]

Nolan wouldn't commit to the sequel straight away. In interviews, he dodged the question, wryly asking, "How many good third movies in a franchise can people name?"[13] His producer and wife Emma Thomas explains that this was not mere performance nor negotiation tactic. "Chris really had to think about whether or not he wanted to do that," she insists, "we were very happy with the way we had tied up *The Dark Knight*."[14]

When Nolan circled back around to the idea of directing a third Batman film, he approached from a novel angle. He had historically insisted that his films be self-contained and allowed to stand on their own as complete experiences of themselves.[15] But his plan for the *Dark Knight* sequel quickly evolved into a film that would not stand on its own in the same way that *Batman Begins* and *The Dark Knight* had. "I kept wondering about the end of Bruce's journey, and once David and I discovered it, I had to see it for myself," Nolan says. "We had come back to what we had barely dared whisper about in those first days in my garage. We had been making a trilogy."[16] The *Dark Knight* trilogy almost seems like an accidental trilogy.

*The Dark Knight Rises* has a decidedly reflective and almost nostalgic tone, featuring a number of recurring characters and actors from both *Batman Begins* and *The Dark Knight*. The film makes a point to include references to key events and characters from both films, with Nolan consciously deciding to conceal these affectionate touches from pre-release publicity. Cillian Murphy reprised his role as Jonathan Crane, playing a judge presiding over show trials.[17] Despite the fact that Ra's Al Ghul had died at the climax of *Batman Begins*, Liam Neeson had a cameo as an apparition visiting Bruce Wayne.[18] Aaron Eckhart filmed no new material for the film, but pictures of the actor (and quick flashback shots of Harvey Dent after his monstrous transformation) play a key role in the *Dark Knight Rises* plot.[19]

However, there is one notable omission from this extended cast reunion in *The Dark Knight Rises*. There had been some early speculation that the film might recast the Joker following the death of Heath Ledger, especially from actor Gary Oldman.[20] But Nolan made it clear very early in the process that the Joker would not be appearing in *The Dark Knight Rises* in any capacity.[21] He made a decision not to address the character in any form: "That is something I felt very strongly about in terms of my relationship with Heath and the experience I went through with him on *The Dark Knight*. I didn't want to in any way try and account for a real-life tragedy. That seemed inappropriate to me."[22] The only *Dark Knight Rises* material to hint at the fate of the Joker was the tie-in novelization written by Greg Cox, which suggested that the character was the sole resident of Arkham Asylum.[23]

Nolan decided to return to *Batman Begins* to find appropriate villains for *The Dark Knight Rises*, creating a strong sense of continuity between the first and last movies in the series.[24] Nolan recalls,

> Moving on to *Dark Knight Rises*, I knew that the League of Shadows had to come back. I knew that we had to return to *Batman Begins* and those philosophical ideas of Ra's Al Ghul, those challenges— that all had to come back. And I also was looking for a very physical adversary because that's something that neither Ra's Al Ghul, the Scarecrow or the Joker really represented: a massive physical threat. David Goyer and I started looking through the history of the comics, and we fixed on Bane.[25]

In many ways, *The Dark Knight Rises* represents a return to the focus on Bruce Wayne that had defined *Batman Begins*, following the shift in focus to the dynamic between

Batman and the Joker in *The Dark Knight*.[26] As with *Batman Begins*, there is an hour of runtime in *The Dark Knight Rises* before Bruce Wayne dons the iconic cape and cowl, with the story focusing quite heavily on the character's psychology. It makes sense that *The Dark Knight Rises* should explicitly mirror Bruce Wayne and Batman in its antagonists. Talia Al Ghul and Bane are effectively positioned within the narrative as counterparts to the lead character, twisted reflections to the hero who serve to split his two personas into two distinct characters. Their presence informs Bruce's arc and comments upon his character.

Talia Al Ghul is an alternate version of Bruce Wayne, one without Batman.[27] She lost her parents at a young age, and channeled her anger into something greater than herself.[28] Much like Bruce cultivates a public persona for the benefit of Gotham and to serve his own agenda, Talia Al Ghul creates her own approximation of a Gotham City socialite by playing the role of Miranda Tate. Talia is a version of Bruce who has allowed her anger and rage to control her, who never transcended them in the way that Bruce did through the creation of Batman.[29] Talia is a reflection of Bruce without Batman, somebody who simply wants to make the world hurt in retribution for the pain that it has caused to her.

In contrast, Bane is a mirror to Batman without Bruce Wayne. Much like Ra's Al Ghul in *Batman Begins*, Bane was a relatively recent addition to the *Batman* mythos, by the standards of the 70-year-old franchise. The character had been created by writer Chuck Dixon and artist Graham Nolan specifically for the *Knightfall* event during the nineties. The writers working on the *Batman* line needed a villain to break Batman's back and to incapacitate him, and so decided to create a new character to fill that role.[30] Bane proved surprisingly popular and was quickly adapted into other media. He memorably appeared in *Batman: The Animated Series* only a month after the end of *Knightfall*, an impressively quick page-to-screen transition.[31] Less than five years after his first appearance, Bane appeared as one of the primary villains in the maligned *Batman & Robin*. Dixon was less than impressed with how his creation was employed.[32]

While Bane is a character associated with brute strength and the physical snapping of Bruce's vertebrae, he is not unique in the *Batman* canon in terms of the physical threat that he poses to the vigilante; there are other Batman villains (like Killer Croc) who are stronger than the hero.[33] Similarly, Bane is not the only *Batman* villain to physically incapacitate the hero, with Bruce ending up in a wheelchair over the course of the story *Blind Justice*.[34] It has been argued that what truly defines Bane as an iconic *Batman* villain is that the character represents the most successful attempt to create an evil counterpart to the Caped Crusader, that Bane is the most convincing execution of the concept of "an evil Batman."[35]

Even in his debut appearance in *Knightfall*, Bane is defined in terms that explicitly mirror Batman. He is an orphan who grew up in adversity and focused upon a symbol to transcend the mortal world. When he decided to take on Batman, he launched a campaign worthy of the Dark Knight himself. Unlike other villains who have tried to kill Batman, Bane fought strategically rather than impulsively. *Knightfall* was a gauntlet designed to exhaust Batman and push him to his breaking point so that Bane could easily defeat him in a knockdown physical brawl. Bane took on Batman systematically and efficiently. These aspects of the character carry over from the comic book page into *The Dark Knight Rises*.

*The Dark Knight Rises* repeatedly and explicitly parallels and contrasts Bane with Batman.[36] The film redesigns the comic book character's iconic luchador mask in order to emphasize the way in which it covers the mouth, the small canisters of painkiller gas looking almost like the sharp teeth of an animal.[37] In doing so, the mask provides a visual contrast with the mask worn by Batman, which covers everything *except* the character's mouth, which could be seen to emphasize Bruce's humanity beneath the mask.[38] One of the prisoners who lived with Bane explains why the villain would cover his face in such a way: "The mask keeps the pain at bay."[39] The prisoner is describing the literal pain caused by a botched surgery to heal a facial wound, which is regulated by small capsules of painkiller gas. However, in keeping with Nolan's tendency to layer the literal with the metaphorical, it also works as a metaphor for Bruce's relationship to Batman, the superhero persona allowing Bruce to focus on something beyond his own emotional pain.

In *Batman Begins*, Bruce first encountered bats in a cave on the grounds of Wayne Manor. As a child, the bats terrified him. As an adult, he embraced the creatures. *Batman Begins* hints that the very idea of Batman was waiting in that cave for Bruce, visiting briefly with him before his parents' death and serving to inspire him in his later adventures. In *The Dark Knight Rises*, Bane emerges from a hole in the ground "in a more ancient part of the world," a narrative choice that explicitly parallels the villain with Batman. Nolan's direction underscores the thematic connection between the cave and the pit through editing and framing, inviting the audience to make the association between these formative locations for these two characters. Given the narrative arc of *The Dark Knight Rises*, and its anxiety about the toll that being Batman has taken on Bruce, the film suggests an equivalence between Bane's prison and Batman's cave. Bruce must pull himself out of both, a literal rising.[40]

Nolan fixates upon the idea of Batman as a mythic figure, to the point that *The Dark Knight Rises* features a recurring motif of characters etching bat symbols in chalk on walls and benches as if trying to conjure the Caped Crusader to life. Bane is cast in a similar light, cultivating a mythology around himself. His reputation precedes him at the start of the film, when Central Intelligence Agency representatives salivate at the prospect of information that might lead them to Bane.[41] Similarly, Bane is a legend within the prison where he later confines Bruce, his past spoken about in hushed tones and half-remembered fragments. Bruce pieces together an inaccurate history of Bane from his time with the other inmates, who speak about Bane in the same way that the citizens of Gotham speak about Batman.

If Bane is a counterpart to Batman, then he is an example of the concept of Batman without Bruce to anchor it. Bane has no civilian identity of which to speak.[42] "No one cared who I was until I put on the mask," Bane states in his introductory scene. His lack of humanity or identity proves to be his undoing. He is defeated at the climax of *The Dark Knight Rises* when Bruce smashes his mask, providing an effective contrast to the way in which Bruce survived the breaking of Batman's mask during their first clash. Broken, Bane concedes that he never escaped the prison. All of the mythology that Bane has so carefully cultivated is a lie, because there is no human basis for any of these stories.[43]

The mythology attributed to Bane seems to be a result of Talia Al Ghul and Bane working in collaboration, as two sharing one life in a way that seems to literalize the divide between Bruce and Batman.[44] It was Talia who escaped the prison, just as it must be Bruce who pulls himself back into the light. *The Dark Knight Rises* seems to suggest that Bruce and Batman only ever worked because they were so integrated into one another. Talia Al Ghul and Bane literalize the idea of Bruce and Batman as two separate identities; they demonstrate that one could never have functioned without the other. Even with their identities closely intertwined, Talia Al Ghul and Bane are fundamentally dysfunctional. *The Dark Knight Rises* seeks to reconcile Bruce and Batman, so that both may move on.

Key to Nolan's decision to make a sequel to *The Dark Knight* was an understanding that the third film in the series would serve as a definitive ending for this iteration of the character. "Unlike the comics, these things don't go on forever in film and viewing it as a story with an end is useful," Nolan said of his creative choices with regards to the film that would become *The Dark Knight Rises*.[45] Jonah Nolan elaborated, "I think what we endeavored to do was not the complete story of Batman but our complete story of this character."[46] From the outset, *The Dark Knight Rises* was conceived as the end of the line for this version of the character. In fact, it honored ideas that Nolan had discussed with Goyer as early as the planning stages of *Batman Begins*. "The final scene of *The Dark Knight Rises* is exactly that scene we talked about then," Goyer recalls. "It remained completely unchanged. We both knew in our hearts that we were onto something special."[47]

This was an important creative decision in a number of respects. Most obviously, it served to delineate Nolan's *Dark Knight* trilogy from the source material, serving as an illustration of some of the key differences between films and comic books. Comic book characters exist in perpetuity, with many iconic characters having been in continuous publication for decades without any real change in their age or their *status quo* on the printed page.[48] On the comic book page, the Marvel Universe has been around since at least 1961,[49] but those 57 years of history has only taken up between five or ten years in the history of those characters.[50]

To be fair, comic book publishers will occasionally tell stories that hint towards an ending for these iconic characters. Frank Miller's miniseries *The Dark Knight Returns* unfolded in a hazy future where Bruce Wayne had retired from his career as the Caped Crusader, coming out of the shadows one last time. Similarly, Mark Millar and Steve McNiven's *Old Man Logan* featured an apocalyptic future in which the comic book hero Wolverine had vowed to never again pop his iconic claws. However, even these seemingly final stories surrendered to the narrative inevitability of ongoing serialized storytelling. Miller produced two sequels to *The Dark Knight Returns*.[51] Meanwhile, Millar teased the continuing story of his futuristic Wolverine in his other work with the publisher,[52] while Marvel would eventually launch *Old Man Logan* as an ongoing series under the pen of writer Jeff Lemire.[53] In comic books, even endings are seldom *truly* endings.[54]

This is the opposite of how films work. Films normally have endings, even if those endings are ambiguous and even if sequels are developed. More than that, films are affected by the passage of time and by factors affecting the production team. Time may move at a different rate on screen, but it moves at the same pace for everybody off-screen. Actors grow old and die, writers and directors move on. As such, live action cinema could never perfectly recreate the perpetual *status quo* associated with comic books. This passage of time is particularly important to Nolan as a director, emphasized both in his storytelling and in his technique.[55]

While pulp characters in film cannot continue in a perpetually frozen *status quo* like their comic book counterparts, only rarely do films acknowledge this inevitable reality. Cinematic adaptations of iconic characters tended to cycle through stories by rotating the lead actor with a minimum of fuss, an unspoken assumption that the audience would not wonder why James Bond changed from Sean Connery to George Lazenby back to Sean Connery and then to Roger Moore.[56] Production teams are very rarely afforded the opportunity to bring closure to their takes on iconic characters, instead gracelessly shuffled off the franchise to make room for a new take with a minimum of fuss. Closure is reserved for iconic characters in prestige pieces.[57]

While Nolan was developing the *Dark Knight* trilogy, there was a change taking place in how crowd-pleasing blockbusters were approaching the issue of long-form storytelling. The James Bond franchise had historically avoided any real sense of long-form continuity from one installment to the next.[58] However, with Daniel Craig's assumption of the iconic role in 2006, films like *Casino Royale* and *Quantum of Solace* would interconnect and overlap in increasingly intricate ways.[59]

The Marvel Cinematic Universe launched with *Iron Man* in 2008, the same year *The Dark Knight* was released. The goal was to create a shared universe of comic book characters drawn from the pages of Marvel Comics, who could interact with one another and appear across several franchises.[60] The Marvel Cinematic Universe was based in large part around adapting familiar comic book narrative devices for the big screen.[61] It included concepts like legacy characters,[62] an elaborate secret history[63] and gigantic crossover events.[64]

As Nolan was working on *The Dark Knight Rises*, the Marvel Cinematic Universe was building to its first crescendo. Released a few months before *The Dark Knight Rises*, *The Avengers* brought together characters from a variety of standalone feature films as part of an epic struggle for the fate of the world. *The Avengers* was a *massive* box office success, earning over a billion dollars in less than 20 days.[65] Its success cast a long shadow, much as *The Dark Knight*'s success had done.[66] Other studios looked upon the success of the Marvel Cinematic Universe and made plans to cultivate their existing properties to emulate that success. Fox conspired to build a shared universe of their X-Men properties.[67] Sony hoped to build out from Spider-Man.[68] Universal looked to revive their classic monster movie franchises as a more modern shared universe.[69] Even Warner Brothers looked to develop their DC properties into a cohesive universe.[70]

This shift towards shared universes represented a fundamentally different way of building blockbuster films and franchises. In particular, this model took a lot of power out of the hands of individual writers and directors. Jon Favreau was in charge of Tony Stark's development in *Iron Man* and *Iron Man 2*, but he had to be aware of larger plans to handle the character in *The Avengers*. Joss Whedon noted that he lacked a lot of creative freedom while working on *The Avengers: Age of Ultron*, being forced to include narrative elements that did not satisfy his storytelling but instead fed the demands of the shared universe.[71] The storytelling in the Marvel Cinematic Universe has been likened to that of a TV series, where the vision of individual writers and directors is largely secondary to the overarching vision of producers and showrunners.[72]

Marvel Studios earned a reputation among directors for being difficult to work with in pursuit of the cohesion of their conjoint franchises.[73] Director Edgar Wright was forced to abandon his ambitious plans for *Ant Man* because he could not find a compromise with the corporation.[74] Director Patty Jenkins parted ways with the company after being unable to realize her vision for *Thor: The Dark World*.[75] Director Ava DuVernay declined to direct *Black Panther* for fear of how her vision might be compromised by the demands of the studio.[76]

Other companies developing their shared universes employed similar methods. Zack Snyder is credited as the director of Warner Brothers' *Justice League*, but a lot of the film was reshot and edited by Joss Whedon, leading to a tangible clash of styles in the finished product.[77] Whedon lost several key battles with the studio on those reshoots.[78] The emergence of the cinematic shared universe in the early twenty-first century typically invested creative power in people who weren't overseeing individual films. In many cases, these were figures with a minimal amount of experience in the practicalities and mechanics of making movies.[79]

A large emphasis of these modern blockbusters was also placed on fidelity to source material and to appeasing the expectations of an eager fan base. Studios imagined that this fidelity might carry over to the frozen time depicted in the source material, that these shared universes and intellectual properties might remain an evergreen source of income without any definitive endings or closure.[80] Even as actors' contracts expired and even as they aged beyond their roles, Marvel Studios made it clear that it would not reboot its shared cinematic universe.[81] There would be no endings for these stories, because they were all so densely integrated into one another that no writer or director's story was ever truly their own.[82] Even when characters' stories did seem to reach logical end points, the gravity of the shared universe inevitably pulled them back into action.[83]

All of this serves to make *The Dark Knight Rises* feel like a film that exists out of time. While *The Dark Knight* arrived at the perfect cultural moment, *The Dark Knight Rises* seems out of step with the pop cultural landscape into which it was released. In terms of blockbuster storytelling, *The Dark Knight Rises* is a movie about endings at a time in popular culture when blockbuster franchises were positioning themselves as perpetual second acts. A certain amount of fandom backlash was directed at the decision to offer a clear and definitive ending to Bruce Wayne's arc that began with *Batman Begins*.[84] Even directly following the release of *The Dark Knight*, Nolan had been explicit in his desire to keep his version of Bruce Wayne cleanly separated from any attempt to indulge in crossovers or to build shared universes.[85]

In some respects, the definitive ending of *The Dark Knight Rises* seemed designed to give Warner Brothers the creative freedom to repurpose the character of Batman as part of their shared cinematic universe. While there was some idle speculation that Warners might try to tether their shared universe to Nolan's vision by carrying over Joseph Gordon Levitt to their *Justice League* franchise, this never came to pass.[86] In fact, Ben Affleck would be announced as Christian Bale's successor in the role of Bruce Wayne and Batman just over a year after the release of *The Dark Knight Rises*.[87]

Nolan remained on board as a producer on the films intended to launch Warner Brothers' shared universe, *Man of Steel* and *Batman vs. Superman*, helping to select director Zack Snyder and contributing to the story.[88] But he was rather uninvolved in their day-to-day production.[89] The handful of creative decisions credited to Nolan in shaping this shared universe emphasize his desire to retain a traditional cinematic form even in the modern blockbuster landscape, most obviously the vetoing of the post-credit teaser scenes that undercut the idea of a given movie as a single self-contained unit of narrative.[90]

The fact that *Dark Knight Rises* is a blockbuster that offers a clear and definitive ending for a beloved pop cultural institution makes it seem like an oddity in the context of the big-budget cinema around it. However, the decision to build it as a film with such an ending arguably distinguishes the *Dark Knight* trilogy from these perpetual ongoing movie franchises and allows the three films to be seen a cohesive unit encapsulating an important moment in America's cultural history.[91]

*The Dark Knight Rises* feels like a movie out of time in more than just its rejection of contemporary trends in superhero cinematic storytelling. The movie's political subtext seemed strange and uncomfortable in the context of mid–2012. *Batman Begins* and *The Dark Knight* were undoubtedly blockbuster superhero movies that aligned with the tenure of President George W. Bush and the War on Terror.[92] These were stories about terrorism in urban environments and the power of fear to suppress and divide a population, something that Nolan candidly acknowledges of his films.[93] However, a lot had changed in the four years since *The Dark Knight*'s release.

President Barack Obama was elected in November 2008 and assumed office in January 2009. His election was treated as a triumph of hope and optimism over fear and uncertainty.[94] His Obama relatively high approval rating at the start of his term provided a sharp contrast with the approval rating of President Bush at the end of his term.[95] Towards the end of his tenure, President Bush posted the highest disapproval rating of in the history of the Gallup polling organization.[96] The American public seemed ready for a change.

While the language and imagery of the War on Terror continued to populate blockbuster entertainment, there was a recurring suggestion that popular culture was ready for more optimistic storytelling. Obama would become renowned as a president uniquely engaged with (and reflected in) popular culture.[97] If the gritty and grounded storytelling of *Batman Begins* and *The Dark Knight* spoke to the tone of the Bush era, then perhaps the hopefulness associated the Obama era could be found in J.J. Abrams' bright and cheerful reboot of *Star Trek* in 2009.[98] Nolan would arguably explore that nostalgic rekindled optimism in his next project, *Interstellar*, but it did place *The Dark Knight Rises* in a very strange position chronologically.

*The Dark Knight Rises* was a blockbuster building on *Batman Begins* and *The Dark Knight*, so it inevitably carried over some of the subtext and themes that defined the earlier series entries. More than that, after the political debates inspired by *The Dark Knight* about the War on Terror, audiences were predisposed to look for political subtext within *The Dark Knight Rises*.[99] There were rumors (later denied by the studio) that Nolan would film sections of *The Dark Knight Rises* against the backdrop of the "Occupy Wall Street" protests in New York City.[100] These rumors colored a lot of the political commentary on *The Dark Knight Rises*, with journalists making sly references to "Occupy Gotham" as early as the release of the teaser trailer.[101]

Nolan denies that his *Dark Knight* trilogy was intended as overtly political cinema. "The films genuinely aren't intended to be political," Nolan insists. "You don't want to alienate people, you want to create a universal story."[102] Nolan elaborates on that idea,

"People often interpret the films as political; they're not. They are examining social issues, and we're really pleased to have been able to follow the threads."[103] This seems a rather ambiguous distinction, inviting the audience to determine how a film engaging with "social issues" might do so without being "political."[104]

Nolan's attempts to deflect from the political subtext of *The Dark Knight Rises* are not entirely convincing. "We're going to get wildly different interpretations of what the film is supporting and not supporting, but it's not doing any of those things," Nolan contended. "It's just telling a story."[105] He seems to suggest that the film's politics exist quite separate from its content, projected onto the film by the audience watching the film and responding to it.[106]

Regardless of Nolan's intent, *The Dark Knight Rises* was received as an overtly political movie in the context of its release. Many commentators read it as a right-wing critique of left-wing populist movements like Occupy Wall Street, insisting that Nolan was arguing against justifiable public outrage at the political and financial establishment in the wake of the Great Recession.[107] Indeed, right-wing news sources proudly claimed *The Dark Knight Rises* as a triumphant ode to conservatism in the face of liberal decadence.[108] Critics at liberal news sources described the *Dark Knight* trilogy as "much more explicitly right-wing than almost any Hollywood blockbuster of recent memory"[109] and specifically critiqued *The Dark Knight Rises* as "an evil masterpiece."[110] While these readings were understandable reflexive takes on a movie about a billionaire crimefighter grappling with a populist movement, they somewhat missed the intricacies of Nolan's arguments.

Nolan is undoubtedly a conservative filmmaker with a small "c," in the style of other filmmakers like the Coen Brothers.[111] Nolan has confessed to a fear of disorder, personified by the Joker as "the threat of pure anarchy" in *The Dark Knight*.[112] He is not a radical filmmaker who seeks to tear down the established political order in revolutionary violence, and *The Dark Knight Rises* affirms that anti-revolutionary sentiment. According to Nolan,

> I'm not being disingenuous when I say that we write from a place of "What's the worst thing our villain Bane can do? What are we most afraid of?" He's going to come in and turn our world upside down. That has happened to other societies throughout history, many times, so why not here? Why not Gotham? We want something that moves people and gets under the skin.[113]

That fear of anarchy and revolution is a broader reflection of Nolan's more intimate and personal themes, the confusion and chaos that defined Leonard in *Memento* extrapolated across an entire cityscape. It is almost a cliché to suggest that the personal is political, that political beliefs are often a reflection of individual values.[114] But in this case, it seems fair to read *The Dark Knight Rises* as an extension of Nolan's self-confessed fear of loss of control.[115] This fear plays out across the film, most notably in the recurring imagery of cracking ice that runs from the title card through to the frozen river that borders the city in the third act; *The Dark Knight Rises* seems constantly troubled by the notion that civilization is nothing more than a thin sheet of ice covering an infinite abyss of anarchy.[116]

Allowing for this conservative personal outlook, it is worth considering the decisions Nolan made when it came to building a motion picture trilogy around Batman. The American superhero is an inherently conservative figure, a lone vigilante fighting to preserve the *status quo* in the face of corrupt and ineffective institutions.[117] Nolan understands that this is the framework that he has inherited in developing a trilogy of films about a billionaire who moonlights as a masked vigilante. "The corruption that drives Bruce Wayne to become Batman is very extreme," Nolan explains. "So, you know, your concept of 'Does the end justify the means?' shifts according to the backdrop. And so the challenge of *Batman Begins* was to make us okay with the idea of vigilantism."[118]

Accepting the inherent conservatism of the superhero genre at face value, it is worth considering how Nolan gently tweaked that existing template. One of the stock criticisms of *Batman* as a concept is that the character romanticizes the image of an angry billionaire who beats up poor and mentally ill criminals in his spare time.[119] This might explain why the *Dark Knight* trilogy repeatedly engages with the idea of Bruce Wayne's privilege; the character spends extended portions of both *Batman Begins* and *The Dark Knight Rises* isolated from his financial fortune.[120] Asked whether Bruce Wayne would have voted for Mitt Romney in the 2012 presidential election, Nolan cheekily responded, "Before or after Bruce goes broke?"[121]

It should also be noted how much time *The Dark Knight Rises* devotes to deconstructing the conservative reading of the end of *The Dark Knight*. Certain journalists and commentators had interpreted the end of *The Dark Knight* as an endorsement of the moral compromise that defined so much of the Bush era, with Bruce Wayne and Jim Gordon conspiring to cover up horrific crimes committed by Harvey Dent in order to preserve the public's faith in their institutions.[122] However, *The Dark Knight Rises* reveals that this romantic lie has a cost: Bane and Talia Al Ghul use this lie in order to destroy everything that Bruce has built and to undermine the social fabric of Gotham.[123] *The Dark Knight Rises* is in many ways a firm rejection of any strongly conservative reading of *The Dark Knight*.

Fitting with the idea of *The Dark Knight Rises* as the most explicit follow-up within Nolan's filmography, it makes sense that extended portions of the film should be given over to the director acknowledging and engaging with commentary on his earlier work. Nolan has stated that he pays little heed to Internet criticism of his films, accepting that most of these criticisms amount to other people's subjective interpretations of his work:

> I try not to be reactive in what I'm doing. It's not as hard to keep your reactions in proportion as you might think, and the reason for that is because yes, a bad review or a particular criticism will make you angry, and you'll be happy when somebody says they like the film—but you get both reactions to every film, no matter who you are, and it's the same movie! So there's a very natural kind of perspective that comes in about other people's responses, which is they're very, very subjective, just as mine are to a lot of movies I watch, so, you don't want to be reactive to that.[124]

At the same time, Nolan's work on *The Dark Knight Rises* and *Interstellar* often feels like reactions to common critiques of his earlier films. Perhaps these shifts were not a direct response to external criticism, instead the result of introspection and analysis. Nevertheless, *The Dark Knight Rises* and *Interstellar* both find Nolan pushing outside his comfort zone and compensating for certain common critiques of his earlier work. In particular, *The Dark Knight Rises* is notable for the development that it affords to its female leads, which stands in marked contrast to the underdeveloped female characters in the earlier *Batman Begins*, *The Prestige* and *The Dark Knight*. If *Inception* found Nolan exploring his own reliance upon dead wives as a convenient storytelling tool, then *The Dark Knight Rises* finds the writer and director trying to look beyond that.

When *The Dark Knight Rises* introduces its two female leads, they are cast in familiar (and problematic) terms as the Virgin and the Whore. Wealthy socialite Miranda Tate invested a lot of money in clean energy and hosts lavish charity balls to provide for the city's less fortunate. Selina Kyle is a seductive and playful thief who steals Martha Wayne's pearls and engages in a cheeky flirtation with Bruce. The opening act of the movie seems to suggest both characters as potential love interests for Bruce.[125] To a certain extent, this is true. Bruce does sleep with Miranda around the halfway point and elopes with Selina Kyle to Italy at the end.

But Nolan subverts this set-up in a number of interesting ways. Miranda is introduced as a virtuous and sympathetic character, with the third act suggesting that she is to serve as a hostage that Bane might use against Batman. However, the film's climax reveals that Miranda is the villainous mastermind behind the entire attack on Gotham. More than that, she is Talia Al Ghul, the daughter of Ra's Al Ghul. Despite the stories that Bruce heard, it was not Bane who escaped from the Pit, it was Talia. Nolan uses gender-neutral language in recounting that backstory to play upon the gendered assumptions of the audience and preserving the surprise reveal that it was Talia, not Bane, who managed that feat.[126] There is a credible argument to be made that Talia is the primary villain of the film, in that it is her emotional arc that drives the plot, and that the stereotypically hypermasculine Bane is ultimately her henchman.

At the same time, Selina Kyle is perhaps Nolan's most complex female character.[127] She has a great deal of agency and power within the *Dark Knight Rises* narrative, and the film is very invested in the choices that she makes.[128] In some ways, Selina serves to put a human face on the soul of Gotham City, a soul that is ultimately inspired to make the choice to do the right thing by Bruce's example. She is a complex character who serves the same function as the ferries at the end of *The Dark Knight*. Much like the ferries were caught up in the existential struggle between Batman and the Joker, Selina finds herself caught in the wrestling match between Bane and Batman. She initially betrays Bruce to Bane in order to get a clean break with her life, but eventually decides to risk her life in service of the greater good.[129] Selina is very much the moral compass of *The Dark Knight Rises*, a human character caught in the middle of an epic battle for the soul of Gotham City. In that respect, it reveals a lot about the film's politics that she is both in massive debt and a wanted criminal while still filling that role.

*The Dark Knight Rises* arrived on the tail end of a massive financial crisis that had begun in 2007 and 2008.[130] Even beyond the immediacy of that financial crisis, income inequality between the richest and poorest members of American (and global) society had dramatically increased over the prior three decades.[131] Nolan had written *The Dark Knight Rises* with a keen eye on that inequity, even if the script had been written before populist movements like Occupy Wall Street had given voice to public unrest.[132] In many ways, *The Dark Knight Rises* was a response to the events that motivated Occupy Wall Street rather than a response to the political movement itself. According to Nolan,

> We were writing years before Occupy Wall Street, and we were actually shooting at the time that it arose, but I think the similarities come from Occupy being a response to the banking crisis in 2008. We were sitting there in a world where, on the news, we were constantly being presented with what-if scenarios. Like: "What if all the banks go bust?" "What if the stock market is worth nothing?" These questions are terrifying, and we were taking the view that we should be writing about what's most frightening.[133]

The primary influence on Gotham City's descent into anarchy in *The Dark Knight Rises* was Charles Dickens' *A Tale of Two Cities*.[134] As with a lot of the more overtly political material in *The Dark Knight*, this connection originated with Jonathan rather than Christopher Nolan.[135] Jonathan explains the choice of inspiration: "*A Tale of Two Cities* was the most harrowing portrait of a relatable, recognizable civilization falling to pieces."[136] It also makes a certain amount of sense given Dickens' origins as a writer of the sort of long-form serialized fiction that could be seen as a distant ancestor of modern comic books.[137] There are countless references to *A Tale of Two Cities* in *The Dark Knight Rises*. Gordon reads a eulogy to Bruce Wayne from the book.[138] Bane can be briefly seen knitting, establishing a thematic connection to Madame Defarge from the book.[139] The character names Stryver and Barsad appear in both *A Tale of Two Cities* and *The Dark Knight Rises*.[140]

*The Dark Knight Rises* might perhaps be described as a tale of *three* cities, with the film using Los Angeles, New York and Pittsburgh to stand in for the fictional Gotham City.[141] It is the only film in the trilogy not to shoot in Chicago.[142] It has been argued that the move away from Chicago represents a conscious shift in emphasis, that Pittsburgh's more blue collar aesthetic appealed more strongly to the themes of the story that Nolan want to tell.[143] Similarly, the use of Manhattan and Wall Street play into this idea as a clear contrast to the blue-collar areas of Pittsburgh.[144]

Regarding the decision to change the look and feel of the city in each of the three films, Nolan says,

> It's not really so much that the actual city changes in the three films, it's that the genre of the movies changes slightly, and we look at Gotham in a slightly different way. *Batman Begins* is very much an origin story, and Gotham is viewed in quite symbolic, quite romantic terms. With *The Dark Knight*, we really switched genres. We're looking at the media, the police, the wealthy, the poor; Gotham takes on that sort of crime epic idea of what a city is. Then, in *Dark Knight Rises*, we really move more into the disaster movie.[145]

*The Dark Knight Rises* has a noticeably different texture from *The Dark Knight*, which in turn had an appreciably different feel than *Batman Begins*. In many ways, *The Dark Knight Rises* could be seen as a sweeping social epic about class and revolution in a contemporary American city.[146] It was very much inspired by classical filmmaking. Michael Caine has compared Nolan's work on the film to that of legendary director David Lean, responsible for the epics *The Bridge on the River Kwai*, *Lawrence of Arabia* and *Doctor Zhivago* as well as the Dickens adaptations *Great Expectations* and *Oliver Twist*.[147] Nolan directed cinematographer Wally Pfister to watch *Battle of Algiers* to prepare for the film, and *Battle*'s influence can be clearly seen towards the end.[148]

As much as the *Dark Knight* trilogy is a relatively cohesive narrative of itself, Nolan works hard to ensure that each of the three films has a distinct flavor and style. It would be easy to effectively make the same movie three times, but each of the three is markedly different in how it approaches the material, the characters and the city itself. *Batman Begins* was a superhero origin story, *The Dark Knight* was a multifaceted crime epic and *The Dark Knight Rises* is a story about revolution and inequality in contemporary America.

*The Dark Knight Rises* is sympathetic to the populist uprising in Gotham and quick to condemn its wealthy citizens for failing in their responsibility to their fellow man. The narrative's most sympathetic viewpoint characters are orphan and police officer John Blake and indebted thief Selina Kyle. Blake's second scene finds him investigating the death of homeless people washed up in the city's storm drains, poor people forgotten by the state who "aged out" of what few social protections exist. Kyle spends a significant portion of the film condemning Bruce for his indifference to the plight of the poor people around him. Even Bruce is wary of the grand gestures of charity made by the wealthy and powerful in Gotham.[149]

There is a certain ambivalence towards the idea of Bruce Wayne as Batman. In particular, *The Dark Knight Rises* is wary of the amount of power that he has concentrated and consolidated in himself. *The Dark Knight Rises* makes a strong case that he has forsaken his civic responsibility as Bruce Wayne more than his crime-fighting obligations as Batman. After all, Gotham has been freed of the blue-collar crime represented by Carmine Falcone in *Batman Begins* and Sal Maroni in *The Dark Knight*, but remains in the grip of John Daggett's white-collar crime. John Blake accuses Bruce of turning a blind eye to the suffering of the poor and disenfranchised.[150] In contrast, Bruce's decision to dress up as Batman to take on Bane leads to unequivocal disaster, distracting law enforcement from Bane's escape at the Gotham Stock Exchange.[151]

Bruce makes an effort to consolidate various weapons and technologies in Wayne Tower, where he can control them.[152] This ultimately allows these weapons to fall into the hands of Bane, demonstrating how self-defeating Bruce's attempts to control such power might be.[153] *The Dark Knight Rises* goes so far as to suggest that Bruce's decision to allow Ra's Al Ghul to die at the end of *Batman Begins*—rather than keeping him alive to face justice—is directly responsible for the chaos that Bane and Talia Al Ghul visit upon Gotham City. *The Dark Knight Rises* is arguably even more skeptical about vigilantism than *Batman Begins* and *The Dark Knight*.

*The Dark Knight Rises* repeatedly suggests that Bruce is a poor choice to be Batman specifically *because* of his wealth and privilege. When trapped in the pit, Bruce struggles to understand how a small child could possibly have made a jump that proves impossible for a grown man. "You told me a child did it," Bruce remarks to his caretaker. "No ordinary child," his caretaker reflects. "A child born in hell; forged from suffering; hardened by pain; not a man from privilege." Eventually, Bruce determines that he needs to make the jump *without* a rope dragging him back. *The Dark Knight Rises* makes the rope as a metaphor for rejection of fear, but it might also reflect the material privilege in which Bruce is anchored and by which he is protected. This reading is consistent with certain anti-capitalist threads that Nolan seeded in both *The Prestige* and *Inception*.[154]

The caretaker's description of the child who escaped from the Pit in some ways applies to the character of John Blake. *The Dark Knight Rises* implies that Blake would make a better or more convincing Batman than Bruce, in large part because he comes from poverty and because he is more connected to the real world than Bruce.[155] The ending suggests that for the concept (or the mythology) of Batman to endure, it needs to extend beyond Bruce himself towards something more egalitarian and inclusive.[156]

All of this glosses over the populist revolt that is led by Bane. Even ignoring how Nolan addresses the right-wing readings of *The Dark Knight* and the class issues baked into Bruce Wayne as a premise, Bane's organized revolution against Gotham's wealthy citizens was readily interpreted as a right-wing screed against the perceived evils of socialism.[157]

Once again, this seems like a very superficial read of the character, the plot and the dynamics at play.

*Batman Begins* presented Ra's Al Ghul as a stock comic book version of fascism. *The Dark Knight* introduced the Joker as an exaggerated take on anarchism.[158] *The Dark Knight Rises* presents Bane and Talia as something closer to nihilists.[159] This is particularly clear when the villains are contrasted with their direct predecessor. In *Dark Knight*, the Joker claims to be engaged in "the battle for Gotham's soul" and seeks to prove to Batman and Gotham City that "the only sensible way to live in this world is without rules." He wanted to be vindicated through Gotham, he wanted to create a city that existed in his own image and validated his own cynical perspective on human nature. Bane and Talia's plan is not based on validating their worldview. This is merely a smokescreen: They are destroying Gotham as revenge upon Bruce for killing Ra's Al Ghul.[160] For all that Bane talks about liberating Gotham, the city would always have been destroyed by the detonation of the reactor. For all that Bane talks of empowering Gotham's ordinary citizens, he stacks the deck towards the darker side of human nature by freeing thousands of criminals and arming them with assault rifles.[161]

Much has been made of the way *Dark Knight Rises* appropriates imagery associated with populist left-wing movements like Occupy Wall Street, but most critiques of the film's politics tend to gloss over the skewering of neo-conservative iconography. In particular, *Dark Knight Rises* makes a point to present Bane's occupation of Gotham in terms that evoke U.S. military intervention in Iraq and Afghanistan, right down to the use of desert camouflage in a movie that takes place in an urban environment with a climax unfolding in the dead of winter.[162] Bane's speeches to the world, promising freedom and stability while surrounded by advanced military technology, evoke the iconography of President Bush's infamous "Mission: Accomplished" speech.[163] Even Bane's language evokes the way in which U.S. military intervention in Iraq and Afghanistan would be discussed, vowing, "Now, we come here not as conquerors, but as liberators, to return control of this city to the people."[164]

Nolan rejects the idea that Bane should be interpreted as a right-wing critique of left-wing ideals. Instead, Nolan contends that the film should be read as a critique of a particular political methodology that is rooted in populism. "If the populist movement is manipulated by somebody who is evil, that surely is a criticism of the evil person," Nolan contends. "You could also say the conditions the evil person is exploiting are problematic and should be addressed."[165] This seems like a reasonable position, more aligned with political centrism than with traditional right- or left-wing divisions. He is advocating for constructive discussion rather than violent revolution to address social issues.[166] This position is arguably best articulated by Gordon's appeal to Foley, which hinges on Nolan's small-c conservatism, the argument that the onus is on society to fix itself. "This only gets fixed from the inside!" Gordon insists.

In spite of allegations of right-wing leanings, it is entirely possible to read *The Dark Knight Rises* as a prescient commentary upon the wave of right-wing populism that spread across the western world in 2016.[167] (The film is set in late 2016.[168]) There are any number of direct parallels between Bane's revolution and the right-wing populist movements that led to Donald Trump's election and the referendum vote for Brexit.[169] Bane's relationship to John Daggett calls to mind the relationship between Trump and the political establishment within the Republican Party, with various members of the establishment stoking the paranoia and resentment that would become the cornerstone of Trump's voter coalition, finding themselves completely powerless in the face of a primal force that they had enabled and abetted.[170] Trump even appeared to allude to Bane's rhetoric in his inaugural address.[171]

Much like Bane, Trump ascended to power on the back of a populist movement powered by resentment, while doing little to actually help the people most in need of assistance.[172] In this light, *The Dark Knight Rises* feels like a prescient critique of the reactionary populism that powered movements like Trumpism or Brexit.[173] Nolan is not engaging with any specific right- or left-wing ideas, but is instead playing with broader concepts of populism and revolution. In that respect, the knee-jerk criticisms of the perceived political leanings of *Dark Knight Rises* feel somewhat outdated. The film is a much broader and more symbolic meditation on populism and its consequences.

As much as Nolan has cultivated a reputation for grounded realism, he has always embraced symbolism and metaphor in his storytelling. This is particularly true in this phase of his career, with *Inception*, *The Dark Knight Rises* and *Interstellar* each operating as much on metaphorical logic as on precise plotting. It could be argued that *The Dark Knight Rises* is his most symbolism-laden work and the least grounded film in his filmography.[174] This is a movie titled *The Dark Knight Rises*, in which Bruce Wayne literally pulls himself out of a pit of despair. Near the beginning, Alfred describes a fantasy that he used to have, only for the closing minutes of the film to play out that fantasy for the audience.[175] Perhaps building off the exploration of his own plotting and storytelling in *Inception*, the plotting of *Dark Knight Rises* is appreciably looser than in many of Nolan's other films, with greater emphasis on allegory and symbolism.[176] In fact, unlike most of Nolan's other films, there were reportedly large sections cut from *The Dark Knight Rises*, which may explain why it feels a lot broader than Nolan's other films.[177]

Given that Nolan's very precise plotting and attention to narrative detail had been part of what endeared him to a certain type of movie fan, it is no surprise that *The Dark Knight Rises* became one of the director's most polarizing films.[178] It was a success by any objective measure: It received positive reviews,[179] earned over a billion dollars globally[180] and was listed as one of the ten films of the year by the American Film Institute.[181] But a very vocal strain of online criticism reacted very strongly to perceived flaws in its internal logic.[182] One of the most persistent criticisms was how Bruce managed to get back to Gotham after escaping from the pit in the third act.[183] Of course, the logical answer to this perceived plot hole is either "Because he is Batman" or "Most likely in the same way that he got half-way around the world while traveling in *Batman Begins*."[184]

*Memento* and *The Prestige* attracted a devoted fan base to Nolan through their meticulous plotting and attention to detail. The extreme reaction to the "plot holes" within *Dark Knight Rises* might be seen as the other side of the coin. Internet culture has given voice to obsessive and detail-oriented fandoms, with entire sites and brands dedicated to documenting plot holes in popular films.[185] The video channels (Screen Junkies' "Honest Trailers," CinemaSins' "Everything Wrong With…," etc.) accrue millions of hits for sarcastic takedowns of popular films.[186] Although this nitpicking criticisms has long been part of the Internet's cultural landscape, they looked to breaking into the mainstream around the time that *Dark Knight Rises* was released.[187] These sorts of criticisms were also leveled at Ridley Scott's *Prometheus*, which had been released several weeks earlier.[188]

The tone of the critical conversation is interesting. Observing these reactions, it appears more widely acceptable to criticize *The Dark Knight Rises* for failing to explain how Bruce got back to Gotham than it is to suggest that the movie is too long and awkwardly paced. Similarly, it seems to be more reasonable to criticize *Prometheus* for having a panicked character run in the wrong direction than to debate the necessity of making an *Alien* prequel in the first place. There has been considerable speculation about what has given rise to this nitpick-driven critical culture. Some might say that it is a reflection of a larger ironic and self-aware culture.[189] Others might contend that it is the result of critics who feel uncomfortable expressing their true opinions in the form of a bolder critical essay.[190] Others may argue that these nitpicks are simply stand-ins for a deeper sense of dissatisfaction that the critic in question cannot clearly articulate.[191]

However, it might also be argued that this obsession with nitpicking plays into the same fascination with objectivity that drives the Internet's fixation upon Rotten Tomato scores and star ratings. Critical opinions are inherently subjective. It is often possible to debate critical observations back and forth without any clear resolution; even accepting a critical observation as objective fact, it is possible to argue about how that detail should be interpreted or contextualized without any objectively "right" answer. One writer called the 165-minute *Dark Knight Rises* "astonishingly bloated—and unforgivable in a film that spends a long, ponderous hour getting started."[192] Other critics agree that it's "a complex, expansive tale [that takes its time] putting the elements in place."[193] Neither critical position is objectively right or wrong. These are not statements of fact, they are arguments; they are either convincing or unconvincing to the reader.

However, plot holes and nitpicks present the illusion of objectivity. The notion of objectivity has always been a point of contention in terms of film criticism.[194] However, the weight attached to that concept has increased in an era of established brands and intellectual property, where fannish engagement with a feature film often begins long before the movie enters production.[195] Commentators want to believe that their favorite media is objectively good, that they are correct in their judgment and that everybody who disagrees is wrong—and can be *shown* to be wrong. This informs a lot of discourse related to high-profile releases across media. In video games, the GamerGate movement is fixated on the notion of "objective reviews" that are designed to shut down debate of complex social and political factors around the work in question.[196] Many critics of fan-friendly feature films are accused of "bias" when they offer a negative review, as if subjectively blinded to some objectively verifiably truth.[197] Nolan is in many ways the perfect director for this cultural moment, his films treading that fine line between objective documentation and subjective perspective, his films populated with characters trying to impose some framework upon their world in order to force it to align with their perspective.

If Nolan is correct to think of plot as information, then plot holes are objective gaps in information; they are tangible in a way that abstract critical arguments are not. The film either fills in all the blanks or it doesn't, and it can be objectively marked on those terms.[198] Like the cold hard figures provided by review aggregators like Rotten Tomatoes and Metacritic, plot holes and nitpicks provide the illusion of an objective and indisputable criticism.[199] In some ways, this criticism of the perceived narrative gaps within *The Dark*

*Knight Rises* exists as the other side of the coin from the attention that Nolan garnered through his construction of elaborate and ambiguous plot mechanics in *Memento*, *The Prestige* and *Inception*. Both that praise and this criticism of Nolan engage with the idea of plot as the most important aspect of modern filmmaking, in large part because it is the easiest to criticize in terms that can considered "objective."

*The Dark Knight Rises* signaled the beginning of something approaching a minor critical backlash to Nolan's work. There were already hints of this backlash in response to *Inception*.[200] In fact, there were rumblings of discontent before *The Dark Knight Rises* had even been released.[201] The cacophony around the release of the movie made it difficult to properly take stock of the film as a piece of cinematic entertainment rather than a cultural event.[202] However, Nolan's work following *Inception* has undoubtedly been subject to an almost reflexive backlash from certain quarters of the critical establishment and the Internet's film community that is impossible to avoid in discussions of the director's work.[203] To be fair, this is arguably an expected stage in the life of any successful and influential director, from Spielberg to Hitchcock to Kubrick.[204] However, those directors did not exist in an environment where the Internet was constantly churning out think pieces and where advertising revenue was driven by sensational headlines.

There are several reasons why *The Dark Knight Rises* became a logical place for this backlash to kick into high gear. Nolan had enjoyed critical and commercial success with *The Dark Knight* and *Inception*, coming off the back of a very successful career as an artful director on the low-key *Memento* and *Insomnia*; as such, his celebrity was reaching critical mass.[205] While *The Dark Knight* had revolutionized superhero movies, *Dark Knight Rises* seemed outdated when compared to something like *The Avengers*.[206] More to the point, Nolan's brand had been established with tightly plotted and well-constructed genre pieces, while *The Dark Knight Rises* was a lot looser in its structuring and a lot broader in its construction.

Other outside factors made *Dark Knight Rises* an appealing choice for a backlash. The film itself seemed to be overshadowed by bigger stories outside its own narrative. Nolan's more over-eager fans had established themselves as part of the cultural landscape, issuing death threats to critics who presumed to give *Dark Knight Rises* a bad review.[207] Nolan had refused to bluntly and effectively disavow those more hardcore devotees in contemporary interviews.[208] The death of Heath Ledger cast a long shadow over the production and the finished film.[209] A Colorado theater hosting a midnight premiere became the site of mass shooting that left 12 people dead and 70 injured.[210] Although the perpetrator was subsequently found to have a history of mental health issues, there was some discussion about whether he might have been inspired by *The Dark Knight*.[211]

*The Dark Knight Rises* is an epic in many ways, a film that seems much larger than its 165-minute running time, casting an impressive shadow across popular culture. It rounds out a trilogy at the center of Nolan's first ten films, and serves as a capstone on three of the most influential and important blockbusters of the twenty-first century. A divisive and polarizing film, it remains a source of contention to this day. It feels very much like a definitive ending. Much like *Inception* found Nolan evaluating his own storytelling and his own favored narrative tropes, *Dark Knight Rises* finds Nolan wrapping up his take on the franchise that established him as a blockbuster director. *Dark Knight Rises* was about closure, as much for the director as for the lead character.

Nolan was credited as a producer on Warners' later DC adaptations *Man of Steel*, *Batman vs. Superman* and *Justice League,* but there was never any real sense that he was eager to remain entangled in the world of the Caped Crusader. *The Dark Knight Rises* is a fond farewell to an old friend and a parting of the ways.

Pressed on the possibility of some nostalgic reunion in the far future, Nolan simply responds, "I know I'm done with Batman."[212]

# 9

## *Interstellar*

*Interstellar* is Christopher Nolan's most American film.

His engagement with American popular culture is not surprising. As children, he and Jonathan Nolan split their time between Chicago and London; the former spent more time in London, the latter in Chicago.[1] Like a lot of British children, Christopher grew up surrounded by American pop culture, with many of his defining memories involving *2001: A Space Odyssey* and *Star Wars*. These would become fundamental to who he was. "Movies become indistinguishable from our own memories," Nolan says. "You file them away and they become very personal."[2]

Nolan's films have always balanced his connection to both the U.K. and the U.S. *Memento* and *Insomnia* were both essentially frontier films about the vast American wilderness and its lack of memory.[3] *Batman Begins* used British studio sets to create an American metropolis,[4] while *The Prestige* used Los Angeles to double for nineteenth-century London.[5] Nolan's *Dark* Knight trilogy emphasized the globetrotting nature of the character and his Gothic European influences. *Inception* featured a character who could not return to America but who dabbled in dreams that looked like set pieces from American blockbusters, all unfolding during a flight from Sydney to Los Angeles.

However, *Interstellar* is a film that is unequivocally American. The feature originated as a project with director Steven Spielberg.[6] Spielberg is practically an American institution.[7] It could be contended that Spielberg "is contemporary American cinema, for good or ill."[8] Spielberg was attached to the project in the early years of the twenty-first century, at a point when he was engaged in making the science fiction blockbusters *A.I.: Artificial Intelligence*, *Minority Report* and *War of the Worlds*.[9] The film makes a great deal of sense in that context, although Spielberg wasn't the director who brought it to the screen.

The project that would become *Interstellar* became Christopher's film by a circuitous route. Jonathan was drafted onto the project as a writer in March 2007.[10] When Spielberg moved his production company Dreamworks to Disney, the project was effectively orphaned at Paramount.[11] Nolan stepped in, which meant that *Interstellar* would be his first film since *The Prestige* to be distributed in the U.S. by a studio other than Warner Brothers. Warners bartered international distribution rights from Paramount, at a very high cost that symbolized their faith and investment in Nolan as a director.[12]

Part of what drew Nolan to the project was the genre and the scale involved, the strong connection that existed between the premise and the blockbusters on which he had grown up. "I always loved science fiction," Nolan says. "It has really been an ambition of mine: If I ever had the opportunity to get involved in a large-scale science fiction project, something about exploring our universe, I would try to seize the opportunity."[13] As a child, Nolan's first attempts at filmmaking had been stop-motion science fiction epics inspired by *Star Wars* and spliced together with footage of real-life NASA launches to add production value.[14] *Interstellar* afforded Nolan the opportunity to revisit that premise as a professional film director working on an impressive budget with a great deal of creative freedom.[15]

However, Nolan was also conscious of the fact that he was inheriting a project from Spielberg and ensured that the director would remain an influence on the finished film. "I do liken it to the blockbusters I grew up with as a kid," Nolan says. "A lot of them by Spielberg. I don't like talking about Spielberg too much because he was the director on the project before me and I don't want to keep coming back to that, but the truth is, there's a great spirit to films like *Close Encounters* [*of the Third Kind*] and *Jaws* that I really wanted to try and capture, because I haven't seen it in a very long time."[16]

As a director, Nolan had been heavily influenced by Spielberg. *Batman Begins* had been a clear effort to reconstruct the sort of eighties blockbusters that Spielberg had produced, right down to the fixation on dysfunctional father-son dynamics.[17] *Inception* deconstructs such blockbuster storytelling with a dynamic between Robert and Maurice Fletcher that could easily have been lifted from a Spielberg film. With that in mind, Nolan was an easy fit for a feature film that had originally been conceived as a Spielberg vehicle.

*Interstellar* is packed with Americana. The casting of Matthew McConaughey in the lead role taps into the strong sense of national identity running through the film. Nolan had worked with popular American lead actors before: Al Pacino on *Insomnia* and Leonardo DiCaprio on *Inception*. However, neither leading performer conveyed the "old timey Americana" that McConaughey so effortlessly embodies.[18] With his thick Texan accent and his ability to convey fundamental decency, McConaughey exudes an all-American charm.[19]

While Nolan had cast Pacino and DiCaprio as morally ambiguous protagonists, Cooper is very much a character tailored to McConaughey's persona. Nolan characterized Cooper as an "everyman," in contrast to more specifically defined characters like Dormer or Cobb.[20] This caused McConaughey some minor frustration in attempting to characterize Cooper. McConaughey:

> I remember Chris saying, "He's the Everyman." I remember walking away going, "Who is the Everyman?!" It's harder to define today than at any time. I basically decided to trust in what I personally feel about it, trust in how I feel about family, trust in how I feel about adventure. I had to make it personal. I had to say, "Guess who the Everyman is in this movie, McConaughey? You."[21]

Even beyond the casting of McConaughey, Cooper inhabits a world steeped in American iconography and imagery. *Interstellar* is set in a hazily defined future, but the production design of the Earth-based sequences consciously evokes a hazily defined past. "We wanted to see these vast skies and rolling landscapes which are very North American," production designer Nathan Crowley says of the Cooper homestead.[22] The rural setting of these early scenes evokes the idealized American imagery of Norman Rockwell.[23] According to Nolan, even the emphasis on corn taps into the same "all–American iconography" that had "always been so potent in the Superman myth."[24]

Part of the retro feel of these sequences was a result of Nolan's investment in verisimilitude, his desire to ground the movie in something tangible and demonstrable. His desire to present an apocalyptic threat was drawn from history, presenting an environmental catastrophe modeled on the Dust Bowl of the '30s. This sense of verisimilitude was enhanced by the use of real interview footage from Ken Burns' documentary *The Dust Bowl*, which (according to Nolan) "[Ken] very kindly let me use some excerpts from because even though it's a science fiction film, I wanted the feeling of dread, the feeling of imbalance between the human race and the planet to be real and credible."[25] Nolan clarifies that the environmental catastrophe presented in *Interstellar* is actually less severe than the historical events that inspired it. "We really had to scale back from the reality of what those things were actually like in the Dust Bowl because you look at the photographs, and it actually seems too crazy. I was always fascinated with the idea of presenting what seems like a science fiction doomsday scenario on this sort of big scale that's actually less than [what] really happened in America."[26]

*Interstellar* is driven largely by a nostalgic affection for the American space program, and for NASA in particular. Unlike other twenty-first century films about deep space missions, *Interstellar* eschews of the idea of a multinational team in favor of more old-fashioned American exceptionalism.[27] *Interstellar* arrived at a time when American popular culture was yearning for a return to the simplicity and idealism of the sixties, with nostalgia permeating all facets of life. At the cinema, *Star Trek*, *X-Men: First Class* and *The Man from U.N.C.L.E.* sought to transport audiences back in time to a bright and idealistic version of the sixties.[28] On television, *Mad Men* and *Pan Am* offered a more nuanced and complicated exploration of the decade.[29] This nostalgia might have been tied to a broader cultural nostalgia, with the 2008 election of President Barrack Obama likened to the election of John F. Kennedy in 1960, a charismatic outsider who appealed to young voters with his message of hope and optimism.[30] If *The Dark Knight Rises* was a belated Bush-era blockbuster with its exploration of the economic crash and the legacy of the War on Terror, then *Interstellar* could be considered Nolan's film for the Obama era.

This broader sixties nostalgia also gave rise to a more specific yearning. During the space race, public opinion was strongly divided on the merits of investment in space travel; the only time that the majority of the public supported the program was for a few months around the time of the moon landing.[31] But the American public's support for space travel has slowly increased since the mid-nineties.[32] The private companies Virgin Galactic and SpaceX looked to step into the void left by reduced public investment in space travel.[33] SpaceX appealed to nostalgia in their branding, with advertisements and publicity pitches designed to evoke mid-twentieth century science fiction.[34] *Interstellar* very clearly belongs to this same tradition, even if its American iconography stretches back further than the fifties or sixties.

*Interstellar* is very careful in how it approaches the idea of nostalgia. Nolan's films are always wary of the dangerous lure of empty nostalgia and the trap that it represents.[35] In its early scenes, *Interstellar* makes it clear that its appeal to the past is not unquestioning or uncompromising. Cooper is not happy to see mankind regress to an agrarian society, and resentful of a culture that refuses to value scientific knowledge.[36] *Interstellar* rejects any form of nostalgia that would reject scientific or cultural progress, as Cooper expresses his frustration with two school officials who believe that the moon landing was faked as "propaganda."[37] The nostalgia at work in *Interstellar* is something more specific, a yearning for a time when the future offered infinite possibilities and potential.

"We used to look up in the sky and wonder at our place in the stars," explains Cooper of his affection for the past. "Now we just look down and worry about our place in the dirt." Writer Jonathan Nolan elaborates upon that sense of lost potential and the desire to recapture it: "I grew up in [the era of] Apollo space travel, we were promised jetpacks and fucking teleportation and instead we got fucking Facebook and Instagram. That's a bummer."[38] *Interstellar* longs for a return to a past when it seemed like anything was possible.[39]

Contemporary science fiction seems to be dominated by apocalyptic futures in which mankind has condemned itself to extinction, often as a result of its own arrogance or hubris.[40] In the later years of the twentieth century and into the twenty-first, science fiction seemed to trade hope and optimism for cynicism and despair.[41] In the early years of this century, most depictions of mankind's future depicted civilizations that had either collapsed (*Mad Max: Fury Road*, *The Road*, *Book of Eli*, *Elysium*, *I Am Legend*) or were in the process of collapsing (*Logan*, *Dawn of the Planet of the Apes*), with relatively few science fiction films daring to imagine a world was functional, let alone *better* than the modern world.[42] Very few people believed Vice-President Dan Quayle's infamously mangled promise that "the future will be better tomorrow."[43]

*Interstellar* does take place against the backdrop of a horrific future. It suggests that mankind is facing extinction owing to food shortages, that basic medical technology is no longer available, that the environment has turned against humanity. More than that, the dialogue repeatedly suggests that mankind actively made things worse in the decades leading up to the film. Sitting at a baseball game, Cooper idly ruminates, "In my day, people were too busy fighting over food to even play baseball." In a conversation with Professor Brand, Cooper hints at the factors that informed the government's decision to shut down NASA: "I heard they shut you down, sir, for refusing to drop bombs from the stratosphere onto starving people." This is certainly a bleak future.

*Interstellar* takes place several years after this collapse, and the film suggests that some form of civilization has reasserted itself. Schools and colleges still exist. Farming communities use advanced technology like automated harvesters. Military technology like robot soldiers and orbital drones have been repurposed to make them "socially responsible." In a meeting with Murph's teacher and principal, Cooper says, "I still pay my taxes. Where's that money go? There's no more armies." There is a strange sense of optimism running through *Interstellar*, even in the midst of a global apocalypse.

This optimism was an important part of the film for Nolan, a conscious rejection of the cynicism and nihilism associated with most apocalyptic narratives. Nolan says,

> I am an optimist, and I think this film is very optimistic. When you look at the world these characters are living in in the beginning, it's not a post-apocalyptic *Mad Max* scenario. It's bucolic, agrarian, and a simple way of life, and people are coping. When you look at people all over the world and what they have to deal with, society copes very well, and human beings are good at coming together and making the best out of situations. I worry about things, but at the same time, I have a lot of faith in people coming together to solve problems.[44]

Nolan has confessed that the breakdown of society is one of his core fears.[45] This is reflected in the characters of the Joker (*The Dark Knight*) and Bane (*The Dark Knight Rises*). But *Interstellar* remains inherently optimistic about society's capacity to endure horrific shocks and senseless brutality. There is a paradoxical optimism to its dystopia.[46]

This is a recurring theme in Nolan's work. One of the more consistent criticisms of Nolan as a writer-director is that his work is inherently nihilistic.[47] To be fair, nihilism is often a critical charge leveled at directors carving out their own identities and mapping their own moral philosophies; for example, the works of Quentin Tarantino[48] and the Coen Brothers[49] are frequently accused of nihilism. It is easy to understand how certain critics would read Nolan's work as nihilistic. *Memento* ends with the implication that Leonard is doomed to live in a self-perpetuating cycle of violence for all eternity. *The Prestige* reveals that Alfred Borden drove his wife to suicide and that Robert Angier is responsible for mass murder. *The Dark Knight* closes on the suggestion that a lie is more comforting than the truth. *Inception* suggests that the emotional catharsis offered by stories is nothing more than cynical manipulation.

But even Nolan's darker films are not completely bleak in outlook. *Memento* suggests that Leonard has doomed himself through the compromises and choices that he has made. *Insomnia* suggests that Will Dormer can find some redemption in death, and that Ellie Burr will not make the same mistakes. *The Prestige* reunites Alfred Borden with his daughter, having decided to leave the world of obsession and magic behind. *Inception* also suggests that emotional catharsis has a real value to the person affected—even if it is the result of cynical manipulation.

More than that, there is a very strong thread of humanism running through Nolan's films. He genuinely believes that people are good and that civilization is both worth protecting and strong enough to withstand attacks upon it. *Batman Begins* has Bruce firmly reject the worldview of Ra's Al Ghul, insisting that Gotham City can be redeemed. *The Dark Knight* climaxes with a scene in which the Joker tries to force the passengers aboard two ferries to blow one another up, to prove that they are nothing more than animals; despite immense pressure, nobody aboard either boat flicks the detonator to destroy the other first.

*Interstellar* is perhaps the clearest expression on Nolan's humanism. In many ways, it can be read as a pseudo-religious film, right down to the dominance of the organ on the soundtrack.[50] It has been described as a "secular end times myth."[51] *Interstellar* arrived at a time when the major Hollywood studios were attempting to figure out how to construct Biblical epics for an increasingly agnostic audience, as demonstrated by the arrival of both Darren Aronofsky's *Noah* and Ridley Scott's *Exodus: Gods and Kings* within the same year as *Interstellar*.[52] In fact, *Interstellar* is very much an exodus movie, about a chosen people being guided by an invisible hand towards their new home.[53]

In its own way, this theme ties back into the Americana that permeates *Interstellar*. Although the mission most obviously evokes the Biblical narrative of *Exodus*, it also evokes uniquely American ideals like "manifest destiny."[54] Central to American identity is the idea that the settlers are a chosen people, that their fate has been guided and shaped by some force beyond mortal reckoning that provided them with a vast continent and ensured the nation's historic good fortune.[55] The "eye of providence" gazes upon Americans even from the face of the dollar bill.[56] *Interstellar* characters frequently talk about their destiny and their purpose in similar terms, as if being directed by some outside force that guides their course. "Something sent you here," Professor Brand tells Cooper as he tries to convince the pilot to sign on to the mission. "They chose you." Cooper seems assured of the mission's potential, about what is "meant" to be as dictated by some unseen force. "Mankind was born on Earth, it was never meant to die here." Explaining the phenomenon that guided him to NASA, Cooper says, "I hesitate to term it supernatural, but it definitely wasn't scientific."

As demonstrated by *The Prestige*, Nolan is skeptical about the idea of superstition and mysticism, arguing that these are largely comforting stories constructed to make the material world bearable. It makes sense that *Interstellar* invests its faith in humanity rather than some inscrutable divine authority. The climax reveals that the wormhole was not constructed by gods or aliens, but by a more evolved form of humanity. The messages that sent Cooper and Murph to NASA were not directions from some mysterious force beyond mankind's comprehension, but instead communicated through the love of a father for his daughter. In the world of *Interstellar*, the mysterious "they" is indistinguishable from the recognizable "us." Cooper clarifies it in exposition: "They didn't bring us here at all. We brought ourselves." He elaborates, "Don't you get it yet, TARS? I brought myself here!"

*Interstellar* adopts the language of a spiritual blockbuster, to the point that it might even be (very loosely) paralleled with John Milton's *Paradise Lost*.[57] But it employs these tropes in service of what might be described as a secular humanism.[58] *Interstellar* believes that human beings are creatures of infinite potential who have the capacity to transcend their limitations when faced with impossible situations.

Stanley Kubrick's iconic science fiction film *2001: A Space Odyssey* was a huge influence on Nolan as a child.[59] Nolan borrowed several shots from *2001* for *Interstellar*, most notably the sequences set in space that fixed the camera's perspective to the plane of a rotating ship.[60] Similarly, *Interstellar*'s trips through the wormhole and into the black hole evoke the more abstract "Star Gate" sequence in *2001*.[61]

Nolan is quite candid about the stylistic debt that he owes to Kubrick's early science fiction masterpiece:

> The shadow of *2001* hangs over anything vaguely in this genre. You're daunted by it but also inspired by it. This is absolutely my attempt to recreate the feeling of going to see that film with my dad when I was seven at the Odeon in Leicester Square in London when it was re-released. That feeling of otherworldliness. That scale. You can't make this film pretending *2001* doesn't exist. You have to embrace it. There's no way not to. You have to just dive in.[62]

Nolan contends that all children should have the opportunity to watch *2001*.[63] The director's first trip to the Cannes Film Festival was not to showcase one of his own films, but to introduce a restored print of *2001* for its fiftieth anniversary.[64]

*Interstellar* feels almost like an act of catharsis in terms of Nolan's relationship to Kubrick. The comparison between Nolan and Kubrick has become a critical cliché.[65] Both directors straddled the Atlantic, cultivating an identity that is at once British and American. Both are appreciated by film fans for their "meticulous planning, fierce intelligence and ambitious reach."[66]

Nolan seems to recognize something of himself in the way that Kubrick could cultivate an *auteur* persona while working within the confines of the established studio system:

I think anyone who is working [for the studios] looks to Kubrick as the great example of someone who is able to make films that were very personal to him, very idiosyncratic, with a great degree of passion, while collaborating with the studios and making what he did fit within the economic models of their times.[67]

In terms of basic craft, there is a very tangible difference between the way in which Nolan and Kubrick approach cinema. Kubrick honed his craft as a photographer, and so his filmmaking is built around perfectly constructed shots designed to convey all the necessary information to the audience.[68] Nolan honed his skills as a director making corporate videos on a tight schedule, and so conveys narrative information through skillful editing rather than meticulous framing.[69]

One of the most enduring criticisms of Nolan's technique has been that his framing and composition are imprecise.[70] This is a fairly significant contrast with Kubrick's more meticulous craft. According to Nolan,

There is such an inherent calm and inherent trust of the one powerful image, that he makes me embarrassed with my own work, in terms of how many different shots, how many different sound effects, how many different things we'll throw at an audience to make an impression. But with Kubrick, there is such a great trust of the one correct image to calmly explain something to the audience. There can be some slowness to the editing. There's nothing frenetic about it. It's very simple. There's a trust in simple storytelling and simple image-making that actually takes massive confidence to try and emulate.[71]

Nolan made an effort to address this criticism in *Interstellar* and to adopt a cinematic style closer to Kubrick's technique than to his own traditional approach. According to Nolan, *Interstellar* "was the first time where I said, 'What is the image? What is the one shot that says everything?'" He has suggested that his eager pursuit of that one Kubrickian image in *Interstellar* is partially responsible for the film's length; whenever he tried to cut some of those images from the film, "it subverted the tone of the movie."[72]

Kubrick is a much more abstract director than Nolan. Kubrick refused to explain the basic meaning of *2001*, leading to decades of speculation from audiences about what the film actually meant.[73] While Nolan built ambiguity into the endings of *Memento* and *Inception*, his narratives tend to be very straightforward and very clearly articulated within the movie itself. *Interstellar* could reasonably be read as a more explicit and literal interpretation of (and response to) *2001*, unlikely to generate as much confusion and ambiguity as Kubrick's science fiction epic.[74]

One frequent comparison between Nolan and Kubrick fundamentally misunderstands Nolan as a filmmaker: the suggestion that both Nolan and Kubrick might be described as "cold" and "detached" directors.[75] This is perhaps an accurate description of Kubrick, who only decided against ending *2001* with a nuclear holocaust primarily because he had ended his previous film (*Doctor Strangelove, or How I Learned to Stop Worrying and Love the Bomb*) with a nuclear holocaust and did not want to repeat himself.[76] *The Washington Post* eulogized Kubrick as "cinema's unsurpassed cynic."[77]

Nolan firmly rejects the notion that his films are unemotional:

I started reading a few years ago that my films have been cold or whatever. I mean, I can tell you when we screened *Inception* for people, they'd come out crying; when we screened *The Dark Knight Rises*, people would come out in tears and the studio guys would be wiping their eyes. We've always had very emotional responses to the films, right back to *Memento*. I think Guy Pearce's performance in that film is extremely moving; my work is very technical, very precise, possibly cold, but he gives it this emotional center that affected people and it would not have been a success without that.[78]

What's interesting about Nolan's emotionality is the way in which he tends to insulate his films from raw sentimentality; his characters often seem one or two degrees removed from pure emotional engagement. This is perhaps most obvious in the way in which the director tends to imbue objects with emotional weight, allowing them to serve as literal stand-ins for emotional connections that may not intrude directly into the narrative.[79] In *Memento*, Leonard tries to remember his wife by having a prostitute interact with her possessions, and turns his body into a literal reminder of a love long lost. In *Insomnia*, Will Dormer reads emotion into the physical traces on Kay Connell's body. In *Batman Begins*, Bruce fixates upon his father's stethoscope. In *The Dark Knight*, Harvey Dent has his lucky coin. In *Inception*, Cobb uses his dead wife's top as his totem to guide him home. In *Interstellar*, Cooper connects with a daughter separated across time and space through a watch that he left behind.

Similarly, Nolanian protagonists are typically motivated by fear and loss; perhaps even the fear of loss itself.[80] In *Memento*, Leonard loses himself in a conspiracy narrative of his own making in response to the death of his wife. In *Batman Begins*, Bruce struggles to find some meaning in the world after to the death of his parents. Robert Angier's obsession with Alfred Borden in *The Prestige* is motivated by the unanswered questions around the death of his wife, questions that he pursues to the end of the film. In *Inception*, Robert Fischer seeks some reconciliation with his dead father while Dom Cobb wants to return home to his children. In *The Dark Knight Rises*, Alfred wonders whether Bruce will ever pull himself out of a pit of despair.

Nolan rarely tackles strong emotions directly. "I try not to be overly manipulative— or I try not to be obvious about it," he says. "That gives people a little more freedom to interpret the movies their way, bring what they want to it."[81] Nolan's films arguably bury their emotion in safe places, locked away and out of sight.[82] These choices have led to accusations that Nolan is a very repressed filmmaker, a director who implies or infers emotion rather than tackling it directly. Nolan's films occasionally toy with this idea, most obviously with the character of Cobb in *Inception*, whose repressed emotions keep bubbling to the surface and causing chaos for those around him.[83]

There is perhaps some truth in the observation that Nolan has difficulty properly calibrating the emotional content of his films, that he is more invested in the mechanics of cinematic storytelling than in the intangible emotional aspects. "A lot of my job is what you might call scientific," he says. "I have always tried to pour myself into the technical side of filmmaking, the things I can control. I relate to the struggle to quantify the elements that are giving you an emotional response. That always feels impossible to me. But I keep trying. A film being more than the sum of its parts is a true mystery."[84] In some ways, *Inception* was an exploration of that idea, with Cobb's team trying to mechanically engineer an emotional catharsis for Robert Fischer.

Nevertheless, Nolan's films have a very strong emotional element to them. It frequently seems like Nolan insulates his films from raw emotions like love and passion as a way of conceding their power. By telling stories about the fear of losing something beloved, or about objects that represent an unarticulated love, he implies that the love at the root of these stories is almost too strong to be tackled directly; that this unspoken love is something that would warp and break the narrative, exerting an impossible gravity that could not be contained within the frame. Love is a force with a power that can inferred by the way in which it acts upon the physical and rational universe. Like the sun, this love is so powerful that it is inadvisable to look directly at it, but its presence is keenly felt.

*Interstellar* literalizes this idea within Brand's monologue about the idea of love as a universal constant. "Love is the one thing we're capable of perceiving that transcends dimensions of time and space," Brand insists. Later, without a hint of irony, *Interstellar* suggests that love is a primal force like gravity.[85] *Interstellar* is undoubtedly Nolan's most explicitly sentimental and emotional film.[86] This arguably fits within the context of *Interstellar* being Nolan's most American film.[87] "I have been shocked to realize how much more emotional this film is," Nolan remarked about how *Interstellar* compares to the rest of his filmography.[88] His wife, producer Emma Thomas, agrees, "Whenever I read that Chris' films are 'unemotional,' I don't agree, but I do find this one to be more emotional."[89]

In a strange way, *Interstellar* is also Nolan's most personal film. When Jonathan Nolan visited his brother's production, he was surprised at how many childhood memories it evoked: "We used our *Star Wars* toys to create stop-motion space epics. On *Interstellar*, I remember standing on the set in one of the spaceships, thinking, "Isn't it odd that this feels so natural?" It felt extraordinary to me, to realize we hadn't yet made this film we'd been making since we were kids—and we were finally doing it."[90] *Interstellar* feels like the culmination of a long circuitous journey.[91]

Despite the fact that *Interstellar* began life as a film to be directed by Steven Spielberg and written by Jonathan Nolan, the finished product is undoubtedly a Christopher Nolan film. It is not an example of Nolan tackling somebody else's work in the same way that he did with *Insomnia*. In fact, Christopher and Jonathan worked separately on the script rather than collaboratively, with Christopher extensively rewriting his brother's earlier draft. Nolan says,

> Every collaboration I've had with Jonathan on a script has been different because of our different circumstances and how we worked on it. This one is very unique in that he worked for a very long time on it without me being involved and then he got very busy doing other things, so I sort of said, "Look, can I take this and combine it with some other ideas I've been working on?" So it was a bit more along the lines of him going "Okay, take a shot, see what you do." Then I showed him what I'd done and luckily he seemed reasonably happy with it. So it was a different kind of collaboration for us.[92]

Although the brothers are reluctant to break down every aspect of the script in order to allocate credit, Jonathan concedes that Christopher tweaked a lot of the middle section:

> The nature of our collaboration is just you're wise not to try to unpack too carefully or pick apart who did what or who added what. But Chris and I had both, since we were kids, thought about this kind of film. And he brought to it a perspective on what if you're reducing it to anything, you realize the second act of the film is very much composed of his ideas."[93]

Tellingly, the second act of the film contains a number of very personal cues for Nolan, in particular a fixation upon drowning and suffocation.[94] On the first planet that the team visits, made of water, they discover that the astronaut dispatched there drowned within minutes of landing. The second planet that they visit has solid clouds and a nitrogen-rich atmosphere, with Cooper almost suffocating when Mann attacks him.[95]

Nolan has acknowledged "a deep fear of the sea."[96] Asked what he would most regret leaving behind were he to journey into space, Nolan quickly responds, "I would miss the wind. I would miss air."[97]

However, the most personal themes of *Interstellar* are related to family. One of the most fundamental changes that Nolan made to his brother's script was to change the gender of Murph, to make the focal child Cooper's daughter rather than son.[98] "When I started the film, I was single, or rather, I wasn't married; my wife and I were dating at the time and didn't have kids," recalls Jonathan Nolan. "Now, I have a daughter, and it's almost impossible to watch on that level."[99]

All of Nolan's films have codenames, designed to protect them from prying eyes. Some of these codenames are more effective than others, but Nolan still likes to disguise as much of the production as possible.[100] *Interstellar* went into production with the codename *Flora's Letter*.[101] Flora Nolan is the eldest daughter of Nolan and Emma Thomas. Actor Jessica Chastain of the shoot, "One day, I noticed this girl. She was really shy and sweet. I went up to her, and she told me her name. And she was Chris' daughter. All of the clues fell into place. You had to be a little bit of a detective, and when I figured it out, I was incredibly moved: *Interstellar* is a letter to his daughter."[102]

Nolan has a long history of assigning codenames to his projects in honor of his children. *The Dark Knight* was *Rory's First Kiss*, *Inception* was *Oliver's Arrow*, *The Dark Knight Rises* was *Magnus Rex*. Nolan is quite candid about the subtext implied by that motif, and by the way in which it plays into the plot of *Interstellar*, which finds a father abandoning his children to chase his passion into space. Nolan says,

> There is a lot of guilt for that.... The very sadness of saying goodbye to people is a massive expression of the love you feel for them. For me, the film is really about being a father. The sense of your life passing you by and your kids growing up before your eyes. Very much what I felt watching Richard Linklater's *Boyhood*, an extraordinary film, which is weirdly doing the same thing in a completely different way. We are all engaged in the biggest mystery of all, which is just living through time.[103]

In fact, this arguably cuts right to the emotional core of Nolan's films. His films are worried about time slipping away, about the loss of precious moments and memories, about losing hold of something fundamental and important.[104] They repeatedly distort and dilate time, exploiting film's capacity to speed up or to slow down events in a way that mirrors human experience.[105] In these narratives, events occur out of order, or at different speeds. Cause and effect are separated from one another, characters insulated from their loved ones by time, trauma coming before violence. Most importantly, Nolan uses formal techniques to remind his audience that time is more than just an objective measurement of hours, minutes and seconds. It is the subjective experience of living in the world, where days can fly by or where minutes can seem like hours.

Russian director Andrei Tarkovsky described the art of filmmaking as "sculpting in time," although he emphasized the capturing of the passage of time within a single frame and expressed distaste for the use of editing to simulate such movement.[106] In contrast, Nolan uses editing and crosscutting to underscore the gaps that exist within perceptions of time.[107] This manipulation of time does not exist in the abstract, with Nolan's films often literalizing this distortion and dilation.[108]

This fear of lost time permeates Nolan's work.[109] He worries about characters who are frozen in time, as the world moves on around them. "I'm not afraid of death," confessed

Brand in *Interstellar*. "I'm an old physicist. I'm afraid of time." In *Memento*, Leonard explicitly compares his difficulty creating new memories to being stuck in the same moment for all eternity. "How am I supposed to heal if I can't feel time?" In *Inception*, time goes slower the deeper that the characters journey into their dreams, allowing them to live entire lifetimes while only hours have passed in the real world. In *Interstellar*, Cooper has the opposite problem, with time moving much slower as he approaches the event horizon of the black hole.

Once again, *Inception* and *Interstellar* seem to ironically mirror one another. *Inception* deconstructed the sort of cathartic feel-good ending that *Interstellar* offers without a hint of irony. Both *Inception* and *Interstellar* serve as metaphors for Nolan's commitment to filmmaking, albeit examining the trade from different angles. *Inception* explores how films distort time by condensing incredible spans of story into a few hours of runtime through the clever use of editing and speed ramping and narrative ellipses. *Interstellar* suggests the view from the opposite side of the camera, a father absent from his family for an extended period of time despite only having a few hours of film to show for it. Cinema becomes a device that bends time, both in the real world where it is produced and in the fictional world that it creates.

Nolan's early films focus on husbands and children who feel the separation of time from their loved ones: Leonard who feels separated from his wife in *Memento*, Bruce who feels separated from his parents in *Batman Begins*, Robert Angier who loses his wife in *The Prestige*, Harvey and Bruce who mourn Rachel in *The Dark Knight*.[110] Nolan's later films tend to fixate upon parents who have become separated from their children.[111] Cooper is the most obvious example in *Interstellar*, but he is mirrored in Cobb from *Inception*. Even *The Dark Knight Rises* makes a point to build its emotional catharsis around Alfred's paternal relationship to Bruce, focusing on his anxieties about his failures as a surrogate father. Mr. Dawson has a similar arc in *Dunkirk*, embarking on the rescue mission as a way of remembering and honoring his lost son.

In some ways, this shift away from widowers and orphans towards parental anxieties marks another transition in Nolan's filmmaking style. With this emphasis on parents separated from their children, his films tend to have happier endings. *Memento* ended with the implication that Leonard was destined to repeat his murder of Teddy indefinitely, without any way of moving past his anger or his grief. *Insomnia* ended with the death of Will Dormer, and perhaps even the release of all the criminals he had helped to convict. *Batman Begins* and *The Dark Knight* suggested that there would be no happy ending for Bruce Wayne.

Starting with *Inception*, the films became more optimistic in their conclusions. At the end of *Inception*, Cobb no longer cares whether he is awake or dreaming; it is an ambiguous ending, but one which allows the character his happiness.[112] At the end of *The Dark Knight Rises*, Alfred gets a chance to see that his surrogate son has let go of his anger and grief to live a better life. At the end of *Interstellar*, Cooper is reunited with Murph just in time for her to forgive him for his absence and to encourage him to continue pursuing his dream rather than remaining at her deathbed. Given how hard Cooper worked to reunite with Murph, it is debatable whether or not that emotional release is properly earned.[113]

This was a change that Christopher Nolan made to his brother's script. Originally,

Jonathan had imagined a much bleaker conclusion to the science fiction epic. His script ended with Cooper trapped inside the black hole after sending the information back to Earth; no time travel, no reunion with Murph, no pursuit of Brandt.[114] This would also arguably have been more in keeping with the original suggestion of grounding the film in close-to-real-world physics, as travel back in time is very much on the extreme fringe of what physicists believe to be possible.[115]

Nolan made a choice early in the creative process that *Interstellar* would be a story more about the power of paternal love than about the rational rules of physics. According to Jessica Chastain,

> When I watch the film now, I still don't understand everything in it, but the main part of this film isn't about science. It's about love. You have to feel it. If you go into the movie—even though the scope is large with space travel—at its core, it's a story about a father and a daughter. If you let it wash over you, that is enough.[116]

This emotional core is perhaps best reflected in the soundtrack. Nolan recruited frequent collaborator Hans Zimmer to work on the score without giving him the script or even a sense of the plot mechanics. "Before I began," Zimmer recalls, "Chris said to me, 'Hans, I will write one page of text for you. And you will give me just one day. Just write whatever comes to you from this one single page.'"[117] On the page was a short story containing only two lines of dialogue, "I'll come back" and "When?" It also included a reference to a conversation that Nolan and Zimmer had shared years earlier. "There was no movie to be made, there was no movie to discuss, we were talking about our children," Zimmer recalls. "I said, 'Once your children are born, you can never look at yourself through your eyes any more, you always look at yourself through their eyes.'"[118] These themes very clearly carry through to the finished film, echoing dialogue in the scene between Cooper and Murph right before Cooper leaves to go on that mission.

Reflecting *Interstellar*'s emphasis on emotionality above rationality, it embraces its soundtrack. Indeed, the soundtrack was so loud that it reportedly broke an IMAX cinema sound system in San Francisco.[119] Audiences complained about not being able to hear the dialogue over the organ.[120] However, the soundtrack does a lot of the movie's heavy thematic lifting, serving to represent the raw power of emotion that cannot be conveyed through expository dialogue or conveyed through familiar character beats; the soundtrack exerts the same force upon the narrative as Brand insists that love exerts upon the universe.[121]

*Interstellar* transforms its emotionalism into a strength, firmly rejecting cynical arguments that would choose rationality ahead of raw emotion. Cooper is presented as a character capable of doing incredible things in order to protect his children.[122] Cooper and Romilly dismiss Brand's suggestion to visit Edmunds' Planet because they feel that she is prioritizing her emotional attachment to Edmunds ahead of the mission; Brand concedes that they are correct in their assessment of her motives, but *Interstellar* ultimately reveals that Brand was entirely correct to choose Edmunds ahead of the more rational choice, Mann.

When Cooper and Romilly decide to visit Mann, they discover that he has set up base on a seemingly inhospitable world. "Our world is cold, stark," Mann warns his fellow travelers, using the sort of adjectives traditionally applied to rational science fiction. In theory, Mann represents a triumph of a rationalist worldview; he is a man without any emotional attachments and therefore can be trusted to make objective decisions.[123] Looking at the 12 astronauts sent on the mission, Cooper asks, "None of them had families, huh?" Brand responds, "No. No attachments. My father insisted. They all knew the odds against ever seeing another human being again." It reflects the logic behind suggestions of sending elderly people on one-way missions to colonize Mars.[124]

*Interstellar* quickly reveals that Mann is emotionally unstable. His lack of emotional attachment to anybody on Earth did not insulate him from selfishness and shortsightedness. In fact, Mann's lack of any strong bond to a human being affected by the crisis on Earth only enabled and abetted his selfishness. He lured the astronauts to his planet and potentially doomed the entire human race, because he could not conceive of empathy for anybody but himself. "I tried to do my duty, Cooper, but I knew the day that I arrived here that this place had nothing. And I resisted the temptation for years, but I knew that, if I just pressed that button, then somebody would come and save me." In contrast, Cooper's emotional connection to Murph allows him to look beyond his own immediate needs and make tough decisions to protect her. *Interstellar* suggests that humans are incapable of completely rational thought.[125] Instead, emotional connections give people something to care about beyond themselves.

In some ways, Nolan fundamentally changed *Interstellar* from its original premise. It had started as an eight-page pitch by physicists Kip Thorne and Lynda Obst, who imagined a relatively accurate feature film about the astrophysics of black holes, wormholes and time dilation.[126] After Nolan inherited the project, he made a point to maintain a lot of the attention to scientific detail that defined the original pitch.[127] Thorne was actively involved with the production and fielded questions from the director about what was and was not possible within the framework of existing scientific understanding.[128] Nolan and Thorne spent weeks arguing about the possibility of faster-than-light travel, an argument that Thorne eventually won.[129] In this way, *Interstellar* might be considered to belong to the literary tradition of "hard" science fiction, science fiction more rooted in concepts considered to be within the realm of possibility than to outlandish concepts like faster-than-light travel.[130]

This embrace and support of heightened emotional engagement is particularly interesting in the context of hard science fiction, where there is a traditional and historical tendency to value rational, scientifically verifiable facts ahead of emotional intuition.[131] It suggests a rejection of the logical aesthetic associated with hard science fiction. This narrative choice arguably represents a deliberate subversion of gendered norms in terms of science fiction, where "hard" science fiction has traditionally been considered masculine over more "soft" genres like fantasy.[132] This gendered division in science fiction is arguably reflected in stereotypical fandom activities: Male fandom tends to fixate upon trivia and statistics, while female fandom engages with character relationships and fan fiction.[133]

Nolan undermined that expectation, creating a hard science fiction story that acknowledges and valorizes emotion over supposed rationality. The film is consciously playing with gender norms by casting Matt Damon as the idealized hard science fiction hero who is helpfully named Dr. Mann. He is the archetypal protagonist of a hard science fiction narrative, a lone explorer with no human connections and with the fate of the world resting on his shoulders, facing a cold and hostile world that he must bring to heel.[134] It makes a strong statement that the most important decisions and discoveries necessary to preserving the human race are made by female characters Amelia Brand and Murphy Cooper. It is especially pointed that one of these women makes an important (and ultimately correct) decision after being reprimanded by her male colleagues for being too emotional. This can be seen as part of a broader trend in Nolan's post–*Inception* films, to develop and expand his female characters.[135]

It is important not to exaggerate the extent of this shift. Cooper is undoubtedly *Interstellar*'s protagonist and Matthew McConaughey is the credited lead in the film.[136] However, the narrative makes a point to stress that he exists largely as a "ghost" to his daughter Murph; he is a phantom and a source of inspiration.[137] In some respects, Nolan has wryly gender-flipped his conventional "lost love" role in *Interstellar*: Cooper is perhaps closer to Catherine in *Memento* or Mal in *Inception* than he is to Dormer in *Insomnia* or Bruce in *Batman Begins*. While Cooper is much more developed than other absent characters, and has much greater agency within the plot, *Interstellar* represents a clear effort by Nolan to humanize an archetype that has been one of his most common recurring tropes. In the second act, *Interstellar* treats both Cooper and Murph as protagonists within their own stories, with their own agency and arcs.

*Interstellar* is a huge movie. It is the longest of Nolan's first ten feature films, clocking in at nearly 170 minutes.[138] It had a long and storied history, stretching eight years from conception to release, with even the nearly three-hour runtime feeling like the time dilation that Cooper would have experienced close to the black hole.[139] The movie had a lavish large-scale production, which involved location shooting in both Canada and Iceland.[140] The computer rendering of the artificial black hole was so elaborate that it led to actual scientific breakthroughs.[141] Although smaller in terms of budget and cultural impact than *The Dark Knight* or *The Dark Knight Rises*, there is a credible argument to be made that *Interstellar* is the biggest movie that Nolan ever made.

And yet in spite of all of that, it remains a curiously intimate piece. It is a logical extension to the stop-motion *Space Wars* films that Nolan had filmed as an eight-year-old. More than that, it is a story of an absent father constructed by a parent worried about his absences from the lives of his children. It is a movie that opens on a slow push through a young girl's bedroom, and imagines eternity reflected in an infinite array of these bedrooms offering a glimpse of lost moments and fleeting contact. This is the central paradox of *Interstellar*, a film that it is at once an intergalactic epic and personal family film.

Like its writer-director, *Interstellar* is a film of contradictions.

# 10

## *Dunkirk*

*Dunkirk* is perhaps Nolan's most British film, at least in terms of subject matter.

Dunkirk is a uniquely British phenomenon. The evacuation of over 300,000 British and French soldiers from Dunkirk in May and June 1940 has become part of the British folk history of the Second World War. While historian Joshua Levine points out that many Americans would look upon an incident like the Battle of Dunkirk as a "terrible defeat,"[1] oral historian Penny Summerfield argues that Dunkirk occupies "an iconic place in British culture."[2] Churchill's speech to the House of Commons in the wake of the evacuation has become one of the most enduring and iconic wartime speeches in history.[3] "Dunkirk spirit" has entered the popular lexicon to describe the never-say-die attitude that often manages to snatch some minor victory from the jaws of massive defeat.[4]

Like several of Nolan's films, *Dunkirk* can trace its roots to a personal experience for the director. In the late nineties, Nolan and Thomas embarked upon a boat trip across the English Channel with a college friend. "We used to go for trips on a friend's boat at weekends, usually around the south coast, but it was Easter weekend so we had a bit of extra time and he suggested Dunkirk," recalls Thomas.[5] Weather conditions transformed what should have been a pleasant day trip into a 19-hour ordeal. Nolan: "It was a very intense experience, and no one was dropping bombs on us."[6] These events prompted an interest in the history of the actual Dunkirk evacuation that had taken place during the summer of 1940.

The idea developed and expanded over time. "It percolated for many years," Nolan says. "About five or six years ago, Emma started giving me first-hand accounts of people who had been there. That opened up something in me in terms of how you might address this story."[7] Thomas had studied history at university, and the Battle of Dunkirk had always held considerable interest to her.[8] She provided her husband and producing partner with a copy of Joshua Levine's *Forgotten Voices of Dunkirk*, which inspired him to begin assembling a narrative built from these first-hand accounts.[9] Levine became a historical consultant on the film, and even wrote a book about the film's relationship with the historical events that inspired it.[10]

Nolan and Thomas were keenly aware of the fact that *Dunkirk* would deal with what amounted to part of British mythology and identity. "As British people, it carries a very special resonance, there's no question," Nolan says.[11] In pitching the film to Warner Brothers, both Nolan and Thomas were adamant that it had to feature British actors and could not cast American performers.[12] The cast ultimately featured in *Dunkirk* would be predominantly British.[13]

The Britishness of *Dunkirk* provides a clear contrast with the strong Americana of *Interstellar*. If *Batman Begins* and *The Prestige* played with the relationship between Nolan's two homes *within* their individual narratives and productions, *Interstellar* and *Dunkirk* provide an interesting conversation across two distinct films. In some ways, in these successive films, Nolan is consciously playing with the national myths of the two countries that he considers to be home.[14] The mythic place that the evacuation of Dunkirk holds in British popular consciousness could be said to mirror the esteem in which American popular culture holds NASA and the space race.

In terms of this dichotomy between the two films, it is perhaps informative that *Interstellar* is a science fiction film that unfolds explicitly in the future while *Dunkirk* is the first historical film in Nolan's filmography. The futuristic, high-concept premise of *Interstellar* could be seen to represent the United States as a nation that has historically been defined by its obsession with the future.[15] In contrast, the period setting of *Dunkirk* might be seen to reflect Britain's longstanding engagement with its own past as a source of strength and identity in an increasingly uncertain world.[16] *Interstellar* is about an American-led mission to save the human race.[17] In contrast, *Dunkirk* is about a historical battle in which the mere act of survival itself becomes a substitute for victory.[18]

Nolan's films are typically about myths and stories, whether those constructed by individuals or by larger entities, whether personal or political: *Following* is about a frame job, trapping the lead character in a compelling and convincing story; *Memento* is about a man who constructs his own narrative on the edge of the American frontier; *Insomnia* is about two competing narratives of two different crimes; the *Dark Knight* trilogy is about the construction, deconstruction and reconstruction of a mythology by a larger culture; *Inception* is about a man who journeys through dreams; *Interstellar* is about the resurrection of NASA to save mankind.

*Dunkirk* stands out because it is the first of these films to tackle a myth anchored firmly in reality. Nolan: "I think the reason I was drawn to Dunkirk was not necessarily those qualities of it being historical, of it being an epic—it was about the story. The story just grabbed me."[19] Nolan's films always suggest a tension between objective and subjective reality, between how events happened and how they are perceived to have happened, but *Dunkirk* is Nolan's first film in which an objective reality actually exists beyond the confines of the movie itself. "This is the first time I've taken on a real-life event, and there's a huge responsibility that comes with that," he states.[20]

While in pre-production, Nolan made a point to meet with veterans of the Battle of Dunkirk and hear their first-hand accounts.[21] Several incidents in the film are drawn directly from personal accounts, most notably the sequence in which a despondent soldier sheds his supplies and wades into the water in a doomed attempt to swim home.[22] When the film was finished, the world premiere was attended by veterans of the Battle of Dunkirk,[23] with some moved to tears by the feature film.[24] Actor Kenneth Branagh joked that the veterans' biggest criticism of the film was that it was louder than the battle that had inspired it.[25]

However, Nolan was also interested in exploring the gaps that exist between the mythic construct and the historical reality of the evacuation of Dunkirk: "You receive the story first in its more mythic, somewhat oversimplified terms. The more you find out about the reality of the evacuation, the more you find out about the messy historical truth of the thing."[26] In this way, *Dunkirk* feels very much like an extrapolation of the exploration of personal myths in *Memento* and of cultural myths in *The Dark Knight*, exploring similar thematic ground through the lens of history.

One of *Dunkirk*'s most interesting aspects is how it eschews the conventions that audiences have come to expect from war movies. In publicity leading up to *Dunkirk*'s release, Nolan was adamant that it should not be treated as a conventional war film.[27] "I didn't view this as a war film," he said. "I viewed it as a survival story."[28] The cinematic language of *Dunkirk* avoids many of the familiar beats of war movies; nobody ever presents a picture of their sweetheart, no recruit outlines "the first thing [they're] gonna do when [they] get home…," no officers provide neat exposition over lovingly detailed maps for the audience's benefit.[29] The subject matter of *Dunkirk* might be war, but its genre defies easy classification.

In some respects, this fits with Nolan's particular strengths and interests. He has come to be classified as a "genre" director, with a strong interest in *noir* and science fiction.[30] His decision to follow the epic science fiction movie *Interstellar* with a historical war movie was seen as surprising by some Internet observers for this reason.[31] But Nolan's commitment to suspense is a consistent through-line in his career, and it makes sense that he would frame *Dunkirk* in these terms.

Nolan consulted classic war movies during pre-production. He even borrowed Steven Spielberg's own print of *Saving Private Ryan*, although he made a choice to develop his film in other directions so as to avoid competing with Spielberg.[32] As usual, Nolan cited a number of key inspirations for his film: *Greed, Sunrise, All Quiet on the Western Front, Foreign Correspondent, The Wages of Fear, The Battle of Algiers, Ryan's Daughter, Alien, Chariots of Fire, Speed, Unstoppable*.[33] Only two of these films could be considered war films in the traditional sense, with a much greater emphasis on the art of creating and maintaining suspense.[34] On *Dunkirk*, Nolan's biggest influence in terms of storytelling was completely removed from the war genre: "*Wages of Fear* was the most direct influence on how we went about shooting the film, in thinking about things in suspense terms."[35]

Divorced from its historical context, *Dunkirk* can be seen as something close to a survival horror film.[36] It is a story about attractive young characters struggling to stay alive in a hostile environment while stalked by a hazily defined and largely unseen threat. The opening scenes set the tone, when Tommy and his friends are ambushed while walking through the eponymous town. Nolan shoots the scene in such a way as to evoke panic and terror: The enemy soldiers are unseen, and the camera puts the audience in the position of this unseen predator as it chases Tommy though the urban environment out towards the beach.[37]

This suspense plays throughout the film. *Dunkirk* literally has a ticking clock on the soundtrack, Nolan providing recordings of his own watches to help Hans Zimmer build a distinctive soundscape.[38] The soundtrack makes use of the aural illusion known as "the Shepard tone" in order to create the sensation that the pitch is constantly rising, feeding into this idea of constantly escalating tension.[39] The Shepard tone had been incorporated into several of Nolan's earlier works: Composer David Julyan had employed it on *The*

*Prestige*[40] and sound editor Richard King had used it in the sound design of the Batpod in *The Dark Knight*.[41] However, Nolan incorporated the Shepard tone into the narrative mechanisms of *Dunkirk*. "I wrote the script according to that principle," he remarks. "I interwove the three timelines in such a way that there's a continual feeling of intensity. Increasing intensity. So I wanted to build the music on similar mathematical principals. So there's a fusion of music and sound effects and picture that we've never been able to achieve before."[42]

*Dunkirk* was designed to synchronize the sound design to the soundtrack, as if to give the film a heartbeat that might echo in the score. "Richard gave the music department his engine tracks for the boats, so that they could be put into exact rhythm with the music and with this ticking clock," Nolan reveals. "Everything is in sync. It's the furthest we've gone with the tight synchronization or the inextricable linking of sound, music and picture. That's one of the reasons why the film is short. I sort of realized that it would be exhausting for an audience to maintain for too long."[43]

*Dunkirk* is a relatively short film, particularly by the standards of Nolan's filmography. It is the director's shortest film since *Following*.[44] This is particularly noticeable given that *Dunkirk* followed *The Dark Knight Rises* and *Interstellar*, his two longest films.[45] This abbreviated length was a choice on the part of the writer-director. "It was about half the length," he says. "It was a 76-page script, a very short script. I really wanted to be telling the story through images, first and foremost. For me, this film was always going to play like the third act of a bigger film."[46] Nolan stresses that *Dunkirk* was always structured to play like the climax of a film like *The Dark Knight Rises* or *Interstellar*: "What I wanted to do was take what I call the snowballing effect of the third act of my other films, where parallel storylines start to be more than the sum of their parts, and I wanted to try to make the entire film that way and strip the film of conventional theatrics."[47]

*Dunkirk* is a film that cuts away its first two acts in order to reach a state of perpetual climax.[48] Nolan has a longstanding preference for crosscutting as a narrative technique, both as a tool to enable protective editing and as a means to escalate tension within a narrative. In some ways, *Dunkirk* is the culmination of this approach to filmmaking: It is an entire film that is effectively one gigantic crosscut sequence, in contrast to Nolan's other films which are stories that build towards (and are occasionally interspersed with) such sequences. *Dunkirk* takes a conventional Nolan narrative and then strips out everything that is not climax. When Emma Thomas first saw the film, she told her husband, "This, to me, is like an art house movie pretending to be a studio film." He responded, "You can't tell anyone that, you can't tell the studio that."[49] But many critics made a note of the movie's art house tendencies upon its release.[50]

In keeping with this experimental style, Nolan originally considered filming *Dunkirk* without a script. "I said, 'I don't want a script,'" Nolan reveals. "Because I just want to show it, it's almost like I want to just stage it. And film it. And Emma looked at me like I was a bit crazy and was like, okay, that's not really gonna work."[51] Thomas recalls her reaction being a bit blunter: "My immediate response was, 'You're insane.'" She elaborates, "But I completely understood where he was coming from. He had said from the beginning that he wanted to do something experimental and explore the boundaries of cinema."[52]

*Dunkirk* is an atypical historical film in a number of respects. Most obviously, it avoids showcasing its setting or its world-building. There is very little dialogue or exposition.

Much of the dialogue is obscured or distorted by ambient noise.[53] Nolan likened the storytelling in *Dunkirk* to the manner in which silent films conveyed narrative:

> The stripped-down running time, the very short script, really was a function of there being so little dialogue in the film. But you only have to look at the silent era to understand how movies weren't built on dialogue, they were built on the image. It's a powerful argument for trying to tell the story that way.[54]

After its release, online film fans reedited *Dunkirk* as a silent movie to showcase the efficiency of its visual storytelling independent of dialogue.[55]

In some ways, this could be seen as a larger trend within this stretch of Nolan's filmography, with the director pushing himself to improve and to broaden his technique. Although not a dialogue stylist in the same manner as Quentin Tarantino, Nolan has conventionally been seen a director who leans heavily on dialogue as a storytelling tool. He is very fond of exposition. The success of *Batman Begins* and *The Dark Knight* arguably popularized the trend of incorporating thematic exposition into blockbusters through dialogue.[56] Nolan has said that *Inception* is a story that is built around very carefully structured and delivered exposition.[57] So the conscious move away from dialogue within *Dunkirk* reflects his willingness to continually push himself as a filmmaker and to respond to perceived weaknesses within his work[58]:

> I took a lot of risks and did a lot of things that were outside my comfort zone with *Dunkirk*. I removed a lot of my safety nets, particularly in the screenwriting area where I'd become, I think, fairly proficient in the use of dialogue to express backstory and character. And when I wrote this screenplay, I decided to remove all that and look at it in a different way.[59]

This lends *Dunkirk* an almost abstract quality. One of the issues with building a gigantic summer blockbuster around the evacuation of Dunkirk was that the events were largely unknown to American filmgoers. "Some at Warner Bros knew the events, or knew them vaguely, some of them had never heard of them at all," Nolan says of his original pitch.[60] In the build-up to the release of the film, there was some concern that audiences would be unfamiliar with the cultural context of the story.[61] In fact, the film's stubborn refusal to provide exposition or background information led to criticism from some reviewers.[62] There is some small suggestion that *Dunkirk*'s refusal to provide the sort of exposition expected in a war movie may have harmed its chances with awards voters.[63]

*Dunkirk* throws the audience into the situation without providing any superfluous context or unnecessary detail. Despite the painstaking attention to detail involved in the production, there is a sense watching *Dunkirk* that the movie is somewhat removed from the particulars of the events that it is depicting. It seems almost like an expanded metaphor for the insanity of war, as perceived by those caught in the midst of it. Nolan says of his approach, "I wanted to give the audience the point of view of someone who didn't necessarily understand or couldn't possibly know the global or geopolitical implications of the event they were passing through."[64]

*Dunkirk* depicts the beach as a place where the laws of reason and sanity are suspended. As boats and planes cross the channel to support the troops, they can only perceive the beach as a cloud of black smoke rising ominously on the horizon. It is a horror and a monstrosity, but they cannot avert their eyes. "There's no hiding from this," Mr. Dawson warns the Shivering Sailor, and he is speaking abstractly as much as literally.

Indeed, Mr. Dawson suggests his own moral responsibility for travelling to Dunkirk: He wonders, "Men my age dictate this war. Why are we allowed to send our children to fight it?"

This absurdity is perhaps best expressed in the imagery on the beach, the soldiers lining up facing the sea, waiting for ships that may never come and arranged in such a way as to make them easy prey for enemy fighters. The concept of "the Mole" allowed the *Dunkirk* script to click into place for Nolan:

> It's eight feet wide, a kilometer long, and thousands of men had to queue up on this thing, not knowing whether there was a boat at the end of it. Dive bombers would come and shoot them and bomb them. They had nowhere to go. They just had to stand out there, and take it. That's in image that, once I heard about it, I felt like, "That's gotta be on film. Somebody has to put that on film." Because it's just horrifying and unique.[65]

But the appeal of the Mole was not its basis in historical fact, but its metaphorical and abstract quality. "The mole represents this Kafka-esque and incredibly relatable nightmare," Nolan insists. "The problem with war films in general is that most of us are lucky enough to not have to experience those events. So sometimes it's hard to relate. But we've all found ourselves in the pedestrian and everyday version of getting in some ridiculous line. And you don't know who to ask and you don't know what the hell is going on."[66] This gets to the heart of how *Dunkirk* approaches its subject matter, in a manner that is designed to ground the horrors of war in subjective personal experiences and powerful abstract imagery rather than trivia and factoids. Nolan tried to provide the audience with a visceral and emotional experience.[67]

This carries over to how he approaches the characters. They are decidedly underdeveloped and underexplored. Many are anonymous to the audience, and the audience would be forgiven for not catching the names of some of the characters who *are* named.[68] The lead character (such as there is a lead character) is named "Tommy," which was a slang nickname for British infantrymen; the equivalent would be for an American war movie to name its protagonist "Joe."[69] The *Dunkirk* characters are very much abstractions, much like the environment around them.

Roger Ebert argued that cinema is "the most powerful empathy machine in all the arts."[70] There is some limited scientific research to support this argument, suggesting that watching movies can build empathy.[71] This makes a certain amount of sense: The gigantic screen becomes a window into another world, an opportunity for audiences to glimpse lives and experiences beyond their own immediate surroundings. This is another small reason why diversity in popular culture is desirable; it allows audiences to build empathy with people who do not look like them or share their experiences.[72] Recent years have seen a considerable push on prestigious and high-profile movies emphasizing the importance of empathy for experiences outside those of the audience.[73] In its own way, *Dunkirk* deserves to be part of that conversation, serving as an exploration of the most primal forms of empathy and compassion.

Nolan and Thomas made an effort to avoid casting recognizable names and faces. According to Thomas,

> At the very beginning, we had told them that we only were going to cast completely fresh faces. We, of course, ended up managing to nab some amazing actors with vast experience, but certainly, at the beginning, we had said that we didn't want to have any name actors.[74]

There is some small irony in the fact that Nolan cast international superstar Harry Styles in a supporting role, despite claiming not to know much about his public profile.[75] Tom Hardy, probably the most bankable actor in the cast, spends the overwhelming majority of the film with a mask obscuring his features.[76]

This anonymity effectively prevents the audience from forming an empathic bond with the characters based on their identity or their history. Instead, it creates a more visceral and immediate emotional connection based on the experiences through which these people are living. "*Dunkirk* is all about physical process, all about tension in the moment, not backstories," says Nolan. "It's all about 'Can this guy get across a plank over this hole?' We care about him. We don't want him to fall down. We care about these people because we're human beings and we have that basic empathy."[77] In some ways, this contextualizes *Dunkirk* as a spiritual companion to its fellow Best Picture nominees *Get Out* and *The Shape of Water*, in that it asks the audience to invest their empathy in something very different from their everyday experiences.

Nolan's emphasis on that primal emotional connection in *Dunkirk* could be seen as a development of the approach that he adopted with *Interstellar*. Arguably Nolan's most overtly emotional narrative, *Interstellar* is rooted in the emotional separation of a family and arguing that love is a force at work in the universe equivalent to gravity or time. *Dunkirk* adopts a similar approach, albeit with less exposition and backstory. *Dunkirk* asks (and trusts) the audience to make a primal emotional connection with the characters based purely on the horrors that they are experiencing rather than the finer details of their day-to-day lives. Nolan:

> What we decided to do was to really try and live in the moment of the experience ... the very immediate and human desire to survive. It's the most human movie I've ever made because it's about the desire for survival. We wanted to tackle that and make what I refer to as a very present tense narrative where you're in the moment with the characters. You're not necessarily spending too much time discussing who they were before or who they will be after.[78]

The idea is that these characters are human beings, and so are deserving of empathy and compassion by virtue of that basic fact rather than by any particulars of their identities or backgrounds.

In many ways, the experiences and motivations of *Dunkirk*'s characters are intentionally kept basic. "Home" is something of an arc word playing across the film, even though none of the soldiers outline exactly where "home" is in any greater detail than Great Britain. "Home" is an abstract concept, a life that exists beyond the hell of this particular battlefield. Similarly, *Dunkirk* places a strong emphasis on the fear of drowning. Even more than gunfire or artillery shells, the water seems to threaten to swallow various characters whole; the downed fighter, the men on the sinking ship, the water filling the cargo hold, the medical transport leaning in against the jetty. There is a visceral quality to the sequences in which characters struggle underwater.[79]

In keeping with the abstract sensibility of the film, these are recurring motifs in Nolan's work. Many of his protagonists are desperately looking to get "home," whether in a literal or an abstract manner.[80] Drowning and suffocation recur within Nolan's filmography, with characters often trapped underwater struggling to breathe.[81] In some ways, *Dunkirk* serves to bring these two recurring motifs back around; "home" represents life outside this hell, while drowning represents perhaps the most basic form of death as the victim takes his last gasp of air.[82]

For all the emphasis that *Dunkirk* places on the idea of empathy, it has received criticism for issues of representation. Some critics objected to the almost complete absence of women.[83] Others responded to the perceived lack of minorities among the soldiers on the beach.[84] In many ways, this reflects a broader cultural change, as film criticism in the twenty-first century becomes more socially conscious and more cognizant of issues around race and gender.[85] Modern directors and writers are more open to criticisms on the basis of representation and diversity than their predecessors.[86]

These criticisms seem somewhat short-sighted. The standard criticism is that there were troops from all over the British Empire at the beach, and so the demographics should have been more diverse than those depicted on film. However, historical data suggest that the troops from India would only have represented "a few hundred among hundreds of thousands" at the beach, a fraction of one percent.[87] Given this information, and the film's narrow subjective focus on a handful of soldiers from a very specific set of military divisions among the stranded British forces, it does not seem unreasonable that *Dunkirk* should feature a predominantly white cast.[88]

While these criticisms do not necessarily hold true for *Dunkirk*, they do draw attention to the relative lack of non-white characters in Nolan's larger filmography. His casts tend to be predominantly white, particularly lead and primary characters.[89] That said, there are cases where it seems like Nolan is consciously avoiding certain racial tropes and clichés in his stories.[90] In this respect, there is some small sense that he is improving as his filmography develops, with later films showing more diverse ensembles than earlier films.[91] Still, this is an obvious recurring blind spot in his filmography. Given his efforts to address valid criticisms of his work (whether his perceived lack of emotion or his relative lack of strong female characters) in *The Dark Knight Rises*, *Interstellar* and *Dunkirk*, there is a possibility that he may address this disparity in subsequent films.

Leaving aside the issue of diversity, *Dunkirk* is consciously empathic, designed to provoke a strong emotional response. Its lack of interest in the identities of its central characters and its subversion of familiar war movie tropes serve as a firm rejection of the familiar framework of wartime mythology. Nolan's films consciously pick at and deconstruct myths and narratives, and *Dunkirk* often plays like a brutal deconstruction of the heroic masculine conventions of war stories. In spite (if not because) of its attention to the subjective experience of warfare, it is an absurdist anti-war parable.

An observation often attributed to François Truffaut suggests that it is impossible to make a film that is truly anti-war.[92] In relation to his plans to make a film about the Battle of Algiers, Truffaut could not justify the decision; he argued that "to show something is to ennoble it."[93] There is some truth in this idea. Most war movies in some way glorify combat and present warfare as an act of valor. The armed forces have historically used Hollywood productions as a recruitment tool.[94] Even in films that depict war or combat in a cynical light, popular culture is (understandably and defensibly) conditioned to respect the sacrifices and heroism of soldiers in those situations.[95] On top of all these issues, *Dunkirk* unfolds in the context of the Second World War, which is one of the few major international conflicts that has developed a mythology as a just or moral war.[96]

*Dunkirk* subverts these expectations in a number of different ways. In keeping with its recurring abstraction of war movie conventions, the German soldiers are seldom identified by nationality.[97] Instead, the movie repeatedly defines them as "the enemy," a choice that generated considerable debate and interest.[98] The German soldiers are kept largely out of frame, often sniping at the characters from a distance.[99] Indeed, the propaganda flier at the start of the film was even redesigned from its historical inspiration to remove an explicit reference to the Germans.[100]

Actor Mark Rylance confirms that this was a conscious decision designed to avoid the cliché of the evil Germans and to deny the movie the satisfaction of seeing those villains vanquished. Rylance:

> We had a conversation when [Nolan] approached me about whether the Germans should ever be referred to. He took out any reference to the Germans and just called them "the enemy," which I thought was really good in that it's not a history lesson. And even when you think about it, the Second World War was not a war between the German people and the English people. It was a war against the idea of fascism, the idea that one man, a dictator in this case, or one race of being, the Aryan race, is better than another individual or race of people. And the English had taken advantage of that idea just as much as the Germans in our treatment of African slaves, which was just as cruel and vicious.[101]

Nazis provide neat cinematic shorthand for cardboard villains.[102] *Dunkirk* sidesteps the cathartic pleasures a rigidly defined villain.

*Dunkirk* is also notable as a relatively rare war film that features young actors playing soldiers close to the age of those who would have served in combat.[103] The primary cast was relatively young when filming the movie; Fionn Whitehead was 20 working on the film and Harry Styles was 23. Nolan said of the casting:

> For me making this film, they're very much boys, and that's an important part of the film and what the film is....[104] It was important to me to not do the usual Hollywood thing of having 30-year-olds playing 19-year-olds. We still send our children out to fight wars.... An 18- or 19-year-old doesn't have an expectation of taking on the whole German army. They just don't want to get killed.[105]

In keeping with that portrayal of young soldiers, *Dunkirk* consciously and repeatedly deconstructs the heroic (and conventionally masculine) narratives of war. Even superficially, this is not a war story about a noble battle, whether ending in victory or defeat. Instead, *Dunkirk* is the story of an army in retreat.[106] It is not a story of conventional heroism and valor, with soldiers risking their lives for the greater good. Instead, as David Bordwell points out, "a cynic could call the movie *Profiles in Cowardice*."[107] The primary characters spend the entire movie trying desperately to get away from combat, rather than running towards it. They lie, they bluff, they use wounded soldiers as props, they abandon their units. *Dunkirk* presents an environment in which the only sane response is the breakdown of traditional military structures and a desperate scramble to stay alive.[108]

*Dunkirk* eschews narratives of military heroism for stories of human frailty. The evacuating soldiers rarely acquit themselves with the sort of dignity and grace under pressure associated with military officers in narratives like this; instead, their actions are panicked and desperate.[109] An anonymous French soldier steals the uniform of a dead British soldier to gain passage on a transport out of the combat zone; the Shivering Sailor pushes young George down the stairs, giving him a concussion that leads to his death; when there is too much weight in the boat to ferry everybody to safety, Alex immediately starts planning to throw other soldiers overboard.[110] *Dunkirk* is not a glorious ode to how combat provides an avenue for men to prove themselves. Instead, it is an examination of how warfare reduces and diminishes men, how it strips away their reason and their humanity.

But it also makes a point never to judge these characters for their actions. While never flinching from the horror of these decisions and these actions, *Dunkirk* refuses to condemn its characters for making these choices in the heat of the moment. The anonymous French soldier is treated with compassion, to the point that Alex seems genuinely concerned about him in their final moments together despite threatening to throw him overboard a short time earlier.[111] The Shivering Sailor receives compassion rather than contempt from both Mr. Dawson and Peter, despite his responsibility for George's death.[112] On arriving in Britain, Alex is ashamed of everything that happened in Dunkirk, while the film makes a point to stress that the public has forgiven them.[113]

This juxtaposition between cruelty and compassion, the decision to respond to horror with empathy, underscores the humanism at the heart of Nolan's filmmaking. It has become a critical cliché to describe Nolan as "cold"[114] or "emotionally distant,"[115] which may explain the stock comparisons between Nolan and Kubrick.[116] Nevertheless, this feels like a reductive approach to the director's storytelling. Like *Interstellar* before it, *Dunkirk* is a narrative experience built largely around emotion. It acknowledges its characters' flaws, but also forgives them. *Dunkirk* condemns war as something horrific and grotesque, but never condemns those who have lived through it for the choices that they made to survive.[117] *Dunkirk*'s presentation of war as an environment in which all laws of civilization have been suspended fits with Nolan's recurring anxiety about the collapse of civic order into anarchy.[118]

*Dunkirk*'s politics would become a matter of some discussion. The film was developed and released in the context of a political maelstrom, with a wave of right-wing nostalgic populism sweeping through the United States and Europe.[119] Votes for Donald Trump and Brexit in 2016 affirmed that large sections of the British and American publics yearned to recapture some glorious (and likely imagined) past.[120] In this context, any major cinematic release about the Second World War was likely to generate discussion and discourse, given the status of the Second World War as a justified or heroic conflict in contrast to the ambiguity of Vietnam, Afghanistan and Iraq.[121]

With this in mind, it makes sense that *Dunkirk* was greeted with considerable political skepticism. It was in production during the campaign leading up to the Brexit referendum, wherein the British public voted to become the first nation to leave the European Union.[122] It was released at a time when the British government and the British public were still trying to figure out what it meant for a nation to withdraw from the European Union.[123] *Dunkirk* was a film designed to evoke memories that had a significant patriotic weight for the British public, at a time when those memories had formed the cornerstone of the campaign to leave the European Union.[124] Most superficially, *Dunkirk* was a film about the literal withdrawal of British troops from a German-dominated Europe. As such, *Dunkirk* practically begged to be read in the broader context of Brexit.[125]

In the aftermath of the film's release, it became something of a right-wing rallying cry.[126] Many pro-Brexit commentators and publishers sought to hijack the film as validation of their political viewpoint.[127] Nigel Farage, one of the key architects of the Brexit vote, argued that all British "youngsters" should see *Dunkirk* to instill in them the proper patriotic values.[128] More broadly, Nolan was criticized in certain quarters as a right-wing filmmaker.[129] However, much like criticisms of *The Dark Knight Rises* that read it as an attack upon movements like Occupy Wall Street, this is a very superficial reading.

Most obviously, *Dunkirk* repeatedly stresses the importance of other nations to the war effort. The introductory scene establishes that it is French soldiers holding the line and repelling the advancing enemy.[130] One of the primary characters on the beach is subsequently revealed to have been a French soldier. When Alex leads his friends to the boat stranded on the beach, they discover that the captain is Dutch. "Merchant navy," the flustered pilot responds. "Here to pick you up. To help you." The sequences with Commander Bolton emphasize the importance of the French to holding the port of Dunkirk. Commander Bolton's final decision is a refusal to abandon those foreign soldiers in the midst of the evacuation of British troops. "I'm staying. For the French."[131] The extended excerpt from Churchill's iconic "We shall fight on the beaches" speech makes a point to include Churchill's appeal to "the New World, with all its power and might," a transparent and desperate plea for American support.[132] That passage is often overlooked in more blatantly nationalistic samples and recreations of the speech.[133]

More to the point, *Dunkirk* represents a firm rejection of unquestioning nationalism. It is about attempts to recover from a catastrophic disaster, rather than about committing unreservedly to a destructive course of action. *Dunkirk* arguably has more in common with attempts to prevent (or minimize the inevitable consequences of) Brexit then with the campaign itself.[134] *Dunkirk* is not the story of nationalist triumph as so many right-wing pundits have described it, is the story of survival in the face of a crippling and humiliating defeat.[135]

Nolan has largely avoided getting drawn into discussions about how *Dunkirk* engages with the Brexit debate:

> Dunkirk is an extraordinary story and it's always served as something of a Rorschach test: different people interpret it in different ways. Interpreting the events of 1940 through a modern lens is frankly disrespectful to the people who lived through the real-life events. This is something that happened in 1940, not something that's happening in 2017. Brexit happened while we were shooting and was as much a surprise to us as to everybody else.... As a filmmaker, you can't control the world that your film goes out into.[136]

This is a very fair observation, particularly given the extended production and release cycles for feature films produced on this scale.

At the same time, Nolan offers a somewhat pointed observation on the attempted appropriation of the narrative of Dunkirk by certain political operators. Nolan reflects of the film's potential relevance to modern events,

> Now if you're asking me about what I prefer to call the resonance of the story, to me it's about European unity, the desperate attempt to keep the French in the war. I think the confusion we see today between patriotism and nationalism is extremely tricky. I don't believe that we want any political faction to own patriotism, or to own Dunkirk. These are points of national pride.[137]

Nolan deserves some credit for the way in which his films have resonated with the broader political climate.

From Nolan's perspective, the politics of *Dunkirk* are more abstract and less specific:

> What was important to me, what I get from the story, and why I think it's a very important story to tell now, I think we live in an era that overemphasizes individuality at the expense of what we can do

together. Whether you're talking about in American industry, the fetishization of the individual billionaire vs. a union, just to give you one example. What *Dunkirk* shows you is: We can do so much more with communal heroism. That's what makes it an unusual war story, of civilians and military coming together. But I think that's why it resonates. We are stronger working together, and for some reason, that's become unfashionable.[138]

In some ways, this could be seen as a logical extension of Nolan's approach to the Batman mythos in the *Dark Knight* trilogy, in which the legend of Batman was treated as something maintained and developed by an entire community rather than by a single individual.[139] *Dunkirk* approaches its subject in such a way as to minimize individual contributions and to underscore the net effect of interactions of large groups of people working in collaboration; many of the characters remain anonymous, and most of its primary cast are unknown actors.[140] Critic Matt Zoller Seitz describes *Dunkirk* as "an Ant Farm Picture," and it is an apt description of how the movie's storytelling works.[141] Even Churchill, who looms large over the British cultural memory of the Second World War, is noticeably absent. Instead of using Churchill's later recording of the "We shall fight on the beaches" speech, *Dunkirk* opts to put his words in the mouth of a traumatized young soldier.

This sense of community spirit is reflected in the film's non-linear narrative, specifically in the contours and specifics of that non-linear narrative. Nolan has largely defined himself as a non-linear filmmaker, with audiences and critics expecting temporal games in each of his films.[142] *The Dark Knight* remains his only *truly* linear film, barring a few quick flashback cuts. It is no surprise that Nolan's Second World War epic would adopt his unique strand of non-linear storytelling.[143] Nolan references that narrative structure as his gateway into the story. "I spent some time trying to figure out a structural device that would allow me to retain subjectivity throughout the entire movie," he confesses. "Once I had that structure, that's when I started to write."[144]

*Dunkirk*'s non-linear structure remains one of its most controversial and divisive aspects.[145] Even positive reviews made reference to non-linear storytelling as a perceived narrative crutch employed by the director.[146] The non-linear structure was often treated as a complication in coverage of the film, something that existed quite apart from the story being told.[147]

However, it is worth reflecting on the particulars of this non-linear structure. *Dunkirk* essentially follow three different threads: "The Mole," in which Tommy desperately tries to escape the beach; "The Sea," in which Mr. Dawson crosses the English Channel to help bring soldiers home, and "The Air," in which Farrier flies his fighter plane across the English Channel to provide cover for the evacuation. However, logic insists that these three plots must cover varying amounts of time. The soldiers were longer on the beach than Mr. Dawson was in his boat, and it would take Mr. Dawson longer to cross the English Channel in the *Moonstone* than it would for Farrier in his Spitfire. As such, there is a pragmatic justification for the fact that "The Mole" unfolds over a week, "The Sea" unfolds over a day, and "The Air" unfolds over an hour.[148]

However, what is interesting about the way in which *Dunkirk* balances these storylines is the decision to intercut them. There are other mechanisms to incorporate the necessary information and the required beats into a story like this, such as the use of flashback or exposition.[149] Instead, *Dunkirk* chooses to cut dramatically and dynamically between its three central story threads, offering the audience little indication in the transition that they are moving forward or backwards in time. Flashbacks tend to halt the forward momentum of a film to flesh out the backstory, but *Dunkirk* uses these rapid transitions to propel the movie forward as it jumps between these three storylines and temporal spaces.[150]

*Dunkirk* is a film very invested in the subjective experience of those people living through the event, and hoping to give the audience some emotional sense of what it might be like to process such happenings. Nolan is very invested in the idea of subjectivity, whether in the narratives that characters choose for themselves or the endings that he leaves open for his audiences:

> The tension between subjective storytelling and sort of the bigger picture is always a challenge in any film, particularly when you're taking on, which I never have done before, historical reality. So I really wanted to be on that beach with those guys. I wanted the audience to feel like they are there.[151]

Nolan's films often feature a conflict between a character's subjective interpretation of events and the objective reality of this situation.[152] This often manifests itself in terms of a fractured sense of time; time literally moving at a different pace for these characters than it does for the larger world. This is a recurring motif for Nolan as a filmmaker, whether metaphorically (Leonard in *Memento*[153]) or literally (Cooper in *Interstellar*[154]). This reflects the subjective human experience of time, where time seems to move at different rates for different people in different circumstances, regardless of objective and verifiable measurements imposed upon it.[155]

The timelines within *Dunkirk* create pocket universes for each of the characters, a barrier between the experiences of individuals like Tommy and Mr. Dawson. For most of the film, the characters seem to operate within different worlds isolated from each other, largely independent and disconnected.[156] There is no tangible connection between Tommy's efforts to get on that medical evacuation ship and Farrier's dogfight over the British Channel. In terms of chronology, the outcome of Tommy's earliest attempts to escape the beach had already been decided long before Farrier climbed into his cockpit. The first half of the film even has these plotlines and characters overlap and intersect with one another, but in fleeting ways that seem to emphasize how disconnected they all are.[157]

However, the climax of the film brings all of these plot threads together so that these individual timelines are synched up. At the height of the evacuation, the three timelines converge so that all the central characters are experiencing time at the same rate. Against all odds, it seems like these three different subjective viewpoints are witnessing the same event in the same place at the same time. It is a moment at which all these different threads are wound up together. Given Nolan has used the musical Shepard tone as a metaphor for the film's storytelling, the climax might be described as a symphony in which the various elements converge.[158] This union of the three narrative threads at the climax is mirrored on the soundtrack, when Hans Zimmer weds three separate Shepard tones together to create a harmony reflecting the intersections of the various characters and timelines.[159]

Even more striking is the manner in which the timelines then diverge once again. The characters unite at the climax, then quickly disassemble and go their own ways. Farrier's closing scenes take place only a few moments after the climax, as he is taken prisoner on the beach, intercut with Mr. Dawson's experiences the next day, and Tommy and Alex's experiences beyond that. Time once again moves at a different pace for these characters, suggesting that they are back within their own worlds and that their experiences are once again firmly disconnected and subjective. There is a sense in which the evacuation of Dunkirk was a moment so significant that it was larger than the subjective experiences of any individual who lived through it. It reflects Nolan's attitude towards cinema as an experience that is at once subjective and objective, individual and collective.[160]

When it was first announced and developed, *Dunkirk* seemed like a massive gamble for Warner Brothers. It was a war film with very few recognizable actors, not based on any pre-existing intellectual property. Nolan had managed to find critical and commercial success with original premises in *Inception* and *Interstellar*, but those had been buoyed by the presence of a successful and popular leading actor. On top of that, war films and period films were always a tough sell at the American box office.[161] This accounted for the film's (relatively) modest budget, approximately half of the budget that had been apportioned to *Interstellar*. "We could very easily have made the film for a great deal more money, but we knew that Warner Brothers wouldn't be comfortable with that, and we also knew that we wouldn't have the freedom to make the film the way that we wanted to make it if we made it for any more than we asked them for," says Emma Thomas. "This was the tightest budget of any film we've ever done."[162]

In some respects, the film looked a lot more like a prestigious autumn release than a big summer blockbuster. "You can't think of a less typical summer movie," remarks editor Lee Smith.[163] This sentiment was so widespread that it extended to the film's box office competitors. "In the entire industry, no one understands what [*Dunkirk*] is doing here," reflected Luc Besson, whose *Valerian and the City of a Thousand Planets* opened the same July weekend as *Dunkirk*. "Typically this kind of film—great director, important subject—comes in November, going for Oscars. Why in July? It doesn't make sense."[164] It might not have made sense to Besson, but *Dunkirk* went on to dominate *Valerian and the City of a Thousand Planets* on its opening weekend.[165] *Dunkirk* became both the highest-grossing Second World War film globally[166] and the highest-grossing of the Best Picture nominees at that year's Academy Awards both globally and domestically.[167]

Some of its success seems to be down to Nolan latching onto (and slightly pre-empting) the zeitgeist. When *Dunkirk* was released, there was a hunger for this kind of story that most major studios would never have anticipated when it went into development.[168] After all, the surrounding production of films like *Their Finest*, *Churchill*, *Darkest Hour* and *HHhH* suggests some broader appetite for films about the Second World War.[169] In discussing what inspired them to bring an account of the Dunkirk evacuation to the screen, Nolan and Thomas frequently cited the dearth of movies exploring the evacuation. Nolan:

> Emma and I had talked about the fact that this is one of the most incredible stories in history and that it hadn't been addressed in modern films....[170] As a filmmaker you're looking for gaps in the culture, pop culture at least; you're looking for things that haven't been addressed in movies. And Dunkirk, for whatever reason, has never been addressed in modern cinema.[171]

Ironically, *Dunkirk* coincided with the release of two other major films exploring the evacuation: *Their Finest* and *Darkest Hour*. It seems like there was something in the popular consciousness, and *Dunkirk* skillfully identified it.

More than that, *Dunkirk* demonstrated that Nolan himself was a name who could anchor a summer blockbuster. Much has been written about the decline of star power in the twenty-first century, and about the rise of intellectual property as leverage for these films.[172] However, *Dunkirk* showed that Nolan's name and brand could open a film without the need for either a recognizable leading actor or a familiar intellectual property.[173] This was a conscious part of the marketing campaign. "The entire campaign presented *Dunkirk* as a visceral thriller and an event experience of magnificent scale and originality as only Christopher Nolan can deliver," commented Sue Kroll, Warner Bros Worldwide Marketing and Distribution President.[174]

By his tenth theatrical release, Nolan had arguably cultivated something of a star persona around himself. Interviews and profiles often linked the director to a set of distinguishing identifiers: the video monitor around his neck,[175] the tea in his flask,[176] his lack of an email address or mobile telephone,[177] his strong views on the preservation of film.[178] The *Dunkirk* press cycle added its own set of Nolan-related mythology on top of the already impressive assemblage of trivia; the director had no idea how famous Harry Styles was when the pop star was cast,[179] the director had at one stage considered directing the film without a script.[180] In fact, Nolan had so successfully crafted a distinctive persona that his critics could build on this iconography to create cynical caricatures of the director.[181] Although this sort of information undoubtedly spreads quicker in the age of viral content, it speaks to how firmly Nolan has established his identity, and the extent to which the director is a brand unto himself. *Dunkirk* perhaps marks the point at which Nolan acknowledged himself as the star of his productions.[182]

With this in mind, it makes sense that *Dunkirk* would be the first film to earn Nolan a Best Director Oscar nomination.[183] In fact, *Dunkirk* would become Nolan's second most successful film at the Academy Awards behind *Inception*, and only his second film to secure a Best Picture nomination.[184] This makes a certain amount of sense. *Dunkirk* looks and feels like a film with greater awards cachet than most of the other films in Nolan's filmography. Recent decades suggest that the Academy Awards have a strong bias against genre filmmaking, outside of truly exceptional phenomena like *Lord of the Rings: The Return of the King*.[185] A war film like *Dunkirk* is more likely to be classified as "awards bait" than a science fiction epic like *Interstellar* or a superhero film like *The Dark Knight Rises*.[186] A recurring subtext of some reviews and commentary was that Nolan had elevated himself as a filmmaker simply by switching genres to something regarded as more serious and worthy than his earlier, pulpier films.[187] This seems unduly dismissive of Nolan's body of work as a whole, and a misreading of *Dunkirk* as a far more conventional movie than it is.

Many pundits identified *Dunkirk* as a potential candidate for Best Picture at the Academy Awards, even acknowledging the fact that it had been released outside the usual award release cycle.[188] Ultimately, *Dunkirk* did manage to secure a nomination, one of only two films among that year's nominees to have been released outside of the usual window.[189] The awards nominations for *Dunkirk* and *Get Out* bucked several recurring trends for the major Best Picture nominees: Both were released outside of awards season, both had earned significant amounts of money, both were cultural events unto themselves.[190] In many ways, *Dunkirk* and *Get Out* were the populist contenders for the Best Picture Oscar. This would be important, given the correlation between the ratings of the live telecast and the amount of money earned by the Best Picture nominees.[191] This relationship between box office ratings and live audience makes sense; viewers are more likely to watch the Academy Awards when there is a chance that films they have seen might take home the big prize.[192]

There was poetry in the Best Picture nominations for *Dunkirk* and *Get Out*, a sense that the radical overhaul of the Academy of Motion Picture Arts and Sciences (prompted in part by the overlooking of *The Dark Knight* nine years earlier) had brought meaningful change to the institution. The expanded Best Picture field allowed for a diverse array of contenders, in a wide variety of genres. The expansion and diversification of the membership led to a more representative slate of nominees and even winners.[193] However, there was a sense that Nolan was somewhat disconnected from the race. *Dunkirk* was largely seen as an also-ran from the moment that the nominations were announced, never considered a serious contender for the big prize.[194] According to commentators, Nolan was too traditional a filmmaker for the new generation of awards voters who had been drafted during the tenures of Sid Ganis and Cheryl Boone Isaacs,[195] while also being too experimental and bold for the traditional old-fashioned voters.[196]

*Dunkirk* won prizes for sound mixing, sound editing and film editing. However, Nolan went home empty-handed. In some respects, this "also-ran" quality to *Dunkirk* demonstrated that Academy Awards had not yet managed to reconcile its appeals to both the art house and the mainstream, that the reforms introduced by Ganis to help bring populist crowd-pleasing movies back into contention had not come to fruition.[197] Perhaps demonstrating the failure of the Academy Awards to skillfully bridge these two worlds, the telecast of the Ninetieth Academy Awards attracted the smallest TV audience in the ceremony's history.[198] It seemed like the Academy Awards had lost their grip on the popular consciousness.[199] Perhaps this demonstrated the difficulty in maintaining a singular cohesive popular culture in the twenty-first century, with so many different and competing viewpoints and perspectives.[200] Perhaps the Oscars can no longer serve mainstream culture, because there is no truly mainstream culture in the era of social media "bubbles," "peak television" and "time-shifted viewing," where there is too much media to consume on too many different channels.[201] There are very few "events" in twenty-first century popular culture that are truly universal, very few pieces of entertainment that have enough cultural weight to be ubiquitous.[202] Perhaps the lost cultural cachet of the Academy Awards is another expression of this fractured nature of contemporary pop culture.

Then again, perhaps this speaks to the power of *Dunkirk* and the talent of Christopher Nolan. His films are often about competing and discordant perspectives of the world, a cacophony of viewpoints from characters who are disconnected and adrift. This certainly feels relatable, with an increasing sense that the modern world has lost a sense of shared reality.[203] Nolan's films literalize this anxiety; time does not even move at the same rate for the central characters in *Dunkirk*. However, the power of Nolan as a director is his ability to harness these subjective narratives and turn them into objective spectacle, one of the few working directors with the capacity to craft a legitimate pop culture event. His films represent a canny understanding of the zeitgeist and the popular consciousness, creating narratives that are at once broad and specific; stories that reflect contemporary culture in a manner that always feels like the work of a distinctive craftsman.

At a point in history when the popular consciousness seems fractured and disoriented, this is no small accomplishment.

# Appendix: Interview with Jeremy Theobald

*You didn't study acting at college. You studied physiology? How did you get involved in making films? And how did you come to commit so much time to it? Because it was every weekend, for the better part of a year, making Following?*

Yeah. It was a very active drama society, and very active film society, at UCL. I was at St. Thomas' Hospital Medical School before I was at UCL. I did that for a year, and then took a year out. I suppose I really started acting when I went to St. Thomas.' When I was at school, I didn't do any acting. There wasn't very much opportunity, in terms of the plays that were being put on.

But there was a stage lighting group that I was a part of. I was effectively a technician for external discos and things like that that were on, where I used to rig lights during my teenage years. So I went to college, and at the Freshers' Fair there was a drama society that looked more interesting than some of the other societies. (I didn't play a lot of sport.)

And so at St. Thomas', I did a couple of plays, fell in with a couple of people; we wrote some reviews, I went to the Edinburgh Fringe a couple of times.

*With the reviews?*

I went as an actor, and as a writer. A medical school review show. Quite old school! [Laughs.]

Did that for a year, and dropped out of medical school. Did a year out, selling all sorts of things; running a bar in Islington, working in Hamleys with Tom Hollander, selling those yappie dogs that could to the backflip![1]

Then I went to UCL, and fell in with the drama society there; much bigger, much more organized. Much more earnest, I suppose! And professional, in many ways. A lot of them were English literature students, and so very much into their drama. So, did a bunch of plays there—produced and designed, as well.

I'm just trying to think of some of the people who were there are the time. There's a couple of stand-up comedians—Trevor Lock and Dan Antopolski—who are still treading the circuit. And an actor, Abigail Burdess, that I worked with a number of times. Abi and I did a few plays together.

There was a film society, they were very active. There was a television society, I did some presenting. One of the tech guys in that, Ivan [Cornell], I became friends with and got to know quite well. He introduced me to Chris.

He said that Chris was making a film, and that it had a voiceover part, and asked if would agree to do it. It was literally going to be fifteen minutes; go down to the studio and record a telephone conversation. And that's for a film that Chris didn't finish.

*This was the first attempt at a feature-length film?*
Yes. I think it was filmed in color as well. I think I maybe saw some rushes. I don't think it was finished.

So, I did that. We got on, we chatted about film, we went out and we had dinner, and we talked a bit more, and he said, "I've got a short that I want to do. Would you read it? Would you be interested?"

[This was] unlike all the other film society scripts at the time that I'd read, which were quite surreal ... slamming doors of trains on Euston Station, when trains had doors that could slam. This was witty. It was funny, it was pithy, and it was dark. It had a great twist at the end. [I was offered the] lead part in that. And that became *Larceny*, the ten-minute short that we shot in one weekend in Chris' flat. A Saturday and a Sunday.

We telecined that and it got to the Cambridge Short Film Festival. It screened there, and we went up for that. It was a really good little short.

*It's been described as one of the best short films to come out of UCL.*[2]
I used to have a video tape of it. And I keep meaning to find out from Ivan or from Chris or from Emma if they have a digital copy, because I don't have it any more.

*It's strange, because it seems to be not as readily available as Doodlebug.*
We never released it on anything. I think Chris thought it was too similar to *Following*, that people would think that it was a test bed for *Following*. Which ... it was in a certain way, in that it was testing that we could work as a group together with that particular equipment and get a usable product that had integrity.

But it wasn't, in that—and Chris has said that, and I think there are several quotes of him saying that—everything that you make should stand on its own two feet.[3] It should be a piece of work of itself. It shouldn't be a calling card for something else or a test or a preview of what's to come. Every piece of art is a piece of art, and it has its own integrity in that way.

It was great. I was really pleased with it.

I think when we spoke last time, I struggled to remember when we made *Doodlebug*; I couldn't remember if it was during gaps in *Following*, or whether it was between *Larceny* and *Following*. I think it was during gaps.

The guy was who in [*Larceny*], Mark Deighton, was going to be Cobb in *Following*. But he decided not to do it for personal reasons. In the end, he couldn't commit that amount of time. And so we cast Alex instead. I remember during the shoot on *Following*, that Alex went off to the Edinburgh Fringe. He did a play up there, so he was rehearsing and missing in July/August. So I think we made *Doodlebug* in that time, just to keep our hand in. Something to do.

*I think you described it yourself as a learning experience, working with the camera as opposed to stage work?*

For me, absolutely. It was really different. Everything that you do as an actor, you learn. Every time you commit your face to film, saying words which are somebody else's as a character, you think of the expressions and the way that you say them. Then you watch it back, you say, "I should have done it like this." Or, "I shouldn't have said it like that." Or, "I shouldn't have done that expression. I should have waited." So you learn, every single time.

It was quite a steep learning curve. Because there's no padding, in *Larceny* or in *Doodlebug* or in *Following*. Some of the critiques of *Following* mention this. Philip French, film critic for *The Observer*, said that there's not a single shot in *Following* which is wasted. There's no establishing shots whatsoever. Every single shot matters. It's very, very tight in that sense.

So you've got nowhere to hide as an actor. Certainly in *Doodlebug*, because I'm the only person in it. I'm the only actor. There's no cutaways to another actor, to allow me to regain composure. So that was a great learning experience. And then we fell into *Following*.

Chris said, after *Larceny*, "I've got a feature film that I want to make. And I want to make it on weekends. I've written it with you in mind, as the lead character. And I think it will work, in the way that we did *Larceny*."

[That is,] with an extremely small crew. Effectively a two-hander, for actors in the vast majority of scenes. It's either Bill and Cobb, or Cobb and the Blonde, or Bill and the Blonde. So Chris doing camera, David [Lloyd] doing sound, Ivan as the gaffer, and two actors. I think it's been said that you could fit all of us and the equipment in the back of a London taxi to get to a location where we were filming.[4]

I'm struggling to remember if we actually did that, but I think we must have done it to be able to come up with that! [Laughs.] I think we must have done it once or twice.

I co-produced that with Emma and Chris, from the point of view of bringing in friends who were actors, who I'd acted with when I was at college on stage in the drama society. I brought Lucy in, I brought Alex in, who were two of the best actors in college at the time.

I got a lot of the locations as well. My flat was my flat, or Bill's apartment was my flat. I have seen written in some of the more academic essays on Chris' work (and certainly in some of the forums) that the production design in *Following* was very prescient (in that he went on to work with Warner Brothers, and worked on the *Batman* series, starting with *Batman Begins*, which I was in as well) because I had the Batman logo on the front of my door.[5]

No. It was just a *Batman* sticker on the front of my door. It had been there since the first Batman films, and had been given away in a copy of *Empire* or something like that.

And [the postcard of] *The Shining*, with Chris liking Kubrick and Jack Nicholson being the Joker before, and it's all very interlinked…

No. Those were just posters that I had on my wall. We didn't change anything. Chris just came around and said, "Yeah. This looks like a scummy sort of apartment where [Bill] would live. We'll just use it like this." We changed very little. So all of the stuff on the wall where I was typing was just the stuff that was on the wall. It was undecorated. I'd taken all the wall paper off, filled in the cracks and never bothered painting.

So those sorts of things that are written about films, I think sometimes people can read too much into design. Certainly, for micro-budget films.

*That's apophenia, I suppose. Everything has to fit into some larger pattern. But, in terms of your work as producer, you were responsible for procuring locations. Was that related to the work that you'd been doing earlier—you mentioned you'd been managing a bar in Islington, so did you use that?*

I mean, all of the locations were simply begged and borrowed from friends. The Blonde's apartment is Chris' parents' house in Highgate. There's a "definition of irony" story.

I'll see if I can get it right. It was twenty years ago. So there's two parts to it. The main part—which is the definition of irony—is that there is a scene in which Cobb and Bill go into the Blonde's apartment and steal a lot of things. My character is seen taking a lot of stuff, putting it into a bag and taking it away. And then there's a scene, later in the story, where I'm seen getting that stuff out of the bag; where I'm in my own apartment, and I look at the box. I get the little seahorse out. There's the beads, the candy bracelet that I wrap around my wrist. I look at the photos of Lucy. And I get a candlestick out, and I get a clock out. All well and good.

When we break into the Blonde's apartment, Alex actually smashed the window. It was a one-take, and he had to do it. He had a hammer, and he smashed the window. We couldn't find a key, because "that would be three keys in a row." So, he actually did smash the window. And the neighbors heard it. A few days later, they spoke to Chris' parents and said, "We thought that you were being robbed the other day." [Chris' parents] said, "No, it's fine. It's fine. [Our] son's making a film about burglary." [The neighbors responded,] "Oh, all right. No problem."

Several weeks later, they were actually burgled.

*I think I heard this story, I heard that some of the props were taken?*

Yeah, some of the things that I put into the bag were actually stolen. So when we came to shoot the scene that we did later—and we did shoot it later chronologically as it was part of a different timeline, after I'd had my haircut—of me getting some of the things out of the bag, I couldn't actually get them out of the bag because they had been stolen in a burglary.

*Just on that, in terms of shooting chronologically, you mentioned last time that when you got the script that Chris had obviously written it in the form in which it appears on screen, non-linear...*

Sorry, I don't think that's obvious at all.

I think it's something that shows the sort of brain that he has, regarding two of the things that we talked about. The first thing is that he wrote it non-linear, more or less as it appears. In fact, [the script] is *more* fractured. So, actually, there's three things to talk about.

The first is that, when he wrote it, the original version of the script was more fractured. When we did test screenings, we discovered that we need to do a longer introduction sequence of all of the characters in one timeline, so that the audience could "get" them and understand what was going on, before you started fracturing the timeline and introducing those characters in a different timeline. The original cut, and the original script, had my character in different timelines far earlier on. So we did a longer narration sequence at the start and there was an ADR pick-up—that I can hear, anyway—right at the beginning.

So the point was that he wrote it in fractured timeline. I read it, and I said, "Yes, I get it." Because, when you read books or when you hear stories, there is a fractured timeline going on. But, as an actor, wanting to be able to know what I was doing on what day and what level of emotion I should be playing, I had to take the script apart and put it back together chronologically with all three timelines running sequentially, so I could understand what my character arc was in the whole thing.

I'll come back to the third thing about how Chris' brain works, in the editing as well and the shooting ratio.

In terms of the story and the fractured timeline, Chris always used "the *Jerry Springer* conundrum" or "the *Jerry Springer* example" when he was talking about this. *Jerry Springer*, as a show, worked because he'd have a man come on to tell his story and he'd have a woman come on to tell her story, and then they'd fight and they'd bicker. "Oh, it wasn't like that! It wasn't like that!" Then he'd have a third person come on and tell a *completely different* version of that story.

They never start with, "I got up in the morning, and I brushed my teeth, and I went to the lavatory." It's always "there's an intern with this dress and it's got some stains on it" and then you work backwards to the fact that she worked for Bill Clinton and then the impeachment comes afterwards. The story starts at a point there, and goes backwards and forwards at the same time. Humans are very good at being able to take those jigsaw puzzle pieces of information and put them into a timeline themselves; to work out the story without having to see it sequentially. Sequential storytelling is quite dull.

And the third thing I was going to say: as an example, we talked about the shooting ratio last time. On certain scenes—and the scene that I remember most is the scene where I meet Cobb in the café—we didn't shoot them all the way through in each of the set-ups. There were probably four set-ups there: there's me; there's Cobb; wide; there's the two-shot. And we didn't shoot the scene through on each of those set-ups, because Chris already had it edited in his head. He knew that he was going to start on the wide, so he only needed the first few lines of that and then he would go to Cobb. And he would cut back and forth. So he would say, "I just want you to do up until this line. And then we'll cut there."

Which is very brave as a filmmaker. Because I've known people make short films like that before. I've known an editor try to make a short film like that before which failed because he didn't have any coverage. It's a way of explaining how talented a filmmaker Chris is, because (a.) he knew the coverage he was getting was good enough to use, (b.) it kept the shooting ratio down, and (c.) he already had the film edited in his head beforehand, because he'd written it in fractured timeline already. He knew how it was going to play.

*There are quotes from Chris where he shoots it primarily in his mind's eye before he realizes it, and it's primarily about getting what's in his head captured on film.*[6]

I was thinking, since last time we talked, in Michael Caine's autobiography he talks about somebody doing that. I think it's … Sean Connery and Michael Caine? *The Man Who Would Be King*? Was that John Huston?

I'm fairly sure that in Michael Caine's autobiography, he talks about John Huston doing the same thing; that they didn't run all of the scenes all the way through. He thought it was very clever, the way that he'd already shot the film.

*Just in terms of the shooting ratio. The shooting ratio on* Following *was phenomenal. I think that for every two-and-a-half minutes shot, one minute was actually used in the film. As compared to fifteen minutes shot for every one used being the industry average.*[7] *In terms of your process as an actor, in terms of the spaces that you had, did you rehearse much outside the set? Did you rehearse much on the set?*

Where we could. Where the apartment was my flat, yes we did. It gave us all the opportunity to work out the blocking, and it gave Chris the opportunity to work out where he was going to shoot and how he was going to shoot.

We did a lot of rehearsals in the film society in UCL; just because it had the space, and because it was free, and because it was large. The idea was that when were in a situation where we were unfamiliar, or something would go on, where somebody would trip over a light or a 747 would go over or something that that, that we would just carry on.

We could busk around it, or ad lib around it. We wouldn't just immediately shout "cut!" and that shot would be lost. We would just carry on, so that something usable could come out of it and that during whatever glitch had happened, that you could do a cutaway or use another shot or that you could cover it in some other way. If somebody did forget their lines, we could busk around it or ad lib around it to a place within the scene where it could carry on. So that film wasn't being used spuriously.

The reason for that is because it was incredibly low budget. Chris was buying one roll of 16mm black and white film a week from his own pocket from his job as a media trainer, and getting it processed. We were shooting that one Saturday a week, so that was all we had. When you're shooting on big budget productions, then you have a much greater shooting ratio because you have more funds and access to more film.

I was working on a film recently, and the director was camera-loader for a feature film. He made his first film on off-cuts from camera loading. On big budget features you never start the shot with anything less than, let's say, 200 feet in the can. So if you get to the end of the shot, if there's 235 feet in the can, they'll say reload. There's no point starting a shot with that little film in the camera, because by the time it gets up to speed, you'll only get thirty seconds worth of film before it runs through, you run out, and you have to re-take. The DoP or the second camera assistant will say to reload.

So this guy asked, "Can I have the off-cuts of this unprocessed film?" And they said, "Yeah." So he took them home, and he spliced them together in a dark room. He made a whole new reel out of them, and from that he was able to shoot his own short film.

*In terms of direction, between you and Chris. I read an interview with you and Chris at the Rotterdam Film Festival, where you were talking about the process that you two had. He was saying that he tended to give actors a lot of space to work. He described it as staying out of your way. How did you find working with him as a director?*

Yeah. He is enormously generous, in that he will let you get on with it and do what you want. He's very specific about certain things. He absolutely knows what he wants. That's the film that's already captured in his mind's eye, and that he's written, and which is pre-edited. That he's visualized. So there's certain stuff where he'll say, "No. You have to do it like this, because it's got to cut together with something later on." In terms of an action or something like that.

But there's an enormous freedom in being able to do what it is that you want with a character and to take it in different ways. Sometimes he'll say, "Okay. That's great. That's really interesting. Let's try it at one-and-a-half speed, just so that scene doesn't take ten minutes." Generally, he just lets you get on with it. Unless he sees something that he does want to change. Which is fantastic as an actor, because the last thing you want is a director turning around and saying, "You have to say it like this. Say it exactly like this."

So, yeah, really really fantastic to work with.

*In terms of your work as a producer on the film, but also the extremely low budget on the film. I think the film came in at around £6,000 in total...*

I think it came out at around £3,000. It was around $5,000, so about £3,000, that we actually made it for. And then it took £3,000 to get the neg-cut done and the print made for San Francisco. Which I took over in my hand baggage for the San Francisco Film Festival. Because Chris and Emma had already moved to the U.S. by then.

The whole thing was telecined on Sony Beta, and the cut was done. It was output to VHS in those days, there wasn't a lot done over the internet. There certainly wasn't fast internet. You just sent VHS out to people for the film festivals. And then, when it's accepted, they need a print. So you actually have to go back to the original negative and cut it into the film, and get a print done from that cut negative. Which hadn't been done at that point, because we hadn't needed to and it cost money. So we had to raise some more money to do that. So that's probably what the other £3,000 was for—and getting the grade done on that, as well.

It was certainly prudent. The whole thing was pretty tight.

*You flew over with the print?*

Yeah. The negative and everything was still in London with Ivan in the Framestore. So it had to cut and printed there. I had to take the reels over, in my hand baggage. I put them through the scanner and pray that the process wasn't fogged by the X-ray. They weren't literally in my hands for eleven hours on the flight, but they were in the overhead lockers above me.

*The festival circuit for* Following *lasted quite a while. You took it all over the world. You took it around the U.S., and then Rotterdam was its European premier. But it took a while to get it released in cinemas in England?*

From what I remember—and this timeline could be wrong, or have some gaps in it—we were accepted at San Francisco. We'd applied at a bunch of film festivals. I think that included Sundance to start with, and the programmer there said, "Not for us, but try this one." So, we were accepted at San Francisco. Peter Broderick of Next Wave Films saw it in San Francisco. He was very big into guerrilla filmmaking at the time. He was doing a lot of work around films that were being made for extremely low budgets, under the radar, without the studios, independents; *Clerks* and *Blair Witch* were two examples at the time.

He saw *Following*, said, "This is great. This has the potential to be another of those sorts of films. I'll invest in it; blow it up to 35mm, we'll do a new sound mix, and we'll do a grade on it. I'll take it to Toronto." Which is one of the big four sales festivals, of Berlin, Cannes, Venice and Toronto. We sold distribution there in the U.S., France and the U.K. I think the Dutch came later, after Rotterdam. But at that time, it was still going through festivals. So he took over the festival strategy, to ensure that it was premiering at the biggest festivals that it could for each territory, to then get the best distribution deal.

I think we then chose Rotterdam, and we won the Tiger Award at Rotterdam, which was great. Then, finally, we came back to Edinburgh, and we did Dinard and other festivals in France as well. Various small festivals, to allow the French distributors to spend a little money. We won the Silver Hitchcock Award in Dinard, where Jane Birkin was president of the jury. I think Tom Hollander was on the panel as well and I mentioned to him that we used to sell toys in Hamleys together!

*You got to collect that one?*

I did. Chris and Emma weren't over for that one. It was a very pleasurable experience; they had a proper awards ceremony at the end, with a red carpet and signing autographs. All very bright lights and film stardom.

# Chapter Notes

## Chapter 1

1. The ubiquity of *Batman* is unquestionable; the character is accepted as an iconic piece of pop culture. Even in *Following*, the lead character has a sticker on his door of the logo from the 1989 Tim Burton film.
2. Nolan has discussed this aspect of the film repeated. See, for example: Robert Capps, "Q&A: Christopher Nolan on Dreams, Architecture, and Ambiguity," *Wired*, 29 November 2010; Jeff Goldsmith, "The Architect of Dreams," *Creative Screenwriting*, July/August 2010.
3. Tom Shone, "Christopher Nolan: the man who rebooted the blockbuster," *The Guardian*, 4 November 2014.
4. Scott Feinberg, "Christopher Nolan on *Interstellar* Critics, Making Original Films and Shunning Cellphones and Email," *The Hollywood Reporter*, 3 January 2015.
5. "Chris was the great herald of Star Wars," recalls his brother, Jonathan. "He had gotten to see it in the U.S. several months early. It was a great privilege, being able to stand in the playground, and articulate all of the exciting things to come. The one-man trailer organization." (Tom Shone, "Christopher Nolan: the man who rebooted the blockbuster," *The Guardian*, 4 November 2014.)
6. Scott Timberg, "Indie Angst," *The New Times Los Angeles*, 15 March 2001.
7. Colin Covert, "Christopher Nolan explains his 'cinematic brain' at Walker Art Center," *Star Tribune*, 6 May 2015.
8. Scott Timberg, "Indie Angst," *The New Times Los Angeles*, 15 March 2001.
9. Andrew Purcell, "Christopher Nolan's *Interstellar* brings back the Spielberg-style family blockbuster," *The Sydney Morning Herald*, 7 November 2014.
10. Alistair Harkness, "Interview: Christopher Nolan on *Interstellar*," *The Scotsman*, 10 November 2014.
11. Erik Davis, "The Christopher Nolan-Directed *Star Wars* Movies We'll Probably Never Get to See," Movies.com, 3 November 2014.
12. Katey Rich, "Christopher Nolan Is Still a Huge Star Wars Geek," *Vanity Fair*, 10 November 2014.
13. Ryan Faughnder, "Imax embeds itself with Hollywood directors to make sure you see 'Dunkirk' and 'Transformers' on its screens," *The Los Angeles Times*, 2 May 2017.
14. Casey Cipriani, "Tribeca: Bennett Miller Gets Christopher Nolan to Open Up About the Studio System and His Biggest Fears," *Indie Wire*, 21 April 2015.
15. Jeff Jensen, "*Room 237*: Exploring Stanley Kubrick's *Shining* influence," *Entertainment Weekly*, 6 April 2013.
16. Scott Feinberg, "Christopher Nolan on *Interstellar* Critics, Making Original Films and Shunning Cellphones and Email," *The Hollywood Reporter*, 3 January 2015.
17. Scott Timberg, "Indie Angst," *The New Times Los Angeles*, 15 March 2001.
18. Scott Feinberg, "Christopher Nolan on *Interstellar* Critics, Making Original Films and Shunning Cellphones and Email," *The Hollywood Reporter*, 3 January 2015.
19. Philip Horne, "I taught him—now he directs Pacino," *The Telegraph*, 10 August 2002.
20. "My influences are primarily film based," Nolan has stated, downplaying any influence of adventure novels or comic books or Edgar Rice Burroughs on his work. (Colin Covert, "Christopher Nolan explains his 'cinematic brain' at Walker Art Center," *Star Tribune*, 6 May 2015.)
21. "I got into filmmaking purely as a means of stringing images together, scenes," Nolan recalls. "Then I came to understand narrative. Studying English was a very good way to give myself more grounding in the word." (Scott Timberg, "Indie Angst," *The New Times Los Angeles*, 15 March 2001.)
22. Jeff Goldsmith, "The Architect of Dreams," *Creative Screenwriting*, July/August 2010.
23. Scott Timberg, "Indie Angst," *The New Times Los Angeles*, 15 March 2001.
24. Colin Covert, "Christopher Nolan explains his 'cinematic brain' at Walker Art Center," *Star Tribune*, 6 May 2015.
25. Jeffrey Ressner, "The Traditionalist," *Director's Guild of America Quarterly*, Spring 2012.
26. Philip Horne, "I taught him—now he directs Pacino," *The Telegraph*, 10 August 2002.
27. Matthew Tempest, "I was there at the Inception of Christopher Nolan's film career," *The Guardian*, 24 February 2011.
28. Scott Feinberg, "Christopher Nolan on *Interstellar* Critics, Making Original Films and Shunning Cellphones and Email," *The Hollywood Reporter*, 3 January 2015.
29. Matthew Tempest, "I was there at the Inception of Christopher Nolan's film career," *The Guardian*, 24 February 2011.
30. Nolan's childhood collaborators

Roko and Adrian Belic would go on to become successful filmmakers in their own right. *Genghis Blues*, directed by Roko and produced with Adrian, would go on to earn an Oscar nomination for Best Documentary Feature. Christopher Nolan is credited on *Genghis Blues* for his "editorial assistance." Roko observes that Nolan was a major influence on his career choice, "It's really because Chris Nolan and I were friends when we were kids that I thought about making movies." (Alisa Damaso, "Roko Belic/Filmmaker," *Killer Creatives*, 22 October 2012.)

31. Neil Evans, "Filmmaker Retrospective: The Intelligent Cinema of Christopher Nolan," *Taste of Cinema*, 10 December 2014.

32. Theobald's only feature-length credit remains the lead role in *Following*. Outside of a guest appearance on *The Bill*, Theobald's multimedia output is primarily short films.

33. Interestingly, and very much in keeping with Nolan's recurring fascination with identity and persona, Theobald's three lead characters were all credited in generic terms. Theobald was "The Man" in *Larceny* and *Doodlebug*, and "The Young Man" in *Following*. Theobald would also make a small cameo in *Batman Begins* as "Younger Gotham Water Board Technician."

34. Christopher Hooton described the film as "Kafkaesque," musing, "Aren't student films always?" While Nolan was not a student while making the film, he may not have been immune to the clichés. (Christopher Hooton, "Christopher Nolan's student short film Doodlebug shows the Dunkirk director's humble beginnings," *The Independent*, 10 April 2017.)

35. Around the launch of *Inception*: Kristopher Tapley, "Watch Christopher Nolan's First Short Film *Doodlebug*," *In Contention*, 20 July 2010. Around the launch of *The Dark Knight Rises*: Scott Beggs, "Watch: Christopher Nolan's First Short Film *Doodlebug*," *Film School Rejects*, 13 April 2012. Around the launch of *Dunkirk*: Christopher Hooton, "Christopher Nolan's student short film Doodlebug shows the Dunkirk director's humble beginnings," *The Independent*, 10 April 2017.

36. This is perhaps most obviously evoked in the dream levels within in *Inception*, with characters navigating dreams-within-dreams-within-dreams. As with *Doodlebug*, the bulk of the team seems comfortable with three levels of recursion within the dream, although Cobb pushes further. However, this idea of recursion plays across Nolan's work, particularly with nested stories like those told by the protagonist in *Memento* or those navigated by the protagonists in *The Prestige*.

37. Will Brooker, "Are You Watching Closely?," *The Cinema of Christopher Nolan: Imagining the Impossible* (2015), p. xi.

38. Marlow Stern, "Christopher Nolan Uncut: On *Interstellar*, Ben Affleck's Batman, and the Future of Mankind," *The Daily Beast*, 10 November 2014.

39. Nathalie Sejean, "34 Things Christopher Nolan Shared About Making His First Feature Film and Learning From It," *Mentorless*, 30 December 2013.

40. "Christopher Nolan on *Following*—Conversations Inside The Criterion Collection," *VICE*, 24 August 2014.

41. Chris Jones, "Exclusive Interview with Christopher Nolan and Emma Thomas from our Guerilla Film Makers Archives," *Chris Jones Blog*, 6 August 2010.

42. Matthew Tempest, "I was there at the Inception of Christopher Nolan's film career," *The Guardian*, 24 February 2011.

43. "Christopher Nolan on *Following*—Conversations Inside The Criterion Collection," *VICE*, 24 August 2014.

44. Mike Fleming, Jr., "Slamdance: Christopher Nolan's Advice For Indie Helmers, And Memories Of Papering Main Street With His $6000 Debut Film," *Deadline*, 18 January 2014.

45. Erin McCarthy, "Director Christopher Nolan Discusses Making His First Film, *Following*," *Mental Floss*, 28 November 2012.

46. Janet Maslin, "Following," *The New York Times*, 2 April 1999.

47. Nathalie Sejean, "34 Things Christopher Nolan Shared About Making His First Feature Film and Learning From It," *Mentorless*, 30 December 2013.

48. Tom Shone, "Christopher Nolan: the man who rebooted the blockbuster," *The Guardian*, 4 November 2014.

49. Erin McCarthy, "Director Christopher Nolan Discusses Making His First Film, *Following*," *Mental Floss*, 28 November 2012.

50. "Christopher Nolan on *Following*—Conversations Inside The Criterion Collection," *VICE*, 24 August 2014.

51. Erin McCarthy, "Director Christopher Nolan Discusses Making His First Film, *Following*," *Mental Floss*, 28 November 2012.

52. "Christopher Nolan on *Following*—Conversations Inside The Criterion Collection," *VICE*, 24 August 2014.

53. Sarah Gilmartin, "Oscar was Wilde about books," *The Irish Times*, 12 May 2014.

54. *Memento* features a protagonist who has cultivated a narrative to make sense of his situation; Nolan's *Dark Knight* trilogy is predicated on the creation, maintenance and resolution of a myth; *The Prestige* imagines two artists consumed and devoured by their art; *Inception* features characters who can plant an idea in another person's head.

55. Of course, the reality is somewhat more nuanced than that generalization. It might be fairer to describe movie-making as a socially-sanctioned form of voyeurism, an acceptable and public glimpse into worlds that don't exist. (*See*, for example, Carl Plantinga, *Moving Viewers: American Film and the Spectator's Experience* [2009].)

56. Nolan concedes that he also made a point to open the film with a sequence shot using a dolly; the interrogation sequence between the police officer and the protagonist is much steadier than the rest of the film. Not only does this reinforce the subjective nature of the protagonist's narrative, but Nolan also contends that opening the film with steadier shots reassured the audience that they were in safe hands. ("Christopher Nolan on *Following*—Conversations Inside The Criterion Collection," *VICE*, 24 August 2014.)

57. *Following* is somewhat clumsier than Nolan's later efforts in this regard, its layered and recursive narrative somewhat less elegant than the back-and-forth in *The Prestige*. Although *Following* is framed as the subjective remembrance of the protagonist, this conversation includes several scenes to which the character has not been party, even beyond the climactic reveal cross-cut with the end of the interrogation. Its subjective viewpoint is imperfect.

58. Scott Timberg, "Indie Angst," *The New Times Los Angeles*, 15 March 2001.

59. Xan Brooks, "Punch the keys now! Why cinema keeps churning out films about writers," *The Guardian*, 17 November 2016.

60. Molly Driscoll, "*Hail, Caesar!*:

Here's why Hollywood loves movies about Hollywood," *The Christian Science Monitor*, 2 February 2016.

61. The protagonist attempts to explain himself to the police in the framing sequence, "I'm a writer. Well, I want to be a writer anyway. I was, um, gathering material for my characters."

62. When Nolan wrote *Inception*, one of the first things he did was to devise "the rules of the world." (Mike Fleming Jr, "Oscar: Chris Nolan Q&A About *Inception*," *Deadline*, 7 January 2011.) James Verini argues that Nolan's films are "most satisfying when understood as games, not as novelistic narratives." (James Verini, "Christopher Nolan's Games," *The New Yorker*, 17 July 2012.)

63. Nate Jones, "The Christopher Nolan Style Guide to Wearing Video Monitors Around Your Neck," *Vulture*, 10 November 2014.

64. Closing an interview by remarking on his typical attire, Jeffrey Ressner asked Nolan, "Why get so dressed up?" (Jeffrey Ressner, "The Traditionalist," *Director's Guild of America Quarterly*, Spring 2012.)

65. Rahul Desai, "The Prestige of Christopher Nolan," *The Hindu*, 12 August 2017.

66. "Christopher Nolan on *Following*—Conversations Inside The Criterion Collection," *VICE*, 24 August 2014.

67. Nolan has argued that part of his creative success comes from making movies that he would want to watch as an audience member. "I've always had faith in audiences because I make films that I want to see, and I don't think I'm a particularly neat and special person." (Jonathan Curiel, "Memory serves Nolan/*Memento* director explores similar themes in big-budget follow-up *Insomnia*," *The San Francisco Gate Chronicle*, 19 May 2002.) Nolan also tends to speak about the audience in the first person. "My attitude to the audience is very simple. I am the audience. We are the audience." (Dave Calhoun, "Christopher Nolan interview: 'Another superhero movie? Unlikely. But never say never,'" *Time Out London*, 28 October 2014.)

68. Ironically, Nolan's parents' house was burgled during the production of *Following*, and some of the props to be used during the film's robberies were stolen in real life. Nolan was mildly frustrated because that meant that he did not get to film all the inserts that he wanted. (Trevor Hogg, "Theatre of the Mind: A Christopher Nolan Profile," *Flickering Myth*, 30 June 2010.)

69. As Bruce Diones summarizes, "The film has echoes of Hitchcock classics such as *Strangers on a Train*, but Nolan's story is leaner and meaner than those thrillers." (Bruce Diones, "*Following*," *The New Yorker*, 1999.)

70. For example, Nolan has argued that *Dunkirk* forsakes dialogue in favor of "the language of the Hitchcock thriller" to more effective capture mood. (Stephanie Merry, "*Dunkirk* director Christopher Nolan excels at building suspense. Here's how he does it," *The Washington Post*, 14 July 2017.)

71. "There are masters like Alfred Hitchcock, where there's such an extraordinarily clear control of narrative that's inspiring," Nolan observes of Hitchcock. (Adam Grant, "Christopher Nolan Wants You to Silence Your Phones," *Esquire*, 19 July 2017.)

72. To be fair, even Nolan's performers have been known to indulge these comparisons. Michael Caine reflected, "'He reminds me of Hitchcock, the way that everything is about creating the best moments of suspense." (Will Lawrence, "Christopher Nolan interview for Inception," *The Telegraph*, 19 July 2010.)

73. "So why did audiences feel so uncomfortable?" asks Anthony Maskell of the visceral response to Hitchcock's work in *Psycho*. "It's a simple but revealing explanation. Hitchcock forced them into a position in which they simply did not want to be—the position of voyeur." (Anthony Maskell, "Hitchcock and Voyeurism," *Cherwell*, 22 March 2015.)

74. *See*, for example, "Exhibitionism/Voyeurism/The Look" in Michael Walker, *Hitchcock's Motifs* (2006), p. 164–177.

75. *See*, for example, John Fawell, *Hitchcock's Rear Window: The Well-Made Film* (2001).

76. *See*, for example, Peter J. Dellolio, "Filmic Space and Real Time in Alfred Hitchcock's Rope," *Kinema*, Spring 2009.

77. *See*, for example, Robert Phillip Kolker, *Alfred Hitchcock's Psycho: A Casebook* (2004).

78. See, for example, David Greven, *Intimate Violence: Hitchcock, Sex, and Queer Theory* (2017).

79. This is most explicit in *Frenzy*, which features a rapist who murders women by strangling them with his tie. The depiction of this act sparked controversy and outrage. (Victoria Sullivan, "Does *Frenzy* Degrade Women?," *The New York Times*, 30 July 1972.) However, this motif is present (if sublimated) in a lot of Hitchcock's work, most notably *Rope*. (Joel Gunz, "*Rope* and Sexual Asphyxia," *Alfred Hitchcock Geek*, 18 January 2006.)

80. Michael Wilmington, "Too Much Sex And Violence?," *The Chicago Tribune*, 5 June 1994.

81. It is also one of only two Nolan scripts to use the sexualized insult "cunt," although this may be down to the fact that Nolan's later work is aimed at a broader audience than *Following* or *Memento*.

82. Anne Billson, "Why is there no sex in Christopher Nolan's films?," *The Telegraph*, 15 November 2014.

83. Although *Memento* does feature a scene with a prostitute, she is not paid for sex work; instead, Leonard uses her to re-enact a chaste romantic fantasy. Tellingly, one of the major creative decisions in the remake of *Insomnia* is to tone down the emphasis on the protagonist's sexual dysfunctions; Engström attacks two women over the course of the Norwegian original, including the receptionist, while Dormer is on edge in a more conventional manner.

84. Reflects Jonathan Nolan of the dynamic at play, "I wanted Chris to have Teddy say at the end—which Chris ultimately rejected and in hindsight was right to do so—'You loved your wife, but how much more did you love your dead wife? How much easier is it to love your dead wife?' Having her taken away is much easier; now she's preserved in aspic, as it says in the short story. Locked away in a filing cabinet, she becomes a memory, not a person." (James Mottram, *The Making of Memento* (2002).)

85. It is entirely possible that Bruce Wayne is a virgin before he sleeps with Talia al Ghul in *The Dark Knight Rises*. (John Perich, "Is Batman a Virgin?," *Overthinking It*, 6 December 2012.) Even that sex scene has been described as "laughably chaste," and only serves to weaken Bruce before his back-breaking brawl with Bane. (Anthony Lane, "Batman's Bane," *The New Yorker*, 30 July 2012.)

86. *Interstellar* seems to acknowledge this criticism, with Cooper returning home to reunite with his long-lost offspring like Cobb in *Inception* or Borden in *The Prestige* before escaping at the very end to return

to Brand. However, for a film about the propagation of the human race, *Interstellar* remains pointedly and overtly asexual. Perpetuation of the species is to be conducted using vaults full of pre-prepared embryos. For all the film's fascination with "love" as a transcendent force, it apparently exists quite apart from sex.

87. Erin McCarthy, "Director Christopher Nolan Discusses Making His First Film, *Following*," *Mental Floss*, 28 November 2012.

88. Both Cobb and the Joker consider themselves students of human nature. Cobb takes great pleasure in "breaking in, entering someone's life, finding out who they really are." Repeatedly over the course of *The Dark Knight*, the Joker takes pleasure in trying to reveal who certain people "really" are. At the party, he instructs Batman, "You just take off your little mask and show us all who you really are." In the police interrogation room, he boasts, "In their last minutes, people show you who they really are." He promises to give Gotham "a good look at the real Harvey Dent."

89. Again, Cobb channels the Joker, who tries to corrupt Batman in a similar way. "I have one rule," Batman states. The Joker taunts, "Then that's the rule you'll have to break to know the truth." He elaborates on that truth, "The only sensible way to live in this world is without rules. And tonight you're gonna break your one rule."

90. In some ways, this reflects the way in which horror movies reinforce social norms by punishing their characters for perceived transgressions. (Holly L. Derr, "A Feminist Guide to Horror Movies, Part Two: It's Not Just About Vampires," *Ms. Magazine*, 26 October 2012.) There is also an aspect of this to classic *film noir*, with those who transgress frequently punished for their rejection of social norms. (Sylvia Harvey, "Woman's Place: The Absent Family," *Women in film noir* (1978), p. 22–34.)

91. In *The Prestige*, Fallon is hung so that Alfred might reconnect with his daughter and heal whatever family remains. In *The Dark Knight*, the Joker's chaos and Batman's sacrifice brings the city together. In *Inception*, the loss of Mal inspires Cobb to reconnect with his children. In *The Dark Knight Rises*, Bruce Wayne has everything stripped away from him only to claw it back. In *Dunkirk*, an entire army retreats from the chaos and carnage of war towards something resembling a civilized state.

92. Christopher Campbell, "*Arrival*, *Dunkirk* and the Distraction of Nonlinear Storytelling," *Film School Rejects*, 27 July 2017.

93. Tom Elrod, "Christopher Nolan: What Are We Watching, Exactly?," *Slant Magazine*, 11 August 2010.

94. Janet Maslin, "Following," *The New York Times*, 2 April 1999.

95. Michelle Balaev argues that nonlinear storytelling conveys a sense of how victims experience trauma. "The lack of cohesion and the disturbance of previous formulations of self and reality are sometimes conveyed in the form of an interruptive or nonlinear narrative," Baleav argues. "In addition, a temporally disjointed narrative highlights the struggle of the protagonist to identify the meaning and purpose of an experience." (Michelle Balaev, *The Nature of Trauma in American Novels* (2012), p. xvi.)

96. For example, the protagonist wakes up covered in bruises and with latex gloves stuffed in his mouth at the start of the film; the audience only gets to see that beating unfold towards the climax. Similarly, the Blonde complains about the robbery of her apartment to the protagonist; the audience then gets to see that robbery (and what happened to her missing earring) afterwards.

## Chapter 2

1. Gideon Lewis-Kraus, "The Exacting, Expansive Mind of Christopher Nolan," *The New York Times*, 30 October 2014.

2. Andrew Pulver, "He's not a god—he's human," *The Guardian*, 15 June 2005.

3. Scott Feinberg, "Christopher Nolan on *Interstellar* Critics, Making Original Films and Shunning Cellphones and Email," *The Hollywood Reporter*, 3 January 2015.

4. Leah Zak, "Guillermo del Toro & Christopher Nolan Talk *Memento* & 'Remaining Strange'," *IndieWire*, 9 February 2011.

5. Laura Winters, "Putting Last Things First in a Puzzle About Memory," *The New York Times*, 25 February 2001.

6. Ron Messer, "Tribeca Film Festival: 10 years later, *Memento* Still Confounds—A Report from the 10th Anniversary Screening," *Collider*, 25 April 2010.

7. Renfreu Neff and Daniel Argent, "Remembering Where it All Began: Christopher Nolan on *Memento*," *Creative Screenwriting*, 20 July 2015.

8. Jonathan Nolan, "Memento Mori," *Esquire*, March 2001.

9. Christopher Nolan, *Memento and Following* (2001), p. 233.

10. Erik Davis, "The Christopher Nolan-Directed *Star Wars* Movies We'll Probably Never Get to See," Movies.com, 3 November 2014.

11. Their process was not as collaborative on *Interstellar*, with Christopher inherited and rewriting a project than Jonathan had been working on with Steven Spielberg. (Jeff Jensen, "Inside *Interstellar*, Christopher Nolan's emotional space odyssey," *Entertainment Weekly*, 16 October 2014.)

12. Melissa Anelli, "GU Alum Becomes the *Memento*-Man," *The Hoya*, 16 March 2001.

13. Dave Trumbore, "Secret Science Nerds: Jonathan Nolan's 21st Century Sci-Fi on Big and Small Screens," *The Nerdist*, 30 November 2016.

14. Sallie Baxendale, "Memories aren't made of this: amnesia at the movies," *British Medical Journal*, 18 December 2004.

15. Daniel Fierman, "*Memento* takes film noir in a new direction," *Entertainment Weekly*, 30 March 2001.

16. Jeff Jensen, "Inside *Interstellar*, Christopher Nolan's emotional space odyssey," *Entertainment Weekly*, 16 October 2014.

17. Zach Dionne, "Christopher Nolan Nearing Dimension-Hopping Time-Travel Film *Interstellar*," *Vulture*, 9 January 2013.

18. Angie Romero, "Stars gather for *Interstellar* premiere," *The Chicago Tribune*, 27 October 2014.

19. Brian Tallerico, "A Simple Guide to Westworld's Multiple Timelines," *Vulture*, 30 November 2016.

20. Sam Rosenthal, "How *Interstellar* Director Christopher Nolan Uses Video Games to Create Filmic Puzzles," *IndieWire*, 28 November 2014.

21. The protagonist explicitly talks about establishing "rules" early in *Following*. Batman skirts around breaking his "one rule" at the climax of *Batman Begins*, only for the Joker to push him to breaking point again in *The Dark Knight*. Cobb establishes rules to Ariadne in *Inception*, although Arthur points out how frequently Cobb breaks his own rules.

22. In *Inception*, the dream world is given very clear and very rigidly defined rules. In *Interstellar*, the characters discuss at great length how time works differently on certain planets.

23. Craig Mathieson, "Westworld turned out to be the ultimate puzzle box," *The Sydney Morning Herald*, 15 December 2016.

24. In large part due to its interest in rules and systems, coupled with its exploration of consequence-free violence, *Westworld* works very well as a metaphor for video games. (Adi Robertson, "*Westworld* is a good TV show about a terrible video game," *The Verge*, 17 October 2016.)

25. Chris Nolen, "Paranoid Android: What HBO's *Westworld* Has To Say About Class and Capitalism in America," *Noleo Fantastico*, 14 December 2016.

26. "When Jonah and I were starting the first season, we were asked repeatedly about the science fiction element of the show," observes co-creator Greg Plageman. "Next thing we knew, the Snowden revelations come out, and we're talking to CNN and Smithsonian, and they're asking us how we knew. We thought everybody knew!" (Melenie McFarland, "*Person of Interest* comes to an end, but the technology central to the story will keep evolving," *GeekWire*, 20 June 2016.)

27. "When he first pitched it to me for *The Dark Knight*," recalls Christopher, "I liked the thematic idea, but I found it possibly a little far-fetched. He would talk me through and explain to me why he thought it wasn't far-fetched, and he turned out to be absolutely right in a way that is frankly terrifying." (Marlow Stern, "Christopher Nolan Uncut: On *Interstellar*, Ben Affleck's Batman, and the Future of Mankind," *The Daily Beast*, 10 November 2014.)

28. There are too many articles to list here, given the constant churn of internet pop culture discussion, but some samples: Phil Owen, "*Westworld*: Who Else Might Be a Secret Robot?," *The Wrap*, 21 November 2016; Scott Meslow, "So Which *Westworld* Character is Secretly a Robot?," *GQ*, 6 November 2016; Leah Thomas, "Is The Man In Black A Robot On *Westworld*? The Villain Has A Mysterious Past," *Bustle*, 16 October 2016.

29. It could be argued that the key difference between the revolutions in *The Dark Knight Rises* and *Westworld* is that *The Dark Knight Rises* is tied to social class while *Westworld* explores notions of race. (Aaron Bady, "*Westworld*, Race, and the Western," *The New Yorker*, 9 December 2016.)

30. *Memento* does play with subjective storytelling through Leonard's voice-over and through a number of shots that put the audience in Leonard's position or over his shoulder. However, *Memento Mori* can render this divide more explicit; approximately half of the story is narrated from Earl to Earl, while the other half unfolds in a more objective style.

31. So the driving narrative of *Memento* unfolds between Leonard's murder of Jimmy and his subsequent murder of Teddy, with black-and-white flashbacks to Leonard waiting in the room before murdering Jimmy. In contrast, *Memento Mori* focuses on Earl ruminating upon the murder of the man who killed his wife. There is no second murder or hint at conspiracy, just a tragic sense that he will not even remember this moment.

32. The short story draws the reader's attention to the fact that Earl saw the face of the man who murdered his wife, implying that he could identify him more clearly than his big screen counterpart.

33. This is perhaps most obvious in the closing shot of the spinning top in *Inception*, which suggests that Cobb has ceased to care about objective reality and instead accepted the reality with which he has been presented. Nolan summarised this moment as such in a commencement speech at Princeton. "I want to make the case to you that our dreams, our virtual realities, these abstractions that we enjoy and surround ourselves with—they are subsets of reality. The way the end of that film worked, Leonardo DiCaprio's character Cobb—he was off with his kids, he was in his own subjective reality. He didn't really care anymore, and that makes a statement: perhaps, all levels of reality are valid." Cobb might find a kindred soul in Leonard. (Ashley Lee, "Christopher Nolan Talks *Inception* Ending, Batman and "Chasing Reality" in Princeton Grad Speech," *The Hollywood Reporter*, 1 June 2015.)

34. "Christopher Nolan on *Following*—Conversations Inside The Criterion Collection," *VICE*, 24 August 2014.

35. Renfreu Neff and Daniel Argent, "Remembering Where it All Began: Christopher Nolan on *Memento*," *Creative Screenwriting*, 20 July 2015.

36. Scott Feinberg, "Christopher Nolan on *Interstellar* Critics, Making Original Films and Shunning Cellphones and Email," *The Hollywood Reporter*, 3 January 2015.

37. Andrew Pulver, "He's not a god—he's human," *The Guardian*, 15 June 2005.

38. Renfreu Neff and Daniel Argent, "Remembering Where it All Began: Christopher Nolan on *Memento*," *Creative Screenwriting*, 20 July 2015.

39. Anthony Kaufman, "Christopher Nolan Remembers *Memento*," *IndieWire*, 15 May 2014.

40. Scott Feinberg, "Christopher Nolan on *Interstellar* Critics, Making Original Films and Shunning Cellphones and Email," *The Hollywood Reporter*, 3 January 2015.

41. Chris Jones, "Exclusive Interview with Christopher Nolan and Emma Thomas from our Guerilla Film Makers Archives," *Chris Jones Blog*, 6 August 2010.

42. "Christopher Nolan on *Following*—Conversations Inside The Criterion Collection," *VICE*, 24 August 2014.

43. Carrie Seidman, "Q & A with Oscar-winning cinematographer Wally Pfister," *The Sarasota Herald-Tribune*, 16 October 2012.

44. Valentina Valentini, "*Transcendence* Director Pfister Talks Perseverance: 'Do not give up'," *Indie Wire*, 8 April 2014.

45. Andrew Romano, "How *Transcendence* Director Wally Pfister Became Christopher Nolan's Secret Weapon," *The Daily Beast*, 17 April 2014.

46. Ian Buckwalter, "The Reason Christopher Nolan Films Look Like Christopher Nolan Films," *The Atlantic*, 23 July 2012.

47. Ryan Gilbey, "Remembering Raoul Coutard, the French New Wave cinematographer (1924–2016)," *The New Statesman*, 11 November 2016.

48. Stephen Holden, "Sven Nykvist, 83, a Master of Light in Films, Dies," *The New York Times*, 21 September 2006.

49. Ronald Bergan, "Jack Cardiff," *The Guardian*, 23 April 2009.

50. Other famous collaborations include David Fincher and Jeff Cronenweth, Darren Aronofsky and Matthew Libatique, Mike Leigh and Dick Pope. (Gregg Kilday and Carolyn Giardina, "Roger Deakins and 5 Other Top DPs on Angelina Jolie's Directing Style, Shooting Through

Hurricanes and Film vs. Digital," *The Hollywood Reporter*, 2 December 2014.)

51. "Catching up with Wally Pfister, the Oscar-winning DP and director who got his start as a news cameraman," *Vox Creative*, 2015.

52. "Christopher Nolan on *Following*—Conversations Inside The Criterion Collection," *VICE*, 24 August 2014.

53. In *Inception*, the characters even refer to these small personal objects as "totems."

54. Ciara Wardlow, "Christopher Nolan's Emotional Objects and the *Dunkirk* Exception," *Film School Rejects*, 26 July 2017.

55. "18-Minute Analysis By Christopher Nolan On Story & Construction Of Memento," *Eyes On Cinema*, 20 November 2014.

56. Jeff Goldsmith, "The Architect of Dreams," *Creative Screenwriting*, July/August 2010.

57. "Christopher Nolan on *Following*—Conversations Inside The Criterion Collection," *VICE*, 24 August 2014.

58. "Trauma disrupts the continuity of one's sense of self-sameness and the ongoing flow and trajectory of life course," argues Vito Zepinic. "Trauma can cause a radical shift in the experiential planes and dimensions of the self (i.e., connection, coherence, continuity, autonomy, vitality, energy) and lead to a sense of being ungrounded, uncentred, and without an emotional anchor." (Vito Zepinic, *Hidden Scars: Understanding and Treating Complex Trauma* (2011).).

59. *Memento* underscores just how subjective these traumatic reminders are. The message "John G raped and murdered my wife" is tattooed across Leonard's chest, but backwards so that *he* can read it in the mirror. From the waist down, the tattoos (like the helpful "EAT") are upside down, so that Leonard can read them. Leonard is the audience for his own tattoos. They are a map of trauma that only he can read.

60. William G. Little, "Surviving *Memento*," *Narrative*, January 2005, p. 73.

61. Nolan is very clever in creating this association, in delivering set-up and pay-off, so that even the major plot reveals at the climax feel organic and foreshadowed. The tattoo needle (improvised from a pen and a sewing needle) seems to prefigure the insulin syringe. The shots of Leonard playful "pinching" his wife work well as distorted memories of administering her insulin injection. The opening and closing sequences even consciously mirror shots, as Leonard and Teddy visit the same dilapidated building for Leonard to enact his vengeance.

62. Examples include the broken window on Leonard's stolen car, which is later explained through a confrontation with Dodd; the abandoned truck at the old shack in the opening scene, with the bullets on the seat, which is later revealed as belonging to Teddy; the bruises on Natalie's face established in her opening scene, which are revealed as self-inflicted later on; the scratches on Leonard's face, which are explained in the film's final sequence.

63. The structure has the benefit of being slightly complex, but also very intuitive. Nolan even goes so far as to effectively map a chalkboard diagram of that arc in "18-Minute Analysis By Christopher Nolan On Story & Construction Of Memento," *Eyes On Cinema*, 20 November 2014.

64. Renfreu Neff and Daniel Argent, "Remembering Where it All Began: Christopher Nolan on *Memento*," *Creative Screenwriting*, 20 July 2015.

65. Scott Timberg, "Indie Angst," *The New Times Los Angeles*, 15 March 2001.

66. Geoff Andrew, "Christopher Nolan," *The Guardian*, 27 August 2002.

67. Scott Timberg, "Indie Angst," *The New Times Los Angeles*, 15 March 2001.

68. Kenneth Turan, "Oh, He's Just Playing With Your Mind," *The Los Angeles Times*, 22 January 2001.

69. Tom Shone, "Christopher Nolan: the man who rebooted the blockbuster," *The Guardian*, 4 November 2014.

70. Scott Timberg, "Indie Angst," *The New Times Los Angeles*, 15 March 2001.

71. David Sims, "How *Memento* Set the Framework for Christopher Nolan's Career," *The Atlantic*, 16 March 2016.

72. "DVD sales top VHS sales for first time," *Silicon Valley Business Journal*, 9 January 2002.

73. Stephen Dawson, "Gettin' better all the time: VHS to DVD to Blu-ray," *Sound and Image*, April 2010.

74. DVDs offered the ability to skip backwards and forwards through "chapters," to configure subtitles and to set language.

75. Indeed, many of the most successful early DVDs came with consciously "showy" DVD special features to emphasis the potential of the format. *The Matrix* was the best-selling DVD of its time, shifting over two million copies in the first year of release. (Eileen Fitzpatrick, "Dream Works' *Gladiator* May Be Biggest DVD Yet," *Billboard*, 9 December 2000.) It memorably promised audience members the opportunity to step outside the film in the middle of the narrative to peer behind the scenes by clicking the "red pill" while watching the film itself. (Jacob Beniflay, "*The Matrix*: Packed with Features," *The Tech*, 22 October 1999.)

76. Although not all audience members were appreciative of the immersive experience. (Christopher Borrelli, "*Memento* DVD tests patience," *The Blade*, 23 May 2002.)

77. Justin Morrow, "What Watching *Memento* in Chronological Order Can Teach About Story Structure," *No Film School*, 8 June 2013.

78. E.C. Newburger, "Home Computers and Internet Use in the United States: August 2000," Report P23-207, *U.S. Census Bureau*, September 2001.

79. Tom Lamont, "Napster: the day the music was set free," *The Guardian*, 24 February 2013.

80. One of the film's closing jokes has the title characters using the money garnered from the "Bluntman and Chronic" feature film to hunt down each of the posters who had insulted them on the internet.

81. Matt Singer, "Why Are Christopher Nolan Fans So Intense?," *ScreenCrush*, 14 November 2014.

82. Even ignoring the online fan communities and message boards, online press were willing to dig deep into the film's mysteries and ambiguities. *See*, for example, Andy Klein, "Everything you wanted to know about *Memento*," *Salon*, 28 June 2001.

83. This is explored very well in the chapter "So What Really Happened? *Memento*, Fans and Online Interpretive Strategies" in Claire Malloy, *Memento* (2010), p. 98–111.

84. These fans have occasionally been described in unflattering terms as "Nolanistas," at once a nod to their perceived pretension and their occasional militant outlook. (A. O. Scott, "*Inception* Criticism Raises Questions for Critics," *The New York Times*, 25 July 2010.) Critic Donald Clarke defines such fans as "male, youngish and convinced that the director of

*Batman Begins* is a genius to compare with Jean Renoir." (Donald Clarke, "Harry Styles gets part in *Dunkirk*. Nolanistas blow their top.," *The Irish Times*, 13 March 2016.)

85. James Mottram, *The Making of Memento* (2002), p. 125.

86. Damon Wise, "It's Unforgettable...," *The Observer*, 15 October 2000.

87. This argument is perhaps best articulated in Phillip E. Wegner, *Life Between Two Deaths, 1989–2001: U.S. Culture in the Long Nineties* (2009). The claim is also supported by Timothy Garton Ash, *Facts are Subversive: Political Writing from a Decade Without a Name* (2009). However, there is more casual and mainstream support for this viewpoint; Tom Brokaw, "The day the 21st century 'truly began,'" *NBC Nightly News*, 11 September 2011.

88. For a brief history, *see* Richard Hofstadter, "The Paranoid Style in American Politics," *Harpers*, November 1964.

89. Surveys conducted by Gallup have suggested that a majority of Americans have believed that Kennedy of a conspiracy dating back to the earliest polls in November 1963. By 1976, 81% of Americans believed that the Kennedy assassination was the work of a conspiracy. (Art Swift, "Majority in U.S. Still Believe JFK Killed in a Conspiracy," *Gallup*, 15 November 2013.)

90. David Greenberg, "Watergate Fueled Conspiracy Theories, Too," *Politico*, 17 June 2017.

91. Tom McNichol, "Richard Nixon's Last Secret," *Wired*, 1 July 2002.

92. At one point during the nineties, close to 80% of Americans believed that the United States government was involved in a cover-up involving extra-terrestrial life. ("Poll: U.S. hiding knowledge of aliens," *CNN*, 15 June 1997)

93. Nick Harding, "Truth and Lies: Conspiracy Theories are Running Rampant Thanks to Modern Technology," *The Independent*, 12 November 2011.

94. Philip Wiess, "Clinton Crazy," *The New York Times*, 23 February 1997.

95. Francis X. Clines, "First Lady Levels Attack Against 'Vast Right-Wing Conspiracy,'" *The New York Times*, 28 January 1998.

96. Fringe right-wing grounds were producing popular "documentaries" like *The Clinton Chronicles* or *Circle of Power* to spread these ideas. (David Corn, "Here Come the Crazy Clinton Conspiracies of the 1990s," *Mother Jones*, 20 February 2014.) 300,000 copies of *The Clinton Chronicles* were put into circulation, with about half of them sold. (Murray Waas, "The Falwell Connection," *Salon*, March 1998.)

97. Andrew Calcutt, "The surprising origins of 'post-truth'—and how it was spawned by the liberal left," *The Conversation*, 18 November 2016.

98. This occurred on both sides of the political spectrum. In the nineties fringe right-wing groups used postmodernism to justify Holocaust denial. (*See*, for example, Robert Eaglestone, *Postmodernism and Holocaust Denial* [2001].) At the same time, there was considerable tension about how best to approach discussions about the nuclear bombings of Hiroshima and Nagasaki at the end of the Second World War. (John Kifner, "Hiroshima: A Controversy That Refuses to Die," *The New York Times*, 31 January 1995.)

99. This is perhaps most noticeable through the acknowledgement of past crimes and indiscretions. The legacy of former Nazi turned space pioneer Hubertus Strughold was called into question, particularly how deeply he had been embraced by the United States establishment during the space race. ("Portrait of Nazi Prompts Protest," *The New York Times*, 26 October 1993.) Similarly, Bill Clinton would issue an apology for illegal radiation experiments conducted on an unsuspecting public between 1944 and 1974. (Marlene Cimons, "Clinton Apologizes for Radiation Tests," *The Los Angeles Times*, 4 October 1995.)

100. Charles Krauthammer, "The Unipolar Moment," *Foreign Affairs*, Winter 1990.

101. Francis Fukuyama, "The End of History?," *The National Interest*, Summer 1989.

102. Clive Crook, "Globalization and its critics," *The Economist*, 27 September 2001.

103. Eric Alterman, "Culture Wars," *Rolling Stone*, 19 October 1995.

104. Steven D. Levitt, "Understanding Why Crime Fell in the 1990s: Four Factors that Explain the Decline and Six that Do Not," *Journal of Economic Perspectives*, Winter 2004.

105. Jesenia M. Pizarro, Steven M. Chermak and Jeffrey A. Gruenewald, "Juvenile 'Super-Predators' in the News: A Comparison of Adult and Juvenile Homicides," *Journal of Criminal Justice and Popular Culture*, January 2007.

106. Clifford Cobb, Ted Halstead, and Jonathan Rowe, "If the GDP is Up, Why is America Down?," *The Atlantic*, October 1995.

107. "The further society advances, the more sophisticated its technologies become, the more rational, orderly, safe and peaceful it should become, we would like to believe," Barna Donovan articulates. "But why is there more disorder, instability, uncertainty and chaos? Someone must be responsible for this, the conspiracy theory argues. The dawn of the twenty-first century should be a world advancing towards utopia. However, it's not. Environmental devastation, disease, terrorism, war and economic uncertainties are the order of the day. There must be a hidden hand orchestrating all this misfortune." (Barna William Donovan, *Conspiracy Films: A Tour of Dark Places in the American Conscious* (2011), p. 7.)

108. Dan Berry, "No Stranger to Conspiracy," *The New York Times*, 18 August 2013.

109. The fact that Leonard can remember that story which would have occurred after his accident, but fudges the details so that it happened to somebody else, suggests that it is possible for new events of sufficient emotional power to make a subconscious impression on him. However, Leonard does not have to accept them.

110. This is a classic *film noir* convention, with several classic films like *Somewhere in the Night* and *The Crooked Way* feature amnesiacs investigating their own lives. (William Park, *What is Film Noir?* (2011), p. 25.)

111. Subsequent scenes reveal that Natalie is simply exploiting Leonard, demonstrating how worthless Leonard's love of his wife is, except as a tool to manipulate him.

112. Hal Arkowitz and Scott O. Lilienfeld, "Why Science Tells Us Not to Rely on Eyewitness Accounts," *Scientific American*, 1 January 2010.

113. Ed Yong, "When Memories are Remembered, They Can Be Rewritten," *National Geographic*, 20 May 2013.

114. In some ways, Leonard's exploitation of his condition to justify his self-deception reflects the way in which Nolan structures his films in such a way as to justify their stylistic conceits; the use of slow motion to

represent time dilation in *Inception*, or the backward flow of *Memento*.

115. "The world doesn't disappear when you close your eyes, does it?" Leonard asks Natalie in the restaurant. It is a rhetorical question, but the movie's closing sequence suggests that Leonard has repeatedly asked the question of himself. Driving away from the crime scene, Leonard monologues to himself, "I have to believe that when my eyes are closed, the world's still here. Do I believe the world's still here? Is it still out there?"

116. Discussing the origin of *Inception* on its release in July 2010, Nolan explained "it took me the last 10 years to finish it and get it right." (Iain Blair, "A Minute With: Director Nolan talks about *Inception*," *Reuters*, 15 July 2010.)

117. Both Joe Pantoliano and Carrie-Anne Moss appear in supporting roles in both *The Matrix* and *Memento*. However, to underscore how fragile reality was in nineties cinema, this is the second movie in which Guy Pearce plays a character chasing a fictional construct that he blames for the death of loved one. (In *Memento*, Leonard chases "Johnny G." In *L.A. Confidential*, Ed Exley is haunted by "Rolo Tomassi.")

118. Randy Laist, "The Hyperreal Theme in 1990s American Cinema," *Americana : The Journal of American Popular Culture, 1900 to Present*, Spring 2010.

119. In some ways, Jonathan Nolan's work on *Westworld* could be seen to hark back to these existential crises of the late nineties, with the film unfolding in a virtual reality theme park populated by individuals who have no idea of their situation. "Have you ever questioned the nature of your reality?" is a frequent refrain. This nineties frame of reference did not go unnoticed. (Christopher Hooton, "*Westworld* is *The Truman Show* meets *Groundhog Day* meets *Red Dead Redemption*," *The Independent*, 3 October 2016.)

120. Jean Baudrillard, *L'illusion de la Fin* (1994), p. 9.

121. Jason Farago, "The '90s: The Decade that Never Ended," *BBC Culture*, 5 February 2015.

122. Kurt Anderson, "You Say You Want a Devolution?," *Vanity Fair*, January 2012.

123. Scott Timberg, "Indie Angst," *The New Times Los Angeles*, 15 March 2001.

124. James Mottram, *The Making of Memento* (2002).

125. Of course, there is also no small irony in the fact that Teddy explicitly calls out Leonard for creating mysteries where they don't actually exist, "a puzzle [he] could never solve."

126. "NYCC: *The Dark Knight Rises*—Jonathan Nolan Discusses the Film's End," *IGN*, 13 October 2012.

127. Ian Phillips, "A fan asked Christopher Nolan about the end of *Inception* and he explained why he'd never tell," *Business Insider*, 23 April 2015.

128. Melissa Anelli, "GU Alum Becomes the *Memento*-Man," *The Hoya*, 16 March 2001.

129. Ian Phillips, "A fan asked Christopher Nolan about the end of *Inception* and he explained why he'd never tell," *Business Insider*, 23 April 2015.

130. Tom Shone, "Christopher Nolan: the man who rebooted the blockbuster," *The Guardian*, 4 November 2014.

131. David Sims, "How *Memento* Set the Framework for Christopher Nolan's Career," *The Atlantic*, 16 March 2016.

132. This harks back to Nolan's observations on how narrative gaps in Graham Stiles' *Waterland* draw the audience into the story, which was an obvious influence on his technique. (Jeff Goldsmith, "The Architect of Dreams," *Creative Screenwriting*, July/August 2010.)

133. "NYCC: *The Dark Knight Rises*—Jonathan Nolan Discusses the Film's End," *IGN*, 13 October 2012.

## Chapter 3

1. Scott Beggs, "No Sleep: Revisiting The Christopher Nolan Movie No One Seems to Remember," *Film School Rejects*, 20 July 2012.

2. *See*, for example: Josh Spiegel, "Revisiting *Insomnia*, Christopher Nolan's Most Underrated and Forgotten Film,"/*Film*, 18 July 2017; Thomas Hanrahan, "Before *Dunkirk*, we review Christopher Nolan's forgotten classic, *Insomnia*," Digital Fox, 15 July 2017.

3. Dean Kish, "Interview: Christopher Nolan talks about Insomnia and other future projects," *Showbiz Monkeys*, 7 May 2002.

4. The Writers Guild of America named *Memento* as the one hundredth best script ever written. ("101 Greatest Screenplays," *Writers Guild of America*, March 2005.) The Editors Guild cited it as the fourteenth best edited film ever made. ("The 75 Best Edited Films," *Editors Guild Magazine*, May-June 2012.)

5. The trilogy's cultural impact has been likened to that of the *Godfather* trilogy in exploring contemporary American culture through genre fiction. (Tom Shone, "The *Dark Knight* trilogy as our generation's *Godfather*," *The Guardian*, 20 July 2012.)

6. Somewhat ironically, given that *Insomnia* is the only Nolan film on which Nolan does not have a writing or story credit, *Insomnia* was written and directed by Erik Skjoldbjærg.

7. Dean Kish, "Interview: Christopher Nolan talks about Insomnia and other future projects," *Showbiz Monkeys*, 7 May 2002.

8. Phillip Duncan, "DVDTalk Interview—Christopher Nolan—Director of *Insomnia*," *DVD Talk*, October 2002.

9. Dean Kish, "Interview: Christopher Nolan talks about Insomnia and other future projects," *Showbiz Monkeys*, 7 May 2002.

10. Scott Feinberg, "Christopher Nolan on *Interstellar* Critics, Making Original Films and Shunning Cellphones and Email," *The Hollywood Reporter*, 3 January 2015.

11. "Here, as in *Memento*," reflected film Mick LaSalle, "the director shows how film bright can be as dramatic, oppressive and revealing as film noir." (Mick LaSalle, "Obsession hot and cold/*Insomnia* brings out a new side of weary Pacino," *The San Francisco Gate Chronicle*, 24 May 2002.)

12. Eddie Cockrell, "Sun-drenched film noir," *The Weekend Australian*, 17 August 2013.

13. Geoff Andrew, "Christopher Nolan," *The Guardian*, 27 August 2002.

14. Writer Tyler Sheridan's "frontier" would build upon this idea, with the first two films (*Sicario* and *Hell or High Water*) set on the more traditional desert frontier while the third (*Wind River*) is set on the colder snow frontier. Indeed, many contemporary westerns (such as *The Revenant* or *The Hateful Eight*) have transitioned away from the rugged desert frontier towards a much colder sort of terrain.

15. See, for example, David Melbye, *Landscape Allegory in Cinema* (2010).

16. During his closing mono-

logue, the camera takes in the road ahead of Leonard. Because of his condition, Leonard can travel the same roads over and over, but they will seem fresh and exciting each time. The same road has limitless potential.

17. See, for example, David Hamilton Murdoch, *The American West: The Invention of a Myth* (2001).

18. Frederick Jackson Turner, "The Significance of the Frontier in American History," *Report of the American Historical Association*, 1893.

19. This is a recurring motif in modern westerns, stories that unfold against the backdrop of states like California and Alaska. In *Heat*, Neil McCauley lives in a villa overlooking the Pacific Ocean, and dreams of escaping further west to Fiji. It is clear that McCauley is an outlaw who is running out of time and space in Los Angeles, as order and civilization encroach upon him, this sentiment reinforced by the use of abandoned urban locations like the drive-in movie-theatre that would be demolished to room for condominiums shortly after the film was released. (April Wright, "When Teenagers Stopped Necking at the Drive-In," *Zócalo Public Square*, 12 March 2014.)

20. Jake Coyle, "The new Western? The mind is latest movie frontier," Boston.com, 14 July 2010.

21. Fred Turner, "Cyberspace as the New Frontier?: Mapping the Shifting Boundaries of the Network Society," *Red Rock Eater News Service*, 1999.

22. Indeed, *Interstellar* star Matthew McConaughey would refer to space as "the frontier to the north" in press around the release of the film. (David Itzkoff, "Flight Club," *The New York Times*, 22 October 2014.)

23. Tim Burton's *Batman* famously hinged on marketing that sold the film based on the character's logo rather than the movie title. (Noel Murray, "How the 1989 *Batman* logo helped set the course for superhero movies," *The Dissolve*, 9 October 2013.)

24. Phil Hoad, "Good ol' future boys: *Interstellar* and sci-fi's obsession with Americana," *The Guardian*, 4 November 2014.

25. Joel Silberman, "Why Christopher Nolan's *Interstellar* is good for America," *The Los Angeles Times*, 10 November 2014.

26. *The Prestige* takes place largely in London and features a predominantly British cast, along with a British protagonist in Alfred Borden. At the same time, the movie also travels to America and pits Borden against American magician Robert Angier. As such, unlike the rest of Nolan's films between *Following* and *Dunkirk*, *The Prestige* seems to straddle the Atlantic.

27. Andrew Pulver, "He's not a god—he's human," *The Guardian*, 15 June 2005.

28. Warner Brothers would split distribution rights on *The Prestige* with Buena Vista and on *Interstellar* with Paramount. In both cases, Warners would retain control of international distribution.

29. Matt Prigge, "David Ayer on why he won't be making a director's cut of *Suicide Squad*," *Metro USA*, 5 August 2016.

30. Kim Masters, "*Superman vs. Batman*? DC's Real Battle Is How to Create Its Superhero Universe," *The Hollywood Reporter*, 29 April 2015.

31. Rob Cain, "Even With Star Director Nolan, *Dunkirk* Was A High-Risk Gamble For Warner Bros," *Forbes*, 23 July 2017.

32. Kim Masters, "Warner Bros. Eyes Slimmed-Down Movie Budgets Under Toby Emmerich," *The Hollywood Reporter*, 21 June 2017.

33. David Gritten, "Warner Brothers: ninety years of grit and greatness," *The Telegraph*, 4 April 2013.

34. Geoff Andrew, "Christopher Nolan," *The Guardian*, 27 August 2002.

35. Patrick Goldstein, "Could Chris Nolan have convinced anyone but Warners to make *Inception*?," *The Los Angeles Times*, 19 July 2010.

36. Ben Fritz, "Why Hollywood Loves *Interstellar* Director Christopher Nolan," *The Wall Street Journal*, 30 October 2014.

37. Dean Kish, "Interview: Christopher Nolan talks about Insomnia and other future projects," *Showbiz Monkeys*, 7 May 2002.

38. Tom Shone, "Christopher Nolan: the man who rebooted the blockbuster," *The Guardian*, 4 November 2014.

39. Trevor Hogg, "*Dark Knight*: Lee Smith talks about Christopher Nolan," *Flickering Myth*, 12 December 2012.

40. "180°: Christopher Nolan Interviews Al Pacino" (2002).

41. Jeffrey Ressner, "The Traditionalist," *Director's Guild of America Quarterly*, Spring 2012.

42. Nolan has suggested that his love of cross-cutting is an efficient way of covering up any gaps found during the editing process, with the ability to cut between multiple story threads serving to cover-up any missing material. ("Christopher Nolan on *Following*—Conversations Inside The Criterion Collection," *VICE*, 24 August 2014.)

43. Trevor Hogg, "*Dark Knight*: Lee Smith talks about Christopher Nolan," *Flickering Myth*, 12 December 2012.

44. Phillip Duncan, "DVDTalk Interview—Christopher Nolan—Director of *Insomnia*," *DVD Talk*, October 2002.

45. Trevor Hogg, "*Dark Knight*: Lee Smith talks about Christopher Nolan," *Flickering Myth*, 12 December 2012.

46. Tom Shone, "Christopher Nolan: The man who rebooted the blockbuster," *The Guardian*, 4 November 2014.

47. Geoff Andrew, "Christopher Nolan," *The Guardian*, 27 August 2002.

48. Geoff Andrew, "Christopher Nolan," *The Guardian*, 27 August 2002.

49. In contrast, Dormer happens upon a convenient dog carcass that can serve the same purpose in the remake, without having to kill an innocent animal to exonerate himself.

50. In contrast, Dormer's confrontation with the equivalent character in the remake is not sexually coded; although she shamelessly flirts with him, he terrifies her with a stunt on the road.

51. In contrast, the dynamic between Dormer and Clement is very much asexual. Their most intimate shared scene comes at the climax of the story, when Dormer confesses his indiscretion to Clement and seeks her absolution.

52. Perhaps owing to its status as a production by a much larger studio, *Insomnia* ends on a more uplifting note than *Memento*. Dormer dies, but his death serves as a cautionary tale. While Leonard refused to learn his lesson in *Memento*, engaging in a continuing cycle of death and destruction, Dormer decides to clean the slate in his dying moments. Dying in the arms of Detective Ellie Burr, he refuses to allow her to cover for his sins and to corrupt herself in the way that he did. "Don't lose your way," he implores her.

53. Scott Bowles, "Movies to keep you awake at night," *USA Today*, 24 May 2002.

54. It is also reflected in the way that Nolan uses editing to suggest

Dormer's hallucinations and his increased exhaustion, as well as a sequence towards the end of the film when Dormer (and the audience) are practically blinded by the simple act of turning on a light switch.

55. Geoff Andrew, "Christopher Nolan," *The Guardian*, 27 August 2002.

56. Josh Wigler, "*Dark Knight Rises* Director Christopher Nolan Always Knew 'How To End The Story,'" *MTV*, 23 July 2012.

57. Rob Blackwelder, "Wide Awake & Living a Dream," *Spliced Wire*, May 2002.

58. Geoff Andrew, "Christopher Nolan," *The Guardian*, 27 August 2002.

59. One of the great irony of long takes—especially *absurdly* long takes—is the way in which they distort reality for the audience. A single long take involves placing the camera in a subjective viewpoint, and so should theoretically come closer to capturing how a person sees the world. However, it also requires a great deal of energy for the audience to keep pace. Editing and cutting is about revealing and controlling information, so long takes tend to overwhelm the audience with information and ask them to focus on too much at once. (Scott Kaufman, "How reality becomes a function of film technique in *Birdman*," *The A.V. Club*, 3 March 2015.)

60. *Insomnia* is actually *more* kinetic than Nolan's other films. It has an average shot length of 2.5 seconds, while the median shot length is 1.7. This is appreciable shorter than *Memento*, where the average shot length is 3.5 seconds and the median shot length is 2.4. It is also shorter than *The Dark Knight*, which has an average shot length of 3.1 seconds and a median shot length of 2.3.

61. "These cleverly filmed inserts not only bring to life what happens when a bullet rips through skin, bone and organ, and illustrate the significance of blood splatter or ripped fibres; they also move the story along as well as any conventional cop show car chase or shootout," explains Gerard Gilbert of the technique employed by the television series. (Gerard Gilbert, "*CSI*: The cop show that conquered the world," *The Independent*, 19 December 2006.)

62. Although the use of inserts in this capacity does provide a nice callback to *Following*. Nolan includes a nice quick shot of Dormer putting on latex gloves to examine the body, harking back to the opening shot of his very first film.

63. Then again, it seems a little absurd to single out Nolan's direction of *Insomnia* for being overly literal. The film is about a detective who cannot sleep named "Will Dormer," his surname evoking the French verb for "to sleep." Finch also keeps framed pictures of birds around his apartment, tying into his own name. *Insomnia* is not an especially subtle film, but there is nothing inherently wrong with that.

64. For a more in-depth discussion of this approach, *see* David Bordwell, "Nolan vs. Nolan," *Observations on Film Art*, 19 August 2012.

65. Although somewhat less obvious, Nolan does something similar at the climax of *Batman Begins*, where the director seems to want a third thread to intercut between Gordon in the Batmobile and Batman on the train, so the film features repeated cuts to the staff at Wayne Tower repeating exposition about the water mains.

66. Peter Travers described it as "taut, tense and terrific." (Peter Travers, "*Insomnia*," *Rolling Stone*, 8 May 2002.) Roger Ebert likened it to "a new production of a good play." (Roger Ebert, "*Insomnia*," *The Chicago Sun-Times*, 24 May 2002.)

67. Scott Feinberg, "Christopher Nolan on *Interstellar* Critics, Making Original Films and Shunning Cellphones and Email," *The Hollywood Reporter*, 3 January 2015.

68. For example, Universal Pictures hired Colin Trevorrow to work on *Jurassic World* after his success with the indie film *Safety Not Guaranteed*. Similarly, 20th Century-Fox recruited Josh Trank to work on *Fantastic Four* following his popular indie film *Chronicle*. Disney have entrusted the production of *Star Wars: Episode VIII—The Last Jedi* to director Rian Johnson, best known for a string of low-budget cult films like *Brick, The Brothers Bloom* and *Looper*.

69. Disney hired quirky New Zealand director Taika Waititi to direct *Thor: Ragnarok* based primarily on his popular New Zealand films like *What We Do in the Shadows* or *The Hunt for the Wilderpeople*. The result was a film with greater critical acclaim (92% positive on *Rotten Tomatoes*; 73% on *Metacritic*) and higher box office returns ($752m) than either *Thor* (77%; 57%; $449m) or *Thor: The Dark World* (66%; 54%; $644).

70. Josh Trank's work on *Fantastic Four* might be the most obvious example here. The director was hired by 20th Century–Fox off the strength of his work on the low-budget indie film *Chronicle*. However, *Fantastic Four* was quickly plagued with rumors of creative conflicts and mismanagement. Reportedly, Trank's involvement with the project was minimised by the studio in the post-production phase. (Kim Masters, "*Fantastic Four* Blame Game: Fox, Director Josh Trank Square Off Over On-Set 'Chaos,'" *The Hollywood Reporter*, 12 August 2015.)

71. Disney's management of their *Star Wars* franchise has been ruthlessly efficient and effective when it comes to dealing with directors whose perspectives do not line up with their own. Garth Edwards' *Rogue One—A Star Wars Story* was reportedly heavily reworked in postproduction. (Andrew Liptak, "*Rogue One*'s reshoots show how Disney saved the first standalone *Star Wars* movie," *The Verge*, 15 January 2017.) Similarly, veteran director Ron Howard was brought in to oversee production of *Solo—A Star Wars Story* after original directors Phil Lord and Christopher Miller clashed with the studio. (Kim Masters, "*Star Wars* Firing Reveals a Disturbance in the Franchise," *The Hollywood Reporter*, 26 June 2017.)

72. Director Patty Jenkins walked away from *Thor: The Dark World* over fundamental disagreements with the studio. (Adam Chitwood, "Patty Jenkins' Idea for *Thor 2* Was a Romeo-and-Juliet-Esque Space Opera," *Collider*, 1 June 2017.) This reportedly caused tension between Marvel Studios and Natalie Portman, who did not return for *Thor: Ragnarok*. (Yohana Desta, "Natalie Portman Is 'Done' with *Thor*," *Vanity Fair*, 18 August 2016.) However, Jenkins did move over to Warner Brothers, where she had a much more productive relationship developing *Wonder Woman*. (Julia Alexander, "Wonder Woman team didn't feel pressured to make 'the same' DCU movie," *Polygon*, 28 June 2017.)

73. Ava DuVernay declined to direct *Black Panther* for Marvel Studios because of the commitment involved and the control surrendered. "For me, it was a process of trying to figure out, are these people I want to go to bed with?" she explains. "Because it's really a marriage, and for this it would be three years. It'd be three years of not doing other things

that are important to me." (Ashley Lee, "Ava DuVernay's Advice on Hollywood: 'Follow the White Guys, They've Got This Thing Wired,'" *The Hollywood Reporter*, 18 July 2015.)

74. Interestingly, *Batman Begins* blends the warm orange colours of *Memento* with the cold blue of *Insomnia*, using orange to represent the urban decay of Gotham and blue to capture the remoteness of Tibet. By the time that Nolan returns to Gotham in *The Dark Knight*, the entire city is as cold as those Tibetan landscapes.

## Chapter 4

1. For example, the release dates of Nolan's first three films are quite close together. *Following* secured a small British theatrical run in November 1999, *Memento* secured a limited release in March 2001, while *Insomnia* was released in May 2002. This was a very tight run of films. Barring the one-year gap between *Batman Begins* and *The Prestige*, Nolan would stagger his later output. There was a three year gap between *Insomnia* and *Batman Begins*, and two years between *The Prestige* and *The Dark Knight*, *The Dark Knight* and *Inception*, *Inception* and *The Dark Knight Rises*, *The Dark Knight Rises* and *Interstellar*.
2. Claude Brodesser-Akner, "After Batman 3, Christopher Nolan Wants to Make His Shelved Howard Hughes Biopic," *Vulture*, 11 February 2011.
3. Dean Kish, "Interview: Christopher Nolan talks about Insomnia and other future projects," *Showbiz Monkeys*, 7 May 2002.
4. Geoff Andrew, "Christopher Nolan," *The Guardian*, 27 August 2002.
5. Scott Tobias, "Christopher Nolan," *The A.V. Club*, 5 June 2002.
6. Dean Kish, "Interview: Christopher Nolan talks about Insomnia and other future projects," *Showbiz Monkeys*, 7 May 2002.
7. Liane Bonin, "Jim Carrey will play Howard Hughes," *Entertainment Weekly*, 3 January 2002.
8. Neil Young, "(Michael) Marty and Howard: A Longer Look at Martin Scorsese's *The Aviator*," *Neil Young's Film Lounge*, 31 January 2005.
9. *Armageddon* and *Deep Impact* both dealt with the threat of an imminent asteroid strike on Earth, and were both released in 1998. That same year, *Saving Private Ryan* and *The Thin Red line* were both prestige dramas about the Second World War that went head-to-heat at the Oscars. Pixar and Dreamworks would both release their own films about nonconformist insects that same year, with *A Bug's Life* and *Antz*.
10. Marlow Stern, "Christopher Nolan Uncut: On *Interstellar*, Ben Affleck's Batman, and the Future of Mankind," *The Daily Beast*, 10 November 2014.
11. After the release of Inception, there were rumors that Nolan would follow up *The Dark Knight Rises* by returning to that script, aiming for a release a decade after *The Aviator*. (Terri Schwartz, "Christopher Nolan Soars With Howard Hughes Biopic 10 Years After *The Aviator*," *MTV*, 14 February 2011.) However, this proved not to be the case. (Kofi Outlaw, "Chris Nolan Still Interested in James Bond; Howard Hughes Film Dead," *Screen Rant*, 4 June 2012.) Nevertheless, *The Dark Knight Rises* includes a none-too-subtle allusion to Howard Hughes when Bruce Wayne becomes a recluse and John Daggett dismissively comments, "We all know he's holed up with eight-inch fingernails and peeing into Mason jars." These were references to some of Hughes more extreme neuroses.
12. Joal Ryan, "Razzies Razz *Batman & Robin*," *E! News*, 9 February 1998.
13. Variety Staff, "'Bat' beats up B.O.," *Variety*, 8 July 1997.
14. Mark S. Reinhart, *The Batman Filmography* (2013), p. 190.
15. Rob Leane, "*Batman Triumphant*: examining the sequel that never happened," *Den of Geek*, 21 March 2016.
16. Aaron Couch, "Before *Batman Begins*: Secret History of the Movies That Almost Got Made," *The Hollywood Reporter*, 14 June 2015.
17. The Scarecrow would be the only villain to appear in all three films, and one of only five characters to appear in the complete trilogy; the others are Bruce Wayne, Alfred Pennyworth, Lucius Fox and James Gordon. The character of Fredericks would appear in *Batman Begins* and *The Dark Knight Rises*, but would only appear in the promotional material for *The Dark Knight* rather than the film itself.
18. Whatever about their own merits, the Tim Burton *Batman* movies were adaptations in *very* loose terms. In *Batman*, the Joker murdered the Waynes and created Batman. In *Batman Returns*, the Penguin was a monstrous circus freak while Catwoman appeared to have been reincarnated by cat magic.
19. To be fair, Raimi did have *some* minor experience directing superhero films. He had directed Liam Neeson in *Darkman*, a cult 1990 superhero revenge film.
20. Lance Ulanoff, "Enough, already, with the superhero movies," *Mashable*, 15 July 2015.
21. Matt Peaches, "Steven Spielberg Predicts Superhero Movies Will Die Off Like Westerns," *Esquire*, 5 September 2015.
22. Patrick Shanley, "In the Shadow of Superheroes, Westerns Are (Quietly) Popular," *The Hollywood Reporter*, 28 February 2017.
23. Jeffrey A. Brown, "How Marvel's superheroes found the magic to make us all true believers," *The Observer*, 31 August 2013.
24. See, for example, Liam Burke, "Sowing the Seeds: How 1990s Marvel Animation Facilitated Today's Cinematic Universe" in *Marvel Comics into Film: Essays on Adaptations Since the 1940s* (2016), p. 113.
25. Cassandra Hsiao, "Post-9/11 world: What caused the rise of superhero movies," *The Los Angeles Times*, 16 June 2016.
26. Todd VanDerWerff, "Superhero movies have become an endless attempt to rewrite 9/11," *Vox*, 11 September 2016.
27. Jason Dittmer, "Captain America in the news: changing mediascapes and the appropriation of a superhero" in *Superheroes and Identities* (2016).
28. This perhaps most obvious in the Marvel Comics written during the first decade of the 21st century, when writers and artists attempted to grapple with existential questions relating to the war on terror. Mark Millar and Steve McNiven framed a classic "freedom-versus-security" debate in their massive *Civil War* crossover in 2005, an event that affected almost the entire line. (See, for example, the entire collection of Kevin Michael Scott (ed.), *Marvel Comics' Civil War and the Age of Terror: Critical Essays on the Comic Saga* (2015).) During *Dark Reign*, largely driven by writer Brian Michael Bendis, the heroes of the Marvel Universe found themselves living under a pseudo-fascist and totalitarian regime anchored in notions of homeland security, protecting the country from alien invaders and foreign gods.

29. Elizabeth Sandifer, "An Accurately Named Trilogy I: *Batman Begins*," *Eruditorum Press*, 6 November 2017.
30. Max Nicholson, "Director Boaz Yakin on the Live-Action *Batman Beyond* Movie That Never Was," *IGN*, 14 June 2015.
31. Frank Miller even drafted the script. (Matt Goldberg, "Darren Aronofsky Wanted Joaquin Phoenix to Star in His R-Rated *Batman: Year One*," *Collider*, 15 September 2017.)
32. Mike Cecchini, "The *Batman v Superman* We Never Saw," *Den of Geek*, 17 November 2017.
33. Scott Feinberg, "Christopher Nolan on *Interstellar* Critics, Making Original Films and Shunning Cellphones and Email," *The Hollywood Reporter*, 3 January 2015.
34. Pat Jankiewicz, "Dark Knight Resurrected," *Starlog #337*, August 2005.
35. Colin Covert, "Christopher Nolan explains his 'cinematic brain' at Walker Art Center," *Star Tribune*, 6 May 2015.
36. "*Batman Begins* press conference, part two," *Time Out London*, 16 June 2005.
37. Christopher Nolan and David S. Goyer, *Batman Begins: The Screenplay* (2005), page xxix.
38. Scott Feinberg, "Christopher Nolan on *Interstellar* Critics, Making Original Films and Shunning Cellphones and Email," *The Hollywood Reporter*, 3 January 2015.
39. "*Batman Begins* press conference, part two," *Time Out London*, 16 June 2005.
40. More than that, there is a lot of evidence to suggest that *Superman Returns* is actually a sequel to Richard Donner's original version of *Superman II* (which was restored and released in November 2006) rather than the theatrical cut released by Richard Lester in June 1981
41. Bryan Singer has retroactively acknowledged that perhaps he was *too* faithful to the films that inspired him in crafting *Superman Returns*. (Ed Gross, "*Superman Returns*: Bryan Singer and Brandon Routh look back 10 years later," *Empire*, 26 April 2016.)
42. Leslie Gornstein, "Why does *Superman Returns* have to make so much just to break even?," *E! News*, 15 July 2005.
43. One of the ironies of this contrast between *Superman Returns* and *Batman Begins* is that both films made a roughly equivalent amount of money at the box office. *Batman Begins* made $372m worldwide, while *Superman Returns* made $391m. However, the production budget on *Batman Begins* was only $150m, while the budget on *Superman Returns* was $270m.
44. This is perhaps most evident in the freedom that Warner Brothers afforded Zack Snyder to reinvent Superman in *Man of Steel* and *Batman vs. Superman*, an iteration of the character that consciously rejected the nostalgia of *Superman Returns*. However, in large part due to internet backlash to this provocative interpretation, Warner Brothers would insist on a more nostalgic approach for Snyder's *Justice League* film. The result was a massive commercial disappointment. (Zack Sharf, "*Justice League* Box Office Bomb: Warner Bros. Could Lose Up to $100 Million on Superhero Tentpole," *IndieWire*, 24 November 2017.)
45. Pat Jankiewicz, "Dark Knight Resurrected," *Starlog #337*, August 2005.
46. Spence D., "Batman Vs. Hans Zimmer and James Newton Howard Part 2," *IGN*, 13 June 2005.
47. Working on *Man of Steel*, in the shadow of John Williams' iconic score, Zimmer's mantra was, "Forget anything that's happened before." (Steve Weintraub, "Hans Zimmer Talks *Man of Steel*, How He Crafted the Score, Dealing with the Pressure of Following John Williams, Nolan's *Interstellar*, *Rush*, and More," *Collider*, 6 June 2013.) In the case of the introduction of Ben Affleck's Batman in *Batman vs. Superman*, Zimmer cannily sidestepped the possibility of self-plagiarism by outsourcing the writing of his theme to collaborator Junkie XL. (Rebecca Hawkes, "Hans Zimmer's *Batman vs Superman* dilemma," *The Telegraph*, 4 November 2014.)
48. Louise McCreesh, "Justice League features both the classic *Batman* and *Superman* themes," *Digital Spy*, 13 November 2017.
49. That said, the introduction of Bruce Wayne in the batsuit at the docks does include a nod to the introduction of Bruce Wayne at the start of Tim Burton's *Batman*. In both cases, a confused and terrified criminal demands to know the identity of their attacker. Bruce confidently replies, "I'm Batman."
50. Pat Jankiewicz, "Dark Knight Resurrected," *Starlog #337*, August 2005.
51. Christopher Karr, "The Dark Knight and the Rise of 'Realistic' Superheroes on Screen," *Highbrow Magazine*, 25 July 2012.
52. *Blade Runner* was a conscious and massive influence on several members of the production team, including production designer Nathan Crowley and cinematography Wally Pfister. (Mark Hughes, "Exclusive: Christopher Nolan Talks *Batman Begins* 10th Anniversary," *Forbes*, 30 July 2015.)
53. *The Dark Knight* and *The Dark Knight Rises* are similarly exaggerated. *The Dark Knight* features a sequence in which Bruce somehow manages to pull finger prints off a bullet that was fired into (and shattered within) a concrete wall while Harvey Dent's transformation happens at "two-fifty, fifty-second street," an address worthy of *Batman '66*. Indeed, the climax of *The Dark Knight Rises*, wherein Batman "just can't get rid of a bomb" is a rather cheeky nod to a similar sequence in Adam West's *Batman!* movie.
54. Adam Smith, "The Making Of *Superman*," *Empire #148*, October 2001.
55. Marc Graser and Cathy Dunkley, "The bat and the beautiful," *Variety*, 8 February 2004.
56. Mark Bernardin, "Christopher Nolan on 'Extreme Places' in the Making of *The Dark Knight Rises*," *The Hollywood Reporter*, 27 December 2012.
57. Charlie Jane Anders, "Why *The Dark Knight* Really Is A Science Fiction Film," *io9*, 31 December 2008.
58. Mark Hughes, "Exclusive: Christopher Nolan Talks *Batman Begins* 10th Anniversary," *Forbes*, 30 July 2015.
59. Mark Seymour, "Double Negative Breaks Down *Batman Begins*," *FX Guide*, 18 July 2005.
60. The elevated train is briefly visible in the background of an early establishing shot in *The Dark Knight*, when the bank robbers pick up the Joker at the street corner. However, the train and the Narrows are largely absent from the final two entries in the series.
61. Jim Emerson, "On the whole 'realism' thing...," RogerEbert.com, 26 September 2011.
62. Pat Jankiewicz, "Dark Knight Resurrected," *Starlog #337*, August 2005.
63. Superman is a literal embodiment of the American dream, an immigrant who came to a foreign land and made something of himself. Batman is a member of the aristocracy, and so more invested in

ideas of class than most contemporaneous American pop culture. Indeed, there were reports of an early *Batman* radio pilot where Batman distinguished himself from Bruce Wayne by speaking in a British accent. (Jim Harmon, *Radio Mystery and Adventure and Its Appearances in Film, Television and Other Media* (2003), p. 205.)

64. Finger recalls, "Bruce Wayne's first name came from Robert Bruce, the Scottish patriot. Wayne, being a playboy, was a man of gentry. I searched for a name that would suggest colonialism." (Bob Kane and Tom Andrae, *Batman & Me* (1989), p. 44.)

65. Outside of Nolan himself, the film series overlapped significantly with Scottish writer Grant Morrison's extended run on the titles, *Batman*, *Batman & Robin* and *Batman Incorporated*. Even *Batman Begins* features a minor role for the villain of Victor Zsasz, who was co-created by British writer Alan Grant, who worked on the character in the comics during the eighties and long into the nineties.

66. Bale conceded, "I just feel that Batman is such an American character that in representing him in doing the interviews I don't want to be sounding English because that would be peculiar." (Wilson Morales, "*Batman Begins*: An Interview with Christian Bale," *Black Film*, June 2005.)

67. Jeff Otto, "Set Visit: *Batman Begins*," *IGN*, 3 January 2005.

68. "Want to live like Batman? Real estate website prices Wayne Manor at $32million (but Bat Cave not included)," *The Daily Mail*, 19 July 2012.

69. Andrew Pulver, "He's not a god—he's human," *The Guardian*, 15 June 2005.

70. Indeed, Gotham derived its name from an antiquated nickname for New York City. (Stacy Conradt, "Why Is New York City Called 'Gotham'?," *Mental Floss*, 7 April 2015.)

71. *Batman* writer and editor Denny O'Neil would famous argue that "Gotham is Manhattan below Fourteenth Street at 3 a.m., November 28 in a cold year. Metropolis is Manhattan between Fourteenth and One Hundred and Tenth Streets on the brightest, sunniest July day of the year." (Barry Popik, "'Metropolis is New York by day; Gotham City is New York by night,'" *Barry Pipik*, 29 March 2008.)

72. Devin Gordon, "Q&A: *Dark Knight* Director Christopher Nolan," *Newsweek*, 11 July 2008.

73. It is revealing, for example, that *Interstellar* is his most overtly American work, followed by *Dunkirk*, his most overtly British.

74. Pat Jankiewicz, "Dark Knight Resurrected," *Starlog #337*, August 2005.

75. *Absolute Batman: The Long Halloween* (2007). The influence of *The Long Halloween* on *Batman Begins* is perhaps best encapsulated in the shot of the Scarecrow on horseback, evoking a splash page from Jeph Loeb and Tim Sale's *Batman: The Long Halloween #8*, July 1997.

76. It was, for example, Goyer who suggested the villains for the film, based on his understanding of what Nolan wanted the film to be about and on his own understanding of the character's continuity. (Kelly Konda, "18 Outrageous Facts About *Batman Begins*, In Their Own Words," *We Minored in Film*, 7 November 2014.)

77. Pat Jankiewicz, "Dark Knight Resurrected," *Starlog #337*, August 2005.

78. Scott Feinberg, "Christopher Nolan on *Interstellar* Critics, Making Original Films and Shunning Cellphones and Email," *The Hollywood Reporter*, 3 January 2015.

79. To be fair, this transformation was explored in *Batman: The Mask of the Phantasm*, a feature-length animation from the creative team behind *Batman: The Animated Series* that received a limited theatrical run. However, despite critical enthusiasm, *The Mask of the Phantasm* never found a wide audience.

80. Bruce Wayne makes an offhand reference to how his parents "were murdered by dastardly criminals" in the first episode of the show, *Hi Diddle Riddle!* However, the impact of their death is never really explored or discussed.

81. The opening scene of *Batman* is framed in such a way as to evoke the murder of the Waynes without explicitly replaying it. Both *Batman* and *Batman Forever* feature flashbacks to the murder of the Waynes, although neither film pays particular attention to Bruce's transformation.

82. Umberto Eco explores this "narrative paradox" in "The Myth of Superman," published in *The Role of the Reader: Explorations in the Semiotics of Texts* (1979).

83. Peter David, "The Illusion of Change," *Comics Buyer's Guide #1285*, 3 July 1998.

84. D.L. Thurston, "A Writer Re-Reviews: Thor (and Captain America)," *D.L. Thurston*, 28 September 2011.

85. This is perhaps why so many superhero sequels, like *Superman II* and *X-Men: Days of Future Past*, have the heroes consider resignation or surrender; this allows them to effectively reenact their original heroic arc as they climb back towards superheroism. It might also explain why so many superhero sequels, like *Batman Returns* and *The Amazing Spider-Man II*, devote so much energy to the origins of villains, allowing the story to give the antagonist a three-act arc. This may explain why *Spider-Man II* is such a beloved and effective superhero sequel, in that it does both of those sequel arcs simultaneously and efficiently.

86. *The Man Who Falls* was originally published in *Secret Origins of the World's Greatest Super-Heroes* (1989).

87. See, for example, "Comic Influences on *Batman Begins*," *Batman Online*, 6 March 2016.

88. Any number of sequences within *Batman Begins* consciously mirror set pieces and story beats from *Year One*, down to Bruce returning to Gotham by air and collapsing bruised and beaten on a fire escape after an early botched mission. The characters of Detective Flass and Carmine Falcone are also carried over from *Year One*.

89. While *Year One* is firmly grounded in the world of gangsters and corruption, *Batman Begins* makes a point to effective side-line organized crime at the half-way point to make room for a cult of ninja assassins wielding a weapon of mass destruction.

90. Stax, "The Influences of *Batman Begins*," *IGN*, 24 September 2004.

91. Brian Balchack, "Director David Goyer talks *Blade: Trinity* and *Batman Begins*!," *MovieWeb*, 8 December 2004.

92. Jeff Otto, "David Goyer Interview," *IGN*, 8 December 2004.

93. As Alison Halsall summarizes, "Creator Bob Kane's original concept for the Batman came from a Leonardo da Vinci sketch of a man wearing bat-like wings, and Kane's other sources include Bela Lugosi's *Dracula* and Douglas Fairbanks' performance in *The Mark of Zorro*." (Alison Halsall, "'What Is the Use of a

Book … Without Pictures or Conversations?': Incorporating the Graphic Novel into the University Curriculum" in *Teaching Graphic Novels in the English Classroom: Pedagogical Possibilities of Multimodal Literacy Engagement* (2017), p. 91.)

94. Ty Templeton, *What If Bob Kane Had Gone Ahead And Created Bat-Man Without Bill Finger?* (2014).

95. Bruce muses, "Criminals are a superstitious cowardly lot, so my disguise must be able to strike terror into their hearts. I must be a creature of the night, black, terrible, a … a…" Right on cue, the narration notes, "As if in answer, a huge bat flies in the open window!" Bruce declares, "A bat! That's it! It's an omen… I shall become a bat!" (*Batman (1940) #1*, Spring 1940.)

96. This is most obvious in Frank Miller's work. The first chapter of *Batman: Year One* treats the arrival of the bat as a grand moment that can serve as the issue's cliffhanger. (*Batman (1940) #404*, February 1987.) However there is also an element of this to Bruce's tormented memories of that moment in the opening issues of *The Dark Knight Returns*. (*The Dark Knight Returns #1*, February 1986.)

97. Grant Morrison touches on this idea frequently in his *Batman* run. In *The Butler Did It*, Morrison jokingly runs through a number of other animal-themed motifs as Bruce meditates upon the fortuitous arrival of the bat at that fateful moment. "It could have been worse." (*Batman (1940) #682*, January 2009.) Morrison would also construct the origin story of the bat in *Batman: The Return*. (*Batman: The Return #1*, January 2011.)

98. Spence D., "Batman Vs. Hans Zimmer and James Newton Howard Part 2," *IGN*, 13 June 2005.

99. *The Dark Knight Rises* plays into this idea by fixating on Martha Wayne's pearls, which Bruce keeps locked away in a safe as if trying to preserve some piece of his long-lost mother. Allowing Selina Kyle the opportunity to wear those pearls expresses Bruce's willingness to finally get past that repression.

100. It is somewhat telling that Natalie refers to Leonard as a "freak" in *Memento*, the same sort of language employed by characters to describe the Joker and Batman in *The Dark Knight*. Leonard and Bruce are transformed by their narratives into something "other." Interestingly, Guy Pearce was originally considered for the role of Ra's Al Ghul, which would have played into this idea. (Horatia Harrod, "Guy Pearce interview for *The Rover*: 'acting was a survival thing'," *The Telegraph*, 14 August 2014.)

101. "Are you so desperate to fight criminals that you lock yourself in to take them on one at a time?" Ra's Al Ghul challenges Bruce early in *Batman Begins*. This seems like a fairly accurate description of Leonard's method of coping with his own loss, sinking into the underworld and fighting one "Johnny G" at a time. Ra's Al Ghul suggests that Bruce is in need of something grander than this anger and violence. "Whatever your original intentions, you have become truly lost," he muses. Again, this seems like an accurate summary of where Leonard finds himself by the end (or the start) of *Memento*.

102. Geoff Boucher, "Christopher Nolan says his Batman doesn't play well with others," *The Los Angeles Times*, 29 October 2008.

103. Jeff Otto, "David Goyer Interview," *IGN*, 8 December 2004.

104. Marc Bernardin, "Christopher Nolan on 'Extreme Places' in the Making of The Dark Knight Rises," *The Hollywood Reporter*, 27 December 2012.

105. Indeed, the teasing reference to the Joker at the end of *Batman Begins* is an overt nod to the ending of *Batman: Year One*, in which Commissioner Gordon warns Batman about the Joker's threat to poison the city's water supply. (*Batman (1940) #407*, May 1987.)

106. The idea that the Wayne family attended a screening of *The Mark of Zorro* (1940) has a long history in *Batman* comics, most notably articulated in stories like *The Dark Knight Returns (1986) #1* or *Batman (1940) #459*. Writer James Robinson and artist Tim Sale would even create a Zorro-inspired character in the Cavalier, introduced in *Legends of the Dark Knight (1989) #32*. It even appears in the credit sequences of *Batman vs. Superman*. There is some small irony in this choice, given that the character of Batman actually pre-dates the release of *The Mark of Zorro* by several months. (I.M. Baytor, "The Mark of Zorro," *Gotham Calling*, 20 August 2015.)

107. Geoff Boucher, "Christopher Nolan says his Batman doesn't play well with others," *The Los Angeles Times*, 29 October 2008.

108. Danny Bowes, "Big Screen Batman: *Batman Returns*," *Tor*, 2 February 2011.

109. It does this through a very deft switcheroo where Liam Neeson is introduced in the persona of Henri Ducard and serves the story function of a cynical mentor figure, before resurfacing in the third act as the leader of a band of international assassins.

110. Marc Graser and Cathy Dunkley, "The bat and the beautiful," *Variety*, 8 February 2004.

111. "*Batman Begins* press conference, part two," *Time Out London*, 16 June 2005.

112. Spence D., "Batman Vs. Hans Zimmer & James Newton Howard Part 1," *IGN*, 10 June 2005.

113. Like clockwork, Batman makes his first full appearance a few seconds after the hour mark, pulling Carmine Falcone out of the car to boldly declare, "I'm Batman." This very precise feat of timing does not seem to have been an accident.

114. The earlier live action *Batman* films had generally failed to this. It is possible to incorporate the Joker and Two-Face into thematic commentaries on the character of Batman, as *The Dark Knight* does. However, *Batman* and *Batman Forever* had little interest in doing so with those villains. Perhaps the best structured of the earlier *Batman* films is *Batman Returns*, which does make the effort to explicitly mirror Bruce Wayne and his antagonists. The Penguin is a literal freak, and Burton's film suggests that on some level Bruce resents the Penguin's ability to wear his freakishness on the outside rather than the inside. Bruce and Selina both mirror one another as broken characters who create alter egos, but who are looking for the missing piece in the their lives.

115. For his part, this mirroring is reflected even in the casting. Cillian Murphy concedes that he was one of the "about 6,000 people" who tested for Batman. As such, his casting as the Scarecrow establishes the Scarecrow as an inferior (or unsatisfactory) version of Batman. It is telling that the Scarecrow is the only villain to appear in all three films. (Ian Spelling, "Mask of the Scarecrow," *Starlog #337*, August 2005.)

116. *The Dark Knight* teases the possibility that Bruce has internalized more of Ra's Al Ghul's philosophy than he would readily concede. As the Joker terrorises Gotham, he unironically quotes Ra's Al Ghul

back to Alfred, "The criminal isn't complicated." Of course, *The Dark Knight* makes it very clear that Bruce's absolutism misunderstands the Joker.

117. This recalls the Joker's rewritten origin in Tim Burton's *Batman*, where the character murdered Thomas and Martha Wayne. It also evokes Obadiah Stane in *Iron Man* and Ivan Vanko in *Iron Man 2*, both characters who have strong ties to Tony Stark's father and play a pivotal role in the development of Stark Industries. It also prefigures the introduction of a much older Batman in *Batman vs. Superman*, wherein a cynical and disaffected older Bruce Wayne has begun a descent into nihilism and tries to murder Superman.

118. The superhero genre dates back to the lead-up to the Second World War. Captain America was famously introduced punching Hitler on the cover of *Captain America Comics #1*, March 1941. Jerry Siegel and Joe Shuster imagined Superman giving Hitler and Stalin a piece of his mind in *How Superman Would Win the War*, published in *Look*, 27 February 1940.

119. In *Captain America: The First Avenger*, the character squares off against the Red Skull and HYDRA, which are Nazis-in-all-but-branding so that the movie could be screened in Germany. In *Captain America: The Winter Soldier*, the character faces Nazis-in-all-but-branding who have infiltrated the American government. Even in *The Avengers*, the villainous Loki shows up in Germany and demands that its population kneel before him. "Is this not simpler? Is this not your natural state?"

120. In some ways, the secret history of the League of Shadows as an organization that has carefully manipulated human history faintly echoes the conspiracy theory themes that echoed through *Memento*. It also establishes Ra's Al Ghul as a Nolan antagonist, a character imposing his own structures and narratives on a chaotic world.

121. In this case, the link between the two concepts in the fascist imagination is best evoked through Leni Reifenstahl's *Triumph des Willens*, perhaps better known by its English title, *The Triumph of the Will*.

122. Superheroes have always had a complicated relationship with ideas like democracy and fascism, given that they largely exist as stories about characters with the power to bend the world to their will who operate outside democratic structures. (Glen Weldon, "Superheroes And The F-Word: Grappling With The Ugly Truth Under The Capes," *NPR*, 16 November 2016.)

123. As Elizabeth Sandifer notes, Batman's ideology in *Batman Begins* is defined as "clearly more liberal and rooted in trust in institutions than R'as al Ghul's long manipulation of history to stamp out decadence, since the film ends with Batman's alliance with Rachel and Commissioner Gordon, but it's easy to make too much of this given that fascism and authoritarianism have long depended on liberal institutions." (Elizabeth Sandifer, "An Accurately Named Trilogy I: Batman Begins," *Eruditorum Press*, 6 November 2017.)

124. Although there is a short sequence towards the end of the film where Ra's Al Ghul speaks to Bruce through a gas mask that seems to prefigure Bane's appearance in *The Dark Knight Rises*.

125. *Batman Begins* invests a lot more heavily in Thomas Wayne than in Martha Wayne. Thomas is developed into a reasonably rounded individual, while Martha is underdeveloped. In the original draft of the script, Martha has a total of two lines; this is very much keeping with how the *Batman* mythos has traditionally marginalised Martha. It is in fact easier to list the exceptions to this general principle, the major stories that preference Martha over Thomas: Neil Gaiman and Andy Kubert's *Whatever Happened to the Caped Crusader?* and Frank Miller and Jim Lee's *All-Star Batman and Robin the Boy Wonder*. (David Brothers, "The Grand Unified Theory of Frank Miller's *Batman*: Will, Hope and Tenderness," *Comics Alliance*, 23 August 2011.)

126. Bruce and Alfred argue about Bruce's place in Wayne Manor on his return from Princeton. Bruce refuses to sleep in the "master bedroom," for fear of usurping his dead father.

127. The film signifies Bruce's escape from his father's shadow with the sequence in which Bruce alienates all of his family's friends, followed by the burning down of Wayne Manor, the destruction of Thomas Wayne's stethoscope *and* the demolition of the elevated train which Thomas Wayne had gifted to the city of Gotham decades earlier. Bruce Wayne does not do anything by half-measures.

128. There is no small irony in the retroactive continuity introduced by *The Dark Knight Rises*, which reveals the details of what happened to Ra's family. In particular, it puts a clever twist on the ending of *Batman Begins*, with Bruce Wayne's decision to let Ra's Al Ghul die effectively rendering him as Joe Chill to Talia Al Ghul.

129. *See*, for example, Douglas Mann, "The Hero with a Thousand Faces and its Application to *Star Wars*," in *Understanding Society* (2008).

130. *See*, for example, Lester D. Friedman, *Citizen Spielberg* (2010), p 33–36.

131. See, for example, Sarah Harwood, *Family Fictions: Representations of the Family in 1980s Hollywood Cinema* (1997), p. 73.

132. Susan Jeffords explores various subtexts of the depictions of these relationships in the chapter "Fathers and Sons: Continuity and Revolution in the Reagan Years" in *Hard Bodies: Hollywood Masculinity in the Reagan Era* (1994), p. 64–90.

133. When Carmine Falcone starts rambling about the "Scarecrow" in front of Rachel Dawes, Jonathan Crane dismisses it as a reference to "Jungian archetypes."

134. Freud argues that the roots of human society can be traced back to the murder of the primordial father, and even suggests that guilt over this original sin is the basis of what he described as the Oedipal Complex. (Sigmund Freud, *Totem and Taboo* (1913).) It should be noted that this Freudian reading of Bruce's relationship with his fathers in *Batman Begins* might also play into his relationship with Selina and his mother's pearls in *The Dark Knight Rises*.

135. Andrew Pulver, "He's not a god—he's human," *The Guardian*, 15 June 2005.

136. *Memento* literalizes the character's psychological condition by structuring the film in such a way that the audience effectively experiences the same dissonance. *Insomnia* uses the camera to communicate concepts that mirror the dialogue, flashing lights when Finch talks about the lights that he saw while sleep-deprived and flashing to crime scene details as the detectives talk about them.

137. Scott Timberg, "Indie Angst," *The New Times Los Angeles*, 15 March 2001.

138. *Batman Begins* suffers in some ways from a surplus of information. Vital information is not only articulated, but repeated. This is most notable in the way that the film *repeatedly* draws the audience's attention to Wayne Tower's function as the "unofficial hub" of Gotham City and *repeatedly* emphasizes that the water mains are all centralised through that skyscraper. During the climactic action sequence, *Batman Begins* keeps cutting back to technicians in Wayne Tower talking about how the system is "gonna blow!"

139. "How am I supposed to heal if I can't feel time?" asks Leonard, while dealing with severe emotional trauma and suffering from a psychological condition that affects his perception of time.

140. "A good cop can't sleep at night because he's missing a piece of the puzzle," Burr advises Dormer. "And a bad cop can't sleep because his conscience won't let him." This is clearly mirrored in the fact that Dormer cannot sleep over the course of the film, even if he believes that his insomnia is driven by the region's perpetual daylight.

141. Alfred alludes to this in a later conversation with Bruce. "You're getting lost inside this monster of yours," Alfred warns his young ward after a high-stakes police chase. Indeed, *The Dark Knight Rises* suggests that Bruce's decision to let Ra's Al Ghul die at the end of *Batman Begins* was a mistake that might have been driven by his heightened emotional state in the moment.

142. To be fair, Nolan and Goyer are not the only writers to have literalized this metaphor. Colson Whitehead took the metaphor even further in *Underground Railroad* (2016).

143. In some ways, this literalism-through-dialogue is an extension of Nolan's utilitarian approach to plotting in general and to the Batman mythos in particular. Nolan believes that every element of his film needs to be justified and explained, to the point where the climax retroactively justifies early scenes of Bruce Wayne doing push-ups by trapping the character in a position where that upper body strength is *very* specifically useful. Alfred even acknowledges as much, "What is the point of all those push-ups if you can't even lift a bloody log?"

144. Indeed, Nolan's approach has shades of what some comic book journalists describe as "Johnsian Literalism," named for the comic book writer Geoff Johns and his tendency to turn a literal aspect of a superhero's powers into a metaphor that defines their personality and the world around them. For example: the Flash is a character own moves very fast, so he needs to slow down; Aquaman is a literal fish out of water. (David Uzumeri, "The Geoff Johns Literalism Method: A Primer," *Comics Alliance*, 17 November 2011.)

145. *Skyfall* might be one of the best examples of this influence, wherein discussions of James Bond's advancing years and creeping redundancy play as metaphors for the franchise's insecurities *and* as a literal expression of the toll that spycraft has taken on the lead character. It is worth contrasting the storytelling in *Skyfall* to other Bond movies built around the question of the character's potential redundancy, like *GoldenEye* or *License to Kill*, which tend to deal with the issue in a more abstract manner.

146. In keeping with Nolan's cinematic fascination with presenting abstract and metaphorical concepts in a concrete manner, through inserts and the use of practical effects, *Batman Begins* devotes considerable energy to explaining *how* Bruce developed Batman from an abstract idea into something physical. *Batman Begins* pays particular attention to logistics and mechanics, the ordering of shipments and the fashioning of "batarangs."

147. Indeed, Alfred makes it clear that he could never countenance Batman if it were *only* about satisfying Bruce's desire for revenge or satisfaction. "When you told me your grand plan for saving Gotham, the only thing that stopped me from calling the men in white coats was when you said it wasn't about thrill-seeking."

148. "I wouldn't presume to tell you what to do with your past, sir," Alfred assures Bruce early in the film. "Just know that there are those of us who care about what you do with your future." Similarly, Gordon seems to honestly invest a lot of hope and faith in a man who dresses as a flying rodent. When Bruce asks what Gordon thinks of his enterprise, Gordon responds, "I think you're trying to help."

149. In some ways, this mirrors Grant Morrison's approach to the character in his contemporaneous comic book run. In *The Return of Bruce Wayne*, Morrison has the title character articulate "the first truth of Batman" as, "I was never alone." (*The Return of Bruce Wayne #6*, December 2010.) It also reflects on the reality that the comic book character Batman is the result of decades of collaboration between artists and writers, with each creative team having the opportunity to add something new to the mythos and to deepen or develop the character.

150. This idea is developed in *The Prestige* and *Inception*, both films that engage with the idea of creation as a fundamentally collaborative process.

151. This is part of the central thesis of Todd McGowan's *The Fictional Christopher Nolan* (2012).

152. Archie Bland, "Comic book superheroes: the gods of modern mythology," *The Guardian*, 27 May 2016.

153. There have been entire treatises written on the idea (such as Richard Reynolds, *Super Heroes: A Modern Mythology* (1992)) and it has even become a talking point for actors working the press circuit promoting these films. (Dan Wickline, "Chris Pine Takes A Shot On Marvel And Compares Superhero Films To Modern Myths," *Bleeding Cool*, 2 June 2017.)

154. Perhaps the best exploration of this idea remains Umberto Eco's "The Myth of Superman," published in *The Role of the Reader: Explorations in the Semiotics of Texts* (1979).

155. This is particularly true in the comic books, where various "reboots" serve as metaphorical Ragnaroks to the superhero characters, a point at which one version of the tale ends and another might begin with the emphasis subtle shifted to reflect the modern world. This is also true of big screen superheroes, who are constantly rebooted and re-imagined. Nolan's *Dark Knight* trilogy is itself one reimagining between Joel Schumacher's *Batman & Robin* and Zack Snyder's *Batman vs. Superman*.

156. Most notably, *Batman Begins* does not share the naming convention of *The Dark Knight* and *The Dark Knight Rises*, much like *Raiders of the Lost Ark* does not share the naming convention of *Indiana Jones and the Temple of Doom* and *Indiana Jones and the Last Crusade*. However, its box office returns were also appreciably lower than the two films that followed, being the only film in the series to earn less than one billion dollars.

157. Scott Mendelson, "*Batman Begins* Perfected The Reboot And Saved The Comic Book Movie 10 Years Ago," Forbes, 15 June 2015.

158. Scott Feinberg, "Christopher Nolan on *Interstellar* Critics, Making Original Films and Shunning Cellphones and Email," *The Hollywood Reporter*, 3 January 2015.

159. Adam Rosenberg, "Matthew Vaughn Says *X-Men: First Class* Takes *Batman Begins* Attitude To *X-Men* Universe," MTV, 9 March 2011.

160. Germain Lussier, "Director Alan Taylor Cites *Batman Begins* as Inspiration for *Terminator* Reboot," /Film, 18 October 2013.

161. Indeed, it seems like *Daredevil* and *Iron Fist* inherited different aspects of *Batman Begins*. *Daredevil* got the pick of the material, featuring non-linear storytelling, old-fashioned crime bosses, and an apocalyptic cult smuggling weapons of mass destruction into a major metropolitan city through the docklands. In contrast, *Iron Fist* seemed to get stuck with the leftovers, with the first thirteen episodes of the series finding its emotionally-stunted billionaire protagonist spending far too much time trying to take control of his father's company.

162. Miller was responsible for some of the most influential *Batman* and *Daredevil* stories ever told, and his contributions to both characters shaped the comic book medium during the eighties. Indeed, the reimagining of the League of Shadows in *Batman Begins* owes a lot to Frank Miller's creation of "the Hand" during his original run on *Daredevil*.

163. In an interview with Charlie Rose, Nolan explained his reluctance to commit publically to a potential sequel, "I don't want to jinx this one, I've put everything I can into this film, and I want to see what people are going to think of this film." (Jett, "*Begins* update for 6/18/05," *Batman on Film*, 18 June 2005.)

## Chapter 5

1. "Fiction winners," *The James Tait Black Prizes*, 25 August 2016.

2. Dave Langford, "*The Prestige*," *The New York Review of Science Fiction #98*, 1996.

3. Dan Shewman, "Nothing Up Their Sleeves: Christopher & Jonathan Nolan on the Art of Magic, Murder, and *The Prestige*," *Creative Screenwriting*, September/October 2006.

4. Emanuel Levy, "*Prestige* with Christopher Nolan," *Emanuel Levy*, 16 October 2016.

5. "*Memento* director turns to magic as *Batman* stalls," *The Guardian*, 17 April 2003.

6. Ryan Hill, "Exclusive Interview: Author Christopher Priest On His New Novel and Christopher Nolan," *Screen Invasion*, 11 April 2014.

7. "*Memento* director turns to magic as *Batman* stalls," *The Guardian*, 17 April 2003.

8. Jeff Goldsmith, "*The Prestige* Q&A: Interview with Jonathan Nolan," *Creative Screenwriting*, October 28, 2006.

9. Ryan Hill, "Exclusive Interview: Author Christopher Priest On His New Novel and Christopher Nolan," *Screen Invasion*, 11 April 2014.

10. "Christopher Nolan's Magic Hour," *Empire*, 9 December 2005.

11. To be fair, there is a shorter gap between the wide releases of his earlier films like *Following*, *Memento* and *Insomnia*, but this compressed timeline is explained by the fact that *Following* and *Memento* both worked the festival circuit before going on wide release. Remarked Nolan of the belated release of *Following*, "Yeah, it dribbled out slowly over about two years, but I think I was 30 when it first was released." (Scott Feinberg, "Christopher Nolan on *Interstellar* Critics, Making Original Films and Shunning Cellphones and Email," *The Hollywood Reporter*, 3 January 2015.)

12. The budget on *The Prestige* ($40m) was considerably closer to the production budget of *Memento* ($9m) rather than *Batman Begins* ($150m).

13. "Christopher Nolan's Magic Hour," *Empire*, 9 December 2005.

14. Rebecca Murray, "Christian Bale Talks About *The Prestige*," About.com, 16 October 2006.

15. Caine even has a voice cameo in *Dunkirk* as the leader of squadron of fighter planes. Nolan reflected, "It's shocking to me that a lot of people haven't [recognised him], when he has really one of the most distinctive voices in cinema. I wanted very much to squeeze him in here. It's a bit of a nod to his character in *Battle of Britain*. And also, it's Michael. He has to be in all my films, after all." (Stephen Whitty, "Chris Nolan on *Dunkirk*, and leaving the *Dark Knight* behind," NJ.com, 16 July 2017.)

16. Pamela McClintock, "Cinema Con: Christopher Nolan Talks *Interstellar*, Plugs Film Over Digital in Hollywood Reporter Q&A," *The Hollywood Reporter*, 36 March 2014.

17. Nolan had reportedly sought to recruit Crowley to work on *Inception*, but he was otherwise engaged with work on *Public Enemies* and *John Carter*. (Gerald Kennedy, "Tech Support Interview: The look of *Inception*," *In Contention*, 16 December 2010.) Crowley did also do a lot of the original production design on the pilot to Jonathan Nolan's *Westworld*. (Carolyn Giardina, "Emmys: How *Westworld*'s Production Designer Invented the Future in an Eerie Amusement Park," The Hollywood Reporter, 6 June 2017.)

18. Zsolt Biro, Attila Tihanyi, Zsolt Berkes and Gergely Hubai, "David Julyan," FilmZene.net, 10 November 2006.

19. Merrick, "ScoreKeeper Chats With Composer David Julyan (*Memento*, *The Prestige*)!!," *Ain't It Cool News*, 19 December 2006.

20. Christian Bale headlined the *Dark Knight* trilogy and *The Prestige*; Cillian Murphy appeared in all three *Dark Knight* films, as well as *Inception* and *Dunkirk*; Tom Hardy appeared in *The Dark Knight Rises*, along with *Inception* and *Dunkirk*; Joseph Gordon Levitt appeared in *Inception* and *The Dark Knight Rises*; Anne Hathaway appeared in *The Dark Knight Rises* and *Interstellar*; Marion Cotillard appeared in both *Inception* and *The Dark Knight Rises*.

21. "Q & A: Christopher Nolan," *The Hollywood Reporter*, 12 February 2012.

22. Rebecca Murray, "Christian Bale Talks About *The Prestige*," About.com, 16 October 2006.

23. Karen Wada, "Tricked Out: How production designer Nathan Crowley transformed modern Los Angeles into Victorian London for *The Prestige*," *Los Angeles Magazine*, 1 February 2007.

24. The film used four Los Angeles theatres—the Belasco, the Los Angeles, the Palace, and the Tower—which, according to production designer Nathan Crowley, had not been redesigned "since the '20s and '30s, and a lot of them are built in a Victorian style." (Steffie Nelson, "Magic films pull conjuring tricks," *Variety*, 8 January 2007.)

25. The film does the same thing with Angier's variation on the trick, which is showcased in an incomplete form at the very start of the film, before being discussed in a courtroom, and then is dissected over the subsequent two hours.

26. Mike D'Angelo, "*The Prestige* plays a trick on its audience, hiding

a secret in plain sight," *The A.V. Club*, 19 February 2016.

27. David Julyan's score builds to a clear crescendo, and then cuts to silence to create a disorienting effect. More than that, Angier explicitly discusses how Borden has no idea how best to present his trick.

28. As such, he provides an interesting mirror to Robert Angier, a member of the British aristocracy (as "Lord Caldlow") who masquerades an American so effectively that even Bordon is taken in.

29. Again, this mirrors the details of the plot of *The Prestige*, given Angier's attempt to use a loaded gun on Borden during a bullet-catch.

30. Annetta Black, "Morbid Monday: Chung Ling Soo & the Bullet Trick That Went Horribly Wrong," *Atlas Obscura*, 23 May 2011.

31. Rival magician Ching Ling Foo, an actual Chinese magician from whom Robinson had cultivated his stage persona, threatened to reveal Robinson's charade to the media at a press conference. Foo cancelled the press conference when it became clear that the press was not interested in exposing Robinson's secret. (Frank Cullen, Florence Hackman & Donald McNeilly, *Vaudeville Old & New: An Encyclopedia Of Variety Performances In America* (2004), p. 225.)

32. Although, it should be noted, Borden and Angier were not devoted to the same illusion at the start of their career. The two are only devoted to the same illusion once Angier sees Broden perform "The Transported Man."

33. "She must help me rid ourselves of Angier," he writes of Olivia. He elaborates, "I think she's telling the truth. I think we cannot trust her." In hindsight, the phrasing is quite overt.

34. Christian Bale's performance helps, subtly modulating between the two twins. It is very clear, for example, that Sarah tells the "wrong" twin about her pregnancy, garnering a somewhat muted reaction rather than unreserved enthusiasm. Watching the movie in retrospect, there is a subtle (but often clear) distinction between the two different twins within Bale's performance; one is taciturn and introspective, the other boisterous and emotional.

35. Frequently, modern production teams working on big budget blockbusters with active online fanbases have to actively lie in interviews to preserve the movies' surprises. One of the more obvious examples is the repeated denials from the *Star Trek Into Darkness* production team about the identity of a character subsequently revealed to be Khan Noonien Singh. This strategy was problematic, as director J.J. Abrams subsequently conceded. (Rob Bricken, "J.J. Abrams admits lying about *Star Trek 2*'s Khan was a mistake," io9, 2 December 2013.)

36. Twists from pre-existing works seem to be excluded from modern pop culture's speculation-driven model of reporting, such as major plot developments in the first few seasons of *Game of Thrones*, like the death of Ned Stark or the betrayal at the Red Wedding.

37. The evidence would seem to suggest that the production team could not have preserved the ambiguity without outright lying. Marion Cotillard had to straight-up lie about the identity of the character in the pre-publicity cycle for *The Dark Knight Rises* in order to preserve the integrity of the film itself. (Jill Pantozzi, "Yes, Marion Cotillard Had To Lie About Her *Dark Knight Rises* Role," *The Mary Sue*, 29 November 2012.)

38. Merrick, "ScoreKeeper Chats With Composer David Julyan (*Memento, The Prestige*)!!," Ain't It Cool News, 19 December 2006.

39. "Christopher Nolan's Magic Hour," *Empire*, 9 December 2005.

40. Rebecca Murray, "Christian Bale Talks About *The Prestige*," About.com, 16 October 2006.

41. It has also been suggested that Tesla's decision to test the device on Alley's cat is an homage to the testing of the transportation device on a cat in the original version of *The Fly*. (Barry B. Luokkala, *Exploring Science Through Science Fiction* (2015), p. 143.

42. Behind the scenes, the transporter was a plot contrivance "born out of necessity, deadlines and a meagre budget." It was too expensive to land a shuttlecraft on an alien planet every week, and the transporter provided a quick and effective way to get the characters to alien worlds. (*How William Shatner Changed the World*.)

43. There were horrific accidents in *Star Trek: The Motion Picture* and "The Darkness and the Light" (*Star Trek: Deep Space Nine*). There were characters split into duplicates in "The Enemy Within" (*Star Trek*) and "Second Chances" (*Star Trek: The Next Generation*). There were characters combined in "Tuvix" and "Drone" (*Star Trek: Voyager*).

44. The franchise never really explored this idea on-screen, however it has preoccupied fans from the earliest days of the franchise. It is a major point of discussion between characters (and even plays into the plot) in James Blish's *Spock Must Die!* (1970), the first *Star Trek* tie-in novel aimed at adults.

45. Incidentally, Jonathan Nolan would do something similar with *Westworld*. Although the show looks and feels like a western, it is a meditation upon another popular science-fiction plot device that has featured heavily on *Star Trek* over the years. If *The Prestige* is the ultimate "transporter malfunction" story, then *Westworld* is the ultimate "holodeck malfunction" story; although it should be noted that both stories examine the initial concept at face value, before exploring its dysfunction and inherent horror.

46. *The Prestige* actively teases its audience by flashing back to the image as its second-last shot, as if to boast about how it put the answers to all of its mysteries up-front.

47. The audience has only heard his name spoken aloud once, by Angier in Colorado Springs.

48. Another example is the fact that the film opens with its closing scene. Cutler's opening monologue is set against a sequence of him playing with Jess Borden. The end of the film reveals that this is the final scene in the story chronologically, with Cutler keeping an eye on Jess before the surviving Borden twin collects her.

49. Even thematically, the reveal about Robert Angier is set up with the recurring motif of crushed birds. Most of the film's "disappearing bird" tricks involving killing the bird and replacing it with a doppelganger, which is exactly what "The Real Transported Man" does with Angier every night. This motif is set up in the opening scenes.

50. "Behind The Magic With *Prestige* Cast," *Access Hollywood*, 24 October 2006.

51. This certainly fits some definitions of magic. Dai Vernon famously argued of his profession, "In the performance of good magic, the mind is led on step by step to ingeniously defeat its own logic." *The Prestige* is structured in such a way as to play into this idea. (Ricky Jay, *Jay's Journal of Anomalies* (2001), p. 147.)

52. Cutler explains the dangers to both Borden and Angier after their first performance together, and

Borden repeats the warning to Sarah when he offers her a demonstration and reveals the nature of the trick.

53. In the early sequences, the protagonist is rough around the edges and wears a leather jacket; in the middle sections, the protagonist has remodelled himself with a haircut and suit based on Cobb; in the final sections, the protagonist has been bruised and battered by Cobb. As a result, the audience is able to quickly figure out where a particular event falls in the movie's chronology.

54. The film pivots on the murder of Jimmy; the black-and-white scenes in the motel room lead *forwards* towards the murder, while the color scenes lead *backwards* towards the murder.

55. This may explain in part why Gotham is so orange in *Batman Begins*. In *The Dark Knight* and *The Dark Knight Rises*, Gotham has the same bluish hue that *Batman Begins* applies to the Tibetan mountains. This may also signify Bruce's increasing emotional remove.

56. Nolan reinforces this subjectivity through the way in which he presents these characters reading these documents; the camera often seems to peer in, as if voyeuristically studying these voyeurs. *The Prestige* is nothing if not reflexive.

57. Certain scenes play out repeatedly across the narrative, from differing perspectives. For example, Olivia's betrayal of Borden to Angier is subsequently reversed, revealed to be Olivia's betrayal of Angier to Borden.

58. David Bordwell, "Revisiting Inception," *Observations on Film Art*, 12 August 2010.

59. Jonathan Dent, *Sinister Histories: Gothic Novels and Representations of the Past, from Horace Walpole to Mary Wollstonecraft* (2016), p. 41.

60. It is also reflected in the characters' fixation on documentation of their methods, the diaries and the notes that are treated as currency in the world of *The Prestige*.

61. This is *especially* notable in the manner in which *The Prestige* completely cuts the framing story from the original novel, which focused on the descendants of the protagonists.

62. This is right down to the frequent disclaimers and warnings that tend to appear on such films, providing an objective framework through which they might be understood, akin to the notes of fictitious editors on "discovered manuscripts." (David Bordwell and Kristin Thompson, *Minding Movies: Observations on the Art, Craft, and Business of Filmmaking* (2011), p. 190.)

63. Steve Rose, "*Cannibal Holocaust*: 'Keep filming! Kill more people!'," *The Guardian*, 15 September 2011.

64. Dave Trumbore, "*The Blair Witch Project* Effect: How Found Footage Shaped a Generation of Filmmaking," Collider, 16 September 2016.

65. Alexandra Heller-Nicholas, *Found Footage Horror Films: Fear and the Appearance of Reality* (2014), p. 89–90.

66. Kevin J. Wetmore, Jr., *Post-9/11 Horror in American Cinema* (2012), p. 59.

67. Slavoj Žižek, *Welcome to the Desert of the Real!: Five Essays on September 11 and Related Dates* (2002), p. 16–17.

68. Indeed, the most horrific and chilling interpretation of Angier's "The *Real* Transported Man" is that Angier's decision to drown himself in the same model of tank as Julia reflects an obsession with recreating and reexperiencing what his wife felt in her dying moments.

69. Of course, subsequent plot developments make it quite clear that it is possible that Borden (or at least the version of Borden writing the diary and being held at gunpoint) might not actually know.

70. Neal Conan, Jane Harman and Robert Kagan, "How 9/11 Changed How Americans View The World," *Talk of the Nation*, 10 September 2012.

71. Kevin J. Wetmore, Jr., *Post-9/11 Horror in American Cinema* (2012), p. 202–203.

72. Jon Schwarz, "Why Do So Many Americans Fear Muslims? Decades of Denial About America's Role in the World," *The Intercept*, 18 February 2017.

73. Psychohistorian Charles B. Strozier argued, "Psychologically, the felt experience of the people within the disaster was that it was an apocalyptic event." (Pythia Peay, "The Traumas of 9/11 and its Effects on the American Psyche," *Psychology Today*, 10 September 2015.)

74. It has been suggested that almost half of Americans believe some conspiracy theory about 9/11. (Tia Ghose, "Half of Americans Believe in 9/11 Conspiracy Theories," *Live Science*, 13 October 2016.) These conspiracy theories are a way of making sense of chaos and trauma. (Ilan Shrira, "Paranoia and the Roots of Conspiracy Theories," *Psychology Today*, 11 September 2008.)

75. Kurt Anderson, "How America Lost Its Mind," *The Atlantic*, September 2017.

76. William Davies, "The Age of Post-Truth Politics," *The New York Times*, 24 August 2016.

77. Deepak Chopra and Anoop Kumar, "Reality Appears Incurably Split—Now What?," *The Huffington Post*, 17 July 2017.

78. If "the man in the box" is the copy who remains in the machine and "the prestige" is the copy created across the room, then the Angier at the end of the story has continuity through neither. The first time that he uses the device, "the man in the box" shoots "the prestige" with a gun. However, during his stage show, "the man in the box" is killed every night and "the prestige" survives. As such, the version of Angier at the end of the film is neither "the man in the box" nor "the prestige," but some twisted and mangled amalgamation of the two.

79. *The Prestige* consciously fudges and fictionalises (and heightens) the real-life conflict between the two, elevating it to near-mythic levels. (Maggie Ryan Sandford, "AC/DC: The Tesla-Edison Feud," *Mental Floss*, 10 July 2012.)

80. MaryAnn Johanson, "Conjuring Up Movie Magic in *The Prestige* and *The Illusionist*," MTV, 12 October 2006.

81. For a more thorough exploration of the film's Marxist commentary, see Todd McGowan's *The Fictional Christopher Nolan* (2012), p. 113–115.

82. It is subsequently revealed that Cutler would never dream of selling on the secret, and simply wants to keep the secret hidden. However, the fact that the judge accepts this logic so readily underscores the capitalist principles under which this world operates.

83. Rebecca Murray, "Christian Bale Talks About *The Prestige*," About.com, 16 October 2006.

84. Marcel Mauss, *General Theory of Magic* (2001), p. 110–111.

85. Mike D'Angelo, "The rational wonders of Christopher Nolan," *The Dissolve*, 14 November 2014.

86. Andy Serkis has compared Tesla to Frankenstein in interviews and press around the film. ("*The Prestige*—Andy Serkis interview," *IndieLondon*, October 2006.)

87. Nolan makes a similar argument in *Inception* in relation to Robert Fischer's attempt to reconcile with his father. *Inception* suggests that the emotional catharsis at the end of narratives is simply an attempt to offer audiences something that life itself does not.

88. Kester Brewin, "*The Prestige*—Religion as Illusion [2]," *Kester Brewin*, 28 June 2012.

89. Studies reveal that religious and superstitious belief provide a framework through which believers might make sense of events in their lives. (Kansas State University, "Insight offered into superstitious behavior," *ScienceDaily*, 2 September 2010.)

90. Nigel Barber, "The Security Blanket Concept of Religion," *Psychology Today*, 2 July 2012.

91. Peter Beaumont, Jo Revill and John Hooper, "'With religion I began to make sense of the world,'" *The Observer*, 23 December 2007.

92. This is a matter of frequent discussion and debate. (Mark Lorch, "Can you be a scientist and have religious faith?," *New Humanist*, 10 June 2015.) Indeed, there is evidence to suggest that a slim majority of American scientists do hold religious beliefs. (Robert Lamb, "Are Scientists Atheists?," *Discovery*, 23 November 2010.)

93. Polling and statistics suggest that there is a major correlation between religious belief and climate change denial, for example. (Cary Funk and Becka A. Alper, "Religion and Views on Climate and Energy Issues," *Pew Research Centre*, 22 October 2015.) The same is true of religion. ("Overview: The Conflict Between Religion and Evolution," *Pew Research Centre*, 4 February 2009.)

94. Bush tended to frame his arguments for the War on Terror in religious terms, and there are secondhand accounts of Bush arguing he was following divine will in liberating Iraq. (Rupert Cornwell, "Bush: God told me to invade Iraq," *The Independent*, 7 October 2005.)

95. Blair has conceded that his religious faith was key to understanding the larger world. (Peter Beaumont, Jo Revill and John Hooper, "'With religion I began to make sense of the world,'" *The Observer*, 23 December 2007.) His former mentor has suggested that his support of the War in Afghanistan and the War in Iraq was informed by this faith. (Jonathan Wynne-Jones, "Tony Blair believed God wanted him to go to war to fight evil, claims his mentor," *The Telegraph*, 23 May 2009.)

96. Indeed, the film's use of Nikola Tesla arguably plays into this broader debate. Tesla has long been seen as a misunderstood genius by certain scientific-minded individuals, and a cult figure of scientists. As such, *The Prestige* transforms the character into an avatar for scientific progress and understanding itself. (Tom de Castella, "Nikola Tesla: The patron saint of geeks?," *BBC Magazine*, 10 September 2012.)

97. Fred Topel, "Christopher Nolan on *The Prestige*," *CanMag*, 23 October 2006.

98. Eric Kohn, Mike D'Angelo and Keith Uhlich, "Critical Consensus: Mike D'Angelo and Keith Uhlich on *The Dark Knight Rises*, Christopher Nolan, and Batman's Next Move," *IndieWire*, 20 July 2012.

99. It should be noted that Nolan's protagonists don't generally suffer for trying to impose a structure or set of rules on the rational world, they suffer for *breaking* and *transgressing* those rules that they imposed upon themselves. The protagonist in *Following* is lured into a trap when he breaks his own rules. When Bruce allows Ra's Al Ghul to die in *Batman Begins*, violating his code, he sets in motion the plot of *The Dark Knight Rises*. Leonard's system of notes and structures in *Memento* is quite impressive, and only falls apart when he starts intentionally creating gaps in it. Cobb repeatedly breaks his own rules in *Inception*.

100. Emanuel Levy, "*Prestige* with Christopher Nolan," *Emanuel Levy*, 16 October 2016.

101. Phillip Duncan, "DVDTalk Interview—Christopher Nolan—Director of *Insomnia*," *DVD Talk*, October 2002.

102. *Following* is about a writer who becomes a voyeur. *Memento* is about a man who fashions his life into a narrative. The *Dark Knight* trilogy finds Bruce Wayne breathing life into a larger-than-life spectacle. *Inception* is perhaps the most literal-minded of these "films about films." Even *Interstellar* is about Nolan's difficulties reconciling the films that he produces with his time away from his family.

103. "The Making of *The Prestige*" (2005).

104. Variety Staff, "*The Prestige*, Christopher Nolan, Jonathan Nolan," *Variety*, 17 December 2006.

105. Jonathan R. Olson, "Nolan's Immersive Allegories of Filmmaking in *Inception* and *The Prestige*," in *The Cinema of Christopher Nolan* (2015), p. 44–61.

106. Rebecca Murray, "Christian Bale Talks About *The Prestige*," About.com, 16 October 2006.

107. "He's kind of keeping tight-lipped about if he'd be interested in doing a second one," reflected Christian Bale during interviews publicising *Batman Begins*. (Stephanie Sanchez, "Interview with Christian Bale," *Web Wombat*, June 2005.)

108. Evan Jacobs, "Batman Begins Producer Talks About a Possible Sequel," *MovieWeb*, 10 August 2005.

109. "I would certainly love to do something on this scale again because I've enjoyed it," Nolan reflected after completing *Batman Begins*. "But I would also be interested to go back to something smaller as well. I mean, I think there are advantages to different scales of filmmaking. You wouldn't want to do just one thing." ("Complete *Batman Begins* L.A. Junket Roundtable Interview: Christopher Nolan & Emma Thomas," Groucho Reviews, June 2005.)

110. Indeed, comic book fans would jokingly refer to *The Prestige* as "*Batman vs. Wolverine*," in a nod to the stars' two most iconic roles. (J. Caleb Mozzocco, "*Batman vs. Wolverine*: The Movie," *Every Day is Like Wednesday*, 20 October 2006.)

111. Madison Vain, "David Bowie: Christopher Nolan remembers directing him in *The Prestige*," Entertainment Weekly, 19 January 2016.

112. Nathan Rabin, Josh Modell, and Noah Cruickshank, "The slinky vagabond: 15 notable David Bowie cameos," *The A.V. Club*, 11 March 2013.

113. Erin McCarthy, "Andy Serkis & the Evolution of Performance Capture Tech," *Popular Mechanics*, 27 July 2011.

114. "*The Prestige*—Andy Serkis interview," *IndieLondon*, October 2006.

115. It should be noted that while Borden's trick imposes a heavy burden on the people around him, including his family, these burdens exist within a familiar framework of Nolan's body of work. Borden is the recurring obsessed-with-his-work-to-the-point-of-alienating-his-family patriarch tends to pop in Nolan's films; he is similar to the character of Dom Cobb from *Inception* or Cooper in *Interstellar*. However, Angier exists in a different class altogether.

116. Jeffrey Ressner, "The Traditionalist," *Director's Guild of America Quarterly*, Spring 2012.

117. Natalie Wolchover, "Why CGI Humans Are Creepy, and What Scientists Are Doing about It," *Live Science*, 18 October 2011.

118. See, for example, "The Designed Photograph: Computer Generated Imagery (CGI) in Car Photography," Peter Smith and Carolyn Lefley, *Rethinking Photography: Histories, Theories and Education* (2015), p. 357–369.

119. It could also be argued that the device "breaks" the narrative in other ways, tying back to why the twist surrounding "The *Real* Transported Man" is so effective. To the audience, *The Prestige* looks and feels like a period drama. The introduction of a device from a science-fiction movie like *The Fly* or a series like *Star Trek* into that world is uncanny, a gross distortion of the popular memory of the past.

120. Doris Gassert, "*Presti*digitation: Some Reflections on Cinema in the Digital Age," in *Film in the Post-Media Age* (2012), p. 207–227.

121. Adam Chitwood, "Fincher, Spielberg, Nolan and More on Film vs. Digital, On-Set Tempers," *Collider*, 13 October 2015.

122. Jen Yamato, "Christopher Nolan's *Interstellar* To Open Two Days Early In 35mm, 70mm," *Deadline*, 1 October 2014; Alissa Wilkinson, "*Dunkirk* is playing in a lot of formats. Here's how each affects your viewing experience," *Vox*, 20 July 2017.

123. Peter Sciretta, "How *The Dark Knight* Went IMAX," /Film, 14 July 2008.

124. Even Quentin Tarantino, another firm advocate of film over digital, made a point to work with digital before confirming his opinion. Tarantino directed a short sequence of Robert Rodriguez and Frank Miller's *Sin City* using the technology. (Michael Fleming, "Inside Move: Tarantino's wages of *Sin*," *Variety*, 28 June 2004.)

125. "Christopher Nolan on *Following*—Conversations Inside The Criterion Collection," *VICE*, 24 August 2014.

126. Christopher Borrelli, "Christopher Nolan interview, about *Interstellar*," *The Chicago Tribune*, 31 October 2014.

127. Ron Magid, "Industrial Light & Magic retools its technologies to finish *Star Wars: Episode II*," *American Cinematographer*, September 2002.

128. "From *Collateral* to *Blackhat*, Michael Mann has redefined digital cinema," *The National Post*, 19 January 2015.

129. Brian Ashcroft, "The Man Who Shot *Sin City*," *Wired*, 1 April 2005.

130. Michael Odmark, "The Close-Up: David Fincher Talks Filmmaking at NYFF48," *Film Society Lincoln Centre*, 28 August 2015.

131. Charles Matthau, "How Tech Has Shaped Film Making: The Film vs. Digital Debate Is Put to Rest," *Wired*, January 2015.

132. Ben Sachs, "How David Fincher and Gyorgy Palfi, two different filmmakers, use digital video to uncanny effect," *Chicago Reader*, 13 October 2014.

133. Daniel Curtis, "Can celluloid lovers like Christopher Nolan stop a digital-only future for film?," *The New Statesman*, 23 August 2017.

134. This tangibility is a huge part of the appeal; the promotion for Christopher Nolan's *Dunkirk* included handing out "an exclusive free collectible 70mm film strip" to those attending 70mm screenings. (*See*, for example, Irish Film Institute, "Dunkirk 70mm Opening Week—on sale July 7th," *Evensi*, 29 July 2017.)

135. Geoffrey Macnab, "Film vs Digital? In the same way that a new generation of music lovers are rediscovering vinyl, cinema enthusiasts are discovering, or rediscovering, celluloid," *The Independent*, 31 August 2017.

136. Calum Marsh, "Reel devotion: Digital may have won the war, but the desire and love for film remains bigger than nostalgia," *The National Post*, 27 January 2017.

137. Again, reflecting Nolan's preference for inserts to give texture to his stylized worlds, or his desire to use in-shot effects to ground stories that otherwise embrace the fantastical. Nolan's films embrace illusion and subjectivity, but they build from a tangible and grounded foundation.

138. In this context, it is worth noting that the Nolans' adaptation of *The Prestige* does slightly change the nature of the device employed by Angier. The novel suggests that the human soul or consciousness is a single indivisible object. In the source novel, when the copy is created, the original is rendered a lifeless husk. The film changes this so that both the original and the duplicate are both clearly self-aware, which ironically has the effect of making Angier's trick even more uncanny and horrific.

## Chapter 6

1. *Interstellar* clocks in at two hours and forty-nine minutes; *The Dark Knight Rises* is two hours and forty-five minutes. In comparison, *The Dark Knight* is a relatively lean two hours and thirty-two minutes.

2. Reports put the budget of *The Dark Knight Rises* at about $250m. *The Dark Knight* cost a more modest $165m. (Chris Begley, "*The Dark Knight Rises* will cost at least $250 million to make," *Batman News*, 12 May 2011.)

3. Pamela McClintock, "Box Office Milestone: *Dark Knight Rises* Crosses $1 Billion Worldwide," *The Hollywood Reporter*, 2 September 2012.

4. *Rotten Tomatoes* lists reviews for *The Dark Knight* as 94% positive. On the next tier of Nolan's filmography, reviews for *Memento*, *Insomnia* and *Dunkirk* are 92% positive. However, *Metacritic* grades *The Dark Knight* at 82 out of a possible 100, in contrast to *Dunkirk* with a 9.4.

5. It is his highest graded work on *IMDb*, ranked in the websites user-generated top ten films of all time. The user rankings on *Metacritic* grade it as 8.9 out a possible 10, tied with *The Prestige* and *Memento*.

6. Mark Bernardin, "Christopher Nolan on 'Extreme Places' in the Making of *The Dark Knight Rises*," *The Hollywood Reporter*, 27 December 2012.

7. Jett, "*Begins* update for 6/18/05," *Batman on Film*, 18 June 2005; Stephanie Sanchez, "Interview with Christian Bale," *Web Wombat*, June 2005.

8. Dan Jolin, "The Making Of Heath Ledger's Joker," *Empire Magazine*, December 2009.

9. "All I can really say is it's a film we're talking about doing," Nolan would cryptically assure interviewers in the months following the release of *Batman Begins*. (Stax, "Villains Set for Batman Sequel?," *IGN*, 12 October 2005.)

10. "Batman Sequel Title & Casting Confirmed!," *Coming Soon*, 1 August 2006.

11. Indeed, *The Dark Knight Rises* is the only other sequel in Nolan's filmography, despite speculation about the possibility (and desirability) of a sequel to *Inception*. (Jeff Ames, "Warner Bros. Dreaming of a Sequel to

Christopher Nolan's *Inception*?," *Collider*, 22 October 2010.)

12. Examples include Jon Favreau jumping straight from *Iron Man* into *Iron Man 2*, or the Russo Brothers moving from *Captain America: The Winter Soldier* on to *Captain America: Civil War* on to *The Avengers: Infinity War*, or Marc Webb leaping from *The Amazing Spider-Man* directly into *The Amazing Spider-Man 2*. None of these directors took the time to develop any of their personal projects between the films.

13. This sort of horse-trading seems to be the norm in contemporary Hollywood, with talent leveraging their own desired projects against the studio's desires and needs. Journalist Kevin Lincoln has argued that this is the logic that explains Ben Affleck's willingness to join the cast of *Batman vs. Superman* and *Justice League*, in return for the freedom to pursue his own passion projects like *Live By Night*. (Kevin Lincoln, "Sad Ben Affleck, Like Batman, Has Seen the Future and Doesn't Like What It Holds," *Vulture*, 30 March 2016.)

14. Scott Feinberg, "Christopher Nolan on *Interstellar* Critics, Making Original Films and Shunning Cellphones and Email," *The Hollywood Reporter*, 3 January 2015.

15. Dan Jolin, "The Making Of Heath Ledger's Joker," *Empire Magazine*, December 2009.

16. The Joker had been introduced as a fairly grim killer with a clown motif in *Batman (1940) #1* (Spring 1940), but had developed over the years. During the Silver Age, he was a figure of camp fun, perhaps best embodied by Caesar Romero in *Batman!* During the Bronze Age, writer Denny O'Neal and artist Neal Adams worked hard to make the character threatening again in stories like *The Joker's Five-Way Revenge* (*Batman (1940) #241*, September 1973). Jack Nicholson had played the character in Tim Burton's *Batman*, while Mark Hamill played the role in *Batman: The Animated Series*. Comic book writer Grant Morrison would try to cheekily reconcile these various interpretations of the character in *The Clown at Midnight* (*Batman (1940) #663*, April 2007), a comic released over a year before *The Dark Knight*, suggesting that the Joker was constantly reinventing himself to reflect the times in which he lived. This approach arguably even explains the Joker in *The Dark Knight*.

17. Jonathan Nolan, "Christopher Nolan: The Movies. The Memories. Part 6: Jonathan Nolan on *The Dark Knight*," *Empire*, July 2012.

18. "Paul Bettany Added to Joker Shortlist," Hollywood.com, 24 June 2005.

19. Matt Dentler, "Will Sean Penn Be The Joker?," *IndieWire*, 24 June 2005.

20. Rodrigo Perez, "Christopher Nolan Says Heath Ledger Initially Didn't Want To Be In Superhero Or Batman Movies: 6 Things Learned From The FSLC Talk," *IndieWire*, 29 November 2012.

21. Jett, "Ledger on The Joker, Bale: No To The Same 'Old Road'," *Batman on Film*, 11 September 2006.

22. Rodrgo Perez, "Christopher Nolan Says Heath Ledger Initially Didn't Want To Be In Superhero Or Batman Movies: 6 Things Learned From The FSLC Talk," *IndieWire*, 29 November 2012.

23. Jett, "Ledger on The Joker, Bale: No To The Same 'Old Road'," *Batman on Film*, 11 September 2006.

24. Katie Calautti, "Christopher Nolan Reflects on his Batman Trilogy, Heath Ledger & More," *Comic Book Resources*, 3 December 2012.

25. Germain Lussier, "Trivia: Christopher Nolan Met With Heath Ledger For the Lead Role in *Batman Begins*," */Film*, 29 November 2012.

26. Alice Vincent, "In 2006, nobody wanted Heath Ledger to play the Joker," *The Telegraph*, 26 May 2016.

27. Dan Jolin, "The Making Of Heath Ledger's Joker," *Empire Magazine*, December 2009.

28. Christopher Hooton, "A look inside Heath Ledger's sinister 'Joker journal' for *The Dark Knight*," *The Independent*, 10 August 2015.

29. Indeed, there was some tasteless speculation that Ledger had invested himself too much in the character and that the role had played some small part in his tragic death by overdose. (Joe Neumaier, "Jack Nicholson warned Heath Ledger on 'Joker' role," *New York Daily News*, 24 January 2008.) This has since been rightly dismissed by his family. (Andrea Mandell, "*The Dark Knight*'s Joker did not kill Heath Ledger, says sister," USA Today, 3 May 2017.)

30. *Batman (1940) #1*, Spring 1940.

31. "We arrived at it in our own way by researching a lot of the more recent Joker stuff, and thinking about what this icon is when viewed through the prism of *Batman Begins*," Nolan explains. "When viewed in the world we created, in the tone we created. And what we arrived at is somebody who is quite a serious guy, really, considering his name's the Joker and that turned out to be quite similar to his original conception." (Stax, "*IGN* Interviews Christopher Nolan," *IGN*, 6 December 2007.)

32. Jerry Robinson's contributions to the creation of the Joker were long obscured and overlooked. Indeed, *The Dark Knight* marked the first time that Warner Brothers and DC Comics explicitly acknowledged him as a co-creator of the iconic character. (Michael Uslan, *The Boy Who Loved Batman: A Memoir* (2011), p. 230.)

33. The Joker was intended to be killed off at the end of that second story in that first issue, but editor Whitney Ellsworth insisting on revising his final panel to suggest that the character had survived. (Brian K. Eason, "*Dark Knight* Flashback: The Joker, Part I," Comic Book Resources, 11 July 2008.) The Joker would appear in nine of the first twelve issues of *Batman*. (Geoff Boucher, "The Joker returns to *Batman* pages, building on 72-year history," The Los Angeles Times, 1 August 2012.)

34. Mark S. Reinhart, *The Batman Filmography* (2013), p. 11.

35. Jonathan Nolan, "Christopher Nolan: The Movies. The Memories. Part 6: Jonathan Nolan on *The Dark Knight*," *Empire*, July 2012.

36. Christopher Nolan, " Christopher Nolan's Top 10," *The Criterion Collection*, 29 January 2013.

37. Rebecca Murray, "Writer/Director Christopher Nolan Talks About *The Dark Knight*," Thought Co., 13 August 2008.

38. For example, unlike many other iterations of the character, the Joker does not have access to any "Joker toxin" or "Joker venom." This may have been a conscious effort to distinguish the character from the Scarecrow, who uses "fear toxin" in both *Batman Begins* and *The Dark Knight*.

39. Dan Jolin, "The Making Of Heath Ledger's Joker," *Empire Magazine*, December 2009.

40. "Dressing the Joker," *IGN*, 25 February 2008.

41. "Joker's Wild," *Wizard Universe*, 8 February 2008.

42. Aoife Barry, "Why the epic Dunkirk was the hardest film Christopher Nolan has made," *The Journal*, 17 July 2017.

43. Tom Shone, "Christopher

Nolan: the man who rebooted the blockbuster," *The Guardian*, 4 November 2014.

44. Scott Bowles, "For now, Nolan and Batman will rest in *Dark* glory," *USA Today*, 7 December 2008.

45. To pick one minor example from *The Dark Knight*, Nolan did not have to cut anything from the film to secure a PG-13 rating, despite how uncomfortable some of the violence is. Nolan managed tone so effectively that he carried the film as close to the line as possible without needed to trim anything off. (Rebecca Murray, "Writer/Director Christopher Nolan Talks About *The Dark Knight*," *Thought Co.*, 13 August 2008.)

46. Geoff Andrew, "Christopher Nolan," *The Guardian*, 27 August 2002.

47. Dan Jolin, "The Making Of Heath Ledger's Joker," *Empire Magazine*, December 2009.

48. In some ways, this happens quite literally. Some of the video footage recorded by the Joker was actually directed by Heath Ledger. (Margaret Maurer, "*The Dark Knight*: 15 Behind The Scenes Secrets About Heath Ledger's Joker," *ScreenRant*, 27 February 2017.)

49. Forrest Wickman has described the director's tendency to put the camera at 90° or 180° off the horizontal plane as Nolan's "signature shot." Indeed, Nolan likes to literally twist the audience's perspective by rotating the camera. He incorporates it into the action shots in *Inception*, but it also recurs in movies like *Memento* and *Interstellar*. (Forrest Wickman, "Christopher Nolan's Favourite Shot, and How It Reflects What His Movies Are Really About," *Slate*, 7 November 2014.) In *The Dark Knight*, Nolan uses the shot repeatedly. Harvey Dent's face is rubbed in the gasoline at a 90° angle from the horizontal plane, while the Joker shoots his last threatening video at 180° and eventually wrestles the camera around to face him at that angle at the very end.

50. The "180° rule" refers to the idea that all shots in an on-screen conversation should pivot around a 180° radius so as to avoid disorienting the audience and to provide a sense of visual continuity. It should feel like the audience is sitting on one side of the conversation. This is a foundation rule of movie-making. Breaking it is traditionally used to disorient the audience or to create a sense of unease and imbalance. In the interrogation scene, the breaking of the rule symbolises a shift in the power dynamics of the scene. (Srikanth Kanchinadham, "Why Christopher Nolan Broke The 180 Degree Rule In *The Dark Knight*!," *Jamuura*, 6 January 2016.)

51. The production team were still getting used to working with IMAX cameras when shooting the opening scene, and so the initial take was slightly out of focus. They reshot the scene in focus, but were not able to recreate the magic of that initial reveal. As a result, the first (slightly out of focus) take marks the audience's first proper introduction to the Joker. (Rodrigo Perez, "Christopher Nolan Says Heath Ledger Initially Didn't Want To Be In Superhero Or Batman Movies: 6 Things Learned From The FSLC Talk," *IndieWire*, 29 November 2012.)

52. David Chen, "Hans Zimmer and James Newton Howard On Composing the Score to *The Dark Knight*," */Film*, 8 January 2009.

53. Blair Jackson, "Batman Rides Again: *The Dark Knight*," *Mix*, 1 July 2008.

54. Elizabeth Sandifer, "An Accurately Named Trilogy II: *The Dark Knight*," *Eruditorum Press*, 13 November 2017.

55. Stax, "*IGN* Interviews Christopher Nolan," *IGN*, 6 December 2007.

56. Sonny Bunch, "Movies: Gotham City's war on terror," *The Washington Times*, 18 July 2008.

57. Commentators have likened the blending of pulp storytelling, popular appeal and social allegory in Nolan's *Dark Knight* trilogy to the way in which Francis Ford Coppola used *The Godfather* films to explore seventies America. (Tom Shone, "*The Dark Knight* trilogy as our generation's *Godfather*," *The Guardian*, 20 July 2012.)

58. Kyle Buchanan, "Is It Possible to Make a Hollywood Blockbuster Without Evoking 9/11?," *Vulture*, 13 June 2013.

59. Todd VanDerWerff, "Superhero movies have become an endless attempt to rewrite 9/11," *Vox*, 11 September 2016.

60. Indeed, a surprising number of these stories attempt to construct a more wholesome and heroic version of 9/11. In *Man of Steel*, the heroes pilot a plane into the world engine in a heroic suicide mission to save the world. In *The Defenders*, it is revealed that the heroes have to save Manhattan itself by destroying one of the island's skyscrapers to help solidify the island's foundations.

61. This is most obvious in blockbusters like *Cloverfield*, *The Avengers* and *Batman vs. Superman*, which offer a grittier and dustier depiction of urban devastation than equivalent nineties films like *Independence Day* or *Armageddon*. (Robbie Collin, "From *Cloverfield* to *Batman v Superman*: how did the 9/11 terrorist attacks change cinema?," *The Telegraph*, 21 March 2016.)

62. Although interdimensional portals over cities are nothing new in cinema, dating back to *Ghostbusters* (1984) at the very latest, they did become a lot more common in the twenty-first century; *The Avengers*, *Thor: The Dark World*, *Teenage Mutant Ninja Turtles: Out of the Shadows*, *Ghostbusters* (2016), *Doctor Strange*, *The Avengers: Infinity War*. (Kevin Lincoln, "Let's Call a Moratorium on Inter-Dimensional Portals in Movies, Shall We?," *Vulture*, 7 November 2016.)

63. There is Malekith's suicide attack upon Asgard in *Thor: The Dark World*, the urban devastation caused by the Vengeance tearing through San Francisco in *Star Trek Into Darkness*, the plane colliding with the world engine in *Man of Steel*.

64. Dent brands the Joker as a terrorist during the news conference at which he turns himself in, and Alfred uses the descriptor when explaining to Rachel how Bruce is willing to let Dent take this action.

65. John Ip, "*The Dark Knight*'s War on Terrorism," *Ohio State Journal of Criminal Law*, September 2011, p. 209–229.

66. Mike M. Ahlers, "U.S. 9/11 panel: Hijackers may have had utility knives," *CNN*, 27 January 2004.

67. Jeremy Chapiro, "Why we think terrorism is scarier than it really is (and we probably always will)," *Vox*, 28 March 2016.

68. The Joker is correct that (relatively minor) disruptions like his terrorist attacks have longer-lasting repercussions on the popular consciousness than "acceptable" or "expected" loss of life through conventional gun violence or warfare. Terrorism has killed far fewer people in the United States than gun violence, but terrorism is a source of greater fear because it exists outside an organized framework. (Jenny Anderson, "The psychology of why 94 deaths from terrorism are scarier than 301,797 deaths from guns," *Quartz*, 31 January 2017.)

69. As John Ip argues, there's a credible argument to be made that Ra's Al Ghul's organized League of Shadows with its terrorist attacks against a "decadent" culture is a *slightly* more accurate depiction of these organizations. The League of Shadows seems to have a reason and a motivation beyond the terror itself, seems to recruit and radicalise young men in pursuit of its goals, and Ra's Al Ghul also plans to ram a means of public transport into a skyscraper to devastate a city. (John Ip, "*The Dark Knight*'s War on Terrorism," *Ohio State Journal of Criminal Law*, September 2011, p. 213–214.)

70. Most obviously, comic book blockbusters have a tendency to fall back on nihilism as a motivation for large-scale antagonists, who seem to engage in destruction and devastation for the sake of it. *See*, for example, Kaecilius in *Doctor Strange*, Malekith in *Thor: The Dark World* and arguably Ultron in *Avengers: Age of Ultron*. It is perhaps revealing that the big villain of the first twenty-odd films in the Marvel Cinematic Universe is Thanos, a character whose primary motivation in the comic books is to murder the universe as a gift to his beloved, the anthropomorphic personification of Death herself.

71. Jon Schwarz, "Why Do So Many Americans Fear Muslims? Decades of Denial About America's Role in the World," *The Intercept*, 18 February 2017.

72. To be fair to *The Dark Knight*, the legacies of imperialism and colonialism lurk at the very edges of this story. In particular, the action that finally inspires the mob to accept the Joker's offer is Batman's unilateral military action in Hong Kong to recover Lau. As Lau points out, Hong Kong is Chinese soil, even if was also one of the last overseas colonies of the British Empire. Even today, Hong Kong remains caught between two worlds. (Nick Frisch, "Twenty Years After the Handover to China, Hong Kong Remains a City on the Edge," *New Yorker*, 30 June 2017.)

73. Paul Hechinger, "*Dark Knight* Director Christopher Nolan Talks About Keeping Batman Real," *BBC America*, December 2012.

74. *Batman (1940) #1*, Spring 1940.

75. Justine Toh, "The tools and toys of (the) War (on Terror): Consumer desire, military fetish and regime change in *Batman Begins*," *Scan: Journal of Media Arts and Culture*, 2009. Interestingly, *Inception* would reveal that the technology used by Cobb and his associates had also initially been developed for military use.

76. Less than two weeks after 9/11, President Bush would describe terrorism as "a threat to our way of life." ("Text: President Bush Addresses the Nation," *The Washington Post*, 20 September 2001.) Years later, President Obama would reject this argument, insisting that it was important not to "overinflate" these terrorist organizations by treating them as "an existential threat to the United States or the world order." ("Pres Obama on Fareed Zakaria GPS," *CNN*, 1 February 2015.)

77. As Elizabeth Sandifer suggests, the most logical interpretation of this story is that Alfred was working as a mercenary during the country's post-colonial civil wars. (Elizabeth Sandifer, "An Accurately Named Trilogy II: *The Dark Knight*," *Eruditorum Press*, 13 November 2017.) It is an interesting acknowledgement of the violent consequences of colonialism in the context of the film, which perhaps ties into the terrorism metaphor at the heart of *The Dark Knight*. As with Bruce's adventure to Hong Kong to recover Lau, Alfred's story places the legacies of imperialism and colonialism close to the heart of the story.

78. Arthur Rizer and Joseph Hartman, "How the War on Terror Has Militarized the Police," *The Atlantic*, 7 November 2011.

79. Richard Jackson, "Political Language, Policy Formulation and the Practice of Torture in the War on Terrorism: Implications for Human Rights," Paper presented at the annual meeting of the American Political Science Association, Marriott, Loews Philadelphia, and the Pennsylvania Convention Center, Philadelphia, PA, Aug 31, 2006.

80. There were reports that the torture-heavy television series *24* was very popular among real-life enhanced interrogation experts, for example. (Hilary Neroni, "*24*, Jack Bauer, and the Torture Fantasy," in *The Subject of Torture: Psychoanalysis and Biopolitics in Television and Film* (2015), p. 95–114.)

81. Jason Bittel, "This Technology From *The Dark Knight* Could Become Reality," *Slate*, 19 June 2013.

82. Vicky Gan, "How TV's *Person of Interest* Helps Us Understand the Surveillance Society," *The Smithsonian Magazine*, 24 October 2013.

83. Carole Cadwalladr and Emma Graham-Harrison, "Revealed: 50 million Facebook profiles harvested for Cambridge Analytica in major data breach," *The Guardian*, 17 March 2018.

84. Andrew Klavan, "What Bush and Batman Have in Common," *The Wall Street Journal*, 25 July 2008.

85. In fact, a considerable portion of *The Dark Knight Rises* is given over to disputing and deconstructing this superficial reading of the film's politics, to the point that the characters in *The Dark Knight Rises* make a point to reverse almost every major compromise that was made at the end of *The Dark Knight*.

86. To be fair, this points to a broader issue in socially-commentary-driven criticism, where it is assumed that the depiction of any action (particularly by a story's protagonist) is an endorsement of this action. This is a very superficial and knee-jerk approach to criticism, one that often refuses to engage with the work as a whole. Director Kathryn Bigalow would wade into this debate over controversy surrounding the depiction of torture in her film *Zero Dark Thirty*. (Ben Child, "Kathryn Bigelow and Mark Boal respond to *Zero Dark Thirty* torture row," *The Guardian*, 8 January 2013.)

87. Roy Greenslade, "Why a 'war' on terrorism will generate yet more terrorism," *The Guardian*, 30 November 2015.

88. One such example is Donald Trump's executive order that attempted to limit access to the United States by travelers from Muslim-majority countries. This was a potent recruiting tool for extremist organizations. (Eliza Mackintosh, "Trump ban is boon for ISIS recruitment, former jihadists and experts say," *CNN*, 31 January 2017.)

89. "Joker's Wild," *Wizard Universe*, 8 February 2008.

90. Jeffery Goldberg, "The Obama Doctrine," *The Atlantic*, April 2016.

91. In *Batman Begins*, Ra's Al Ghul talks metaphorically about "a cleansing fire" needing to purge Gotham, while a literal fire burns down Wayne Manor. In *The Dark Knight Rises*, Bane repeats the mantra that "the fire rises" as he plots to unleash anarchy upon the streets of Gotham.

92. The line is rendered tragic and ironic by the unfortunate passing of Heath Ledger, which means that the last image of the Joker in the *Dark Knight* is the character

dangling upside down and laughing manically to himself. Indeed, there is some sense that Heath Ledger would have appeared in the sequel to *The Dark Knight* had he not passed away. (David Crow, "Heath Ledger wanted to do another Batman movie as The Joker," *Den of Geek*, 5 May 2017.)

93. Later in the sequence, when Detective Stephens physically abuses the Joker, it turns out to play *right into* the character's hands. The Joker manages to subdue Stephens, force his way out of the interrogation room, and set of a bomb in the Major Crimes Unit.

94. Scott F. Stoddart, "New Visions/New Vistas: Christopher Nolan's Batman Trilogy and the New Western" in *The New Western: Critical Essays on the Genre Since 9/11* (2016), p.229–244.

95. In *Batman Begins*, Ra's Al Ghul builds his whole philosophy around the idea that "the criminal is not complicated." However, the League of Shadows still has to carefully foster and create crime in Gotham to justify their attempted mass murder. If the criminal is not "complicated," it seems illogical to weaponized "economics" to drive the city to the brink of collapse. In *The Dark Knight Rises*, Bane cultivates a reputation as the only person to ever have escaped the pit and as the leader of the League of Shadows. Ultimately, he is neither. As with the Joker, Bane is subdued once his hypocrisy is exposed and his myth is demolished.

96. The film seems to imply that the Joker is unsure whether Harvey Dent is Batman at this point in the film. He seems to believe that Dent might be Batman after the confrontation at the party, but doesn't seem especially surprised when Batman shows up to stop his attack on the police convoy.

97. It could reasonably be argued that the Joker is advancing game theory throughout *The Dark Knight*. In the opening sequence, the Joker has clearly set up the robbery in such a way as to evoke "the Pirate Puzzle," in which a group of pirates argue with (and murder) one another in order to secure a greater share of their profits. (Presh Talwalkar, "Game Theory in *The Dark Knight*: the opening scene (spoilers)," *Mind Your Decisions*, 19 August 2008.) However, the ferry game at the climax is a somewhat muddled variation on the classic "Prisoner's Dilemma," which the movie signifies by using actual prisoners. (Michael A. Allen, "The Dark Knight and Game Theory," *The Quantitative Peace*, 19 July 2008.)

98. "See, I'm not a monster," the Joker promises Batman. "I'm just ahead of the curve." However, given how his final scheme plays out, *The Dark Knight* seems to suggest that Joker was trying to assure himself as much as Batman, to justify his own monstrosity by projecting it on to the world at large.

99. When the Joker insists upon "half" of the mob's money in return for killing Batman, they respond by demanding, "Are you crazy?" The Joker very quietly responds, "No I'm not... No, I'm not."

100. "When the chips are down these civilized people, they'll eat each other," the Joker had promised Batman in an earlier scene.

101. Dan Jolin, "The Making Of Heath Ledger's Joker," *Empire Magazine*, December 2009.

102. This plot device was inspired by a line from Alan Moore and Brian Bolland's *Batman: The Killing Joke* (May 1988). In that story, the reader witnesses an origin story for the character, before the villain concedes, "If I'm going to have a past, I prefer it to be multiple choice!"

103. *The Dark Knight* does include a number of quick flashes to earlier scenes, but the story progresses in a straight line. *Inception* distorts its sense of time through flashbacks in dreams; *The Dark Knight Rises* features an extended flashback to Bane's origin, and then reveals it to be Talia's; *Interstellar* finds Cooper travelling through time; *Dunkirk* unfolds in three different time periods, each moving at a different speed. Interestingly, though, *The Dark Knight* does not entire escape Nolan's non-linear sensibilities. Somewhat cheekily, the opening shot of the first trailer for *The Dark Knight* was the closing shot of the film, meaning that the first footage that most audiences saw of *The Dark Knight* was the last footage in the film.

104. Michael Colan, "Dream A Little Deeper: The Narrative Storytelling Style Of Early Christopher Nolan Films," *MoviePilot*, 15 May 2017.

105. Harvey Dent's election as Gotham's new District Attorney, his relationship with Rachel, and Bruce's plan to undermine the mob by providing Gordon with "lightly irradiated bills" are all events building from *Batman Begins* that happen off-screen before the start of *The Dark Knight*.

106. During the attempted blackmail, Reese makes an off-hand reference to how Bruce has "got the entire RND department burning through cash claiming it's related to cell phones for the army." This is unrelated to substance of Reese's blackmail, but is important in setting up the surveillance device that will be revealed the movie's climax. So Fox has to then bring it up with Bruce in his next scene with the character, which happens to involve the fingerprint and the bullet.

107. Indeed, the way in which the short thwarted-blackmail scene throws off the subtle rhythm of the bullet montage might be best reflected in the discussion and debate around what exactly is happening during that sequence. The scene logic is quite clear, but disrupting the flow of information disorients the audience. (Ray Wgner, "Basic Movie Science: *The Dark Knight*," *Birth. Movies. Death*, 5 July 2012.)

108. During the Joker's attack on the convoy, for example, Gotham seems to be bustling. When the batmobile is destroyed, it lands near some workers enjoying a late evening snack. When the batpod whirls through traffic, the film makes a point to focus on the people *inside* these cars. When Batman is forced to take a diversion through a shopping center, Nolan includes lots of shots of by-standers dodging out of the way.

109. For example, this is quite clear during Batman's attack on the Prewitt Building. While Gordon is receiving a threatening phone call from Dent, Nolan includes a quick reaction shot from two snipers within earshot, both of whom are clearly surprised to hear Gordon talking to Dent on the phone, as any rational person in this fictional world would be.

110. Demonstrating Nolan's attention to detail, even the identities of Maroni's informants within the police department are carefully seeded much earlier in the film when Dent warns Gordon about "working with scum like Wuertz and Ramirez." Ramirez's sick mother is even alluded to twice before being revealed as Maroni's leverage over her, once in conversation with Gordon and again when Alfred pulls up all officers with relatives in hospitals.

111. Stax, "*IGN* Interviews Christopher Nolan," *IGN*, 6 December 2007.

112. Kristopher Tapley, "Christopher Nolan Talks Michael Mann's

*Heat* With Cast and Crew at the Academy," *Variety*, 7 September 2016.

113. Stax, "*IGN* Interviews Christopher Nolan," *IGN*, 6 December 2007.

114. In a feature for the magazine *Empire*, Dan Jolin described *The Dark Knight* as "the *Heat* of comic-book movies." (Dan Jolin, "*The Dark Knight*," *Empire*, July 2008.) Nolan himself would argue that *The Dark Knight* took on "that sort of crime epic idea of what a city is." (Mark Bernardin, "Christopher Nolan on 'Extreme Places' in the Making of *The Dark Knight Rises*," *The Hollywood Reporter*, 27 December 2012.)

115. Both Gordon and Maroni react with a mixture of awe and horror to what has happened to Gotham over the course of the film. Maroni reacts to the scarring of Dent with genuine discomfort, "It's too much…" Gordon appears close to a nervous breakdown by the climax of the film.

116. *See* for example, Dan Hassler-Forest, *Capitalist Superheroes: Caped Crusaders in the Neoliberal Age* (2012), particularly "Introduction," p. 1–20.

117. Both *The Dark Knight* and *The Dark Knight Rises* rank among the top twenty highest grossing films at the United States box office, along with *The Avengers* and *Avengers: Age of Ultron*. Worldwide, *The Avengers*, *Avengers: Age of Ultron*, *Iron Man 3* and *Captain America: Civil War* all rank within the top ten.

118. In November 2017, following the release of *Justice League*, there were estimates of thirty-five major superhero movies planned over the next four years. In many cases, the studios had simply marked release dates on calendars without any further detail. (Adam Chitwood, "Upcoming Superhero Movie Release Dates: From 2017 to 2021," *Collider*, 23 November 2017.)

119. Graeme McMillan, "Steven Spielberg Says Superhero Movies Will Go 'the Way of the Western'," *The Hollywood Reporter*, 2 September 2015.

120. Mark Sweney, "Even superheroes may not be able to save Hollywood's desperate summer," *The Observer*, 26 August 2017.

121. Chris Ager, "Are There Too Many Superhero Movies for Hollywood to Handle?," *ScreenRant*, 22 August 2014.

122. According to producer Kevin Feige, the key to staving off superhero fatigue is "to keep things fresh and to keep things unexpected." (Ana Dumaraug, "Kevin Feige On Superhero Fatigue: Marvel Keeps Things 'Fresh'," *ScreenRant*, 23 July 2017.) Under his direction, Marvel has done this in part by skillfully blending genres. This process arguably began during "Phase II" of their superhero franchise-building, which began with *Iron Man 3* in May 2013. In 2014, the studio blended the genre with paranoid political thrillers in *Captain America: The Winter Soldier* and with space opera in *Guardians of the Galaxy*. In 2015, despite a troubled production, *Ant-Man* positioned itself as a superhero heist movie.

123. Emanuel Levy, "*Dark Knight, The*: Expanding Film's Scope and Locations," *Emanuel Levy*, 29 July 2008.

124. Dan Palmer, "Mies's Gotham," *Confessions of a Preservationist*, 29 July 2008.

125. Owen Williams, "The Cinematography Of *The Dark Knight*," *Empire*, 19 July 2012.

126. Emanuel Levy, "*Dark Knight, The*: Expanding Film's Scope and Locations," *Emanuel Levy*, 29 July 2008.

127. Peter Sciretta, "How *The Dark Knight* Went IMAX,"/*Film*, 14 July 2008.

128. Iain Stasukevich, "Batman to the Max," *American Cinematographer*, August 2012.

129. Mark Wilson, "A Rare Tour of IMAX Cameras," *Gizmodo*, 28 May 2009.

130. Mike Seymour, "*Dark Knight*: Imax, Effects and That Bike," *FX Guide*, 21 July 2008.

131. Debra Kaufman, "Marrying IMAX and 35mm in *The Dark Knight*," *Studio Daily*, 14 July 2008.

132. Mekado Murphy, "The Imax Difference, Blockbuster Size," *The New York Times*, 13 July 2012.

133. Jordan Raup, "*Interstellar* Will Feature Over an Hour of IMAX Footage; New Stills and Spots Arrive," *The Film Stage*, 15 October 2014.

134. Greg Harmon, "Christopher Nolan's *Dunkirk* will feature 79 awe-inspiring minutes of IMAX footage," *Cultjur*, 6 July 2017.

135. Jeffrey Ressner, "The Traditionalist," *Director's Guild of America Quarterly*, Spring 2012.

136. Chris Begley, "Warner Bros. wants *Batman* in 3D?," *Batman News*, 25 September 2010.

137. Mike Fleming Jr, "Oscar: Chris Nolan Q&A About *Inception*," *Deadline*, 7 January 2011.

138. Jeffrey Ressner, "The Traditionalist," *Director's Guild of America Quarterly*, Spring 2012.

139. Xan Brooks, "Is James Cameron's 3D movie *Avatar* the shape of cinema to come?," *The Guardian*, 20 August 2009.

140. Somewhat ironically, despite becoming the highest grossing movie of all time, *Avatar* left a very understated cultural footprint, almost disappearing from the cultural radar in the space of under a decade. (Ed Power, "*Avatar*: how the biggest film of all time got left behind," *The Telegraph*, 15 April 2016.)

141. Brendon Connelly, "How the film industry blew it with 3D," *Den of Geek*, 24 June 2016.

142. Jordan Magrath, "Director's Spotlight: Christopher Nolan," *Film Equals*, 4 November 2014.

143. Scott Mendelson, "*Gravity* Passes $100M In IMAX," *Forbes*, 7 February 2014.

144. Chris O'Falt, "How the New *Star Wars* Movie is Bringing Celluloid Back to Cinema," *IndieWire*, 14 December 2015.

145. Brent Lang, "*Avengers: Infinity War* to Be Shot Entirely With Imax Cameras," *Variety*, 7 may 2015.

146. Iain Stasukevich, "Batman to the Max," *American Cinematographer*, August 2012.

147. The blu ray edition of *The Dark Knight* recreates some of the effect of the IMAX version of the film, the aspect ratio adjusting to take in the whole screen for the sequences shot on IMAX. (Richard Lawler, "Expect *The Dark Knight*'s IMAX sequences on Blu-ray," *Engadget*, 17 July 2008.)

148. Although, as David Bordwell notes, Nolan's framing and composition were never particularly precise even before he started shooting in IMAX and protecting for the more conventional 2.39:1 ration. (David Bordwell, "Nolan vs. Nolan," *Observations on Film Art*, 19 August 2012.)

149. Jim Emerson, "*Dark Knight* Quiz #1: What's wrong with this picture?," RogerEbert.com, 10 January 2009.

150. Jim Emerson, "The framing of *The Dark Knight*," RogerEbert.com, 12 January 2009.

151. Stephanie Zacharek, "*The Dark Knight*," *Salon*, 17 July 2008.

152. "Christopher Nolan on *Following*—Conversations Inside The Criterion Collection," *VICE*, 24 August 2014.

153. Indeed, these criticisms of Nolan arguably exist in a larger critical context, with a broader move

away from more traditional and formal methods of storytelling in cinema. There is an understandable anxiety that Hollywood is losing a large part of its artistic history and craft in this transition. This is perhaps best explored in David Bordwell's *The Way Hollywood Tells It Story and Style in Modern Movies* (2006).

154. Indeed, another frequent criticism of Nolan's filmmaking is his tendency to include more cuts than are strictly necessary in seeking to convey information to the audience. (A.D. Jameson, "More on *Inception*: Shot Economy and 1 + 1 = 1," *Big Other*, 4 October 2010.) However, the popularity of Nolan's films and the success that they have enjoyed with mass audience while embracing relatively abstract concepts like dreams and time travel suggest that Nolan communicates their information quite efficiently. It may not elegant, but it is effective.

155. Zachery Brasier, "Why Christopher Nolan Is Not The New Stanley Kubrick," *Seroword*, 4 December 2015. (Of course, there are *many* reasons why the comparisons between Kubrick and Nolan are unconvincing, but in formal terms Kubrick is a much more precise director with the camera.)

156. It could, for example, be argued that Kubrick's distinct visual style developed through his photography and informed his cinematic compositions. (Philippe Mather, *Stanley Kubrick at Look Magazine: Authorship and Genre in Photojournalism and Film* (2013).)

157. This is perhaps most obliviously notable in his preference for the one-point perspective in his work, a technique also favored by later formalists like Paul Thomas Anderson and Wes Anderson. (Sarah Salovaara, "The 'One-Point Perspective' in Stanley Kubrick's Work," *Filmmaker Magazine*, 21 March 2014.)

158. For a point of comparison, there was outrage among fans of the director when Warner Brothers released a high-definition remaster of *Barry Lyndon* with a *slightly* wrong aspect ratio. Kubrick desired for the film to be seen at an aspect ratio of 1.66:1, but the blu ray presented the image at a ratio of 1.78:1. On most high definition monitors, that difference would amount only an additional thirty-six rows of pixels at the top and bottom of the screen; a relatively miniscule difference, certainly much smaller than the difference between IMAX ratio of 1.78:1 and the theatrical ratio of 2.35:1 employed on *The Dark Knight*. Although *Barry Lyndon* was one of Kubrick's least popular films, this became a minor controversy. (Josh Zyber, "*Barry Lyndon* Aspect Ratio Controversy Solved," *High-Def Digest*, 28 June 2011.)

159. Anne Billson, "Action sequences should stir, not just shake," *The Guardian*, 5 November 2008.

160. Jim Emerson, "In the Cut, Part I: Shots in the *Dark (Knight)*," RogerEbert.com, 8 September 2011.

161. This may explain the quick cuts and the inserts that Nolan uses during his fighting sequences, offering audiences a literal blow-by-blow account of the action rather than simply standing back and taking it all in.

162. Lynden Barber, "Sound and Fury," *The Australian*, 30 October 2010.

163. For example, the big action beat at the climax of *Captain America: Civil War* is the brawl at the airport, but this devolves into a quieter confrontation between Steve, Bucky and Tony in the Russian silo. The big action beat of *Star Trek Into Darkness* involves the mission to stop the Vengeance from destroying the Enterprise, but this subsequently devolves into a wrestling match between Spock and Khan through twenty-third century San Francisco. In *SPECTRE*, the climax involves a plan to stop the sinister "Nine Eyes" programme going active, but then develops into a hunt through the ruins of MI6 in which Bond shoots down Blofeld's helicopter with a pistol.

164. "*Premiere* Features *Batman Begins*," *SuperHeroHype*, 9 May 2005.

165. Stax, "*IGN* Interviews Christopher Nolan," *IGN*, 6 December 2007.

166. Roger Ebert, "The Dark Knight," *The Chicago-Sun Times*, 16 July 2008.

167. Catherine Elsworth, "*The Dark Knight*: Heath Ledger's Batman movie smashes box office records," *The Telegraph*, 20 July 2008.

168. Dave McNary, "*Dark Knight* breaks $1 billion mark," *Variety*, 20 February 2009.

169. Jonathan Nolan, "Christopher Nolan: The Movies. The Memories. Part 6: Jonathan Nolan on *The Dark Knight*," *Empire*, July 2012.

170. *Transformers: Dark of the Moon*; *Thor: The Dark World*; *Transformers: The Last Knight*. Indeed, even *Teenage Mutant Ninja Turtles: Out of the Shadows* alludes to the word "Dark" in its title.

171. Kristen Acuna, "Every Big Movie Keeps Showing Us This Same Scene Over And Over Again," *Business Insider*, 12 November 2013.

172. Scott Mendelson, "Why Hollywood Needs To Rewatch *The Dark Knight*," *Forbes*, 27 August 2014.

173. Alex Hess, "*The Dark Knight*: my most overrated film," *The Guardian*, 14 November 2014.

174. Aaron Couch, "The Unexpected Humor in Christopher Nolan's *Batman* Movies," *The Hollywood Reporter*, 10 February 2017.

175. "The Dark Knight Effect," *Empire*, 13 July 2012.

176. Peter Sciretta, "IMDb Watch: Are *Dark Knight* Fanboys Burying *The Godfather*?," */Film*, 28 July 2008.

177. "Batman fans beat *Godfather* with 'rank trick'," news.com.au, 23 October 2009.

178. It is worth noting how seismic this shift was. *The Godfather* had been the highest rated movie on the list since September 1999, displaced for a month in January 2002 by *The Lord of the Rings: The Fellowship of the Ring*. Since its ascent to the number one slot in August 2008, *The Shawshank Redemption* has yet to be displaced. (This manuscript went to print a decade after that shift.)

179. Matt Singer, "*Dark Knight Rises* Critic Receives Death Threats," *IndieWire*, 16 July 2012.

180. "*Batman*: death threats made to reviewers," *The Telegraph*, 19 July 2012.

181. Matt Singer, "Why Are Christopher Nolan Fans So Intense?," *ScreenCrush*, 14 November 2014.

182. See, for example, Josh Tyler, "Note To Awards Givers: Ignore *The Dark Knight* At Your Own Peril," *Cinema Blend*, December 2008.

183. Jim Emerson, "Critics better love *The Dark Knight*—or else!," RogerEbert.com, 13 December 2008.

184. Sasha Stone, "The State of the Race: The Inevitable *Knight*," *Awards Daily*, 11 August 2008.

185. This tension was articulated in Brandon Valentine's reflection on the perceived snub of *The Dark Knight* at the Golden Globe Awards, when he suggested that the film had been overlooked because awards voters refused to "believe that any film with a comic-book superhero as its protagonist cannot be taken seriously as award-worthy drama." (Murray Pomerance, *The Last Laugh: Strange Humours of Cinema* (2013), p. 197.)

186. Even professional journalists and critics would subscribe to this logic, arguing that *The Dark Knight* effectively "showed movie fans and critics alike that superhero films could, and should, be taken seriously." (Bill Ramey, "Heroes Of The Year: *Dark Knight Rises* Director Christopher Nolan," *MTV*, 19 December 2012.

187. Miller revolutionized the genre in the late eighties by introducing sex and violence into superhero comic books. "I felt that superhero comics had really been held back by a misperception that they were just for kids," the writer reflected in hindsight. ("The Evolution of *Batman*," *AMC*, June 2007.)

188. "Superhero comics are, for better or worse, taken *very* seriously these days," reflected journalist Abraham Riesman of the impact of books like *The Dark Knight Returns* and Alan Moore and Dave Gibbons' *Watchmen*. (Abraham Riesman, "The Single Most Important Year in Superhero History Was 1986," *Vulture*, 26 October 2016. Emphasis original.)

189. Jackson Ayres, "When Were Superheroes Grim and Gritty?," *The Los Angeles Review of Books*, 20 February 2016

190. Jason Guriel, "*Batman: The Killing Joke* Predicted the Bleak State of Superheroes," *The Atlantic*, 22 July 2016.

191. Julian Darius, "Why Comics Have Failed to Achieve Real Respect," *Sequart*, 17 October 2011.

192. John Horn, Doug Smith and Nicole Sperling, "Unmasking Oscar: Academy voters are overwhelmingly white and male," *The Los Angeles Times*, 19 February 2012.

193. Gregory Ellwood, "Oscar 2009: Why the *Dark Knight* snub? The Academy is old, stupid," *Hitfix*, 23 January 2009.

194. "The more happy meals and candy and cereal boxes that your film is plastered across, the less chance you have of being taken seriously at the end of the year," reflects analyst Jeff Bock. (Brent Land, "How Much Has Changed Since Oscar Expanded Best Picture Nominations?," *Variety*, 21 February 2017.)

195. The total box office gross of the Best Picture winners (and nominees) trended downwards in the first decade of the twenty-first century, with the notable exception of 76th Academy Awards in March 2004 when Peter Jackson's *The Lord of the Rings: The Return of the King* took home the title. (Matthew Belinkie, "Analysing Oscar," *OverthinkingIt*, 17 February 2009.) The five Best Picture nominees at the 81st Academy Awards in March 2009 grossed a total of $353m. This was less than the domestic take of *The Dark Knight*, let alone its worldwide total.

196. Mark Graham, "Oscar Turns Its Nose Up at *Revolutionary Road*, *The Dark Knight*," *Vulture*, 22 January 2009; Lewis Wallace, "Why So Serious? Oscars Snub *Dark Knight* for Top Awards," *Wired*, 23 January 2009; Gregg Kilday, "*Dark Knight's* best picture snub no surprise," *The Hollywood Reporter*, 22 January 2009; Ben Child, "The week in geek: The *Dark Knight*'s Oscars snub is a disgrace," *The Guardian*, 28 January 2009.

197. Tim Robey, "Oscar nominations 2009: a list of surprises," *The Telegraph*, 22 January 2009.

198. Malina Saval, "'The Reader," *Variety*, 30 January 2009.

199. Peter Finch won an Oscar for his work on *Network*. (Gregg Kilday, "Heath Ledger wins posthumous Oscar," *The Hollywood Reporter*, 22 February 2009.)

200. Luke Owen, "*Logan* will never get an Oscar nomination, because comic book movies will never get Oscar nominations," *Flickering Myth*, 6 January 2017.

201. Julian Sancton, "Would Heath Ledger Win If He Were Alive?," *Vanity Fair*, 27 January 2009.

202. "How come comic book movies never get nominated?" Jackman jokingly declared, riding a prop Batpod. "How can a billion dollars be unsophisticated?" Extending the gag, Jackman's opening number consciously glossed over *The Reader*. "*The Reader*. I haven't seen *The Reader*. I was gonna see it later, but I fell behind. My batmobile took longer than I thought to design."

203. The Best Picture category had originally included ten nominees, but had been cut to five nominees since the 17th Academy Awards in March 1944. (Richard Corliss, "Why the Oscars Need 10 Nominees," *Time*, 25 June 2009.)

204. Noel Murray, "The Pros & Cons Of Expanded Best Picture Nominations," *The A.V. Club*, 25 June 2009.

205. *See*, for example, Kevin Fallon, "Why *The Hunger Games* Has a Shot at the Best-Picture Oscar," *The Atlantic*, 27 March 2012; Glen Weldon, *The Caped Crusade: Batman and the Rise of Nerd Culture* (2017), p. 252.

206. Gregg Kilday, "Academy Revises Best Picture Rules; Can Be 5 to 10 Nominees," *The Hollywood Reporter*, 14 June 2011.

207. Stephen Galloway, "Oscars: Academy Weighing Return to Five Best Picture Nominees (Exclusive)," *The Hollywood Reporter*, 3 March 2015.

208. As observers were fond of pointing out, before *Argo*'s win at the 85th Academy Awards in February 2013, *Driving Miss Daisy* was the only "modern" Best Picture winner not to have also earned a Best Director nomination. (Christopher Rosen, "Best Picture Win Without A Best Director Nomination? For *Argo*, *Zero Dark Thirty* It Could Be Tough," *The Huffington Post*, 15 January 2013.)

209. Michael Schulman, "Shake-up at the Oscars," *The New Yorker*, 27 February 2017.

210. Stephen Galloway, "Oscars: The Academy's Terrific New Membership List Faces Long-Term Problems," *The Hollywood Reporter*, 30 June 2016.

211. Scott Feinberg, "Academy's New Voting Rules Raise Questions, Concerns and Anger Among Members," *The Hollywood Reporter*, 23 January 2016.

212. Chris Lee, "Christopher Nolan's *Inception* Oscar Snub," *The Daily Beast*, 15 February 2011.

213. Other inductees involved in the production of *Inception* were actor Ellen Page, production designer Guy Hendrix Dyas, sound engineers Lora Hirschberg and Ed Novick, and visual effects designers Paul Franklin and Mark H. Weingartner. (Dave Karger, "Motion Picture Academy invites 178 new members, including Russell Brand, Jesse Eisenberg, and Beyonce Knowles," *Entertainment Weekly*, 17 June 2011.)

## Chapter 7

1. Dave itzkoff, "A Man and His Dream: Christopher Nolan and *Inception*," *The New York Times*, 30 June 2010.

2. Cole Haddon, "Interview: Christopher Nolan Talks *Inception*," *MTV* 12 July 2010.

3. John Hiscock, "*Inception*: Christopher Nolan interview," *The Telegraph*, 1 July 2010.

4. Jen Yamato, "Chris Nolan and Guillermo del Toro: 10 Highlights From Their *Memento* Q&A," *MovieLine*, 5 February 2011.

5. Chris Ryan, "You're Waiting for a Train," *The Ringer*, 19 July 2017.

6. Cole Haddon, "Interview: Christopher Nolan Talks *Inception*," *MTV* 12 July 2010.

7. Ben Fritz, "The 365 Days of Summer Movies," *The Wall Street Journal*, 27 April 2017.

8. Matt Singer, "When Did March Become Part of Summer Movie Season?," *Screencrush*, 1 March 2017.

9. Kirsten Acuna, "Movie Studios Are Setting Themselves Up For Huge Losses," *Business Insider*, 6 March 2013.

10. Statistics indicate that the decline to second weekend in the 1980s was about 15.7%, growing to 21.5% in the 1990s. By 2012, the average second weekend decline for a major release was 49.1%. As a result, a lot of a movie's long-term box office fortunes are determined by its opening weekend returns. (Jim Pagels, "Why *Batman* Had No Competition at the Box Office," *Slate*, 23 July 2012.)

11. Jason Bailey, "How the Death of Mid-Budget Cinema Left a Generation of Iconic Filmmakers MIA," *Flavourwire*, 9 December 2014.

12. Scott Mendelson, "Box Office: *Blade Runner 2049* Is A Bomb Because Of Its Budget," *Forbes*, 15 October 2017.

13. Matthew Garrahan, "The rise and rise of the Hollywood film franchise," *The Financial Times*, 12 December 2014.

14. Lauren Duca, "Everything Is A Sequel Now, And It's Your Fault, America," *The Huffington Post*, 18 June 2015.

15. David Goldman, "Disney to buy Marvel for $4 billion," *CNN*, 31 August 2009.

16. "Disney buys *Star Wars* maker Lucasfilm from George Lucas," *BBC News*, 31 October 2012.

17. Adam Rogers, "You Won't Live to See the Final Star Wars Movie," *Wired*, 17 November 2015.

18. Aaron Hatch, "'Original' Films in Hollywood: Deconstructing the Backlash Against American Cinema," *The Artifice*, 2 March 2016.

19. Mark Harris, "The Day the Movies Died," *GQ*, 10 February 2011.

20. In 2011, the year following the release of *Inception*, there were 27 major sequels released, setting a new record. (Edward Davis, "Is Hollywood Afraid Of *Inception* & Original Ideas? 2011 Breaks Record For Sequels With 27 Films," *IndieWire*, 17 February 2011.)

21. The first of these three iterations was overseen by Sam Raimi and starred Toby Maguire; *Spider-Man* (2002), *Spider-Man II* (2004), *Spider-Man III* (2007). The second of these iterations was directed by Marc Webb and starred Andrew Garfield; *The Amazing Spider-Man* (2012), *The Amazing Spider-Man II* (2014). The third iteration was launched in conjunction with Marvel Studios, with Tom Holland taking on the role in *Captain America: Civil War* (2016).

22. Justin Kroll, "Ben Affleck Is the New Batman," *Variety*, 22 August 2013.

23. There are unconfirmed reports that the budget on the film may have extended past the reported figure to somewhere near $200m. (Richard Corliss, "Box Office: *Inception* Gets an Immaculate Reception," *Time*, 18 July 2010.)

24. Patrick Goldstein, "Could Chris Nolan have convinced anyone but Warners to make *Inception*?," *The Los Angeles Times*, 19 July 2010.

25. Jeremy Kay, "Christopher Nolan's Inception delivers dream result for Warner Bros," *The Guardian*, 19 July 2010.

26. Robert Trussel, "From pop culture to politics, nostalgia is everywhere," *Kansas City Star*, 15 November 2015.

27. Indeed, several authors have contextualized this particular strong push towards nostalgia as a response to the trauma of 9/11 and the War on Terror. (Matthew Leggatt, *Cultural and Political Nostalgia in the Age of Terror: The Melancholic Sublime* [2017].)

28. Pat Saperstein, "Why Nostalgia Rules the Internet and You Can't Escape *Full House*," *Variety*, 19 August 2015.

29. Brian Raftery, "Enjoy the Early–'00s Nostalgia Wave—It Might Be the Last Revival," *Wired*, 24 May 2017.

30. Charlie Lyne, "How nostalgia took over the world (and why that's no bad thing)," *The Guardian*, 9 July 2016.

31. It could be argued, for example, that Donald Trump built his successful presidential campaign around an idealized past that never existed, harking back to the romanticized popular conception of the fifties. Similarly, one explanation offered for the Brexit vote in the United Kingdom is that nit was rooted in a strong sense of nostalgia for Britain's former position as a world power. (Cathal Kelly, "The new Age of Nostalgia," *The Globe and Mail*, 23 December 2016.)

32. Mike Fleming Jr, "Oscar: Chris Nolan Q&A About *Inception*," *Deadline*, 7 January 2011.

33. Jim Emerson, "Inception: Has Christopher Nolan forgotten how to dream?," RogerEbert.com, 17 July 2010.

34. A. O. Scott, "This Time the Dream's on Me," *The New York Times*, 15 July 2010.

35. Ciara Wardlow, "The Synergy of *Inception* and *Paprika*," *Film School Rejects*, 2 March 2017.

36. Mike Fleming Jr, "Oscar: Chris Nolan Q&A About *Inception*," *Deadline*, 7 January 2011.

37. Adam Grant, "Christopher Nolan Wants You to Silence Your Phones," *Esquire*, 19 July 2017.

38. Some of the criticisms of *Inception* honed in on the fact, but declined to explore it. "Nolan is a literal-minded man," reflected critic David Denby. "Cobb's intercranial adventures aren't like dreams at all—they're like different kinds of action movies jammed together." However, he seemed to miss that this was precisely the point. (David Denby, "Dream Factory," *The New Yorker*, 26 July 2010.)

39. Lydia Marinelli, "Screening Wish Theories: Dream Psychologies and Early Cinema," *Science in Context*, March 2006, p. 87–110.

40. F.E. Sparshott, "Vision and Dream in the Cinema," *Philosophic Exchange*, Summer 1971.

41. Robert T. Eberwein, *Film and the Dream Screen: A Sleep and a Forgetting* (1984).

42. Uri Hasson, Yuval Nir, Ifat Levy, Galit Fuhrmann, Rafael Malach, "Intersubject synchronization of cortical activity during natural vision," *Science*, March 2004.

43. "Suddenly about a year ago while making *Hour of the Wolf*, I discovered that all of my pictures were dreams," reflected the legendary Swedish director. "Of course I understood that some of my films were dreams, that part of them were dreams.... But that all of my pictures were dreams was a new discovery to me." ("Introduction to Ingmar Bergman" (1967), a television documentary produced by Lewis Freedman, quoted in Marcha Kinder, "*From the Life of Marionetters* to *The Devil's Wanton*: Bergman's Creative Transformation of a Recurrent Nightmare," *Film Quarterly*, Spring 1981, p. 26.)

44. Stephen Prince, *The Warrior's Camera: The Cinema of Akira Kurosawa* (1999), p. 4.

45. "I always say, I hardly ever

have gotten ideas from dreams," contends Lynch of his inspirations. "I love dream logic. I love the feel." (Jake Folsom, "8 Bits of Wisdom from David Lynch's 53-Minute Interview," *IndieWire*, 3 December 2014.)

46. This is reflected in the tendency to begin stories *in media res*, a technique of which Nolan is particularly fond. Indeed, the audience begins *Inception* with little idea of where they are or what is going on, with Cobb washed up on a beach. However, the audience accepts these confusing images as cinematic convention.

47. Scott Foundas, "Christopher Nolan interview: Can *Inception* director save the summer?," *San Francisco Weekly*, 14 July 2010.

48. Jeffrey Ressner, "The Traditionalist," *Director's Guild of America Quarterly*, Spring 2012.

49. Geoff Boucher, "*Inception* Breaks into Dreams," *The Los Angeles Times*, 4 April, 2010.

50. See, for example, Martin Scorsese's ruminations upon the topic. (Juan Rodriguez Flores, "Theater movies will always be a communal experience for Martin Scorsese," *Latino Weekly Review*, 9 January 2017.)

51. Scott Foundas, "Christopher Nolan interview: Can *Inception* director save the summer?," *San Francisco Weekly*, 14 July 2010.

52. By positioning Cobb as the central figure in the narrative, it could be argued that Nolan most definitely subscribes to *auteur* theory.

53. Ariadne even literally builds scale models of her dream landscapes, like real-life production designers would do.

54. The film suggests as much during his transformation into Browning, with the character sitting in front of a set of mirrors that resemble an actor's dressing room.

55. Jeff Jensen, "*Inception*: Behind the scenes of a movie about movies—and the mind of its maker," *Entertainment Weekly*, 24 July 2010.

56. Geoff Boucher, "*Inception* Breaks into Dreams," *The Los Angeles Times*, 4 April, 2010.

57. It should also be noted that logo of Christopher Nolan and Emma Thomas' production company Syncopy also includes a maze design.

58. Christian Metz, *The Imaginary Signifier* (1982), p. 48–49.

59. Consider, for example, the way in which Nolan cites *Waterland* as an influence on his work for the way that it relies upon the reader to fill in the gaps in its narrative. (Jeff Goldsmith, "The Architect of Dreams," *Creative Screenwriting*, July/August 2010.) Similarly, Nolan has argued that many political readings of his work exist as projections of the audience's perspective. Pressed on the politics of *The Dark Knight Rises*, Nolan suggested such interpretations were inherently subjective. "We're going to get wildly different interpretations of what the film is supporting and not supporting, but it's not doing any of those things. It's just telling a story." ("Christopher Nolan: *Dark Knight Rises* Isn't Political," *Rolling Stone*, 20 July 2012.)

60. The five levels are: (a.) the real world on the plane; (b.) the car chase with the van; (c.) the hotel level with Arthur; (d.) the snowy mountains; (e.) the collapsing subconscious. Five levels of recursion. Robin Dunbar has argued that five levels of recursion is the most that an average audience can handle, citing examples like *Othello* and *The Judge and his Hangman*. (Robin Dunbar, "The Social Brain: Mind, Language, and Society in Cultural Perspective," *Annual Review of Anthropology* (2004), p. 164–81.

61. "The audience doesn't understand what it means but it gives something a visceral resonance," Nolan explained in an interview with *Film Comment*. (Amy Taubin, "Dream Work," *Film Comment*, July/August 2010.) Nolan has also conceded that he appreciated being "forced" to use slow motion by the plot of *Inception*. (The Treatment, "Christopher Nolan: *Inception*," KCRW, 14 July 2010.)

62. It is very similar to the way in which *Following* justifies its (cost-dictated) shaky handheld black-and-white aesthetic by constructing a *film noir* psychological thriller or the way in which *Memento* justifies its use of black-and-white as a means to distinguish between the two separate time flows.

63. Kristin Thompson and David Bordwell, "*Inception*; or, Dream a Little Dream within a Dream with Me," *Observations on Film Art*, 6 August 2010.

64. Scott Timberg, "Indie Angst," *The New Times Los Angeles*, 15 March 2001.

65. Jeff Goldsmith, "The Architect of Dreams," *Creative Screenwriting*, July/August 2010.

66. Robert Capps, "Q&A: Christopher Nolan on Dreams, Architecture, and Ambiguity," *Wired*, 29 November 2010.

67. Steve Weintraub, "Christopher Nolan and Emma Thomas Interview *Inception*- They Talk 3D, What Kind of Cameras They Used, Pre-Viz, WB, and a Lot More!," *Collider*, 25 March 2010.

68. Marc Bernardin, "Marvel, *Star Wars*, *Harry Potter* and more: Why the movie star no longer shines as bright as the franchise," *The Los Angeles Times*, 17 June 2016.

69. Brent Lang, "Why *The Revenant* Proves Leonardo DiCaprio May Be Hollywood's Biggest Star," *Variety*, 10 January 2016.

70. Journalist Katey Rich has jokingly referred to DiCaprio's efforts to fill out his "Great Living Director" Bingo Card. (Katey Rich, "Leonardo DiCaprio To Play A Martial Arts Expert In Potential Spy Franchise," *Cinema Blend*, 4 October 2011.)

71. Many famous people tell stories about how they were inspired by images and stories that they saw on screen. Mae Jemison was inspired to become an astronaut by seeing Nichelle Nichols on the original *Star Trek*. (Camille Jackson, "The Legacy of Lt. Uhura: Astronaut Mae Jemison on Race in Space," *Duke Today*, 28 October 2013.) Chris Carter decided to work in television and film after a screening of *Raiders of the Lost Ark*. (Andrew Dention, "*X-Files* Uncovered: An Interview with Chris Carter," *Rolling Stone Rock & Roll Yearbook*, 1995.)

72. Jeff Goldsmith, "The Architect of Dreams," *Creative Screenwriting*, July/August 2010.

73. This applies even outside of the primary plot. *Inception* reveals that Cobb has already performed inception on another individual, his deceased wife Mal. He discusses how she reacted to "a simple little idea that changed everything."

74. Of course, there are exceptions to this rule. However, there has also been a lot of time and energy devoted to the study of storytelling archetypes. Consider the ubiquity of the three-act structure or the influence of the Joseph Campbell monomyth. (See, for example, Christopher Vogler, *The Writer's Journey: Mythic Structure for Writers* (2007).)

75. It has been argued that the emergence of archetypal blockbuster storytelling in the late seventies and into the eighties overlapped with a nostalgic yearning in the American

psyche that yearned for a simpler and more straightforward time in the wake of Vietnam and Watergate and leading towards the election of Ronald Reagan. (See, for example, Keith Booker, "Star Wars," in *Alternate Americas: Science Fiction Film and American Culture* (2006), p. 109–125.)

76. The films of Lucas and Spielberg are perhaps the most obvious examples here; *Star Wars*, *Close Encounters of the Third Kind*, *E.T.: The Extra-Terrestrial*. (Michael S. Kimmel discusses this cultural moment in *Manhood in America: A Cultural History* (2006), p. 211–212.)

77. Pat Jankiewicz, "Dark Knight Resurrected," *Starlog #337*, August 2005.

78. To be fair, it might be slightly more accurate to contend that Maurice Fischer is an archetypal Spielbergian father figure. Even *60 Minutes* host Lesley Stahl has acknowledged that "the workaholic, absent father" is a fixture of Spielbergian cinema in films from *E.T.* to *Indiana Jones and the Last Crusade* to *Hook* to *War of the Worlds*. This element even informs subplots in otherwise unrelated movies, like *The Adventures of Tintin* or *Lincoln*. (Prachi Gupta, "Five things you probably didn't know about Steven Spielberg," *Salon*, 22 October 2012.)

79. *Inception* makes it clear that Robert has sought out other surrogate relationships in an effort to compensate for that paternal absence, most notably with his godfather (and his father's legal counsel) "Uncle Peter" Browning.

80. This literalisation of emotional absence is a recurring motif in Spielberg films. *Indiana Jones and the Last Crusade* kicks into high gear when Henry Jones goes missing. *Hook* involves a workaholic father disappearing into a fantasy world. At the climax of *Close Encounters of the Third Kind*, Roy Neary leaves his family behind to journey to the stars.

81. Indeed, Spielberg's recurring emphasis on the inevitable reconciliation between father and son is an interesting and telling choice in his approach to Campbellian monomyth. Spielberg tends to favor atonement with father over the more overtly sexual and feminine "hero's sexual union with the goddess-mother of the world." Spielberg is even more keenly focused on father-son relationships than Campbell. (Harold Schechter and Jonna Cormely Semeiks, "Campbell and the 'Vanilla-Frosted Temple': From Myth to Multiplex" in *Uses of Comparative Mythology: Essays on the Work of Joseph Campbell* (2015), p. 188.)

82. The film's grey hyper-capitalist future recalls the aesthetic of Spielberg's twenty-first century Kubrick-influenced films like *A.I.* and *Minority Report*. The chase through Mombasa evokes the chase through Cairo in *Raiders of the Lost Ark*.

83. With this in mind, it is telling that *The Dark Knight Rises* builds to the image of Alfred finding his surrogate son living happily ever after, putting the audience in the subjective position of a father who wants what is best for his child. *Interstellar* opts to tell the story from both sides, with one plot thread focusing on Coop and one thread built around Murph. In *Dunkirk*, the most developed character is arguably Mister Dawson, who takes part in the rescue mission as a way of metaphorically reconnecting with a son who died in the earlier days of the conflict.

84. Psychologists have noticed that people tend to narrativise their own lives, by trying to impose their own reason and logic upon events outside of their control to provide a deeper meaning or purpose to their struggles. (Julie Beck, "Life's Stories," *The Atlantic*, 10 August 2015.)

85. Indeed, one of the more popular interpretations in the film is that Cobb's team effectively performs an inception on Cobb himself, that he is as much a subject for this mission as Fischer himself, and that Ariadne is introduced to him with the express purpose of helping him get past his issues and come home. (Bilge Ebiri, "The Hidden 'Inception' Within *Inception*," *Vulture*, 18 July 2010.)

86. For a more thorough exploration of Aristotle's use of the term and the concept, see Gregory Michael Sifakis, *Aristotle on the Function of Tragic Poetry* (2001).

87. Ari Hiltunen, *Aristotle in Hollywood: The Anatomy of Successful Storytelling* (2002).

88. Catherine Shoard, "When it comes to films we love a true story. Just not too much reality," *The Guardian*, 19 November 2015.

89. Steven James Snyder, "The Great Inception Debate: Alive? Dead? Both?," *Time*, 19 July 2010.

90. Josh Spiegel, "Why Fan Theories Are Destroying Film Discourse," *Movie Mezzanine*, 5 September 2015.

91. Padraig Cotter, "How fan theories changed the way we watch movies and TV," *Little White Lies*, 5 February 2017.

92. This trend could be reflected in any number of ways, from the emphasis on review aggregators like *Rotten Tomatoes* or *Metacritic* to provide an absolute and objective measure of film's relative value through to the fixation on "objective" reviews by fan-centric movements like *Gamergate* or the accusation of "bias" thrown against film critics who harbour opinions different than the accuser.

93. *Memento* generated all manner of speculation and theorizing. (Andy Klein, "Everything you wanted to know about *Memento*," *Salon*, 28 June 2001.) Similarly, fans watching *The Dark Knight* would theories about whether minor characters were secretly cameos from more high-profile figures in the *Batman* mythos; was "Mister Reese" a phonetic hint that the character was *really* "Mister E. Nygma," the Riddler? (Mitch Uppman, "Coleman Reese From *The Dark Knight* Was The Riddler?! Check Out These 6 Convincing Batman Fan Theories!," *Movie Pilot*, 3 February 2016.) Fans even speculated on whether Alfred's glimpse of Bruce Wayne at the end of *The Dark Knight Rises* was "real" in the context of the narrative. (Katey Rich, "What Really Happened At The End Of *The Dark Knight Rises*?," *Cinema Blend*, 22 July 2012.)

94. Abrams recalls a literal "mystery box" that he purchased at a New York magic shop as a child, with no idea what it contained. He has still declined to open it, even decades later. Abrams explains, "It represents infinite possibility. It represents hope. It represents potential." (Moira Macdonald, "Two good docs, and J.J. Abrams' 'mystery box,'" *The Seattle Times*, 1 June 2011.)

95. Perhaps the best example of this is in the second season cliffhanger in *Sherlock*. In "The Reichenbach Fall," the title character seems to fall to his death. However, the third season premiere, "The Empty Hearse," devotes a lot of time and energy to exploring certain fan theories about how the character might have survived such a fall. (Brendon Connelly, "Sherlock Lives—Reality And Fan Fiction In 'The Empty Hearse,'" *Bleeding Cool*, 1 January 2014.) Moffat affectionately acknowledged some of the overly elaborate fan theories as "a measure of nonsense." (Roth Cornet, "*Sherlock*: Steven Moffat on the Fake Death, if

the Series Has Gone Meta, Character Vs. Mystery-Driven Stories," *Doctor Who* Crossover," IGN, 26 January 2014.) However, Moffat's tendency to play with fan theories and speculation can frequently be seen in his season-long arcs on *Doctor Who*, in which the show repeatedly reveals that its central characters are people rather than mysteries.

96. Edward Davis, "Christopher Nolan Says Stop Trying To Figure Out The Purposely Ambiguous Ending Of *Inception*," *IndieWire*, 1 December 2010.

97. Ben Child, "Christopher Nolan explains *Inception*'s ending: 'I want you to chase your reality,'" *The Guardian*, 5 June 2015.

98. Mike Symonds, "Film Crit Hulk SMASH: Christopher Nolan & The Cruelty Of Time," *Birth. Movies. Death*, 26 July 2017.

99. This idea is reflected in the opening scenes with the squashed bird, where a canary is killed during a magic trick, and a replacement offered up at the end of the trick. However, the audience does not care about the canary that was killed, because they choose to believe that it was the same canary that appeared at the end of the illusion. Robert Angier's "The *Real* Transported Man" does something similar.

100. In particular, *Dunkirk* engages with the idea of this distorted narrative of events as a national myth, standing in contrast to the *Dark Knight* trilogy's exploration of broader political mythology, *The Prestige* as a meditation upon religion, and *Inception* as an exploration of cinematic narrative.

101. This is not a radical notion by any measure, this is part of the human experience. It has been frequently discussed and debated; see, for example, Jonathan Gottschall, *The Storytelling Animal: How Stories Make Us Human* (2012).

102. Indeed, it is telling that *The Dark Knight* never quite manages to come up with a convincing response to the Joker's criticisms of organized society, in particular its indifference to violence so long as that violence can be contextualized as "all part of the plan." The film instead suggests that the cohesion of society itself, and the protection that cohesion affords, is of enough intrinsic value that it can withstand the Joker's assaults upon it.

103. "We should charge Fischer a lot more than Saito for this job," Eames wryly observes of their mission. Indeed, the final shot of Eames and Fischer at the top level of the dream, on the shore of the river, suggests that even Eames is genuinely affected by Fischer's emotional reconciliation with his father.

104. There were a host of articles on the subject from all across the world: Andrew Pulver, "Is Christopher Nolan the new Stanley Kubrick?," *The Guardian*, 15 July 2010; Olivier Delcroix, "Christopher Nolan, le nouveau Kubrick?," *Le Figaro*, 5 August 2010; Bilge Ebiri, "Which Kubrick-Compared Director Is the Most Kubrickian?," *Vulture*, 7 December 2010.

105. Matthew Belinkie, "Does Christopher Nolan Have a Woman Problem?," *Overthinking It*, 29 July 2010.

106. There are some exceptions, of course. Although *Insomnia* focuses on an investigation into the murder of a young woman, Will Dormer's decision to frame Wayne Dobbs was motivated by the murder of a young boy. Although Bruce loses both parents in the mugging in *Batman Begins*, he seems more motivated by the loss of his father than by the death of his mother.

107. Mathilda Gregory, "Want to give your male lead some depth? Give him a dead wife," *The Guardian*, 24 July 2010.

108. Janelle Asselin, "Gail Simone: The Comics Alliance Interview, Part One—Batgirl, Birds Of Prey, And Women In Refrigerators," *Comics Alliance*, 1 December 2014. The title of the trope originates from a plot beat in *Green Lantern (1990)* #54 (August 1994) when a villain killed the hero's love interest and left her in a refrigerator as a taunt to the eponymous superhero. That same villain would later try to top himself by putting the same hero's mother in an oven. (*Green Lantern (1990)* #180, October 2004.)

109. Katie Rife, "This 'Women In Refrigerators' supercut is downright chilling," *The A.V. Club*, 14 August 2014.

110. After all, *Memento* reveals that Leonard's account of his wife's death is a fabrication designed to prevent him from processing his own responsibility and guilt. This theme might have been better developed with a line that was cut from the finished version of the film, wherein Teddy challenges Leonard that he is more in love with the idea of his deceased wife than he ever was with woman herself. "You loved your wife, but how much more did you love your dead wife? How much easier is it to love your dead wife?" (James Mottram, *The Making of Memento* (2002).)

111. Even in *The Prestige*, the rivalry between Angier and Borden begins with the death of Julia McCullough. Angier blames Borden for his wife's death. However, over the course of the film, the rivalry develops into something else entirely. Angier becomes obsessed with Borden's performance of "The Transported Man."

112. It is debatable whether this approach is objectively "better" or "worse" than the more conventional motivation afforded by "women in refrigerators." It acknowledges that such female characters are often broad ideals rather than fully formed characters, and embraces the subtext of the trope head-on while making a point to criticize the masculine characters who adhere to such conventions. At the same time, it does mean that many of Nolan's early films lack strong and well-developed female characters with their own agency and personality outside of the obsessions of male protagonists. Perhaps the most developed female characters in Nolan's first six films are Natalie from *Memento* and Ellie Burr from *Insomnia*, which is a disappointing tally.

113. Nolan himself discusses the character in archetypal terms. "The character and her relationship to Cobb's psyche is the literal manifestation of what the femme fatale always meant in film noir—the neurosis of the protagonist, his fear of how little he knows about the woman he's fallen in love with, that kind of thing," he explains of Mal. Mal was never intended as a character in her own right, but instead as a literal extension of Cobb's psyche. (Robert Capps, "Q&A: Christopher Nolan on Dreams, Architecture, and Ambiguity," *Wired*, 29 November 2010.)

114. While there is a relative dearth of strong and well-developed female characters in Nolan's early filmography, they become much more prominent in his later films. There are arguably more well-developed female characters in the two films following *Inception* than there had been in the six films preceding it; Selina Kyle and Talia Al Ghul in *The Dark Knight Rises*, Brand and Murph in *Interstellar*.

115. Mal was obviously a woman, but the bulk of her appearances in

*Inception* are as the manifestation of a male character's subsconcious.

116. This is particularly interesting in the context of *Inception* as a metaphor for filmmaking and the decision to position Cobb as the "director" in the metaphor. It evokes what would become the discussion around various sexual harassment scandals in the second decade of the twenty-first century, particularly in the entertainment industry. These exposes suggested that male actors and producers would often work with (and enable) abusers, who they protected through silence. (Susanna Schrobsdorff, "When Men See Other Men Behaving Badly," *Time*, 19 October 2017.)

117. Indeed, it is Ariadne who points out the moral ambiguity of what the team is attempting to do to Robert Fischer, while all her male colleagues seem entirely comfortable with poisoning his healthy relationship with Peter Browning in pursuit of their agenda.

118. Talia is arguably a more nuanced and developed version of Mal, right down to the decision to cast Marion Cotillard in the role. Selina Kyle is a more nuanced and developed version of Ariadne, serving as a voice of reason to an obsessive protagonist. The female characters in *The Dark Knight Rises* are arguably still archetypes, but they are more developed archetypes than those featured in *Inception*, suggesting an iterative process.

119. Maria, "Inception, or, Leo angsts about family and chicks," *The Hathor Legacy*, 10 August 2010.

120. Of course, this being a Christopher Nolan movie, Mal is cast as a strangely chaste "Whore." Mal oozes a certain classic *film noir* sexuality, in terms of her costuming and the manner in which Cotillard plays the seductive and emotionally volatile projection. However, it should be noted that the relationship between Cobb and Mal seems curiously asexual; even leaving aside Mal's plot to frame her husband for her death, it seems strangely believable that the couple should spend their anniversary in two separate hotel rooms.

121. Even before the audience is introduced to Ariadne, the script makes it clear that she will be making her own choices over the course of the film. When Cobb asks his father-in-law to introduce him to a promising new student, he explains, "You know what I'm offering. You have to let them decide for themselves." Over the course of the film, Ariadne operates with more autonomy than her male colleagues like Arthur or Eames.

## Chapter 8

1. Jeff Eames, "Warner Bros. Dreaming of a Sequel to Christopher Nolan's *Inception*?," *Collider*, 22 October 2010.
2. When the topic was broached, Nolan reflected, "I've always liked the potential of the world. It's an infinite, or perhaps I should say an infinitesimal world that fascinates me." (Mike Fleming, Jr., "Oscar: Chris Nolan Q&A About *Inception*," *Deadline*, 7 January 2011.)
3. Chris Agar, "Joseph Gordon-Levitt Shoots Down The Idea of *Inception 2*," *Screen Rant*, 29 June 2017.
4. Gordon's conversation about "escalation" at the end of *Batman Begins* is very much a broad outline of one of the key thematic arcs in *The Dark Knight*, tied to the character of the Joker who was seeded in the playing card reveal.
5. What prior knowledge is necessary is articulated early and explicitly, for example the ascent of Sal Maroni to the top of the city's organized crime following the incarceration of Carmine Falcone in *Batman Begins*. The character of Rachel Dawes was recast from Katie Holmes to Maggie Gyllenhaal between *Batman Begins* and *The Dark Knight*, while Jonathan Crane shows no obvious scarring or side effects from getting tasered in the face at the end of *Batman Begins* when he reappears in *The Dark Knight*.
6. While a lot of this material is covered by exposition, a lot of knowledge is assumed. The opening scene of *The Dark Knight Rises* finds Jim Gordon providing a eulogy for Harvey Dent before skipping forward eight years in time, which would seem to rely on the audience's familiarity with the character from *The Dark Knight*.
7. The Pit in *The Dark Knight Rises* only really makes sense in thematic symmetry with the well from *Batman Begins*. The climax of *The Dark Knight Rises* overtly and explicitly mirrors the climax of *Batman Begins*, right down to Batman leading a full-frontal assault on the League of Shadows as a distraction for a more tactical strike by Jim Gordon to undermine their plan.
8. Brian Cronin, "Movie Legends Revealed: Did Ledger's Death Alter Plans For Joker in *Dark Knight Rises*?," *Comic Book Resources*, 30 September 2015.
9. David Crow, "Heath Ledger wanted to do another Batman movie as The Joker," *Den of Geek*, 5 May 2017.
10. Mark Hughes, "Did Christopher Nolan Originally Intend for the Joker to Appear in *The Dark Knight Rises*?," *The Huffington Post*, 19 July 2012.
11. Dave Trumbore, "*The Dark Knight Rises*: Could Leonardo DiCaprio Have Starred as the Riddler?," *Collider*, 1 June 2012.
12. Favourites for the iconic villain that was frequently cited (but never materialized) included Eddie Murphy and Johnny Depp. (Ben Child, "Eddie Murphy might just actually be *Batman 3*'s Riddler," *The Guardian*, 19 December 2008; Anita Singh, "Batman sequel to *The Dark Knight*: Johnny Depp to play The Riddler?," *The Telegraph*, 31 July 2008.)
13. Geoff Boucher, "Christopher Nolan on *Dark Knight* and its box-office billion: 'It's mystifying to me'," *The Los Angeles Times*, 27 October 2008.
14. Marc Bernardin, "Christopher Nolan on 'Extreme Places' in the Making of *The Dark Knight Rises*," *The Hollywood Reporter*, 27 December 2012.
15. Stax, "IGN Interviews Christopher Nolan," *IGN*, 6 December 2007.
16. Jody Duncan Jesser and Janine Pourroy, *The Art and Making of The Dark Knight Trilogy* (2012).
17. Interviewed a few weeks before the release of the film, Murphy was deliberately coy about his potential involvement in the film. "Let's not be impatient," Murphy advocated. "People are so impatient. Some things [spoilers are] great for, but other things ... isn't it so great to go and see a film that you haven't seen a script for, that you haven't seen on set videos, that you haven't read spoilers for, that you just go in and you just are in it? That's what it should be." (Terri Schwartz, "Cillian Murphy on Christopher Nolan: 'He's set the bar for all sorts of superhero franchises'," *IFC*, 20 June 2012.)
18. Neeson recalls the particulars of his small appearance, "I was on set for two hours, I think. And then Chris said, 'Don't tell anybody you were here.'" (Ryan Lamble, "Liam Neeson interview: *Taken 2*, *The Dark Knight Rises*, comedy and biscuits," *Den of Geek*, 1 October 2012.)

19. "I never intended to come back," Eckhart argued in interviews around the time, although he did joke about sucker-punching the director when he was not invited to work on the film. (Brian Warmoth, "Anne Hathaway Will Be 'Wonderful' In *Dark Knight Rises*, Says Aaron Eckhart," MTV, 26 February 2011.)

20. B. Alan Orange, "Eclusive: Will Chris Nolan Recast the Joker for *Batman 3* or Will the Riddler Take His Place?," *MovieWeb*, 29 June 2008.

21. Russ Fischer, "No Surprise: Christopher Nolan Emphatically Says The Joker Won't Return in *Batman 3*," /Film, 4 June 2010.

22. Christopher Rosen, "*Dark Knight Rises*: The Joker Won't Appear In Batman Finale," *The Huffington Post*, 5 June 2012.

23. The novelization does somewhat hedge its bets, by following that observation with the concession, "Nobody was really sure." (Greg Cox, *The Dark Knight Rises: The Official Movie Novelization* [2012].)

24. Because the Joker is not even mentioned and because Harvey Dent only appears in quick flashbacks and photographs, *The Dark Knight Rises* somewhat glosses over the villains of the second film in the series.

25. Mark Bernardin, "Christopher Nolan on 'Extreme Places' in the Making of *The Dark Knight Rises*," *The Hollywood Reporter*, 27 December 2012.

26. One of the more common criticisms of *The Dark Knight* is that the Joker is much more dynamic and engaging character than Bruce Wayne in the context of the story. While *The Dark Knight* certainly develops the character of Bruce Wayne, the Joker serves as the magnetic core of the story. Even Christian Bale acknowledges that Heath Ledger overshadowed him. "Heath turned up, and just kind of completely ruined all my plans," Bale recalls. "Because I went, 'He's so much more interesting than me and what I'm doing.'" (Kevin Polowy, "Christian Bale Disappointed in His *Batman* Performances," Yahoo, 2 March 2016.)

27. Interestingly, at the same time that Christopher Nolan was reinventing the character of Talia Al Ghul in *The Dark Knight Rises*, comic book writer Grant Morrison was reworking the character in his *Batman Incorporated* runs. Morrison mirrored the relationship between Bruce and Talia on his own parents' divorce. (Brian Truitt, "Grant Morrison recalls life and death of Damian Wayne," *USA Today*, 31 March 2013.)

28. There is an added irony in the fact that Bruce Wayne effectively killed Ra's Al Ghul at the climax of *Batman Begins*, setting in motion a bitter cycle of violence and creating his own warped counterpart.

29. *The Dark Knight Rises* reinforces this contrast when both Bruce and Talia are lying in bed together. As Bruce studies her back, he notices scars that recall his own wounds early in *The Dark Knight*.

30. Todd Matthy, "An Interview with Bane Creator Chuck Dixon," *Todd Matthy*, 15 August 2012.

31. G. Kendall, "When *Batman: The Animated Series* Refused to 'Break' the Dark Knight," *Comic Book Resources*, 9 April 2017.

32. "They had him as almost an imbecile, when in the comics he is extremely smart," complains Dixon of the treatment that Bane received in *Batman & Robin*. (Jerome Madia, "*Batman* comics writer Chuck Dixon happy with portrayal of Bane in *The Dark Knight Rises*," *The Philadelphia Inquirer*, 20 July 2012.)

33. It should be noted that one of the first things that the *Batman* writing staff did on introducing Bane was to have the character cripple Killer Croc, establishing something of an informal sorting algorithm of physically imposing *Batman* villains. (*Batman (1940) #489*, February 1993.)

34. *Blind Justice* serves as something of an interesting nexus point in the *Batman* cinematic canon. It was written by Sam Hamm, who provided the screenplay to Tim Burton's *Batman*. However, it also introduced the character of Henri Ducard, one of Bruce's teachers and the identity assumed by Ra's Al Ghul in the first act of *Batman Begins*. It could also be argued that *Blind Justice* established a template for event storytelling that would inform later stories like *Knightfall*. (Chris Sims, "Blind Justice: How The Writer Of *Batman '89* Provided The Template Of The Modern *Batman* Event," *Comics Alliance*, 1 July 2014.)

35. Chris Sims, "Ask Chris #42: Breaking Down Bane," *Comics Alliance*, 21 January 2011.

36. The film even parallels Batman and Bane in terms of action; Bane's introductory scene features the villain staging a daring mid-air abduction involving an elaborate rescue from a large transport plane, a sequence that evokes Batman's abduction of Lau from Hong Kong in *The Dark Knight*.

37. "I wanted it to be like an animal," explains costume designer Lindy Hemming of the design. "I wanted it to have an animalistic feeling, and I looked at things like Silverback Gorillas and snarling teeth and fangs coming up and fangs coming down." (Steve Weintraub, "Costume Designer Lindy Hemming Talks Catwoman, Redesigning Bane for Nolan's Universe, and More on the Set of *The Dark Knight Rises*," *Collider*, 10 July 2012.)

38. Brent Holmes, "Why They Wear the Mask: The Mouthpieces of Nolan's *Batman* Trilogy," *Kino: The Western Undergraduate Journal of Film Studies*, Volume 4: Issue 1 2013.

39. It has been argued that Bane might be seen as something close to a cyborg, a human being enhanced through technological innovation. (Matt Evans, "Cyborgs, Companion Species, Species, and the General Will: The Deeply Constitutive Relationship Between Bats and Batman" in *Superheroes and Critical Animal Studies: The Heroic Beasts of Total Liberation* (2017), p. 135–150.) If this is the case, Bane's technological augmentation might be contrasted with Bruce's earlier use of a metal endo skeleton to enhance his strength and reflexes; Bane is what Bruce runs the risk of becoming if he pursues this obsession.

40. Thematically, *The Dark Knight Rises* suggests a connection between the prison and the concept of "the Lazarus Pit," a piece of comic book mythology tied to Ra's Al Ghul. In the comics, a body is thrown into the Lazarus Pit only to be resurrected. In *The Dark Knight Rises*, Bruce's resurrection is more metaphorical than literal, but the symbolism carries over. (Siddhant Adlakha, "*The Dark Knight Rises*: Hope & Despair," *Birth. Movies. Death*, 30 November 2015.)

41. Indeed, the opening scene has one of Bane's soldiers describe him as "the masked man" to the CIA operative, another description that could easily be used to describe Batman.

42. Interestingly and coincidentally, "Bane" serves as a phonetic amalgam of bother "Batman" and "Wayne," suggesting that Bane is an incomplete version of the protagonist.

43. This revelation and the manipulation of narrative serves to establish Bane as a Nolanian antagonist

like Ra's Al Ghul or the Joker. Nolan's villains cultivate lies and deceptions, and are often defeated by exposing the lies within their own personal mythologies; Batman defeats Ra's Al Ghul in *Batman Begins* by offering a constructive and optimistic mythology in contrast to his grim fatalism, Batman defeats the Joker in *The Dark Knight* when he comes to understand that the Joker is ultimately seeking validation of his own world view, Batman defeats Bane in *The Dark Knight Rises* when he breaks the villain's mask and forces him to admit that he never escaped the prison.

44. The scripts reinforces this thematic connection by having Bruce repeatedly describe Batman as his "powerful friend," which is consciously mirrored by Talia's description of Bane as her "friend" and "protector" towards the end of the film.

45. Brendan Bettinger, "Christopher Nolan Speaks! Updates on *Dark Knight* Sequel and *Superman Man of Steel*," *Collider*, 10 March 2010.

46. Kirsten Acuna, "Jonathan Nolan Finally Explains Robin's Role In *The Dark Knight Rises*," *Business Insider*, 16 October 2012.

47. Kevin P. Sullivan, "*Dark Knight Rises*: Batman Must Die," *MTV*, 25 June 2012.

48. A quote often attributed to comic book legend Stan Lee suggests that comic book readers only want "the illusion of change" in their beloved characters. As such, most changes to the *status quo* tend to revert back to basics over time. (Peter David, "The Illusion of Change," *Comics Buyer's Guide #1285*, 3 July 1998.) For example, while Nolan was filming his *Dark Knight* trilogy, Grant Morrison was writing a sprawling epic involving the character that dramatically changed its *status quo*. However, that massive saga concluded with everything returning to how it had been before, with Morrison's work on *Batman Incorporated (2012)* feeling like a knowing wry commentary on the gravity exerted by comic book *status quo*. (Oliver Sava, "*Batman Incorporated #13* concludes Grant Morrison's 7-year epic in mythical fashion," *The A.V. Club*, 2 August 2013.)

49. Of course, continuity is a flexible thing; writers and editors would retroactively incorporate comics dating back to the forties in shared Marvel continuity. (Such as *Captain America Comics #1*, March 1941.) However, the most commonly-accepted starting point, and the point at which modern comics continuity really began, was with the publication of *Fantastic Four (1961) #1* in November, 1961.

50. This phenomenon is known as "Marvel Time," which has the effect of keeping its characters largely frozen in time. This means that origins will always take place in the recent past, rather than in their original context. Early comics depicted Tony Stark as an arms dealer during the Vietnam War. (*Tales of Suspense #39*, March 1963.) More recent comics have updated his origin to Afghanistan prior to the Gulf War. (*Iron Man (2005) #1*, January 2005.) Similarly, Frank Castle originally served in the Vietnam War. (*Marvel Preview #2*, August 1975.) However, his updated origin makes him a veteran of the Gulf War. (*Punisher (2011) #4*, October 2011.)

51. Miller handled the first of these sequels, *The Dark Knight Strikes Again*, largely on his own. However, he worked in collaboration with writer Brian Azzarello and artists Andy Kubert and Klaus Janson on *Dark Knight III: The Master Race*.

52. The character appeared in a supporting role in Mark Millar and Bryan's Hitch's run on *Fantastic Four* as "the Hooded Man." The character would be subsequently hinted to be the protagonist of *Old Man Logan*. (*Fantastic Four (1998) #561*, January 2009.)

53. Dave Richards, "Lemire's *Old Man Logan* Explores Marvel's 'Most Scarred Character'," *Comic Book Resources*, 6 November 2015.

54. There are any number of other examples, such the apocalyptic "Maestro" version of the Hulk introduced by Peter David in *The Incredible Hulk: Future Imperfect #1* (December 1992). The character would subsequently becoming a recurring antagonist for the entire Marvel Universe. (*Captain Marvel (2000) #27-30*, March≠May 2002.)

55. Time is a preoccupation within the plots of *Memento*, *Inception*, *Interstellar* and *Dunkirk*. However, time is also a recurring fascination suggested by Nolan's use of crosscutting and editing across threads and locations where time is moving at a different rate. Crosscutting and editing are the ultimate manipulation of time within a cinematic narrative, and these are techniques that clearly interest Nolan as a storyteller.

56. To be fair, certain strains of fandom have spent a long time speculating on various theories about why James Bond looks (and acts) differently from one iteration to the next. (Huw Fullerton, "This one fan theory could change everything you know about James Bond," *The Radio Times*, 29 February 2016.) However, the franchise has only ever winkingly acknowledged the transition, with George Lazenby wryly reflecting in the cold open to *On Her Majesty's Secret Service* that "this never happened to the other fellow."

57. For example, Francis Ford Coppola used *The Godfather, Part III* to bring some closure to the story of Michael Carleone as played by Al Pacino. In contrast, Michael Keaton and Tim Burton did not get an opportunity to bring closure to their interpretation of Batman before making room for Val Kilmer and Joel Schumacher.

58. For example, the death of Bond's wife at the climax of *On Her Majesty's Secret Service* was somewhat glossed over in the teaser to *Diamonds are Forever*. Barring an occasional reference like that made in the teaser to *For Your Eyes Only*, Bond's marriage would be very rarely acknowledged over the course of the series.

59. Chris Ryan, "*Spectre* and the Age of Blockbuster Continuity," *Grantland*, 30 March 2015.

60. Jim McLauchlin, "Kevin Feige on Building the Hit Marvel Movie Machine," *Newsarama*, 11 July 2008.

61. Indeed, this involved a steep learning curve for many filmmakers working with the studio. "It's never been done before and that's kind of the spirit everybody's taking it in," producer Kevin Feige explained of the creative process. "The other filmmakers aren't used to getting actors from other movies that other filmmakers have cast, certain plot lines that are connected or certain locations that are connected but I think for the most part, in fact, entirely everyone was on board for it and thinks that it's fun." (Jami Philbrick, "Exclusive: Kevin Feige Talks Iron Man 2, The Avengers and More," *MovieWeb*, 26 April 2010.)

62. The feature film *Ant-Man* introduces the concept of "legacy characters" to the Marvel Cinematic Universe, characters who use the same codename as an older existing character; examples include Jay Garrick, Barry Allen and Wally West all using "The Flash" or Alan Scott, Hal Jordan and Kyle Rayner using "Green

Lantern." (Chris Sims, "Roasting Old Chestnuts: Our Favorite Comic Book Cliches," *Comics Alliance*, 3 November 2009.)

63. The Marvel Cinematic Universe gradually develops an elaborate alternative history to the real world, with an alternate Second World War in *Captain America: The First Avenger* and a radically different take on Operation: Paper Clip in *Captain America: The Winter Soldier*. This is to say nothing of suggestions about ancient history in *Thor*. This increasingly elaborate continuity that extends beyond an alternate present is a hallmark of comic book continuity.

64. Marvel Studios' plan to launch a series of standalone feature films including *Iron Man*, *The Incredible Hulk*, *Iron Man 2*, *Thor* and *Captain America: The First Avenger* all leading into *The Avengers* clearly evoked the familiar comic book storytelling device of the crossover, when popular characters from several individual titles would come together as part of a single epic narrative. (Mark Beall, "Mark Beall's Geek Beat: Crossover Action Desired," *Moviefone*, 2 May 2006.)

65. *The Avengers* would be tied with *Avatar* and *Harry Potter and the Deathly Hallows, Part 2* as the fastest-grossing movie to one billion dollars. (Christopher Rosen, "*The Avengers*: $1 Billion In Global Box Office After Record Second Weekend," *The Huffington Post*, 13 May 2012.)

66. Borys Kit, "Forget Franchises: Why 2014 Will Be Hollywood's Year of the 'Shared Universe,'" *The Hollywood Reporter*, 6 January 2014.

67. Seb Patrick, "How Fox is building an *X-Men* movie universe," *Den of Geek*, 12 February 2014

68. Seb Patrick, "Will Sony's plans for a *Spider-Man* movie universe work out?," *Den of Geek*, 29 January 2014.

69. Joseph Medina, "Monsters Shared Universe: Writer Jon Spaihts Confirms Present Day *Van Helsing*," *LRM*, 15 July 2009

70. Andrew Dyce, "Why The *Justice League* Can Successfully Launch DC's Movie Universe," *ScreenRant*, 27 October 2012.

71. Ali Plumb, "*Avengers: Age Of Ultron* Spoiler Podcast," *Empire*, 4 May 2015.

72. Joanna Robinson, "Is the Marvel Cinematic Universe Actually the Most Popular TV Show of the Decade?," *Vanity Fair*, 5 December 2017; Todd VanDerWerff, "How Marvel films like *Captain America: Civil War* became the world's biggest TV show," *Vox*, 12 May 2016.

73. Emma Dibdin, "Does Marvel Studios have a director problem?," *Digital Spy*, 23 August 2015.

74. "Suddenly becoming a director for hire on it," muses Wright of the dynamic, "you're sort of less emotionally invested and you start to wonder why you're there, really." (Blair Marnell, "Edgar Wright Reveals Why He Left *Ant-Man*," *The Nerdist*, 24 June 2017.)

75. "You have to make sure that the movie you want to make is fully the right movie for that studio too. It was heartbreaking, but I also knew that it was good," reflects Jenkins of her departure. "I knew that it was good because I didn't think I could make a great film out of their script." (Kate Erbland, "*Wonder Woman* Makes History: How Patty Jenkins Lost the Chance to Direct One Big Superhero Movie and Landed a Better One," *IndieWire*, 1 June 2017.)

76. "I think I'll just say we had different ideas about what the story would be," DuVernay relates. "In the end, it comes down to story and perspective. And we just didn't see eye to eye. Better for me to realize that now than cite creative differences later." (Yolanda Sangweni, "Exclusive: Ava DuVernay Won't Be Directing *Black Panther* Movie," *Essence*, 3 July 2015.)

77. Terri Schwartz, "Justice League Cast on Zack Snyder vs. Joss Whedon's Influence on the Movie," *IGN*, 4 November 2017.

78. Joanna Robinson, "*Justice League* Was Apparently Micromanaged Even More Than We Thought," *Variety*, 24 November 2017.

79. For example, a lot of the "creative direction" of Warner Brothers' *Justice League* was overseen by comic book writer Geoff Johns, whose primary cinematic experience involved working as an assistant to Richard Donner and working on the much-maligned box office bomb *Green Lantern*. (Brent Lang, "DC Shake-Up in the Works After *Justice League* Stumbles (Exclusive)," *Variety*, 7 December 2017.)

80. Adam Rogers, "You Won't Live to See the Final Star Wars Movie," *Wired*, 17 November 2015.

81. Mark Hughes, "Marvel Isn't Rebooting MCU, And Stories Suggesting Otherwise Are False," *Forbes*, 19 October 2017.

82. When stories in these blockbusters did end, they tended to end for particular versions of these iconic characters. *X-Men: Days of Future Past* offered a sense of closure for the cast of the original *X-Men*, *X-Men II* and *X-Men III*, while representing a continuation of the adventures of the cast of *X-Men: First Class*. Indeed, even that ending suggested in *Days of Future Past* was subsequently overwritten by *Logan*, which serves as an exception to this rule in that it does seem to offer a definitive ending to the character of Wolverine as played by Hugh Jackman.

83. For example, many critics and audience members interpreted the end of *Iron Man 3*, wherein Tony Stark heals his heart and destroys all his armour, as a logical endpoint of the character's larger arc. (Emily Asher-Perrin, "Your Pal, The Mechanic: How *Iron Man 3* Stripped Tony Stark of His Armor For Good," *Tor*, 6 May 2013.) However, Tony is still largely the same character in subsequent appearances like *The Avengers: Age of Ultron* and *Captain America: Civil War*. Indeed, the co-writer of *Iron Man 3* even did interviews after the release of the film to assure fans that Tony Stark would still be Iron Man in the films that followed. (Josh Wigler, "*Iron Man 3* Ending Helps *Avengers: Age Of Ultron*, Writer Says," *MTV*, 3 September 2013.)

84. One of the most common fandom-driven complaints about Nolan's *Dark Knight* trilogy is that it depicts a version of Bruce Wayne who was only Batman for a few months between the events of *Batman Begins* and *The Dark Knight Rises*. (Bill Ramey, "The *Dark Knight* Trilogy: So What If Bruce Was Only Batman A Year!," *Batman on Film*, 19 May 2013.) Of course, studies suggest that this is a quite a reasonable approach to take to the character, given the demands that being Batman would take on a supposedly mortal individual. (Janey Tracey, "Science Says Bruce Wayne's Body Could Only Handle 2–3 Years of Being Batman," *Outer Places*, 8 August 2014.)

85. Geoff Boucher, "Christopher Nolan says his Batman doesn't play well with others," *The Los Angeles Times*, 29 October 2008.

86. Kevin Jagernauth, "Sorry, Joseph Gordon-Levitt Won't Be Batman In *Justice League*," *IndieWire*, 28 November 2012.

87. Justin Kroll, "Ben Affleck Is the New Batman," *Variety*, 22 August 2013.

88. Alasdair Wilkins, "Christopher Nolan explains how *Watchmen* paved

the way for *Man of Steel*," *io9*, 23 May 2013.

89. Andrew Dyce, "Henry Cavill Says *Man of Steel* is 'Zack Snyder's Baby' and Not Nolan's," *ScreenRant*, 8 May 2013.

90. According to Snyder, Nolan vetoed the idea because "a real movie wouldn't do that." Nolan has been more diplomatic in stating his case, clarifying, "We shouldn't be chasing other movies, but stay true to the tone of *Man of Steel*." (Tom Shone, "Christopher Nolan: the man who rebooted the blockbuster," *The Guardian*, 4 November 2014.)

91. In this context, it is revealing how often the *Dark Knight* trilogy is compared to monumental works of American popular culture like the *Godfather* films. (Tom Shone, "The *Dark Knight* trilogy as our generation's Godfather," *The Guardian*, 20 July 2012.) "That was a superhero movie as *The Godfather*," reflects writer and director Joss Whedon of Nolan's *The Dark Knight*. (Lauren, Duca, "Here's What Joss Whedon Thinks About The State Of The Superhero Genre," *The Huffington Post*, 16 June 2014.) David Koepp made a similar comparison when talking about how his teenage children approached the film. ("The Dark Knight Effect," *Empire*, 13 July 2012.)

92. John Ip, "*The Dark Knight*'s War on Terrorism," *Ohio State Journal of Criminal Law*, September 2011, p. 209–229; Sonny Bunch, "Movies: Gotham City's war on terror," *The Washington Times*, 18 July 2008.

93. Paul Hechinger, "*Dark Knight* Director Christopher Nolan Talks About Keeping Batman Real," *BBC America*, December 2012.

94. For example, *Rolling Stone* published a commemorative magazine that was titled "Barack Obama and the Triumph of Hope." Studies found that all voters across party lines felt that the election of Barack Obama represented at least "one of the most important advances" for the progress of African Americans in the United States. (Frank Newport, "Americans See Obama Election as Race Relations Milestone," *Gallup News*, 7 November 2008.) The American population was optimistic in the capacity of Obama to accomplish his policy goals. (Jeffrey M. Jones, "Americans Hopeful Obama Can Accomplish Most Key Goals," *Gallup News*, 12 November 2008.)

95. Lydia Saad, "Obama and Bush: A Contrast in Popularity," *Gallup News*, 10 November 2008.

96. Frank Newport, "Bush's 69% Job Disapproval Rating Highest in Gallup History," *Gallup News*, 22 April 2008.

97. Kurt Anderson, "Crossroads; Pop Culture in the Age of Obama," *The New York Times*, 9 August 2009; Nicholas Ferroni, "The First Pop Culture President in History," *The Huffington Post*, 7 November 2012.

98. Dana Stevens, "Go See *Star Trek*," *Slate*, 6 May 2009; Ward Sutton, "A *Star Trek* for the Obama Era," *The Huffington Post*, 7 June 2009.

99. Esther Zuckerman, "Watching *The Dark Knight Rises* and Seeing Politics," *The Atlantic*, 17 July 2012.

100. Ally Semigran, "*Dark Knight Rises* not shooting at Occupy Wall Street," *Entertainment Weekly*, 25 October 2011.

101. Ben Child, "*The Dark Knight Rises* trailer gives us Occupy Gotham," *The Guardian*, 20 December 2011; Conor Dougherty, "Occupy Gotham? *Dark Knight Rises* Trailer Suggests Inequality Theme in Batman," *The Wall Street Journal*, 19 December 2011.

102. Brian Hiatt, "Christopher Nolan: *Dark Knight Rises* Isn't Political," *Rolling Stone*, 20 July 2012.

103. Mark Bernardin, "Christopher Nolan on 'Extreme Places' in the Making of *The Dark Knight Rises*," *The Hollywood Reporter*, 27 December 2012.

104. It seems entirely possible that Nolan was playing with semantics in his classification of *The Dark Knight Rises*. Managing a multi-billion-dollar film franchise involves a great deal of care to avoid provoking an audience wary of an increasingly politicised entertainment landscape. (Conor Friedersdorf, "Why Everything Is Politicized Even Though Most Americans Hate It," *The Atlantic*, 26 March 2013.)

105. Brian Hiatt, "Christopher Nolan: *Dark Knight Rises* Isn't Political," *Rolling Stone*, 20 July 2012.

106. In this regard, Nolan's perspective on political readings of his work might be reflected by the mechanics of dreaming in *Inception*, where the architect builds a world and then the audience populates it with their own subconscious. Nolan seems to be implying that the audience is doing something similar in relation to the politics of *The Dark Knight Rises*.

107. Catherine Shoard, "*Dark Knight Rises*: fancy a capitalist caped crusader as your superhero?," *The Guardian*, 17 July 2012.

108. John Nolte, "*Dark Knight Rises* Review: Nolan Slaps Obama With a Masterpiece," *Brietbart*, 21 July 2012.

109. Ross Douthat, "The Politics of *The Dark Knight Rises*," *The New York Times*, 23 July 2012.

110. Andrew O'Hehir, "*The Dark Knight Rises*: Christopher Nolan's evil masterpiece," *Salon*, 18 July 2012.

111. Todd VanDerWerff, "*Hail Caesar* is the slapstick comedy about economic philosophy you need right now," *Vox*, 6 February 2016.

112. Steve Weintraub, "Christopher Nolan Interview—*The Dark Knight*," *Collider*, 20 July 2008.

113. Brian Hiatt, "Christopher Nolan: *Dark Knight Rises* Isn't Political," *Rolling Stone*, 20 July 2012.

114. Indeed, the phrase originated Carol Hanisch's essay "The Personal is Political" from February 1969, widely circulated in *Notes from the Second Year: Women's Liberation* (1970).

115. Geoff Andrew, "Christopher Nolan," *The Guardian*, 27 August 2002.

116. Nolan glosses over that interpretation of the film's ice symbolism. "It's about interpreting the Batman symbol to do with ice, which comes into play later in the film, not in any massively meaningful way," Nolan contends. "I just like to try to open in the film with some sense of where the thing's going to go." (Kevin P. Sullivan, "*Dark Knight Rises* Opening Image: Christopher Nolan Explains," *MTV*, 22 July 2012.)

117. As Jason Dittmer argues, "superheroes are about the protection of life and property and almost never seek to fundamentally revolutionize the system. Any character that seeks to achieve political or economic praxis is, by comic book convention, characterized as a villain." (Jason Dittmer, "Captain America's Empire: Reflections on Identity, Popular Culture, and Post-9/11 Geopolitics," *Annals of the Association of American Geographers*, September 2005, p. 642.)

118. Brian Hiatt, "Christopher Nolan: *Dark Knight Rises* Isn't Political," *Rolling Stone*, 20 July 2012.

119. This is an accepted part of the character's identity. "I got interested in the class element of Batman," reflects comic book writer Grant Morrison, who was working on *Batman Incorporated* as *The Dark Knight Rises* was released. "He's a rich man who beats up poor people. It's quite a bizarre mission to go out

at night dressed as a bat and punch the hell out of junkies." (Gavin Edwards, "The Super Psyche," *Playboy*, 18 April 2012.)

120. In *Batman Begins*, the character even travels the world and learns to steal. Although he maintains that he never became a criminal, he concedes, "The first time I stole so that I wouldn't starve, I lost many assumptions about the simple nature of right and wrong."

121. Brian Hiatt, "Christopher Nolan: *Dark Knight Rises* Isn't Political," *Rolling Stone*, 20 July 2012.

122. Andrew Klavan, "What Bush and Batman Have in Common," *The Wall Street Journal*, 25 July 2008.

123. This theme is even reflected in smaller and more intimate character threads. *The Dark Knight* featured a sequence in which Alfred burned a letter from Rachel Dawes, in order to protect Bruce Wayne from the truth. However, in *The Dark Knight Rises*, Alfred acknowledges that he made a mistake in trying to insulate his ward from reality. "Maybe it's time we all stopped trying to outsmart the truth and let it have its day," Alfred argues.

124. Scott Feinberg, "Christopher Nolan on *Interstellar* Critics, Making Original Films and Shunning Cellphones and Email," *The Hollywood Reporter*, 3 January 2015.

125. While Bruce has locked himself away from the world, Miranda Tate continues to reach out to him. "She's very persistent," Alfred notes. "And quite lovely, in case you were wondering." Later, Alfred finds Bruce looking into Selina Kyle. "You two should exchange notes over coffee," Alfred quips when Bruce admits to being impressed with the thief's craft.

126. Brian Brutlag, "The Films of Christopher Nolan: *The Dark Knight Rise*," *The Sociologist Dojo*, 25 October 2014.

127. Maria Aspan, "Guest Post: Why Catwoman is the Best Part of *The Dark Knight Rises*," *IndieWire*, 25 July 2012.

128. Natalie Zutter, "With Anne Hathaway In *The Dark Knight Rises*, Christopher Nolan Finally Gets The Bombshell Female Character Right," *Alloy*, 20 July 2012.

129. Selina Kyle is not the only character to make this choice. Peter Foley and all the other police officers ultimately make the same choice at the climax. However, *The Dark Knight Rises* is much more invested in Selina Kyle's character and autonomy, and so uses her to explore that theme in a more intimate manner than *The Dark Knight* had done.

130. Steve Denning, "Lest We Forget: Why We Had A Financial Crisis," *Forbes*, 22 November 2011.

131. Zanny Manton Beddoes, "For richer, for poorer," *The Economist*, 13 October 2012.

132. "Occupy Wall Street" emerged in September 2011, three years after the financial crisis. (Ayesha Kazmi, "How Anonymous emerged to Occupy Wall Street," *The Guardian*, 27 September 2011.) In contrast, *The Dark Knight Rises* had begun *filming* four months earlier, with a story and script *long* completed. (Russ Fischer, "Press Release Pass-On: *The Dark Knight Rises* Begins Filming, No New Info Announced," */Film*, 19 May 2011.)

133. Scott Foundas, "Cinematic Faith," *Film Comment*, Winter 2012.

134. Forrest Wickman, "The Dickensian Aspects of *The Dark Knight Rises*," *Slate*, 21 July 2012.

135. Chris Eggertson, "*Dark Knight Rises* director Christopher Nolan on Bane, grandiosity and secrets revealed," *HitFix*, 9 July 2012.

136. Hugh Hart, "Nolan Vision: Making the Masterful *Dark Knight Rises*," *Wired*, 8 July 2012.

137. Evan Puschak, "The Serial: From Dickens To *Star Wars*," *Nerdwriter*, 13 April 2013.

138. Tom Kutsch, "Batman, America and the politics of fear," *Al Jazeera*, 1 August 2013.

139. Bill Bradley, "One Thing You Didn't Notice About Bane In *The Dark Knight Rises*," *The Huffington Post*, 11 April 2015.

140. The Dickensian quality of the name "Stryver," applied to a clear social striver, is a particularly nice inclusion; it evokes the naming conventions applied to comic book characters like "Edward Nygma" ("E-nigma") and "Victor Fries" ("Mister Freeze").

141. "*The Dark Knight Rises* filming in NY," *The New York Post*, 19 July 2012.

142. Luis Gomez, "Chicago stand-ins steal revenue but not thunder in new *Dark Knight Rises*," *The Chicago Tribune*, 18 July 2012.

143. "A quick shot of the Chicago skyline screams money and prosperity," argues Chicago-based journalist Christopher Borrelli. "A quick shot of Pittsburgh, where a lot of the film was shot, reveals working-class areas within yearning range of gleaming skyscrapers. You'd have to find a pretty wide lens before you could hold the poor of Chicago and the rich of Chicago within the same frame." (Christopher Borrelli, "So you're ready to talk about *The Dark Knight Rises*?," *The Chicago Tribune*, 20 July 2012.)

144. Jonathan Lemire and Kim Stack, "Batman Occupies Wall Street: *Dark Knight* Films Fight Scene Downtown," *New York Daily News*, 5 November 2011.

145. Mark Bernardin, "Christopher Nolan on 'Extreme Places' in the Making of *The Dark Knight Rises*," *The Hollywood Reporter*, 27 December 2012.

146. Nolan himself has described the film as a "revolutionary epic." (Jim Vejvoda, "Nolan: *The Dark Knight Rises* is a Revolutionary Epic," *IGN*, 5 June 2012.)

147. Melena Ryzik, "Michael Caine and Christopher Nolan and Oscar," *The New York Times*, 5 December 2012.

148. Oliver Lyttelton, "Christopher Nolan Talks The Politics & Influences Of *The Dark Knight Rises* & More From the Film's Press Tour," *IndieWire*, 24 July 2012.

149. Attending one such function early in the film, Bruce muses, "The proceeds go to the big fat spread. It's not about charity. It's about feeding the ego of whichever society hag laid this on."

150. The end of the film returns to this idea, with Bruce Wayne deciding to bequeath Wayne Manor to Gotham City "for one purpose, and one purpose only: the housing and care of the city's at-risk and orphaned children."

151. "The police weren't getting it done," Bruce complains to Alfred when the butler objects to that intervention. "Perhaps they might have if you hadn't made a sideshow of yourself," Alfred counters. "You led a bloated police force on a chase, with a load of fancy new toys from Fox." Alfred's criticisms seem valid, particularly since the film watched Foley direct law enforcement's attention away from Bane towards Batman, over Blake's protests.

152. Bruce pointedly refuses to share his technology with law enforcement and civil government. "Aren't the police supposed to be investigating, then?" Alfred protests when Bruce takes matters into his own hands. "They don't have the tools to analyze it," Bruce counters. "They would if you gave them to them," Alfred responds. "One man's

tool is another man's weapon," Bruce replies. The irony of this exchange becomes clear when Bane later uses those same tools to terrorise Gotham, as a direct result of Bruce's arrogance and controlling tendencies.

153. The same is true of the reactor that Bane converts to a nuclear bomb. Bruce keeps it a secret from the world, and refuses to share it with others. This refusal forces him to share it with Miranda Tate, who subsequently turns out to be Talia Al Ghul and then uses the reactor as a weapon to terrorise Gotham. As with Bruce's armoury, there is a sense that this is too much power for one man to hold unchecked.

154. Nolan's work touches on these themes repeatedly. *The Prestige* is on some level a film about monetising wonder to escape a material world. *Inception* imagines a highly corporatised future in which large international businesses seem to have usurped the role of government.

155. Based on the details of his childhood that Blake accounts to Bruce, he was certainly "forged from suffering; hardened by pain; not a man from privilege."

156. "The idea was to be a symbol," Bruce assures Blake around the midpoint of the film. "Batman could be anybody. That was the point." It involves a certain fudging of the logic and justification employed by *Batman Begins*, but it is a logical extension of the same idea.

157. Mark Fisher, "Batman's political right turn," *The Guardian*, 22 July 2012.

158. Elizabeth Sandifer, "An Accurately Named Trilogy II: *The Dark Knight*," *Eruditorum Press*, 13 November 2017.

159. Brian E. Frydenborg, "The Politics of *The Dark Knight Rises*," *Movie Pilot*, 1 January 2013.

160. Although this is revealed at the climax, Gordon hints at Bane's hypocrisy in his conversation with Foley. Bane had earlier promised that the bomb's detonator had been given to an "anonymous Gothamite," but Gordon knows this is nonsense. "You think he's given control of that bomb to one of the people?" Gordon demands. "You think this is part of some revolution? There's one man with his finger on the button. That's Bane." Gordon is ultimately vindicated when it is revealed that Bane has given the detonator to Talia, which is certainly against the *spirit* of his big speech, if not the literal wording. ("Though I'm not ordinary, I am a citizen," she insists.)

161. Bane's rhetoric is gleeful and pointedly disingenuous throughout film. "Gotham is yours!" Bane pledges. "None shall interfere. Do as you please. But start by storming Blackgate and freeing the oppressed!" Despite Bane's assurances that Gotham belongs to its citizens, he immediately *orders* them to free a bunch of prisoners. He also then uses his paramilitary to carry out those orders. Bane's rhetoric suggests that Gotham is in a state of anarchy, but he never seems to surrender any control of the situation.

162. Johan Höglund discusses this interesting and under-discussed aspect of the *Dark Knight* trilogy in "Militarising the Virtual Gothic" in *The American Imperial Gothic: Popular Culture, Empire, Violence* (2014).

163. By 2012, the speech was already understood as a horribly ill-judged and ironic image that completely misrepresented the conflict in question. (Ujala Sehgal, "Eight Years Ago, Bush Declared 'Mission Accomplished' in Iraq," *The Atlantic*, 1 May 2011.)

164. This lines up neatly with right-wing rhetoric on the invasion of Iraq. Dick Cheney famously boasted, "Now, I think things have gotten so bad inside Iraq, from the standpoint of the Iraqi people, my belief is we will, in fact, be greeted as liberators." (*Meet the Press*, 16 March 2003.) The military campaign even capitalized on this narrative, branding military intervention as "Operation Iraqi Freedom," an attempt to cultivate a more benign narrative around the invasion. (Frank Rich, "Operation Iraqi Infoganda," *The New York Times*, 28 March 2004.)

165. Brian Hiatt, "Christopher Nolan: *Dark Knight Rises* Isn't Political," *Rolling Stone*, 20 July 2012.

166. Brian E. Frydenborg, "The Politics of *The Dark Knight Rises*," *Movie Pilot*, 1 January 2013.

167. Henry Bevan, "How *The Dark Knight Rises* foreshadowed the dawn of Trump," *Little White Lies*, 8 January 2017.

168. The film unfolds eight years after the events of *The Dark Knight*, which was released in 2008. (The *Gotham Tonight* segments released to promote *The Dark Knight* and various documentation visible in the film confirm that the sequel was intended to be set in 2008, meaning that *Batman Begins* took place in 2007.) As with the movie's ice imagery, Nolan insists that there was no strong thematic reason for making the gap eight years, he just wanted a significant amount of time to insulate *The Dark Knight* from *The Dark Knight Rises*. "If I had to express it thematically, I think what we're saying is that for Batman and Commissioner Gordon, there's a big sacrifice, a big compromise, at the end of *The Dark Knight* and for that to mean something, that sacrifice has to work and Gotham has to get better in a sense," Nolan explains. "They have to achieve something for the ending of that film—and the feeling at the end of that film—to have validity. Their sacrifice has to have meaning and it takes time to establish that and to show that, and that's the primary reason we did that." (Geoff Boucher, "*Dark Knight Rises*: Christopher Nolan opens up about Bane choice," *The Los Angeles Times*, 12 December 2011.)

169. Indeed, Bane has even been co-opted by various right-wing segments of the internet, with the alt-right engaging in what has become known as "Bane Posting," which consists of mimetic references to the character's iconic dialogue from the film. Indeed, even Aidan Gillen's anonymous CIA official has become a right-wing internet icon. ("Aidan Gillen has accidentally become part of a bizarre 'alt-right meme'," *The Daily Edge*, 29 January 2017.)

170. John Nichols, "The Republican Party Created This Monster," *The Nation*, 8 October 2016.

171. In his address on freeing the prisoners held at Blackgate, Bane vows, "We take Gotham from the corrupt! The rich! The oppressors of generations, who have kept you down with myths of opportunity. And we give it back to you the people." In Trump's inauguration, he spoke of the concentration of power in a disconnected Washington D.C., promising his supporters, "We are transferring power from Washington, D.C., and giving it back to you, the people." The parallels did not go unnoticed. (Dani Levy, "Donald Trump Inauguration Address Compared to Batman Villain Bane's Speech," *Variety*, 20 January 2017.)

172. Of course, Bane ascended to power on the back of class resentment, while studies suggest that Trump's support is rooted in racial resentment. (Jamelle Bouie, "White Elephant," *Slate*, 1 September 2017.) Trump's policies also do very little to help most of his voting base, and

offer no support for the problems that directly affect those voters through heathcare or taxation. (Jennifer Rubin, "The multiple ways Trump is hurting his base," *The Washington Post*, 27 February 2017.)

173. Anatole Kaletsky, "Trump's rise and Brexit vote are more an outcome of culture than economics," *The Guardian*, 28 October 2016.

174. Chris Sims, "Logic and Symbolism In *The Dark Knight Rises*," *Comics Alliance*, 24 July 2012.

175. The tidiness of this symbolism was a source of confusion to some audience members, with some observers wondering whether Alfred *really* saw his fantasy come to life or whether he were simply hopefully imagining it. Christian Bale has argued that the scene in the closing montage should be taken at face value. (Jonathon Dornbush, "Christian Bale talks *Exodus*, explains ending of *Dark Knight Rises*," *Entertainment Weekly*, 9 December 2014.)

176. Alastair Stewart, "The plot holes and symbolism of *The Dark Knight Rises*," *Den of Geek*, 13 June 2014.

177. In particular, costume designer Lindy Hemming has discussed an entire origin story for Bane that is entirely absent from the original film involving training and torture. (Selios Phili, "Style Reconnaissance: *The Dark Knight Rises*'s Lindy Hemming on Bane's Sweet Jackets, Alfred's Old-Man Armani, and Catwoman's Mugler Wardrobe," *GQ*, 6 August 2012.)

178. Post-release coverage of the film tends to include words like "polarizing" and "divisive." (For example: Edward Davis, "Joseph Gordon-Levitt Explains Why There Doesn't Need To Be A Spin-Off Movie From *The Dark Knight Rises*," *IndieWire*, 15 August 2012.) A study of the most divisive movies ranked on *Metacritic* in late November 2017 determined that *The Dark Knight Rises* was the thirty-ninth most divisive movie ever made. (Rosie Fletcher, "These Are the Most Divisive Movies Ever, According to Science," *Esquire*, 25 November 2017.)

179. As of December 2017, *Rotten Tomatoes* has *The Dark Knight Rises* listed at 87% positive, meaning that 87% of film critics consider it to be above average.

180. Mark Hughes, "*The Dark Knight Rises* Tops $1 Billion, Surpasses *The Dark Knight*," *Forbes*, 5 September 2012.

181. Anthony Breznican, "*The Dark Knight Rises* on AFI's best-movies list," *Entertainment Weekly*, 10 September 2012.

182. There are almost too many examples to list, but some samples: Jen Yamato, "Holy Plot Holes, Batman! 9 Logical Gripes With *The Dark Knight Rises*," *MovieLine*, 23 July 2012; SlashFilm Staff, "15 Things That Bothered Us About *The Dark Knight Rises*," */Film*, 23 July 2012; Daniel Carlson, "9 Huge Plot Holes in *The Dark Knight Rises* That Totally Don't Work," *Pajiba*, 24 July 2012.

183. "*The Dark Knight Rises*: 3 Ways Batman Could Have Returned To Gotham," *What Culture?*, 10 September 2012; Darren Franich and Jeff Castro, "*Dark Knight Rises*: 10 Scenes We Wish We'd Seen," *Entertainment Weekly*, 20 July 2012; Mike Ryan, "*The Dark Knight Rises*: 7 Lingering Questions," *The Huffington Post*, 23 July 2012.

184. Several scenes before Bruce makes his escape from the prison, Lucius Fox suggests that the bomb "will go off in twenty-three days." This gives Bruce anywhere up to three weeks to make the journey from the prison to Gotham, which seems reasonable for man of Bruce's resourcefulness—even without his existing resources.

185. John Sutherland, "Nitpicking," *The Guardian*, 13 June 2005.

186. Matt Singer, "Nitpicking the nitpickers," *The Dissolve*, 25 August 2014.

187. Matt Singer, "Nitpicking the *Dark Knight Rises* Nitpickers," *IndieWire*, 26 July 2012.

188. John Kenneth Muir, "Death by a Thousand Nitpicks? *Prometheus* (2012) and the critical reception," *John Kenneth Muir's Reflections on Cult Movies and Classic TV*, 20 June 2012.

189. Elias Bezem, "Millennial Misanthropy: On the modern-day culture of cinema nitpicking," *The Metropolist*, 2 March 2016.

190. Matt Singer, "Nitpicking the *Dark Knight Rises* Nitpickers," *IndieWire*, 26 July 2012.

191. Noel Murray, "Plot holes and politics: Do you need an airtight reason to dislike a movie?," *The A.V. Club*, 1 August 2012.

192. Chris Tookey, "First Review: *The Dark Knight Rises* might be spectacular to look at ... but it's humorless and too long," The Daily Mail, 16 July 2012.

193. Colin Covert, "*Dark Knight Rises*: An epic finale," *The Star Tribune*, 20 July 2012.

194. Ronald Bergan, "Objective film criticism: an impossible task?," *The Guardian*, 3 July 2008.

195. Jason Bailey, "DC Fans Don't Understand What Criticism Is—And Film Media is Partly to Blame," *Flavourwire*, 31 May 2017.

196. Erik Kain, "#GamerGate Wants Objective Video Game Reviews: What Would Roger Ebert Do?," *Forbes*, 28 December 2014.

197. Brian Raftery, "*Justice League*, Rotten Tomatoes, and DC Fans' Persecution Complex," *Wired*, 20 November 2017.

198. The prevalence of this sort of critical outlook can probably be gauged by reference to "The Raiders of Minimisation," the fourth episode of the seventh season of *The Big Bang Theory*. In that episode, a character "ruins" *Raiders of the Lost Ark* by pointing out that the character of Indiana Jones contributes nothing of material value to the plot. Naturally, the episode went viral and generated a lot of attention, suggesting that whether *Raiders of the Lost Ark* was good or bad could be measured by an in-universe performance review of the title character. (Kristy Puchko, "Has *The Big Bang Theory* Ruined Indiana Jones Forever?," *Cinema Blend*, 16 October 2013; Simon Gallagher, "How *The Big Bang Theory* Ruined Indiana Jones For Everyone," *What Cuture?*, 15 October 2013.)

199. The idea that these plot holes and nitpicks can be used to objectively grade movies is perhaps best reflected in *CinemaSins*' "Everything Wrong With..." videos, in which a counter at the top left-hand corner of the screen provides an actual count of the recorded errors so that it might be properly ranked and graded. This is similar to how aggregators like *Rotten Tomatoes* or *Metacritic* reduce a movie's value to a simple score out of one hundred.

200. Heather Horn, "*Inception*: The Backlash Begins," *The Wire*, 21 July 2010.

201. Charlie Jane Anders, "So wait. Is there really a *Dark Knight Rises* backlash?," *io9*, 8 August 2011.

202. Matt Singer, "*The Dark Knight Rises* Beyond the Hype," *IndieWire*, 23 November 2012.

203. Phil Hoad, "Global box office: has the Christopher Nolan backlash hurt *Interstellar*?," *The Guardian*, 12 November 2014.

204. David Crow, "Examining the Christopher Nolan backlash," *Den of Geek*, 25 February 2015.

205. Indeed, the same month that

Nolan released *The Dark Knight Rises*, he was honored with a star in front of Grauman's Chinese Theatre. Not only was Nolan among the youngest honourees, he was one of only eight directors to receive the honor. (Nikki Finke, "Chris Nolan Receives Rare Hollywood Honour," *Deadline*, 8 July 2012.)

206. See, for example, Richard Brody, "*The Dark Knight Rises* vs. *The Avengers*," *The New Yorker*, 22 October 2012; Andrew Pulver, "*The Dark Knight Rises* tries to match *The Avengers* in superheroes battle," *The Guardian*, 8 July 2012; Simon Columb, "Gloomy *Dark Knight* and Shiny *Avengers*," *Flickering Myth*, 8 July 2012.

207. Matt Singer, "*Dark Knight Rises* Critic Receives Death Threats," *IndieWire*, 16 July 2012.

208. Michael Cavna, "*Dark Knight Rises*: In defense of Batman fans, Christopher Nolan remarks on Rotten Tomatoes—and Rush Limbaugh—kerfuffles," *The Washington Post*, 18 July 2012.

209. Heath Ledger's absence was frequently discussed in reviews, for example: Matt Harvey, "*The Dark Knight Rises*: Only Missing A Heath Ledger," *Sabotage Times*, 23 July 2012. Indeed, one of the most frequent sources of fan speculation is how different *The Dark Knight Rises* might have been if Heath Ledger were alive, for example: Kit Simpson Browne, "Just How Different Was Nolan's Third *Batman* Movie Supposed To Be?," *MoviePilot*, 28 October 2014.

210. Anita Busch, "Aurora Theater Shooting, 3 Years Later: When Moviegoers Became Superheroes," *Deadline*, 1 June 2015. The tragedy was also the inspiration for an independent movie titled *Dark Night*, directed by Tim Sutton.

211. Gregory Weinkauf, "Batman, America and Violence: Considerations," *The Huffington Post*, 22 July 2012; Giovanni Fazio, "*The Dark Knight Rises*," *The Japan Times*, 27 July 2012; David Thomson, "Aurora and Batman," *New Republic*, 24 July 2012.

212. Mark Bernardin, "Christopher Nolan on 'Extreme Places' in the Making of *The Dark Knight Rises*," *The Hollywood Reporter*, 27 December 2012.

## Chapter 9

1. Luis Gomez, "Batman's Chicago connection," *The Chicago Tribune*, 22 July 2014.

2. Jordan Crucchiola and Jason Kehe, "The Impact of Borges, *Brazil*, and M. C. Escher on *Interstellar*," *Wired*, 20 November 2014.

3. Geoff Andrew, "Christopher Nolan," *The Guardian*, 27 August 2002.

4. Jeff Otto, "Set Visit: *Batman Begins*," *IGN*, 3 January 2005.

5. Karen Wada, "Tricked Out: How production designer Nathan Crowley transformed modern Los Angeles into Victorian London for *The Prestige*," *Los Angeles Magazine*, 1 February 2007.

6. Michael Fleming, "Space chase pic on Par launch pad," *Variety* 14 June 2006.

7. Indeed, even in the year that *Interstellar* was released, *Forbes* would name Spielberg as "the most influential celebrity in America," with almost half of the American population recognising his influence. (Dorothy Pomeranz, "Steven Spielberg Tops Our List Of The Most Influential Celebrities," *Forbes*, 15 January 2014.)

8. I. Q. Hunter, "Spielberg and Adaptation" in *A Companion to Steven Spielberg* (2017), p. 225.

9. It could also be argued that *Indiana Jones and the Kingdom of the Crystal Skull* also demonstrated Spielberg's engagement with science-fiction storytelling in the first decade of the twentieth century, trading the thirties occult trappings of the original trilogy for weird fifties science-fiction. (J. W. Rinzler and Laurent Bouzereau, *The Complete Making of Indiana Jones* (2008).)

10. Jay Fernandez, "Spielberg, Nolan plan sci-fi project," *The Los Angeles Times*, 24 March 2007.

11. Jeff Jensen, "Inside *Interstellar*, Christopher Nolan's emotional space odyssey," *Entertainment Weekly*, 16 October 2014.

12. Warner Brothers surrendered a share of their *Friday the 13th* franchise and a portion of any cinematic adaptation of *South Park* in return for the rights to distribute *Interstellar* internationally. (Germain Lussier, "Warner Bros. Gave Up *Friday the 13th* and *South Park* Rights for Piece of Christopher Nolan's *Interstellar*," */Film*, 5 June 2013.)

13. Emanuel Levy, "*Interstellar*: Interview with Director Christopher Nolan," *Emanuel Levy*, 22 October 2014.

14. Alistair Harkness, "Interview: Christopher Nolan on *Interstellar*," *The Scotsman*, 10 November 2014.

15. Tom Shone, "Christopher Nolan: the man who rebooted the blockbuster," *The Guardian*, 4 November 2014.

16. Kevin Jagernauth, "Christopher Nolan Talks Influence Of *Close Encounters*, *The Right Stuff*, *2001* And More On *Interstellar*," *Indie Wire*, 29 September 2014.

17. Colin Covert, "Christopher Nolan explains his 'cinematic brain' at Walker Art Center," *Star Tribune*, 6 May 2015.

18. Ned Hepburn, "Matthew McConaughey, *Interstellar*, and the All-American Jacket," *Esquire*, 5 November 2014.

19. In fact, less than two years after the release of *Interstellar*, *People Magazine* would cite Matthew McConaughey as the number one reason to love America. (Elizabeth Leonard, "Matthew McConaughey Is Our #1 Reason to Love America! Inside His Candid Interview," *People*, 22 June 2016.)

20. Alexandra Cheney, "Christopher Nolan on *Interstellar* and Preserving the Theatrical Experience," *Variety*, 26 March 2014.

21. Jeff Jensen, "Inside *Interstellar*, Christopher Nolan's emotional space odyssey," *Entertainment Weekly*, 16 October 2014.

22. Trevor Hogg, "*Interstellar*: Nathan Crowley interview," *3dtotal*, 13 February 2015.

23. Chris Klimek, "*Interstellar*: Stunning And Bold, With Lots Of Corn," *NPR*, 6 November 2014.

24. Indeed, Nolan would consult with director Zack Snyder on how best to manage the corn grown for the film. Snyder had grown three hundred acres of corn for *Man of Steel*, the Superman reboot produced by Nolan. Nolan would then grow five hundred acres of corn for *Interstellar*. (Marlow Stern, "Christopher Nolan Uncut: On *Interstellar*, Ben Affleck's Batman, and the Future of Mankind," *The Daily Beast*, 10 November 2014.)

25. Edward Davis, "Watch: Christopher Nolan On The Colbert Report; Says *Interstellar* Borrows Clips From Ken Burns' *Dust Bowl* Documentary," *IndieWire*, 6 December 2014.

26. Stephen Galloway, "*Interstellar*'s Christopher Nolan, Stars Gather to Reveal Secrets of the Year's Most Mysterious Film," *The Hollywood Reporter*, 22 October 2014.

27. Twenty-first century science-fiction films like *Sunshine*, *Gravity*, *The Martian* and *Life* tend to offer an international perspective on space

flight. There are multiple possible reasons for this. Modern space flight is likely to be an international endeavor featuring heavy involvement from nations like China. (Vikram Mansharamani, "China Is Winning the 21st Century Space Race," *Fortune*, 31 March 2016.) More pragmatically in terms of filmmaking, international markets (especially China) are of increasing importance to box office returns. (Joanna Robinson, "Did You Catch All the Ways Hollywood Pandered to China This Year?," *Vanity Fair*, 5 August 2016.)

28. Darren Mooney, "Opinion: Pop culture is saturated with throwbacks to the 1960s right now—but why?," *The Journal*, 8 November 2014.

29. Alyssa Rosenberg, "From *Playboy Club* to *Pan Am*, When '60s-Era Nostalgia Isn't Enough," *The Atlantic*, 25 September 2011.

30. Obama made considerable effort during his election to secure the support of the Kennedy establishment within the Democratic Party. (Toby Harnden, "Barack Obama is JFK heir, says Kennedy aide," *The Telegraph*, 12 October 2007; Karen Tumulty, "Why the Kennedys Went for Obama," *Time*, 28 January 2008.) However, the comparisons go beyond that; German journalist Christoph von Marschall published a bestselling biography of Obama titled *Barack Obama—Der schwarze Kennedy* (2007), which might be translated as "Barack Obama—The Black Kennedy."

31. Matt Novak, "How Space-Age Nostalgia Hobbles Our Future," *Slate*, 15 May 2012.

32. Studies suggest that the American public were more likely to support the space programme on the fortieth anniversary of the Moon Landing than they would have been on the tenth, twenty-fifth or thirtieth. (Jeffrey M. Jones, "Majority of Americans Say Space Program Costs Justified," *Gallup*, 17 July 2009.)

33. Joel Achenbach, "Does the future of space travel lie with NASA or space entrepreneurs?," *The Washington Post*, 23 November 2013.

34. Kevin Kryah, "Elon Musk's SpaceX Says: Consider Mars for Your Summer Vacation," *Esquire*, 18 May 2015.

35. In *Inception*, for example, Cobb advises Ariadne that she can conjure specific details from memory, but advises her against building entire worlds from memory. *The Dark Knight Rises* is a film largely about Bruce letting go of past trauma, as symbolized by his willingness to take Martha Wayne's pearls out of the locked safe in which they have been kept.

36. In a meeting with officials at Murph's school, Cooper can barely contain his rage. Miss Hanley complains about the money spent on "useless machines," remarking, "If we don't want a repeat of the excess and wastefulness of the 20th century, then we need to teach our kids about this planet, not tales of leaving it." Cooper rather pointedly responds, "One of those 'useless machines' they used to make was called an MRI. If we had any of those left, the doctors would've been able to find the cyst in my wife's brain before she died instead of afterwards. Then she'd have been the one listening to this instead of me which would have been a good thing, because she was always the calmer one."

37. This is a particularly important nuance in an era where nostalgia for a lost America often expresses itself through anti–intellectualism and paranoia. (Francesca Polletta and Jessica Callahan, "Deep stories, nostalgia narratives, and fake news: Storytelling in the Trump era," *American Journal of Cultural Sociology*, July 2017.) *Interstellar* works very hard to distinguish its own nostalgia for space-age optimism from the trappings of more regressive nostalgia.

38. Peter Sciretta, "Interview: *Interstellar* Writer Jonathan Nolan: Real Space Exploration Is 'Fucking Done, We Peaked!,'" */Film*, 6 November 2014.

39. This potential was not just demonstrated by the actual space race itself, but also in the way in which contemporary popular culture engaged with the idea of space travel. *Star Trek* premiered three years before the moon landing, and remains one of the most popular and consistently optimistic portrayals of human space exploration in film and television. (Matthew Daly, "*Star Trek* offers a rare optimistic view of humanity—and its return to TV can do a lot for progressive values," *The Independent*, 6 November 2015.)

40. One need only look at the popularity of zombie apocalypse narratives in television series like *The Walking Dead* or *Fear the Walking Dead*, and in films like *28 Days Later*, *Land of the Dead*, *Zombieland*, *Shaun of the Dead*, *Planet Terror*, the *Resident Evil* franchise, *The Girl With All the Gifts*. These are all stories that imagine the graphic destruction of mankind, and this is only one subgenre of apocalyptic science-fiction.

41. Graeme McMillan, "Where Are Our Bright Science-Fiction Futures?," *Time*, 29 March 2013.

42. Annalee Newitz, "Dear Science Fiction Writers: Stop Being So Pessimistic!," *Smithsonian Magazine*, April 2012.

43. To be fair, some science-fiction films engaged with this premise directly. Brad Bird's *Tomorrowland* was explicitly about the self-fulfilling nature of mankind's preoccupation with imagining apocalyptic futures. (Erin Whitney, "Disney's Futuristic *Tomorrowland* Rejects Dystopian Tropes With An Optimistic Call To Action," *The Huffington Post*, 22 May 2015.)

44. Marlow Stern, "Christopher Nolan Uncut: On *Interstellar*, Ben Affleck's Batman, and the Future of Mankind," *The Daily Beast*, 10 November 2014.

45. Nolan has conceded that "anarchy" is "the thing [he's] most afraid of." (Stax, "*IGN* Interviews Christopher Nolan," *IGN*, 6 December 2007.)

46. Samuel Arbesman, "Science Fiction Frames: *Interstellar* and Dystopian Optimism," *Medium*, 29 June 2016

47. Rob Harvilla, "Tonight, You're Going to Be Part of a Social Experiment," *The Ringer*, 22 July 2017; Armond White, "*Interstellar*: To Insipidness and Beyond," *National Review*, 6 November 2014.

48. Michiko Kakutani, "Culture Zone: Designer Nihilism," *The New York Times*, 24 March 1996; Todd Gitlin, "Revenge of the Nerd," *The New York Times*, 3 March 1996; Bret Easton Ellis, "The Gonzo Vision of Quentin Tarantino," *The New York Times*, 12 October 2015. Tarantino disputes this assertion, "I always thought I didn't have any big moral bounds when it came to so many things," he confesses. "But if you look at my movies, they almost follow the Hays Code. Violence was never a major issue in the old days of Hollywood. You could have as much violence as you wanted as long as the bad guy dies in the end, or denounces his sins. The thing those films specialised in is what I specialise in when it comes to violence." (Godfrey Cheshire, "Hollywood's New Hit Men," *Interview*, September 1994.)

49. Brandon Harris, "On the Coen Brothers and Nihilism," *Gaijin*, 8 September 2008; David Denby,

"Storm Warnings," *The New Yorker*, 15 September 2008; Mike Miley, "The Coen Brothers' Mean Streak," *The Huffington Post*, 18 October 2008. The Coen Brothers would seem to openly mock this recurring charge with the inclusion of actual nihilists as comedic villains in *The Big Lebowski*.

50. The pipe organ on the soundtrack was recorded at London's Temple Church. (Stephen Fortner, "Hans Zimmer on Scoring *Interstellar*," *Keyboard Magazine*, 5 March 2015.)

51. David Crow, "Christopher Nolan's *Interstellar*: A Secular End Times Myth," *Den of Geek*, 1 April 2015.

52. Brent Lang, "From *Noah* to *Exodus*: How Hollywood Fared in its Year of the Bible," *Variety*, 14 December 2014.

53. It is quite explicitly a hand. The characters' first real contact with the mysterious "them" responsible for the wormhole is through a "handshake" with Brand as the ship travels through the wormhole.

54. Anders Stephanson, *Manifest Destiny: American Expansionism and the Empire of Right* (1995).

55. See, for example, the chapter "The Cultural Construction of Nationalism in Early America," in Lloyd S. Kramer, *Nationalism in Europe and America: Politics, Cultures, and Identities since 1775* (2011), p. 125–146.

56. This is the Great Seal, depicting an eye hovering atop a pyramid. On the seal is written, "Annuit cœptis." This might be translated as "[God] has favored our undertakings." (Richard T. Hughes, *Myths America Lives By* (2003), p. 100–101.) The seal was co-designed by Charles Thomson, who argued that "the eye over it and the motto allude to the many signal interventions of providence in favor of the American cause." (Thomas G. West, *The Political Theory of the American Founding* (2017), p. 251.)

57. Megan Garber, "*Interstellar* Isn't About Religion (and Also It Is Totally About Religion)," *The Atlantic*, 12 November 2014.

58. Brett Mccracken, "The Masterful *Dunkirk* Explores a 'Miracle' of History," *The Gospel Coalition*, 24 July 2017.

59. Kevin Polowy, "Christopher Nolan on How *Star Wars* and *2001* Influenced His Space Odyssey *Interstellar*," *Yahoo!*, 7 November 2014.

60. Although, to be fair, these shots were already a visual influence on the rotating hotel scenes in *Inception*. Nevertheless, they create a keen visual continuity between the two films. (Siddhant Adlakha, "*Interstellar* and *2001: A Space Odyssey*—Echoes Through Time," *Birth. Movies. Death*, 3 April 2017.)

61. T.R. Witcher, "Kubrick's indestructible influence: *Interstellar* joins the long tradition of borrowing from *2001*," *Salon*, 22 November 2014.

62. Dave Calhoun, "Christopher Nolan interview: 'Another superhero movie? Unlikely. But never say never,'" *Time Out London*, 28 October 2014.

63. Glenn Whipp, "Christopher Nolan on the power of the people and why 2001 should be required preschool viewing," *The Los Angeles Times*, 4 January 2018.

64. Dave McNary, "Christopher Nolan to Present *2001: A Space Odyssey* at Cannes," *Variety*, 28 March 2018.

65. Roger Clarke, "From *Action Man* to *Batman*," *The Guardian*, 13 July 2008; Andrew Pulver, "Is Christopher Nolan the new Stanley Kubrick?," *The Guardian*, 15 July 2010; Tom Huddleston, "Why Christopher Nolan is not the new Stanley Kubrick," *Time Out London*, 21 July 2010; Tom Elrod, "Christopher Nolan: What Are We Watching, Exactly?," *Slant Magazine*, 11 August 2010; Andrew Pulver, "With *Dunkirk*, Christopher Nolan has finally hit the heights of Kubrick," *The Guardian*, 19 July 2017; Sean Hutchinson, "How *Dunkirk* Proves Christopher Nolan Is Stanley Kubrick's Cinematic Heir Apparent," *Inverse*, 25 May 2016.

66. John Naughton, "Christopher Nolan: the enigma behind *Interstellar*," *The Telegraph*, 8 November 2014.

67. Jeff Jensen, "*Room 237*: Exploring Stanley Kubrick's *Shining* influence," *Entertainment Weekly*, 6 April 2013.

68. Kubrick's perfectionism would occasionally cause his productions to fall behind schedule and to come in over budget. *2001* ended up two years behind schedule. (Michael Moorcock, "'Close to tears, he left at the intermission': how Stanley Kubrick upset Arthur C Clarke," *New Statesman*, 8 January 2017.) When *The Shining* fell behind schedule, it had the knock-on effect of blocking studio space for *Star Wars: Episode V—The Empire Strikes Back*. (Mark Clark, "You'll Find I'm Full of Surprises: Preproduction of *The Empire Strikes Back*" in *Star Wars FAQ: Everything Left to Know About the Trilogy That Changed the Movies* (2015).) Actor Matthew Modine recalled during the shooting of *Full Metal Jacket* that Kubrick's pursuit of perfection would lead him to go "dangerously overboard" and "way behind schedule." (Matthew Modine, *Full Metal Jacket Diary* (2005).)

69. Nolan's approach to filmmaking has ensured that the director has come in ahead of schedule and under budget on his major blockbuster films, which he deems essential to ensuring his creative independence from potential studio interference. (Tom Shone, "Christopher Nolan: the man who rebooted the blockbuster," *The Guardian*, 4 November 2014.)

70. Jim Emerson, "The framing of *The Dark Knight*," RogerEbert.com, 12 January 2009.

71. Germain Lussier, "Christopher Nolan Briefly Discusses *Interstellar* Influences," /Film, 8 April 2013.

72. Jeff Jensen, "Inside *Interstellar*, Christopher Nolan's emotional space odyssey," *Entertainment Weekly*, 16 October 2014.

73. "You're free to speculate as you wish about the philosophical and allegorical meaning of the film—and such speculation is one indication that it has succeeded in gripping the audience at a deep level—but I don't want to spell out a verbal road map for *2001* that every viewer will feel obligated to pursue or else fear he's missed the point," Kubrick explained of the film's more abstract qualities. (Eric Norden, "Interview: Stanley Kubrick," *Playboy*, September 1968.)

74. Brian Welk, "*Interstellar*," *The Sanity Clause*, 10 November 2014.

75. Siddhant Adlakha, "*Interstellar* and *2001: A Space Odyssey*—Echoes Through Time," *Birth. Movies. Death*, 3 April 2017.

76. Douglas Kellner, "Kubrick's *2001* and the dangers of technodystopia" in *Endangering Science Fiction Film* (2015), p. 28.

77. Sharon Waxman and T.R. Reid, "Stanley Kubrick, Cinema's Unsurpassed Cynic, Dies," *The Washington Post*, 8 March 1999.

78. Scott Feinberg, "Christopher Nolan on *Interstellar* Critics, Making Original Films and Shunning Cellphones and Email," *The Hollywood Reporter*, 3 January 2015.

79. Ciara Wardlow, "Christopher Nolan's Emotional Objects and the *Dunkirk* Exception," *Film School Rejects*, 26 July 2017.

80. Mike Symonds, "Film Crit Hulk SMASH: Christopher Nolan & The Cruelty Of Time," *Birth. Movies. Death*, 26 July 2017.

81. Stephen Rebello, "Playboy Interview: Christopher Nolan," *Playboy*, July/August 2017, p. 38.

82. Often, emotional relics are locked away in literal safes; Robert Fischer's toy and Mal's totem in *Inception*, Martha Wayne's pearls in *The Dark Knight Rises*. That security is important to Nolan's protagonists. As Bruce muses, "That's a beautiful necklace. Reminds me of one that belonged to my mother. It can't be the same one because her pearls are in this safe, which the manufacturer clearly explained is uncrackable."

83. Danny Bowes, "*Inception*: The First Blockbuster For Your Mind," *Tor*, 24 May 2011.

84. Jeff Jensen, "Inside *Interstellar*, Christopher Nolan's emotional space odyssey," *Entertainment Weekly*, 16 October 2014.

85. Indeed "gravity" is a Nolan shorthand for abstract concepts that act upon the physical universe. In *The Dark Knight*, the Joker likens "madness" to gravity, suggesting that it similarly offers an irresistible pull.

86. In many ways, the climax of *Interstellar* is a very straight-up and unquestioning execution of the sort of emotional catharsis that Nolan deconstructed at the climax of *Inception*.

87. At the risk of engaging in cultural stereotypes, mainstream American cinema (of the kind defined by *Interstellar*'s original director, Steven Spielberg) has a tendency to embrace sentimentality and emotionality. It could be argued that American culture is more emotive and expressive than British culture. (See, for example, Terry Eagleton, "The Outgoing Spirit" in *Across the Pond: An Englishman's View of America* (2014), p. 44–72.)

88. Tom Shone, "Christopher Nolan: the man who rebooted the blockbuster," *The Guardian*, 4 November 2014.

89. Jeff Jensen, "Inside *Interstellar*, Christopher Nolan's emotional space odyssey," *Entertainment Weekly*, 16 October 2014.

90. Nev Pierce, "Jonathan Nolan Talks *Interstellar*," *ShortList*, November 2014

91. In some ways, that circuitous route is reflected in the plotting of the film. Cooper leaves his family behind to journey into deep space, but eventually returns to them ending up right back in a replica of the farm house that he resented for so long. He then leaves on another adventure, to go and find Brand. Nolan talks about taking the typical call to adventure and "looping it back on itself." (Christopher Nolan and Jonathan Nolan, *Interstellar: The Complete Screenplay With Selected Storyboards* (2014).)

92. Steve Weintraub, "Christopher Nolan, Matthew McConaughey, Anne Hathaway, and More Talk *Interstellar*, the Evolution of the Script, and Grounding the Film with Emotion," *Collider*, 8 November 2014.

93. Peter Sciretta, "Interview: *Interstellar* Writer Jonathan Nolan: Real Space Exploration Is 'Fucking Done, We Peaked!'," */Film*, 6 November 2014.

94. This recurring fascination with drowning can be seen at various points in Nolan's filmography. In *Insomnia*, Dormer gets trapped underwater while chasing Finch. In *The Prestige*, Robert Angier obsesses with the drowning of his wife to the point that he also plans to drown one hundred clones of himself. In *Inception*, a car packed with sleeping characters plunges towards the river, while the opening shot has Cobb washed up on a beach. In *The Dark Knight Rises*, exiled parties wander out on to the ice to be swallowed up by Gotham Bay. In *Dunkirk*, Collins almost drowns in his spitfire and Tommy repeatedly almost drowns while trying to get off the beach.

95. This is mirrored by the situation on Earth. Brand notes that the blight is making the Earth's atmosphere richer in nitrogen. "The last people to starve will be the first to suffocate." Murph later accuses Brand, "You left us here, to suffocate, to starve."

96. Jeff Jensen, "Inside *Interstellar*, Christopher Nolan's emotional space odyssey," *Entertainment Weekly*, 16 October 2014.

97. Stephen Galloway, "*Interstellar*'s Christopher Nolan, Stars Gather to Reveal Secrets of the Year's Most Mysterious Film," *The Hollywood Reporter*, 22 October 2014.

98. Sam Ashurst, "Jessica Chastain's *Interstellar* gender-swap," *Dazed*, 5 November 2014.

99. James Rocchi, "Interview: *Interstellar* Co-Writer Jonathan Nolan on *Close Encounters*, Rewrites & More," *IndieWire*, 4 November 2014.

100. "Chicago journalists smell a Bat in *Rory's First Kiss*," *The Guardian*, 19 July 2007.

101. Charlie James Anders, "Is Christopher Nolan's *Interstellar* really about climate disaster?," *io9*, 31 August 2013.

102. Jeff Jensen, "Inside *Interstellar*, Christopher Nolan's emotional space odyssey," *Entertainment Weekly*, 16 October 2014.

103. Tom Shone, "Christopher Nolan: the man who rebooted the blockbuster," *The Guardian*, 4 November 2014.

104. Mike Symonds, "Film Crit Hulk SMASH: Christopher Nolan & The Cruelty Of Time," *Birth. Movies. Death*, 26 July 2017.

105. Chet Betz, "Christopher Nolan's War on Time," *Paste Magazine*, 30 July 2017.

106. Andrei Tarkovsky, *Sculpting in Time* (1987).

107. Notably, while films like *The Dark Knight*, *Inception* and *The Dark Knight Rises* all use crosscutting to illustrate how characters are connected to one another despite being dislocated in time and space, *Interstellar* uses crosscutting to emphasize the gap that exists between Cooper and his children on Earth. The fight between Mann and Cooper on a distant world is crosscut with Murph's fight against Tom; although the two conflicts parallel one another in thematic terms, emphasizing Cooper and Murph's refusal to give up, they do not connect directly or literally. It could be argued that the entirety of *Dunkirk* is crosscutting, with the three stories briefly aligning at the climax before disentangling again towards the end of the film.

108. James Charisma, "From *Memento* to *Dunkirk*, All Christopher Nolan Movies Are About This One Thing," *Playboy*, 21 July 2016.

109. Interestingly enough, Nolan's recurring fixation with drowning may even play into this theme. In *Heat*, a Michael Mann movie for which Nolan has an avowed fondness, one character shares his recurring dream about drowning. His colleague responds, "You know what that's about?" The dreamer replies, "Yeah. Having enough time."

110. Liz Baessler, "The Evolution of Christopher Nolan's Widowers," *Film School Rejects*, 15 August 2017.

111. Oliver Lytteton, "How Parenthood Is At The Heart Of *Interstellar* & Other Christopher Nolan Films," *IndieWire*, 11 November 2014.

112. Ben Child, "Christopher Nolan explains *Inception*'s ending: 'I

want you to chase your reality'," *The Guardian*, 5 June 2015.

113. Philip Pirrello, "15 Unbelievable Story Beats *Interstellar* Got Away With," *Comic Book Resources*, 12 November 2014.

114. Kyle Hill, "Jonathan Nolan's Ending to *Interstellar* Made A Lot More Sense," *The Nerdist*, 19 March 2015.

115. "There's been a lot of research that's been done on whether the laws of physics permit travel back in time or not, and we've got interesting results but no firm answers," explains scientific advisor Kip Thorne. "In that area Chris made his own rule set, which we discussed at length when he described it to me early last year. And it's a rule set for which I then could find a scientific rationale, but it was a rule set that was much less constrained by the laws of physics because we don't understand the laws of physics in that domain yet!" (Lee Billings, "Parsing the Science of *Interstellar* with Physicist Kip Thorne," *Scientific American*, 28 November 2014.)

116. "Jessica Chastain: *Interstellar* isn't about science, it's about love," *CBS News*, 30 October 2014.

117. WENN, "Christopher Nolan Kept *Interstellar* Plot Secret From Composer," *Contact Music*, 2 April 2014.

118. Tom Shone, "Christopher Nolan: the man who rebooted the blockbuster," *The Guardian*, 4 November 2014.

119. Vince Mancini, "The Trouble With 70 MM…," *Uproxx*, 4 November 2014.

120. Sean O'Neal, "*Interstellar* receiving complaints that it's just too darn loud," *The A.V. Club*, 14 November 2014.

121. Katie Kilkenny, "Why *Interstellar*'s Organ Needs to Be So Loud," *The Atlantic*, 11 November 2014.

122. Cooper's love of his children allows him to find the strength to fight back against Mann long enough to re-establish communication with Brand to warn her that Mann plans to strand them on the surface. Similarly, Cooper's love of his children convinces him to sacrifice himself in the hope of recovering useful data from inside the black hole.

123. Studies suggest that such cold and rational decision-making is largely an illusion and that important and key decisions are often influenced by facts as trivial as the weather. (Vivian Giang, "The Myth Of Rational Decision-Making," *Fast Company*, 6 July 2015.)

124. "Send 60-year-old astronauts to Mars on a one-way trip to save money, say scientists," *The Daily Mail*, 17 November 2010.

125. When Cooper discovers that TARS' honesty setting is only at ninety percent, the robot helpfully explains, "Absolute honesty isn't always the most diplomatic, nor the safest form of communication with emotional beings." The implication is that all humans are emotional beings, even those without overt emotional attachments to others.

126. Daniel Clery, "Physicist who inspired *Interstellar* spills the backstory—and the scene that makes him cringe," *Science Magazine*, 6 November 2014.

127. Jolene Creighton, "The Mind-bending Physics Behind *Interstellar*, with Neil deGrasse Tyson & Christopher Nolan," *Futurism*, 22 May 2015.

128. "One of the things that I found really inspiring about working with [Kip] is that, when I would ask him a question, he would never answer in the moment," recalls Nolan of his relationship with Thorne. "He might give me his initial thought of, 'OK, I don't think that's possible, but let me go away.' He would always go away and spend a couple of days doing his own calculations and talking to other scientists and researching all the different papers that had been published on the subject, and then he would come back with an answer." (Stephen Galloway, "*Interstellar*'s Christopher Nolan, Stars Gather to Reveal Secrets of the Year's Most Mysterious Film," *The Hollywood Reporter*, 22 October 2014.)

129. Adam Rogers, "The Metaphysics of *Interstellar*," *Wired*, November 2014.

130. Alasdair Richmond, "*Interstellar* gives a spectacular view of hard science," *The Conversation*, 10 November 2014.

131. Natalie Zutter, "Why Do We Reject Love as a Powerful Force in *Interstellar*?," *Tor*, 13 November 2013.

132. Madhu Dubey, "Becoming Animal in Black Women's Science Fiction," in *Afro-Future Females: Black Writers Chart Science Fiction's Newest New-Wave Trajectory* (2008), p. 31–32.

133. As with any commentary on gender divisions, this is something of a generalization; there are undoubtedly female fans who like trivia and statistics and male fans who like fan fiction and relationships. However, studies of fandom do suggest that such activities are gendered. (Constance Grady, "Why we're terrified of fanfiction," *Vox*, 2 June 2016; Henry Jenkins, *Textual Poachers: Television Fans and Participatory Culture* (1992).)

134. In some respects, the casting of Matt Damon in the role of "Doctor Mann" invites comparisons to Ridley Scott's *The Martian*, which would be released the following year. Like *Interstellar*, *The Martian* was a science-fiction story that adopted the trappings of hard science-fiction, including a great deal of attention to scientific and procedural accuracy. (Jeffrey Kluger, "What *The Martian* Gets Right (and Wrong) About Science," *Time*, 18 May 2016.) However, *The Martian* has also been criticized for embracing the clichés associated with hard science-fiction that *Interstellar* subverts. It is perhaps too much to argue that *The Martian* is *Interstellar* from Doctor Mann's perspective, but the film adopts a very stereotypically masculine perspective as expected within the framework of conventional "hard" science-fiction. (Katy Waldman, "*The Martian* Glorifies Nerd Dudes. What Does It Have to Offer Nerd Ladies?," *Slate*, 7 October 2015.) Similarly, *The Martian* largely eschews emotion in favor of rationalism. As critic Richard Brody observes, "Scott isn't interested in what Mark is going through emotionally or psychologically—or, for that matter, in who Mark is—but only in what Mark does." (Richard Brody, "What's Missing from *The Martian*," *The New Yorker*, 9 October 2015.) This is to say nothing of the uncomfortable subtext of the recurring gag where Mark hates disco, given the cultural history of the musical style involves a legacy of aggressive hostility towards the genre from straight white men. (Hadley Meares, "The night when straight white males tried to kill disco," *Aeon*, 28 February 2017.)

135. Anna Klassen, "Christopher Nolan's Feminist *Interstellar* Isn't His First Pro-Women Film," *Bustle*, 28 October 2014.

136. Mike Fleming, Jr., "Is Christopher Nolan Giving *Interstellar* Lead To Matthew McConaughey?," *Deadline*, 28 March 2013.

137. Trying to console Murph as he leaves, Cooper assures her, "After you kids came along, your mom said something to me I never quite understood. She said, 'Now, we're just here to be memories for our kids.'

And I think that now I understand what she meant. Once you're a parent, you're the ghost of your children's future." This description of Coop evokes the image of Mal haunting Cobb's subconscious in *Inception*, or Bruce's flashbacks of Thomas Wayne in *Batman Begins*.

138. Simon Brew, "*Interstellar* to be Christopher Nolan's longest film," *Den of Geek*, 29 September 2014.

139. Dave McNary, "Christopher Nolan Starts Shooting *Interstellar*," *Variety*, 13 August 2013.

140. Kristina Skorbach, "6 Things You Probably Didn't Know About *Interstellar*," *The Epoch Times*, 3 November 2014.

141. Adam Rogers, "Wrinkles in Spacetime: The Warped Astrophysics of *Interstellar*," *Wired*, October 2014.

## Chapter 10

1. Kelly Scott, "Why Dunkirk is a source of inspiration for Brits—and filmmakers," *The Los Angeles Times*, 14 July 2017.

2. Penny Summerfield, "Dunkirk and the Popular Memory of Britain at War, 1940–58," *Journal of Contemporary History*, November 2010.

3. Although, interestingly, there is an element folk history at work here as well. People who lived through the Second World War have claimed to have heard Churchill deliver his iconic "we shall fight on the beaches…" speech delivered to the House of Commons on 4 June 1940, despite the fact that no audio recording of the speech exists and it was not broadcast. Churchill would record an audio version of the script in 1949, after the end of the Second World War, arguably cultivating the myth. (Richard Toye, *The Roar of the Lion: The Untold Story of Churchill's World War II Speeches* (2013), p. 70–71.) Indeed, there is some debate over whether or not Churchill's rhetoric helped boost the morale of the British public at the time, in spite of the mythology that has developed around his speeches in the aftermath of the Second World War. (Jasper Copping, "Winston Churchill's speeches were overrated and some 'went down badly'," *The Telegraph*, 20 August 2013.)

4. Rachel Lewis, "Why the British Still Talk About the 'Dunkirk Spirit'," *Time*, 20 July 2017.

5. Steven MacKenzie, "Back to the beaches of Dunkirk," *The Big Issue*, 20 July 2017.

6. Cara Buckley, "Christopher Nolan's Latest Time-Bending Feat? *Dunkirk*," *The New York Times*, 12 July 2017.

7. Andreas Wiseman, "Christopher Nolan explains why *Dunkirk* was a gamble that required a 'leap of faith'," *Screen Daily*, 11 December 2017.

8. Steven MacKenzie, "Back to the beaches of Dunkirk," *The Big Issue*, 20 July 2017.

9. Rebecca Keegan, "Meet the Woman Behind *Dunkirk*," *Vanity Fair*, 16 February 2018.

10. James Barber, "*Dunkirk* Rethinks the War Movie: Historian Joshua Levine Shares His Experiences Working With Director Christopher Nolan," Military.com, 21 July 2017.

11. Gill Pringle and Will Tentindo, "Christopher Nolan and Emma Thomas: Making *Dunkirk*," *FilmInk*, 11 July 2017.

12. Joe Utichi, "For Christopher Nolan's Producer And Partner Emma Thomas, Maintaining A Winning Streak Is Essential," *Deadline*, 23 February 2018.

13. Irish actors Cillian Murphy and Barry Keoghan would be included in the primary cast, but both actors adopt British accents.

14. Indeed, Nolan himself has conceded that his dual citizenship has informed and shaped his creative output. (Sid Smith, "*Insomnia* director Nolan doesn't rest on his *Memento* laurels," *The Chicago Tribune*, 27 May 2002.)

15. This obsession can arguably be traced back to concepts like "manifest destiny" and "providence," reinforced through imagery like the unstoppable railroad engine, suggesting that the relatively young nation's future was promised and assured. (Michael S. Burdett, "The Religion of Technology: Transhumanism and the Myth of Progress," in *Religion and Transhumanism: The Unknown Future of Human Enhancement* (2014), p. 131–148.) It is also reinforced by America's role as a world leader in politics, technology and culture since the end of the Second World War. (Ian Bremmer, "The Era of American Global Leadership is Over. Here's What Comes Next," *Time*, 19 December 2016.)

16. Ishaan Tharoor, "Brexit and Britain's delusions of empire," *The Washington Post*, 31 March 2017.

17. Of course, *Interstellar* is threaded with a nostalgia for old-fashioned optimism and idealism, a weird nostalgia for the future that could be seen to reflect broader contemporary debates about the relationship between nostalgia and futurism in American popular culture. (Samuel Goldman, "Romney and Nostalgic Futurism," *The American Conservative*, 31 August 2012.) Nevertheless, *Interstellar* is still an optimistic science-fiction epic set in the future.

18. Much like the nostalgic futurism of *Interstellar* could be paralleled with contemporary political discourse in the United States, *Dunkirk* arrived at a moment in time when it seemed to tap into the British cultural and political psyche, particularly as it related to the "Brexit" vote. (Rafael Behr, "*Dunkirk* reveals the spirit that has driven Brexit: humiliation," *The Guardian*, 26 July 2017.)

19. Andreas Wiseman, "Christopher Nolan explains why *Dunkirk* was a gamble that required a 'leap of faith'," *Screen Daily*, 11 December 2017.

20. Eric Kohn, "Christopher Nolan Explains Why *Dunkirk* Is His Most Personal Film Yet," *IndieWire*, 21 July 2017.

21. Veteran Vic Viner allegedly told the director that was impossible to accurately convey the subjective experience of living through those events, explaining, "You can't tell anybody what it was like. You had to have been there." (Richard Hartley-Parkinson, "One of final Dunkirk rescue survivors dies aged 99," *The Metro*, 2 October 2016.)

22. Andy Lewis, "Making of *Dunkirk*: Christopher Nolan's Obsessive $100M Re-creation of the Pivotal WWII Battle," *The Hollywood Reporter*, 5 January 2018.

23. Joey Pucino, "Prince Harry meets veterans ahead of *Dunkirk* premiere," *The Sydney Morning Herald*, 14 July 2017.

24. Roisin O'Connor, "*Dunkirk* veteran in tears at Christopher Nolan film premiere: 'It was just like I was there again'," *The Independent*, 24 July 2017.

25. Emma Stefansky, "Dunkirk Vets Say Nolan's Movie Was Louder Than the Real Thing," *Vanity Fair*, 22 July 2017.

26. Eliza Berman, "Christopher Nolan: *Dunkirk* Is My Most Experimental Film Since *Memento*," *Time*, 19 July 2017.

27. Clarisse Loughrey, "*Dunkirk*: Christopher Nolan says his WWII

epic is 'not a war film,'" *The Independent*, 5 April 2017.

28. Brent Lang, "Christopher Nolan Gets Candid on the State of Movies, Rise of TV and Spielberg's Influence," *Variety*, November 2017.

29. David Bordwell, "*Dunkirk* Part 2: The art film as event movie," *Observations on Film Art*, 9 August 2017.

30. Charlie Jane Anders, "Genre Directors Who Have Never Made a Bad Movie," *io9*, 24 July 2012.

31. Even coming up to the film's release, journalist Hoai-Tran Bui argued that *Dunkirk* was a "strange choice" for the director. (Hoai-Tran Bui, "*Dunkirk* Review Round-Up: A Stirring Spectacle That is One of the Year's Best Films," */Film*, 18 July 2017.)

32. Michelle Lanz, "Christopher Nolan didn't want *Dunkirk* to compete with *Saving Private Ryan*," *The Frame*, 29 November 2017.

33. William Earl, "Christopher Nolan Reveals How 11 Classic Films Inspired *Dunkirk*," *IndieWire*, 25 May 2017.

34. Rohan Naahar, "Weekend Binge: The 11 films that inspired Christopher Nolan to make *Dunkirk*," *The Hindustan Times*, 1 September 2017.

35. Jake Coyle, "Q & A: Christopher Nolan on the craft of *Dunkirk*," *The Associated Press*, 2 February 2018.

36. Dan McLaughlin, "*Dunkirk* Is A Horror Movie," *National Review*, 31 July 2017.

37. Nolan's framing underscores the horror and absurdity of the situation. In theory, the beach is a wide open space in comparison to the town itself, but it also represents a trap. The English Channel forms a clear barrier, a reminder of how cornered these troops are even in this wide open space. As such, Nolan frames these scenes with long columns; the flag poles, the make-shift jetties, the queues of soldiers standing around waiting. These columns become bars on a prison cell, demonstrating just how trapped these men are.

38. Aoife Barry, "Why the epic *Dunkirk* was the hardest film Christopher Nolan has made," *The Journal*, 17 July 2017.

39. Christopher Hooton, "The Shepard tone: The auditory illusion that makes Hans Zimmer's *Dunkirk* score so powerful and even shaped the screenplay," *The Independent*, 27 July 2017.

40. Lewis McGregor, "The Power of Sound: Using the Shepard Tone In Filmmaking," *Premium Beat*, 27 July 2017.

41. Blair Jackson, "Batman Rides Again: *The Dark Knight*," *Mix*, 1 July 2008.

42. Jason Guerrasio, "Christopher Nolan explains the 'audio illusion' that created the unique music in *Dunkirk*," *Business Insider*, 24 July 2017.

43. Michelle Lanz, "Christopher Nolan didn't want *Dunkirk* to compete with *Saving Private Ryan*," *The Frame*, 29 November 2017.

44. Running one hour and forty-six minutes, *Dunkirk* is one of only three of Nolan's films to clock in at under two hours; *Following* and *Insomnia* are the other two, and could be considered relatively outliers in his filmography.

45. The difference in length is not merely academic; *Dunkirk* is fifty-nine minutes shorter than *The Dark Knight Rises* and one hour and three minutes shorter than *Interstellar*. Such differences are appreciable.

46. Kevin P. Sullivan, "How Christopher Nolan crafted his WWII masterpiece, *Dunkirk*," *Entertainment Weekly*, 18 July 2017.

47. Jake Coyle, "Q & A: Christopher Nolan on the craft of *Dunkirk*," *The Associated Press*, 2 February 2018.

48. Kristen Thompson, "*Dunkirk* Part 1: Straight to the good stuff," *Observations on Film Art*, 2 August 2017.

49. Joe Utichi, "For Christopher Nolan's Producer And Partner Emma Thomas, Maintaining A Winning Streak Is Essential," *Deadline*, 23 February 2018.

50. Todd McCarthy described the film as "an impressionist masterpiece." (Todd McCarthy, "*Dunkirk*: Film Review," *The Hollywood Reporter*, 17 July 2017.) Ignatiy Vishnevetsky remarked that the film was "a big-boy white elephant art film that is actually a lean and mean suspense set-piece machine." (Ignatiy Vishnevetsky, "Christopher Nolan goes to war in the thrilling *Dunkirk*," *The A.V. Club*, 18 July 2017.)

51. Christopher Nolan, *Dunkirk* (2017).

52. Matt Grobar, "Producer Emma Thomas On *Dunkirk*; Patty Jenkins Talks *Wonder Woman* & Denis Villenueve On *Blade Runner 2049*—The Contenders," *Deadline*, 4 November 2017.

53. On the film's release, there were complaints that the dialogue was too hard to hear. (Chris O'Falt, "*Dunkirk* Is Too Loud For Some Viewers, But Christopher Nolan Says That's the Way He Likes It," *IndieWire*, 26 July 2017.) Nolan responded to such criticism of the sound mix in *Interstellar* by pointing out that dialogue is just one part of the larger sound mix, "I don't agree with the idea that you can only achieve clarity through dialogue. Clarity of story, clarity of emotions—I try to achieve that in a very layered way using all the different things at my disposal—picture and sound. I've always loved films that approach sound in an impressionistic way and that is an unusual approach for a mainstream blockbuster, but I feel it's the right approach for this experiential film." (Carolyn Giardina, "Christopher Nolan Breaks Silence on *Interstellar* Sound (Exclusive)," *The Hollywood Reporter*, 15 November 2014.) *Dunkirk* just carries the same idea even further.

54. Andreas Wiseman, "Christopher Nolan explains why *Dunkirk* was a gamble that required a 'leap of faith'," *Screen Daily*, 11 December 2017.

55. Like Stories of Old, "*Dunkirk* re-edited as a Silent Film—The Power of Visual Storytelling," *YouTube*, 28 July 2017

56. Daniel Clarke, "Show, Don't Tell: Christopher Nolan's Reliance on Dialogue," Seroword, 3 December 2014.

57. Robert Capps, "Q&A: Christopher Nolan on Dreams, Architecture, and Ambiguity," *Wired*, 29 November 2010.

58. This is particularly true in the films that follow *Inception*. The expanded roles for female characters in *The Dark Knight Rise* and *Interstellar* feel very much like a response to criticisms about how the director wrote female characters in earlier films. The strong emotional storytelling in *Interstellar* plays like a conscious rejection of criticisms of Nolan as an unfeeling and cynical technician.

59. Glenn Whipp, "Christopher Nolan on the power of the people and why 2001 should be required preschool viewing," *The Los Angeles Times*, 4 January 2018.

60. Andreas Wiseman, "Christopher Nolan explains why *Dunkirk* was a gamble that required a 'leap of faith'," *Screen Daily*, 11 December 2017.

61. Indeed, this reflected in the number of "explainer" articles that were published about the evacuation

on American pop culture websites in the lead-up to the release of the film. (For example: Nate Jones, "A Clueless American's Guide to the Battle of Dunkirk," *Vulture*, 19 July 2017.)

62. John Podhoretz, "Undone Dunkirk," *The Weekly Standard*, 28 July 2017.

63. A recurring theme of the awards-season "anonymous voter" pieces was a tendency to criticize *Dunkirk* for its perceived lack of clarity. One voter complained that they "learned more about Dunkirk from five minutes of *Darkest Hour* than [they] did from the whole movie *Dunkirk*," as if to suggest that films should be treated as history text books. (Scott Feinberg, "Brutally Honest Oscar Ballot #2: *Get Out* Filmmakers 'Played the Race Card,' 'Just Sick of' Meryl Streep," *The Hollywood Reporter*, 2 March 2018.) Another complained, "I wasn't familiar with Dunkirk in my history, and I didn't know it's in France. And they never explained it." (Michael Musto, "Confessions of an Oscar Voter: Why I Loved *Three Billboards* and Don't Get *Get Out*," *The Daily Beast*, 13 February 2018.)

64. Paraag Shukla, "Exclusive: Christopher Nolan on *Dunkirk*," *HistoryNet*, 5 July 2017.

65. Erik Davis, "Interview: Christopher Nolan on the Extreme Lengths They Took to Bring *Dunkirk* to Life," *Fandango*, 16 July 2017.

66. Bryan Alexander, "Meet the nightmare of Christopher Nolan's *Dunkirk*: The mole," *USA Today*, 19 July 2017.

67. Indeed, Nolan's big pitch for *Dunkirk*, as the director related in interviews leading up to the release of the film, was "virtual reality without the goggles." (Bryan Bishop, "Watch Christopher Nolan explain why he thinks *Dunkirk* in IMAX is like 'virtual reality without the goggles,'" *The Verge*, 12 July 2017.)

68. Cillian Murphy's character is identified only as "Shivering Sailor," despite being important enough to appear in two of the three timelines running through the film. Aneurin Barnard plays a character who is identified as "Gibson" early in the film, but who is later revealed to be an imposter; despite the fact that he is one of the most prominent characters in the film, the audience never learns his real name.

69. For a brief history of the term, and its origins that can be traced back to the eighteenth century, see for example: Tom Carew, *How the Regiments Got Their Nicknames* (1974). Even Nolan himself seems to regard "Tommy" as a name more than a character, talking in interviews about "when we had to search for the lead role we call 'Tommy.'" ("Interview: Christopher Nolan," *Playboy*, 30 August 2017.)

70. Roger Ebert, "Ebert's Walk of Fame remarks," RogerEbert.com, 24 June 2005.

71. Christopher Zumski Finke, "Watching movies may help you build empathy," *Yes! Magazine*, 21 October 2015.

72. Angie Han, "Why Diversity in Film Matters More Than Ever," */Film*, 17 November 2016.

73. In the year that *Dunkirk* was released, *Moonlight* won the Best Picture Oscar at the annual Academy Awards. A large amount of the coverage of the film emphasized the importance of the film in inspiring empathy for viewers who might not have the same pool of life experiences as the protagonist Chiron, a lower-class gay black child growing up in Miami. (See, for example: Angelica Jade Bastién, "The Empathy Machine: Why *Moonlight* Isn't Universal and That's a Good Thing," *Cléo*, 21 April 2017; Imad Pasha, "Empathy, authenticity and resonance in *Moonlight*: why its Best Picture win transcends representation," *The Daily Californian*, 9 March 2017; MaryAnn Johanson, "*Moonlight* movie review: the empathy machine in action (but only if you're watching)," *FlickFilosopher*, 16 November 2016.) The following year, when *Dunkirk* competed for the Best Picture Oscar at the Academy Awards, the award went to *The Shape of Water*, another film largely defined by its capacity to generate empathy for characters who were "othered." (Brian Welk, "Guillermo del Toro Says *The Shape of Water* Teaches Empathy for 'the Other,'" *The Wrap*, 10 February 2018.)

74. Joe Utichi, "For Christopher Nolan's Producer And Partner Emma Thomas, Maintaining A Winning Streak Is Essential," *Deadline*, 23 February 2018.

75. David Canfield, "Christopher Nolan Didn't Really Know Who Harry Styles Was When He Cast Him in *Dunkirk*," *Vulture*, 9 July 2017.

76. Asked about the decision to put Tom Hardy in *another* mask after the mask in *The Dark Knight Rises*, Nolan playfully explained, "I was pretty thrilled with what he did in *The Dark Knight Rises* with two eyes and couple of eyebrows and a bit of forehead so I thought let's see what he can do with no forehead, no real eyebrows, maybe one eye." (Laura Harding, "Christopher Nolan reveals why Tom Hardy likes to cover his face in films," *The Independent*, 16 July 2017.)

77. Stephen Rebello, "*Playboy* Interview: Christopher Nolan on *Dunkirk* & the Creeping Relevance of *The Dark Knight*," *Playboy*, 11 July 2017.

78. Lindsey Bahr, "Q&A: Nolan previews adrenaline rushing war epic *Dunkirk*," *ABC News*, 3 April 2017.

79. Actor Harry Styles confesses that he felt a real and tangible panic while filming the scenes. (Bryan Alexander, "Harry Styles felt real underwater panic shooting terrifying *Dunkirk* scenes," *USA Today*, 15 July 2017.) Much of the critical response to the film emphasized the visceral quality of the film. (Brian Roan, "The Visceral Physicality of Christopher Nolan's *Dunkirk*," The Film Stage, 22 July 2017; Kate Taylor, "Review: *Dunkirk* gives a visceral sense of the danger and desperation of war," *The Globe and Mail*, 20 July 2017.)

80. Cobb in *Inception* and Cooper in *Interstellar* are the most literal examples, but Leonard attempting to recreate his married life with a prostitute in *Memento* and Borden promising to his daughter that he will come back to her in *The Prestige* are also examples.

81. As with a lot of *Dunkirk*, *Interstellar* seems to pave the way to this stylistic choice, featuring both a death by drowning *and* an attempted suffocation. However, *Memento* and *Batman Begins* feature characters suffocating or struggling to breath; both *Insomnia*, *The Prestige* and *The Dark Knight Rises* feature characters who drown or are almost drowned.

82. *Dunkirk* is not the first time that Nolan has made this juxtaposition. The comparison comes up in *The Prestige*. After the death of Julia McCullough in a drowning stunt that goes wrong, John Cutter tries to reassure her widowed husband, Robert Angier, telling a story about an old sailor who drowned and "said it was like going home." In one of the last lines of the film, Cutter confronts Angier and corrects his earlier account. "I was lying. He said it was agony." In some ways, *Dunkirk* feels like that metaphor expanded to the length of a feature film; "home" and "suffocation" juxtaposed as primal expressions of "life" and "death."

83. Mehera Bonner, "I Think *Dunkirk* Was Mediocre at Best, and It's Not Because I'm Some Naive Woman Who Doesn't Get It," *Marie Claire*, 28 July 2017.

84. Sunny Singh, "Why the lack of Indian and African faces in *Dunkirk* matters," *The Guardian*, 1 August 2017.

85. Jaime Weinman, "Hot takes and problematic faves: the rise of socially conscious criticism," *Vox*, 23 April 2017.

86. It should be noted that some of this debate about representation and diversity is retroactive in nature, with various critics and commentators engaging with historic portrayals and venerated artists. For example, Quentin Tarantino has been highly critical of John Ford's treatment of Native American characters within his westerns. (Matt Singer, "Quentin Tarantino Says He Hates John Ford," *IndieWire*, 27 December 2012.) Similarly, there has been retroactive discussion about the behavior of *auteur* directors that would have been tolerated in the past, but would be called out today. (Elahe Izadi, "Why the *Last Tango in Paris* rape scene is generating such an outcry now," *The Washington Post*, 5 December 2016.)

87. John Broich, "What's Fact and What's Fiction in *Dunkirk*," *Slate*, 20 July 2017.

88. In fact, it should be noted that *Dunkirk* depicts greater diversity among the French forces on the beach, particularly noticeable during the stretcher sequence. This arguably fits with the historical record, given that there was much greater representation of French colonies in the French army than Indian troops in the British army at Dunkirk. (Franz-Stefan Gady, "No, India's Army Did Not Play a 'Significant Role' at Dunkirk," *The Diplomat*, 8 August 2017.)

89. Perhaps the most prominent character of color in Nolan's filmography is Lucius Fox, the tech wizard played by Morgan Freeman in *Batman Begins*, *The Dark Knight* and *The Dark Knight Rises*. However, this character originated in the source material, introduced by writer Len Wein and artist John Calnan in *Batman (1940) #307* (January 1979). As such, it seems unreasonable to credit Nolan for this example.

90. For example, casting Liam Neeson as Ra's Al Ghul in *Batman Begin* deftly sidesteps a lot of the orientalism associated with the character.

(Desmond White, "Could Dwayne Johnson's Black Adam Contribute to Orientalism?," *Sequart*, 6 October 2014.) Similarly, in *Interstellar*, the death of the white Doyle before the black Romilly could be seen as a slight subversion of the familiar cliché that "the black dude dies first" in horror and science-fiction films. (Matt Barone, "Fact Check: Do Black Characters Always Die First in Horror Movies?," *Complex*, 31 October 2013.)

91. As Nolan's filmography progresses, characters and actors of color become more prominent. *Inception* features Ken Watanabe as Saito and Dileep Rao as Yusuf, both members of the heist time. *Interstellar* features David Oyelowo in a small, but early and important, role as the school principle and David Gyasi as the scientist Romilly. These are relatively slim pickings in a career spanning two decades and ten films.

92. *See*, for example: Roger Ebert, "*Platoon*," *The Chicago Sun Times*, 30 December 1986; Tom Brook, "Is there any such thing as an anti-war film'?," *BBC*, 10 July 2014; "Your Turn: Truffaut was right," *The Sydney Morning Herald*, 24 October 2011.

93. Quoted in Antoine de Baecque and Serge Toubiana, *François Truffaut* (2000), p. 164.

94. Sometimes the military provides access to production crews in return for exposure and favorable coverage. (Steve Rose, "The U.S. military storm Hollywood," *The Guardian*, 6 July 2009.) In other cases, the link is more blatant; there is strong evidence that the release of *Top Gun* saw recruitment numbers for the United States Air Force soar. (Mark Evje, "*Top Gun* Boosting Service Sign-ups," *The Los Angeles*, 5 July 1986.)

95. James Fallows, "The Tragedy of the American Military," *The Atlantic*, January/February 2015.

96. Frank Newport, "Almost All Americans Consider World War II a 'Just' War," *Gallup*, 3 June 2004.

97. Most of these references are made in relation to characters who are pointedly not German; Alex accuses a Dutch sailor of being a "Kraut" and a "German," and very briefly alludes to the possibility that the French soldier posing as "Gibson" might be a "bloody Jerry."

98. Sonny Bunch, "Hollywood has long denounced Nazis. *Dunkirk* didn't need to remind us what we already know," *The Washington Post*, 16 August 2017.

99. The clearest shot of German soldiers comes towards the very end of the film, as Farrier is arrested on the beach.

100. The original flier features "Les Allies—The Allied" surrounded by "Les Allemands—The Germans." The Version portrayed in the film instead portrays a more generic "we" surrounding "you." (Justin T. Westbrook, "The Real History Behind The Story Of *Dunkirk*," *Gizmodo*, 24 July 2017.)

101. Ashley Lee, "Why Mark Rylance Hopes *Dunkirk* Speaks to Younger Viewers (Thanks to Harry Styles)," *The Hollywood Reporter*, 20 July 2017.

102. To pick an arbitrary example from another big budget summer blockbuster, *Captain America: The Winter Soldier* awkwardly undercut its own criticism of the United States military-industrial complex by revealing that its villains were literal Nazis, from German during the Second World War. (Alyssa Rosenberg, "What *Captain America: The Winter Soldier* gets very wrong," *The Washington Post*, 10 April 2014.)

103. For example, statistics argue that the average age of an American soldier during the Vietnam War was twenty-two years of age. (James Westheider, *Fighting in Vietnam: The Experiences of the U.S. Soldier* (2011), p. 107.) Sean Penn was twenty-nine years old when he played the lead role of such a soldier in *Casualties of War*, and Martin Sheen was thirty-nine years old when he played the lead role of such a soldier in *Apocalypse Now*.

104. Kevin P. Sullivan, "How Christopher Nolan crafted his WWII masterpiece, *Dunkirk*," *Entertainment Weekly*, 18 July 2017.

105. Brian Brooks, "Christopher Nolan Tells New York Crowd He Prefers Blu-ray To Netflix," *Deadline*, 19 July 2017.

106. Noah Berlatsky, "How Christopher Nolan's *Dunkirk* Finds New Ways to Subvert the Tropes of the War Film," *Slate*, 21 July 2017.

107. David Bordwell, "*Dunkirk* Part 2: The art film as event movie," *Observations on Film Art*, 9 August 2017.

108. Indeed, the film's marketing was built around the tagline "survival is victory." (Sean Wist, "Survival is Victory in the New Trailer for Christopher Nolan's *Dunkirk*," *Jo Blo's Movie Emporium*, 14 December 2016; Grant Davis, "Three New *Dunkirk* Banners Show That In War, Survival

Is Victory," *Heroic Hollywood*, 13 June 2017.) This is reflected in the script, with Alex confronts the blind man on returning to Britain. "Well done, lads," the old man states. "All we did is survive," Alex responds. The old man assures him, "That's enough."

109. In terms of Nolan's filmography, there is a sense that the behavior of the evacuating soldiers in *Dunkirk* could be seen to vindicate Bane's cynical view of human nature in *The Dark Knight Rises*, almost literally; from his description of "shipwrecked men turning to sea water from uncontrollable thirst" to those who would desperately "clamber over each other to stay in the sun." Drowning and crushing are recurring motifs of the evacuation in *Dunkirk*.

110. In this context, it is worth noting that the only blood that appears onscreen over the course of the film is the stain on George's forehead. The real wounds in *Dunkirk* are not inflicted by the anonymous "enemy," but by these people on one another.

111. As the soldiers abandon the sinking ship, Alex calls out to the anonymous French soldier.

112. "Is he a coward?" George asks Mister Dawson of the Shivering Sailor. Mister Dawson refuses the label and explains, "He's shellshocked, George. He's not himself. He may never be himself again." Later, when the Shivering Sailor comes to his senses, he seems to remember what happened to George. "The lad," he asks, "will he be okay?" Peter lies in response, having confirmed George's death only moments earlier. A quick reaction shot from Mister Dawson demonstrates his approval for this comforting white lie. At the end, the Shivering Sailor leaves the Moonstone, his violence against George unremarked upon and unpunished; perhaps even forgiven.

113. When the returning soldiers are greeted by an old man at the train station, Alex complains, "That old bloke wouldn't even look us in the eye." However, both Tommy and the audience know that the old man did not look Alex in the eye because he was blind. Alex's contempt and shame is not mirrored in the public. "They'll be spitting at us in the streets," Alex assures Tommy. Instead, the troops are celebrated and validated by the eager public.

114. See, for example, Richard Trenholm, "War epic *Dunkirk* has a stopwatch where a heart should be," *CNET*, 20 July 2017; Mike Symonds, "Film Crit Hulk SMASH: Christopher Nolan & The Cruelty Of Time," *Birth. Movies. Death*, 26 July 2017; Garth Franklin, "Nolan On *Dunkirk* Runtime, Cold Criticisms," Dark Horizons, 9 July 2017.

115. *See*, for example: Jason Fraley, "Review: Christopher Nolan's *Dunkirk* viscerally stunning, emotionally chilly," *WTOP*, 21 July 2017; Megan McArdle, "*Dunkirk* and the Great Films That Won't Be Made," *Bloomberg*, 20 July 2017.

116. Indeed, *Dunkirk* breathed new life into that particular critical cliché; *see*, for example, Andrew Pulver, "With *Dunkirk*, Christopher Nolan has finally hit the heights of Kubrick," *The Guardian*, 19 July 2017; Sean Hutchinson, "How *Dunkirk* Proves Christopher Nolan Is Stanley Kubrick's Cinematic Heir Apparent," *Inverse*, 25 May 2016.

117. There is a sense that this compassion is rooted in the abstraction of war; the understanding that nobody who has not lived through the insanity of war can presume to judge those who have. Nolan explains, "I have not fought in a war. Frankly, it's my worst nightmare to do so. And I have nothing but respect and admiration for people who have been put in that position." (David Jenkins, "Christopher Nolan: 'I've not fought in a war, it's my worst nightmare to do so,'" *Little White Lies*, 13 July 2017.)

118. Nolan has conceded that anarchy is one of his greatest recurring fears. He reiterated this, even in the context of the publicity circuit around *Dunkirk*, "In today's world, anarchy scares me the most." ("Interview: Christopher Nolan," *Playboy*, 30 August 2017.) In some ways, *Dunkirk* might be seen as an extrapolation of this fear as it was expressed in *The Dark Knight* and *The Dark Knight Rises*, in which major American cities collapse into chaos at the machinations of supervillains.

119. Simon Shuster, "Donald Trump and the Populist Revolt in Europe," *Time*, 6 December 2016.

120. Samuel Earle, "The Toxic Nostalgia of Brexit," *The Atlantic*, 5 October 2017.

121. Geoffrey Wheatcroft, "The Myth of the Good War," *The Guardian*, 9 December 2014.

122. Gary Younge, "Brexit: a disaster decades in the making," *The Guardian*, 30 June 2016.

123. To pick various headlines from the day that *Dunkirk* was released: Philip Oltermann, "How Brexit might affect the UK's young tech industry freelancers," *The Guardian*, 21 July 2017; Annabelle Dickson, Charlie Cooper and Maïa de La Baume, "9 ways Britain could stay in the European Union," *Politico*, 21 July 2017; Iain Watson, "Brexit: Is cabinet now united behind transition plan?," *BBC*, 21 July 2017; Chad Bray, "Bank of America Chooses Dublin as Post-'Brexit' European Hub," *The New York Times*, 21 July 2017; Natasha Browne, "UK farm subsidies to be dealt out on 'environmental merit' after Brexit," *AgriLand*, 21 July 2017; Nesrine Malik, "Is this the Brexit banking exodus Theresa May told us couldn't happen?," *The Guardian*, 21 July 2017.

124. Doctor Peter Ammon, the former German ambassador to London explicitly cited the country's mythology of the Second World War as a major influence on the outcome of the referendum. (Patrick Wintour, "German ambassador: second world war image of Britain has fed Euroscepticism," *The Guardian*, 29 January 2018.)

125. This is without even getting into Nolan's long-standing fascinations with myths and nostalgia. *The Dark Knight Rises* had seemed to foreshadow the right-wing populism that came to dominate American politics in the years that followed, while *Interstellar* touched in some small way on the romantic nostalgia that dominated the following election. As such, it would be surprising if *Dunkirk* did not resonate with these developments, even beyond the superficiality of its subject matter.

126. Jason Wilson, "*Dunkirk*: the film that has rightwing writers itching for a culture war," *The Guardian*, 21 July 2017.

127. Allison Pearson, "For Brexit to work, we need Dunkirk spirit not 'Naysaying Nellies,'" *The Telegraph*, 1 August 2017.

128. Tom Peck, "If Nigel Farage thinks it's high time all 'youngsters' are made to see *Dunkirk*, he's entirely missed the point of it," *The Independent*, 31 July 2017.

129. Jonathon Sturgeon, "Tory Porn: The Hobbesian anti-art of Christopher Nolan," *The Baffler*, 25 July 2017.

130. Indeed, Tommy explicitly has to identify himself to the soldiers in French and they subsequently provide covering fire to him as he

runs away from the sounds of gunfire.

131. Indeed, the aspects of the film focusing on Commander Bolton are among the more controversial aspects of the film, from a historical standpoint. The relatives of the real-life James Campbell Clouston argue that he played a role equivalent to that of the fictional Commander Bolton, and were upset at the fact that his name was not used in the film. (Guy Adams, "The real hero of *Dunkirk*: Courage of the piermaster who manned a crucial jetty to organise evacuees for six days and five nights without a break," *The Daily Mail*, 25 July 2017.) Nolan responded to such criticisms, "Clouston has an incredible story we could not do justice to in the film." ("Sons Of Dunkirk Heroes Critical Of Lack Of Movie Recognition For Fathers," *W.E.N.N.*, 25 July 2017.) Similarly, there has been some historical criticism of the sequence in which Commander Bolton opts to remain behind, "because it suggests the French had their own Dunkirk." (John Broich, "What's Fact and What's Fiction in *Dunkirk*," *Slate*, 20 July 2017.) Nevertheless, the choice of this line as Bolton's closing line is an important symbolic gesture on the part of the film.

132. James M. Lindsay, "TWE Remembers: Dunkirk, Operation Dynamo, and Churchill's 'Never Surrender' Speech," *Council on Foreign Relations*, 4 June 2013.

133. Professor Richard Toye identifies this section as "the most important bit," and contends, "Usually, when the recording is played today, it gets cut off after the words 'never surrender.'" (Professor Richard Toye, "'We shall fight on the beaches': 3 things you never knew about Churchill's most famous speech," *History of Government*, 2 December 2013.) As such, the inclusion of that entire section in *Dunkirk* feels a deliberate attempt to place emphasis on the United Kingdom's dependency on foreign aid for its survival.

134. John Wight, "Christopher Nolan's *Dunkirk* And Brexit Or Bust," *The Huffington Post*, 27 July 2017.

135. James Cooray Smith, "Nigel Farage's love for *Dunkirk* shows how Brexiteers learned the wrong lessons from WWII," *New Statesman*, 26 July 2017.

136. Andreas Wiseman, "Christopher Nolan: why *Dunkirk* is anything but a 'Brexit movie,'" *Screen Daily*, 30 November 2017.

137. Robbie Collin, "Christopher Nolan interview: 'To me, *Dunkirk* is about European unity,'" *The Telegraph*, 23 December 2017.

138. Jake Coyle, "Q & A: Christopher Nolan on the craft of *Dunkirk*," *The Associated Press*, 2 February 2018.

139. This is perhaps best demonstrated in *The Dark Knight Rises*, when the city of Gotham keeps the myth of Batman alive through chalk etchings while Bruce Wayne languishes in a foreign prison, but both *Batman Begins* and *The Dark Knight* emphasize that Bruce could never have been Batman on his own; he needed Alfred, Lucius and even Ra's Al Ghul.

140. Even the process of adaptation consciously emphasized communal contribution ahead of individual accomplishment. In response to complaints by the family that Commander James Campbell Clouston had inspired the character of Commander Bolton without being explicitly named in the script, Emma Thomas observed, "We are not changing that fictional name due to the fact that our character was inspired by the stories of several different men." ("Sons Of Dunkirk Heroes Critical Of Lack Of Movie Recognition For Fathers," *W.E.N.N.*, 25 July 2017.) Indeed, it has been suggested that Commander Bolton was *also* inspired by the real-life Captain William Tennant. (John Broich, "What's Fact and What's Fiction in *Dunkirk*," *Slate*, 20 July 2017.)

141. Matt Zoller Seitz, "*Dunkirk*," RogerEbert.com, 21 July 2017.

142. Chet Betz, "Christopher Nolan's War on Time," *Paste Magazine*, 30 July 2017.

143. Indeed, Nolan consciously teased the film's structure quite early in its publicity cycle, indicating that he understood audiences' expectations of his work. (Zack Sharf, "Christopher Nolan Teases Tricky *Dunkirk* Storytelling: 'The Film is Told From Three Points of View,'" *IndieWire*, 28 February 2017.)

144. Andreas Wiseman, "Christopher Nolan explains why *Dunkirk* was a gamble that required a 'leap of faith,'" *Screen Daily*, 11 December 2017.

145. Christopher Campbell, "*Arrival*, *Dunkirk* and the Distraction of Nonlinear Storytelling," *Film School Rejects*, 27 July 2017.

146. David Edelstein, "*Dunkirk* Is A Harrowing War Movie, Muddled By A Convoluted Timeline," *NPR*, 21 July 2017.

147. Sarah Moran, "*Dunkirk*'s Confusing Timeline Explained," *ScreenRant*, 24 July 2017.

148. Were the film presented in a linear manner, the audience would likely spend a full third of the film with Tommy, the next third intercut between Tommy and Mister Dawson, and the final third intercut between Tommy, Mister Dawson and Farrier. This would mean that the film's developed character would not be introduced until the second act, and the film would have to establish Farrier as a character in the middle on already crowded climax where the audience was invested in Tommy and Mister Dawson. On a smaller level, this would lose a number of clever and skillful transitions, such as the cut away from the Shivering Sailor on the boat with Mister Dawson to his brief encounter with Tommy at the beach, and the ensuing dramatic irony.

149. David Bordwell has discussed some of these alternatives, and explored their historical use within the established genre of the war movie, making *Dunkirk*'s refusal to employ such techniques particularly pointed. (David Bordwell, "*Dunkirk* Part 2: The art film as event movie," *Observations on Film Art*, 9 August 2017.)

150. So, for example, the adrenaline from the sequence in which Tommy and "Gibson" try to sneak on board a medical evacuation ship carries over into a less immediately tense sequence in which Mister Dawson hijacks his own boat to take part in the evacuation; these events are separated by several days and thirty kilometres, but the editing and the score provide a strong connection and overlap between the two.

151. Jason Guerrasio, "Christopher Nolan explains the biggest challenges in making his latest movie *Dunkirk* into an 'intimate epic,'" *Business Insider*, 11 July 2017.

152. This divide reflects one of the appeals of filmmaking to Nolan, because it creates a similar divide in audience members. As Nolan explains, "What cinema gives you, unlike any other medium, is this fascinating and wonderful tension and dialogue between this intensely subjective experience you're having from the imagery the filmmaker has put up there, and this extraordinarily empathetic sharing of that with audience around you." (Jake Coyle, "Q & A: Christopher Nolan on the craft of *Dunkirk*," *The Associated Press*, 2 February 2018.)

153. The audience experiences *Memento* backwards, but this is revealed to be more than just a clever formal touch. In his closing monologue, Leonard reflects on how disconnected he has become from the regular flow of time. "How can I heal? How am I supposed to heal if I can't feel time?"

154. At one point in *Interstellar*, Cooper presents Murphy with a watch so the pair can measure how differently each will experience time in the months and years ahead.

155. In keeping with the conflict between the emotional and the rational in Nolan's filmography, it has been suggested that the subjective experience of time is tied to the subject's emotional state. (Marc Gozlan, "A stopwatch on the brain's perception of time," *The Guardian*, 1 January 2013.)

156. Narratively speaking, this is similar to the way in which *Interstellar* using physics to emphasize the gulf between Cooper and Murphy, by having the pair experience time moving at a different pace from one another.

157. At one point, the squadron flies over Mister Dawson's boat as he is sailing, but none of the characters involved have any sense of the significance of the event. At another point, Tommy and Alex come into contact the Shivering Sailor trying to get off the beach, but the encounter is fleeting and nothing significant comes of this brief intersection.

158. Alissa Wilkinson, "*Dunkirk* turns a WWII battle into a symphony. It's Christopher Nolan's masterpiece," *Vox*, 21 July 2017.

159. Ed Newton-Rex, "The *Dunkirk* Soundtrack is Way Cleverer Than You Think," *Medium*, 26 September 2017.

160. Nolan has talked about cinema as "one of the ways in which people try to break from their "very singular point of view" to "try to see things from the same point of view." (Scott Foundas, "Christopher Nolan interview: Can *Inception* director save the summer?," *San Francisco Weekly*, 14 July 2010.) He has also discussed the "wonderful tension and dialogue between this intensely subjective experience you're having from the imagery the filmmaker has put up there, and this extraordinarily empathetic sharing of that with audience around you." (Jake Coyle, "Q & A: Christopher Nolan on the craft of *Dunkirk*," *The Associated Press*, 2 February 2018.)

161. Rob Cain, "Even With Star Director Nolan, *Dunkirk* Was A High-Risk Gamble For Warner Bros," *Forbes*, 23 July 2017.

162. Joe Utichi, "For Christopher Nolan's Producer And Partner Emma Thomas, Maintaining A Winning Streak Is Essential," *Deadline*, 23 February 2018.

163. Tim Gray, "How *Dunkirk* Overturned Conventions of Storytelling, Marketing and More," *Variety*, 22 February 2018.

164. Chris Lee, "Everything About *Dunkirk* Screams Oscar—So Why Is It Coming Out in July?," *Vanity Fair*, 17 July 2017.

165. In fact, *Dunkirk* ($50.5m) earned almost three times e as much as *Valerian and the City of a Thousand Planets* ($17m) in its opening weekend, domestically. (Anthony D'Alessandro, "*Dunkirk* Takes Warner Bros Past $1B; *Girls Trip* Record Opening For Malcolm D. Lee; Reasons Why *Valerian* Crashed," *Deadline*, 23 July 2017.)

166. Mansoor Mithaiwala, "*Dunkirk* Becomes Highest Grossing WWII Film at Global Box Office," *ScreenRant*, 15 September 2017.

167. Natlaie Robehmed, "Oscars 2018: How Nominated Movies Rank At The Box Office," *Forbes*, 27 February 2018.

168. Indeed, as the film approached release, even those prognosticators who had faith in the film's box office potential seemed to have difficulty articulating why beyond a broad trust in Nolan's understanding of contemporary movie audiences. On the eve of the film's release, one anonymous insider reflected, "This movie will somehow make money. Don't ask me how, but I am done betting against Chris Nolan." (Anthony D'Alessandro, "How Warner Bros Beat The Period-Film Curse At The B.O. & Positioned *Dunkirk* As A Summer Tentpole," *Deadline*, 23 July 2017.)

169. Some pundits have argued that, in complicated political times, audiences yearn for films that take them back to time periods that are perceived as being less morally ambiguous or uncertain. (Anne T. Donahue, "In Times of Political Turmoil, War Movies Are More Than Just Escapism," *Esquire*, 25 July 2017.)

170. Andreas Wiseman, "Christopher Nolan explains why *Dunkirk* was a gamble that required a 'leap of faith'," *Screen Daily*, 11 December 2017.

171. Cara Buckley, "Christopher Nolan's Latest Time-Bending Feat? *Dunkirk*," *The New York Times*, 12 July 2017.

172. Marc Bernardin, "Marvel, Star Wars, Harry Potter and more: Why the movie star no longer shines as bright as the franchise," *The Los Angeles Times*, 17 June 2016.

173. Rebecca Keegan, "How *Dunkirk*, Summer's Boldest Box-Office Gamble, Paid Off," *Vanity Fair*, 24 July 2017; Adam Chitwood, "*Dunkirk* Soars Past $500 Million at the Worldwide Box Office," *Collider*, 15 September 2017.

174. Anthony D'Alessandro, "How Warner Bros Beat The Period-Film Curse At The B.O. & Positioned *Dunkirk* As A Summer Tentpole," *Deadline*, 23 July 2017.

175. Nate Jones, "The Christopher Nolan Style Guide to Wearing Video Monitors Around Your Neck," *Vulture*, 10 November 2014.

176. Nate Jones, "Here Are Some More Interesting Facts About Christopher Nolan and Tea," *Vulture*, 31 October 2014.

177. Kirsten Acuna, "Director Christopher Nolan Doesn't Have A Cellphone Or Email Address," *Business Insider*, 5 January 2015.

178. Scott Foundas, "Christopher Nolan Rallies the Troops to Save Celluloid Film," *Variety*, 11 March 2015.

179. David Canfield, "Christopher Nolan Didn't Really Know Who Harry Styles Was When He Cast Him in Dunkirk," *Vulture*, 9 July 2017.

180. Kyle Kizu, "Christopher Nolan Wanted to Shoot *Dunkirk* Without a Script," *The Hollywood Reporter*, 4 August 2017.

181. For example, consider Jonathon Sturgeon's introduction to his article on the director's alleged conservative politics, "I like to imagine Christopher Nolan, the Last Tory, on set. He wears periwinkle cufflinks, black pants, and a herringbone waistcoat. He sips at a flask of tea. His soothing air of self-command is not an affectation; it is borne out of a sense of duty to his cast and crew, his family, and, above all, his audience." (Jonathon Sturgeon, "Tory Porn: The Hobbesian anti-art of Christopher Nolan," *The Baffler*, 25 July 2017.)

182. It should be noted that this is a relative rare event, particularly in the modern economic and cultural climate. Even established and venerated directors like Martin

Scorsese have difficulty securing the creative freedom necessary to bring their vision to the screen. Paramount Pictures declined to fund and distribute Scorsese's long-gestating *The Irishman*, starring Al Pacino and Robert DeNiro. Streaming giant Netflix had to step in to fill the gap. (Mia Galuppo, "Martin Scorsese's *The Irishman* Heads to Netflix From Paramount," *The Hollywood Reporter*, 21 February 2017.)

183. Nolan had previously receiving writing nominations for both *Memento* and *Inception*, and had been included on *Inception*'s Best Picture nomination.

184. *Memento* received two Academy Award nominations, and won none. *Batman Begins* earned a single nomination for cinematography, and lost. *The Prestige* received two nominations, and won none. *The Dark Knight* won two of its eight nominations. *Inception* won four of its eight nominations. *Interstellar* won one of its five nominations. *Dunkirk* eventually won three of its eight nominations.

185. Charles Poladian, "Oscar Genre Bias: Why Sci-Fi, Foreign Films And Horror Movies Never Get Best Picture Nominations," *International Business Times*, 22 February 2015.

186. Nolan concedes as much of *Dunkirk*, acknowledging, "Right out of the gate I said this material risks being misconstrued as a period drama, a self-serious war film, awards bait or whatever you might call it." (Josh Rottenberg, "*Dunkirk* director Christopher Nolan on why, in this era of peak TV, he's still all in on movies," *The Los Angeles Times*, 24 July 2017.)

187. *See*, for example: David Fear, "Why *Dunkirk* Is the Christopher Nolan Movie We've Been Waiting For," Rolling Stone, 24 July 2017; Andrew Pulver, "With *Dunkirk*, Christopher Nolan has finally hit the heights of Kubrick," *The Guardian*, 19 July 2017.

188. Adam Chitwood, "Oscar Beat: Is *Dunkirk* a Major Contender?," *Collider*, 25 July 2017; Chris Lee, "Everything About *Dunkirk* Screams Oscar—So Why Is It Coming Out in July?," *Vanity Fair*, 19 July 2017; "Can *Dunkirk* Hang In Through Awards Season?," *Vanity Fair*, 21 July 2017.

189. Indeed, *Get Out* and *Dunkirk* were the two highest grossing Best Picture nominees of the year in question, and perhaps the two films that movie-goers were most likely to have seen before the nominees were announced. These two films accounted for half of the total haul of the other nine nominees. (Marcus James Dixon, "Oscars box office: *Dunkirk* and *Get Out* are biggest money-makers in Best Picture race," *Gold Derby*, 6 February 2018.)

190. Recent years have suggested a familiar pattern for credible Best Picture nominees; prestige dramas that open in limited release and earn very low box office returns. (Chris Lee, "Why the Academy Keeps Giving Oscars to Movies No One Sees," *Fortune*, 29 February 2016.)

191. Aisha Harris, Alex Heimbach, Chris Kirk, and Natalie Matthews-Ramo, "When Box-Office Hits Get Nominated, Do Oscar Ratings Go Up?," *Slate*, 22 February 2013.

192. Brian Moylan, "Does the Oscars boycott explain low ratings? No, but the box office might," *The Guardian*, 1 March 2016.

193. Jordan Peele was the only the third person to score nominations for picture, direction and screenplay with his feature film debut. He was also the first black artist to accomplish this. (Patrick Shanley, "Oscars: *Get Out* Makes History With Nominations for Jordan Peele, Horror Genre," *The Hollywood Reporter*, 23 January 2018.) More than that, he would become the first black writer to win the best original screenplay award. (Sandra Gonzalez, "Jordan Peele is first black screenwriter to win best original screenplay," *CNN*, 5 March 2018.) Rachel Morrison became the first woman to be nominated in the cinematography field, for her work on *Mudbound*. (Kristopher Tapley, "Oscars: *Mudbound*'s Rachel Morrison Makes History as First Female Cinematographer Nominee," *Variety*, 23 January 2018.) Yance Ford became the first transgender director of an Oscar-nominated film, for his work on *Strong Island*. (Jude Dry, "Oscars 2018: Transgender Artists and Stories Earn Historic Nominations for *Strong Island* and *A Fantastic Woman*," *IndieWire*, 23 January 2018.) Perhaps acknowledging a broader arc of these changes to the institution's demographics, Guillermo del Toro became the fourth Mexican-born director to win in the previous five years. (Matt Donnelly, "Oscars: Guillermo del Toro Gets Fourth Mexican-Born Best Director Win in 5 Years," *The Wrap*, 4 March 2018.)

194. Cary Darling, "It's Oscar season—why isn't anyone talking about *Dunkirk*?," *The Houston Chronicle*, 2 March 2018.

195. Asked about the lack of awards success for *Dunkirk*, one anonymous younger voter explained, "It's about not wanting to award people who they felt had been rewarded a lot in the past. Maybe we need to give someone else a chance. I definitely think, whether it was conscious or subconscious, that was happening."(Kyle Buchanan, Stacey Wilson Hunt, and Chris Lee, "We Polled New Oscar Voters: How Are They Changing the Way the Academy Thinks?," *Vulture*, 26 February 2018.) Of course, it should be noted that Nolan had only earned his first directing nomination on his tenth film, and was competing against two directors who had been nominated for their directorial debuts.

196. An anonymous member of the producing branch complained that *Dunkirk* was "a little confusing." (Scott Feinberg, "Brutally Honest Oscar Ballot: *Call Me by Your Name* Is 'Wrong,' *The Post* Got 'Over-Spielbergized,'" *The Hollywood Reporter*, 27 February 2018.) A member of the actors' branch objected that *Dunkirk* was "sometimes confusing." (Scott Feinberg, "Brutally Honest Oscar Ballot #2: *Get Out* Filmmakers 'Played the Race Card,' 'Just Sick of' Meryl Streep," *The Hollywood Reporter*, 2 March 2018.)

197. Sean Fennessey, "Did the Oscars Blow Its Big Bet?," *The Ringer*, 7 February 2018.

198. Josef Adalian, "Does It Matter If This Year's Oscars Were the Least-Watched Ever?," *Vulture*, 5 March 2018.

199. This is a recurring motif of awards season punditry. *See*, for example: Sara McCorquodale, "There's nothing more out of touch than the Oscars and here's the proof," *The Independent*, 10 February 2016; Madeleine Gaudin, "The Oscars are out of touch (and not just because *Lady Bird* lost)," *The Michigan Daily*, 6 March 2018; Ben Child, "Are the Oscars out of touch with what filmgoers want?," *The Guardian*, 22 February 2013.

200. It has been argued, for example, that the advent of streaming as removed a lot of cultural impact of television by stripping away the idea of "watercooler" television, or a shared popular consciousness of major television series. (David Lister, "If we lose the sense of shared experience we get from television,

we lose a cultural bond," *The Independent*, 30 August 2013.)

201. Kathryn VanArendonk, "2016: The Year of TV Bubbles," *Vulture*, 16 December 2016.

202. Dan Kois, "Spoilers: In Defense of the American Watercooler," *Vulture*, 13 March 2008.

203. Kurt Anderson, "How America Lost Its Mind," *The Atlantic*, September 2017.

## *Appendix*

1. Tom Hollander worked at the iconic British toy store Hamleys to support theatre work after he failed to secure a place in drama school. He worked as a toy demonstrator, which he described as "a very actorish thing to do." (Kate Kellaway, "Tom Hollander: 'I go to bed in a mood created by the audience the previous night'", *The Guardian*, 17 February 2017.)

2. The UCLU FilmSoc website entry on *Larceny* described it as "is one of the best (if not the best) shorts of filmsoc recent generations."

3. Nolan has vocally rejected descriptions of his early work as "calling card" films designed to serve as stepping stones to something bigger rather than existing as films unto themselves. The director argues, "When I was going around the festival circuit with *Following*, very often people would refer to my film as 'a calling card film,' and I found that very frustrating. My comment at the time was, 'If you want to make a calling card, you go to Kinkos. You don't spend three years of your life putting a film together.' The act of making that film was "filmmaking," to me, and it was as valid and still is as valid as everything I do today." (Scott Feinberg, "Christopher Nolan on *Interstellar* Critics, Making Original Films and Shunning Cellphones and Email (Q&A)", *The Hollywood Reporter*, 3 January 2015.)

4. Nolan jokes of the shooting experience, "At the time, when we did the festival circuit, I would say that we could fit the entire cast and crew into a London taxi." (Steve Greene, "Christopher Nolan: He Absolutely Will Not Make a Fourth *Batman* Movie", *IndieWire*, 9 June 2012.)

5. The Batman logo on the apartment door in *Following* is one of the film's most discussed and most frequently referenced aspects. (Malika Gumpangkum, "The Cinematic Universes of Christopher Nolan Pt. 1: *Following* (1998)", *Nerdophiles*, 5 November 2014; Julianne Ramsey, "The Great Christopher Nolan Film Re-Watch! Day 1: *Following*", *We Minored in Film*, 6 June 2013; Justin Gerber, Leah Pickett, Michael Roffman, Blake Goble and Dominick Suzanne-Mayer, "Ranking: Every Christopher Nolan Movie from Worst to Best", *Consequence of Sound*, 19 July 2017; Cameron Beyl, "Christopher Nolan's *Following* (1998)", *The Directors Series*, 15 February 2017.)

6. Editor Lee Smith described Nolan's process, "Chris has made the movie [in his head] and then makes the movie in the camera." (Trevor Hogg, "*Dark Knight*: Lee Smith talks about Christopher Nolan", *Flickering Myth*, 4 December 2012.)

7. Nathalie Sejean, "34 Things Christopher Nolan Shared About Making His First Feature Film and Learning From It", *Mentorless*, 30 December 2013.

# Bibliography

Anderson, Kurt. "How America Lost Its Mind." *The Atlantic*, September 2017.
Ash, Timothy Garton. *Facts Are Subversive: Political Writing from a Decade Without a Name*. Yale University Press, 2009.
Balaev, Michelle. *The Nature of Trauma in American Novels*. Northwestern University Press, 2012.
Barr, Marleen S. (ed.). *Afro-Future Females: Black Writers Chart Science Fiction's Newest New-Wave Trajectory*. Ohio State University Press, 2008.
Baudrillard, Jean translated by Chris Turner. *L'illusion de la Fin*. Stanford University Press, 1994.
Booker, M. Keith. *Alternate Americas: Science Fiction Film and American Culture*. Greenwood Publishing Group, 2006.
Bordwell, David, with Kristin Thompson. *Christopher Nolan: A Labyrinth of Linkages*. Self-published, 2013.
Bordwell, David, and Kristin Thompson. *Minding Movies: Observations on the Art, Craft, and Business of Filmmaking*. University of Chicago Press, 2011.
Bordwell, David. "Nolan vs. Nolan." *Observations on Film Art*, 19 August 2012.
Bordwell, David. *The Way Hollywood Tells It Story and Style in Modern Movies*. University of California Press, 2006.
Burger, Alissa (ed.). *Teaching Graphic Novels in the English Classroom: Pedagogical Possibilities of Multimodal Literacy Engagement*. Palgrave Macmillan, 2017.
Cox, Greg. *The Dark Knight Rises: The Official Movie Novelization*. Titan Books, 2012.
Cullen, Frank, Florence Hackman and Donald McNeilly. *Vaudeville Old & New: An Encyclopaedia Of Variety Performances In America*. Psychology Press, 2004.
Donovan, Barna William. *Conspiracy Films: A Tour of Dark Places in the American Conscious*. McFarland, 2011.
Eaglestone, Robert. *Postmodernism and Holocaust Denial*. Icon Books, 2001.
Eco, Umberto. *The Role of the Reader: Explorations in the Semiotics of Texts*. Indiana University Press, 1979.
Falwell, John. *Hitchcock's Rear Window: The Well-Made Film*. Southern Illinois University Press, 2001.
Feinberg, Scott. "Christopher Nolan on *Interstellar* Critics, Making Original Films and Shunning Cellphones and Email." *The Hollywood Reporter*, 3 January 2015.
Firestone, Shulamith, and Anne Koedt (eds.). *Notes from the Second Year: Women's Liberation*. Self-published, 1970.
Freud, Sigmund. *Totem and Taboo*. Beacon Press, 1913.
Friedman, Lester D. *Citizen Spielberg*. University of Illinois Press, 2006.
Fukuyama, Francis. "The End of History?" *The National Interest*, Summer 1989.
Furby, Jacqueline and Stuart Joy (eds.). *The Cinema of Christopher Nolan: Imagining the Impossible*. Wallflower Press, 2015.
Goldsmith, Jeff. "The Architect of Dreams." *Creative Screenwriting*, July/August 2010.
Gibson, Mel, David Huxley, Joan Ormrod. *Superheroes and Identities*. Routledge, 2016.
Gottschall, Jonathan. *The Storytelling Animal: How Stories Make Us Human*. Mariner Books, 2012.
Greven, David. *Intimate Violence: Hitchcock, Sex, and Queer Theory*. Oxford University Press, 2017.
Harmon, Jim. *Radio Mystery and Adventure and Its Appearances in Film, Television and Other Media*. McFarland, 2003.
Harwood, Sarah. *Family Fictions: Representations of the Family in 1980s Hollywood Cinema*. Palgrave Macmillan, 1997.
Hassler-Forest, Dan. *Capitalist Superheroes: Caped Crusaders in the Neoliberal Age*. Zero Books, 2012.
Heller-Nicholas, Alexandra. *Found Footage Horror Films: Fear and the Appearance of Reality*. McFarland, 2014.
Hiltunen, Ari. *Aristotle in Hollywood: The Anatomy of Successful Storytelling*. Intellect Books, 2002.
Hofstadter, Richard. "The Paranoid Style in American Politics." *Harpers Magazine*, November 1964.

Höglund, Johan. *The American Imperial Gothic: Popular Culture, Empire, Violence*. Routledge, 2014.

Ip, John. "*The Dark Knight*'s War on Terrorism." *Ohio State Journal of Criminal Law*, September 2011.

Jeffords, Susan. *Hard Bodies: Hollywood Masculinity in the Reagan Era*. Rutgers University Press, 1994.

Jenkins, Henry. *Textual Poachers: Television Fans and Participatory Culture*. Routledge, 1992.

Jesser, Jody Duncan, and Janine Pourroy. *The Art and Making of The Dark Knight Trilogy*. Harry N. Abrams, 2012.

Kane, Bob, and Tom Andrae, *Batman & Me: An Autobiography*. Eclipse Press, 1989.

Kimmel, Michael S. *Manhood in America: A Cultural History*. Oxford University Press, 2006.

Kolker, Robert (ed.). *Alfred Hitchcock's Psycho: A Casebook*. Oxford University Press, 2004.

Krauthammer, Charles. "The Unipolar Moment." *Foreign Affairs*, Winter 1990.

Leggatt, Matthew. *Cultural and Political Nostalgia in the Age of Terror: The Melancholic Sublime*. Routledge, 2017.

Loeb, Jeph, and Tim Sale. *Absolute Batman: The Long Halloween*. DC Comics, 2007.

Luokkala, Barry B. *Exploring Science Through Science Fiction*. Springer, 2015.

Mann, Douglas. *Understanding Society: A Survey of Modern Social Theory*. Oxford University Press, 2008.

Mather, Philippe. *Stanley Kubrick at Look Magazine: Authorship and Genre in Photojournalism and Film*. Intellect Books, 2013.

Mauss, Marcel. *General Theory of Magic*. Taylor and Francis, 2001.

McEniry, Matthew J., Robert Moses Peaslee, and Robert G. Weiner (eds.). *Marvel Comics into Film: Essays on Adaptations Since the 1940s*. McFarland, 2016.

McGowan, Todd. *The Fictional Christopher Nolan*. University of Texas Press, 2012.

Melbye, David. *Landscape Allegory in Cinema*. Palgrave Macmillan, 2010.

Molloy, Claire. *Memento*. Edinburgh University Press, 2010.

Mottram, James. *The Making of Memento*. Faber & Faber, 2011.

Murdoch, David Hamilton. *The American West: The Invention of a Myth*. University of Nevada Press, 2001.

Neff, Renfreu and Daniel Argent. "Remembering Where it All Began: Christopher Nolan on *Memento*." *Creative Screenwriting*, July 2015.

Nolan, Christopher. *Dunkirk*. Faber & Faber, 2017.

Nolan, Christopher. *Inception: The Shooting Script*. Faber & Faber, 2010.

Nolan, Christopher. *Memento & Following*. Faber & Faber, 2001.

Nolan, Christopher, with David S. Goyer and Jonathan Nolan. *The Dark Knight Trilogy: The Complete Screenplays*. Faber & Faber, 2010.

Nolan, Christopher, and Jonathan Nolan. *Interstellar: The Complete Screenplay With Selected Storyboards*. Faber & Faber, 2014.

Park, William. *What is Film Noir?* Bucknell University Press, 2011.

Pethő, Ágnes (ed.). *Film in the Post-Media Age*. Cambridge Scholars Publishing, 2012.

Pomerance, Murray. *The Last Laugh: Strange Humours of Cinema*. Wayne State University Press, 2013.

Priest, Christopher. *The Prestige*. Hachette UK, 2011.

Reinhart, Mark S. *The Batman Filmography*. McFarland, 2013.

Schatz, J.L., and Sean Parson (eds.). *Superheroes and Critical Animal Studies: The Heroic Beasts of Total Liberation*. Rowman & Littlefield, 2017.

Scott, Kevin Michael (ed.). *Marvel Comics' Civil War and the Age of Terror: Critical Essays on the Comic Saga*. McFarland, 2015.

Shone, Tom. "Christopher Nolan: the man who rebooted the blockbuster." *The Guardian*, 4 November 2014.

Smith, Peter, and Carolyn Lefley. *Rethinking Photography: Histories, Theories and Education*. Routledge, 2015.

Stoddard, Scott F. (ed.). *The New Western: Critical Essays on the Genre Since 9/11*. McFarland, 2016.

Tarkovsky, Andrei translated by Kitty Hunter-Blair. *Sculpting in Time: Reflections on the Cinema*. Texas University Press, 1986.

Timberg, Scott. "Indie Angst." *The New Times Los Angeles*, 15 March 2001.

Toye, Richard. *The Roar of the Lion: The Untold Story of Churchill's World War II Speeches*. Oxford University Press, 2013.

Walker, Michael. *Hitchcock's Motifs*. Yale University Press, 2006.

Wegner, Phillip E. *Life Between Two Deaths, 1989–2001: U.S. Culture in the Long Nineties*. Duke University Press, 2009.

Wetmore, Kevin J., Jr. *Post-9/11 Horror in American Cinema*. Continuum, 2012.

West, Thomas G. *The Political Theory of the American Founding: Natural Rights, Public Policy, and the Moral Conditions of Freedom*. Cambridge University Press, 2017.

Zepinic, Vito. *Hidden Scars: Understanding and Treating Complex Trauma*. Xlibris, 2011.

Žižek, Slavoj. *Welcome to the Desert of the Real!: Five Essays on September 11 and Related Dates*. Verso Books, 2002.

# Index

Academy Awards 82–84, 145–146
*Alien* 114, 133
*All Quiet on the Western Front* 133
amnesia 13
anarchism 70–71, 107, 120–121
*Apt Pupil* 37
Aronofsky, Darren 38, 121
*The Aviator* 36

*Batman* (1989) 39, 45
*Batman & Robin* 37, 39, 101
*Batman vs. Superman: Dawn of Justice* 38, 87, 105, 116
The Battle of Algiers 110, 133
*Blade Runner* 40, 86
*Blade: Trinity* 43
*The Blair Witch Project* (1999) 57
Borges, Jorge 6
Brexit 112–113, 140–141
*The Bridge on the River Kwai* 110
Britain 41, 52, 59, 131–132
budget 30
Bush, George W. 61, 72–73, 106, 108, 112

Caine, Michael 52
Campbell, Joseph 46
*Cannibal Holocaust* 57
capitalism 59–60, 109–110
Carrey, Jim 36
chaos 58, 69–70, 92, 139
*Chariots of Fire* 133
Chicago 3, 5, 13, 26, 29, 40–41, 77–78, 110, 107
*Citizen Kane* 19
*Collateral* 36, 65
computer-generated imagery 24, 40, 64
conservatism 107–108

conspiracy theory 21–22, 58
criticism 79–80, 82, 97, 108, 113–114
crosscutting 7, 11, 34, 79–80, 90, 134
*CSI* 34

*Dark City* 24
*Darkest Hour* 144
deleted scenes 32–33, 113
digital photography 64–66
Disney 86
*Dr. Mabuse* 69
*Doctor Zhivago* 110
Donner, Richard 38
*Doodlebug* 5–6, 15
DVD 19, 20, 32–33, 68

Eastwood, Clint 30, 90
Eischer, M.C. 6
*Esquire* 13
*The Europa Report* 29
*The Evil Dead* 37
*eXistenZ* 24
exposition 3, 8, 14, 17, 19, 34, 47, 48, 79, 90, 133, 134–135

*Fight Club* 20
*film noir* 7–8, 23, 28
filmmaking 62–66, 89, 127
*Foreign Correspondent* 133
frontier 28–29, 41, 117, 132

gender 96–97, 108–109, 128–130, 138
genre 54–55, 76–77, 133
*Get Out* 145–146
*The Godfather* 82
Goyer, David S. 42, 43, 81
*Great Expectations* 110
Great Recession 107, 109
*Greed* 133
*Green Acres* 19

*Harsh Realm* 24
*Heat* 76–77
*HHhH* 144
Hitchcock, Alfred 8–10, 115
Hughes, Howard 36

identity 15
*The Illusionist* 36
IMAX 7, 64, 78–79
*Independence Day* 24
inserts 8, 17, 33
*Insomnia* (1997) 27
internet 20, 29, 54, 58, 82, 93–94, 113

*Jay and Silent Bob Strike Back* 20
the Joker 68–76
Julyan, David 52, 54, 63, 133
*Justice League* 39, 105, 116

*King Kong* (2005) 63
Kubrick, Stanley 30, 80, 96, 115, 122–123, 140

*Larceny* 5
*Lawrence of Arabia* 110
literalism 48, 58, 73, 89, 102, 125
*The Lord of the Rings* 63
*Lost* 93
Lucas, George 4, 46, 65, 79, 86

*Man of Steel* 105, 116
Mann, Michael 36, 65
Marvel Studios 77, 86, 104–105
materialism 59–60
*The Matrix* 24
"Memento Mori" 15–16
memory 23
myth 49, 102, 132–133

narrative 21, 30, 48–49, 59, 74–75, 90, 91–92, 95, 132

Newmarket Films 16, 20, 63
9/11 25, 38, 57–58, 71–72
Nolan, Jonathan 4, 13–16, 51, 69, 117, 118, 125–126, 127–128
non-linear storytelling 11, 18–19, 55–56, 142

Obama, Barack 73, 106, 119
*Oliver Twist* 110

*Paprika* 88, 89
Person of Interest 15
Pfister, Wally 17, 52, 78
*Pleasantville* 24
*Prometheus* 114
*Public Enemies* 65, 77

Raimi, Sam 37
realism 39–40, 64, 65, 113
reality 24, 40–41, 58, 74–75, 95
reboot 49, 81
religion 59, 60–61, 121–122
reshoots 30–31
revolution 15, 107, 112
*Rope* 9
rules 8, 10–11, 14, 23–24, 57, 69, 74, 88

*Saving Private Ryan* 133
second unit 30
self-delusion 23
sequels 67–68, 81, 99
sex 9–10
shared universes 104–105
Singer, Bryan 37, 39

*The Sixth Sense* 20
Smith, Kevin 20
Smith, Lee 30–31, 52, 80
*Snow White and the Seven Dwarves* 4
Soderbergh, Steven 20, 30
*Speed* 133
*Spider-Man* 37
Spielberg, Steven 46, 77, 90, 92, 115, 117, 118, 125, 133
*Star Trek* 55, 86, 106
*Star Wars* 4, 46, 86, 117, 118, 125
*Star Wars: Episode II—Attack of the Clones* 65, 79
*Star Wars: Episode VII—The Force Awakens* 4, 79
structures 10–11, 75–76
subjectivity 8, 16, 18, 23, 24, 31, 32, 40, 56, 75, 89, 114, 135–136, 143
*Sunrise* 133
*Sunshine* 29
superheroes 37, 47, 48, 77, 82, 103, 107–108; origin stories 42
*Superman* (1978) 38, 39
*Superman Returns* 39

*A Tale of Two Cities* 110
*Tanner '88* 17
*Tarantella* 5
Tarantino, Quentin 20, 90
television 19, 86
*Their Finest* 144
Theobald, Jeremy 5
*The Thirteenth Floor* 24

Thomas, Emma 13, 30, 84, 125, 131, 134
3D 78–79, 89
time 24–25, 126–127, 143
trauma 11, 18–19, 43–44, 58, 95–96, 126
*The Truman Show* 24
Trump, Donald 112–113, 140
*2001: A Space Odyssey* 4, 96, 117, 122, 123

University College London 5
*Unstoppable* 133
*The Usual Suspects* 37

verisimilitude 40
*Vertigo* 9
voyeurism 7, 8, 9
*V.R. 5* 24

*The Wages of Fear* 133
War on Terror 37–38, 58, 61, 71–73, 106
Warner Brothers 27, 29–30, 38, 67, 86–87, 117, 144
*Waterland* 5
*Westworld* 14, 15
women in refrigerators 96
Working Title 13

*The X-Files* 21, 93
*X-Men* 37

Zimmer, Hans 39, 44, 70, 128, 133–134

www.ingramcontent.com/pod-product-compliance
Lightning Source LLC
Chambersburg PA
CBHW081555300426
44116CB00015B/2895